Fundamentals in British Politics

Edited by

Ian Holliday
Andrew Gamble
and
Geraint Parry

First published 1999 by
MACMILLAN PRESS LTD
Houndmills, Basingstoke, Hampshire RG21 6XS
and London
Companies and representatives
throughout the world

ISBN 0–333–71096–7 hardcover
ISBN 0–333–71097–5 paperback

A catalogue record for this book is available
from the British Library.

This book is printed on paper suitable for recycling and
made from fully managed and sustained forest sources.

10   9   8   7   6   5   4   3   2   1
08   07   06   05   04   03   02   01   00   99

Copy-edited and typeset by Povey–Edmondson
Tavistock and Rochdale, England

Printed and bound in Great Britain by
Creative Print & Design (Wales), Ebbw Vale

Published in the United States of America by
ST. MARTIN'S PRESS, INC.,
Scholarly and Reference Division
175 Fifth Avenue, New York, N.Y. 10010

ISBN 0–312–22649–7 (cloth)
ISBN 0–312–22650–0 (paper)

Contents

Contents

List of Contributors

Patrick Dunleavy is Professor of Government at the London School of Economics. Educated at Corpus Christi College, Oxford, and Nuffield College, Oxford, he worked at the Open University before moving to the LSE in 1979. He is a long-time editor of the *Developments in British Politics* series, and has published *Democracy, Bureaucracy and Public Choice* (1991) and many other books and papers.

Andrew Gamble is Professor of Politics and Director of the Political Economy Research Centre at the University of Sheffield. Recent publications include *Hayek: The Iron Cage of Liberty*, and journal articles on economic governance, the politics of ownership and comparative political economy.

Ian Holliday is Professor of Policy Studies at the City University of Hong Kong. Recent publications include *The British Cabinet System* (co-authored) and journal articles on British politics and policy. He co-edits the journal *Party Politics*.

Nevil Johnson was from 1969 to 1996 Nuffield Reader in the Comparative Study of Institutions in the University of Oxford and a Professional Fellow of Nuffield College where he is now an Emeritus Fellow. He has written extensively on British and German political institutions, and has a special interest in constitutionalism and the theory of institutions. His books include *In Search of the Constitution* (1977) and *The Limits of Political Science* (1989).

Michael Kenny is Lecturer in Politics at the University of Sheffield. Recent publications include *The First New Left: British Intellectuals after Stalin* and *Rethinking British Decline* (co-edited). He is the author of journal articles on British political thought, ethics and cultural policy, and the insights offered by modern political thought into contemporary international society.

Elizabeth Meehan is Professor of Politics at the Queen's University of Belfast. Recent publications deal with citizenship and the EU, devolution in the UK and British-Irish relations. Examples are 'European Integration and Citizens' Rights: A Comparative Perspective', *Publius: The Journal of Federalism* (1996); 'Citizenship and Social Inclusion', in M. Roche (ed.) *European Citizenship and Social Exclusion*

(1997); 'The Belfast Agreement: Distinctiveness and Cross-Fertilization in the UK's Devolution Programme', *Parliamentary Affairs* (1999).

Michael Moran is Professor of Government in the University of Manchester. He is co-author of the best-selling textbook *Politics UK*, and researches on comparative public policy. His most recent book is *Governing the Health Care State.*

Geraint Parry is the W. J. M. Mackenzie Professor of Government at the University of Manchester. Recent publications include *Political Participation and Democracy in Britain* (co-authored) and *Democracy and Democratization* (co-edited), and journal articles on political theory and political education. He is editor of the journal *Government and Opposition.*

Gillian Peele is Fellow and Tutor in Politics at Lady Margaret Hall, Oxford. She is the author of *Governing the UK* (1995) and a co-editor of *Developments in British Politics 5* (1997) and of *Developments in American Politics 3* (1998).

John Peterson is Jean Monnet Professor of European Politics at the University of Glasgow. Recent publications include *Decision-Making in the European Union* (co-authored), *A Common Foreign Policy for Europe?* (co-edited) and *Technology Policy in the European Union* (co-authored).

Robert Reiner is Professor of Criminology in the Law Department, London School of Economics. Among his recent books are *Chief Constables* (1991), *The Politics of the Police* (2nd edn, 1992) and *Policing* (1996). He was President of the British Society of Criminology from 1993 to 1996. His present research is an ESRC-funded study of changing media representations of crime and criminal justice in Britain since the Second World War.

Martin J. Smith is Professor of Politics at the University of Sheffield. He has published widely on British politics and comparative public policy. His recent publications include *The Core Executive in Britain* and *Quangos, Accountability and Reform* (co-edited).

Robert Thomas is Lecturer in Law at the University of Manchester. He has recently obtained his doctorate on the relationship between English and European Community administrative law, and is currently turning this study into a book.

1
Introduction

GERAINT PARRY

There may seem something paradoxical in asking what are the fundamentals of British politics in this age of anti-foundationalism. In almost every area of political, social or cultural endeavour the fundamentals of the activities are currently called into question. This is the prime characteristic of that multi-faceted phenomenon termed post-modernism. Even if one does not adopt a post-modernist position it needs to be recognised that what appear to have been unquestioned assumptions or principles have been reinterpreted as merely particularly dominant languages or discourses within which an activity is being represented. The claim is more thoroughgoing than the longstanding allegations that world-views are the ideology of a ruling class or the political formula of an elite. There is a recognition that the intellectual world is much more pluralist. Multiple competing viewpoints are available, most of which appear to have a measure of plausibility as explanations of the social world. In this environment it might appear a forlorn task to seek the fundamentals of any activity.

At the same time this very fluidity can give rise to the demand to unearth foundations. The uncertainty, the sense that 'anything goes', prompts commentators and ordinary citizens to look for some markers whereby they can still find their way. Hence politicians, of various hues, talk of going 'back to basics' or of a return to 'fundamental values'. Of course these may be dismissed as themselves political discourses or electoral rhetoric. Nevertheless their significance lies in the politicians' perceptions that this is a rhetoric which is capable of resonating all the more powerfully in a pluralist world. However, and further confounding the difficulty, one reason why calls to go back to basics do resonate is that they are given different meanings by different audiences. We may have varying understandings of what is basic to our lives depending on our generational, cultural or social and economic backgrounds.

Although such extreme pluralism is characteristic of the present time it is important to recognise that a degree of uncertainty as to fundamentals may have been a feature of 'modern' politics since the origins of the modern state in the seventeenth century. The state emerged as a free-standing public power claiming supreme jurisdiction within a given territory. It also assumed certain responsibilities, notably from personal rulers and the church. This combination of capacities and responsibilities might be regarded as definitive of the modern state and hence as fundamental to it. But again difficulties rear themselves. States are to a considerable extent a construction of political elites. Statecraft plays a role in defining what is claimed to be fundamental to the state and to politics in any given era. Competing elites seek to refashion the political arena as well as the activities that go on within it. They may then hope to portray their reconstruction of the arena as something that is built on foundations intended, as all foundations are, to be of long duration. Alternatively, they may prefer to describe their achievements with more apparent modesty as shoring up or extending old, familiar foundations. Edmund Burke caught the essence of such statecraft when he stated that political change should be undertaken in the manner of a sensitive architect who extends an existing building with a design in a similar style.

This latter argument is of particular relevance to the study of the fundamentals of British politics. One of the most common themes in the analysis of Britain is the alleged continuity of its central institutions and practices. A number of these institutions, such as the Crown and Parliament, are linear descendants of medieval politics, leading some writers even to suggest that Britain has never truly been a modern state. Certainly it has not undergone the cataclysmic changes to its institutions brought about either by internal revolution or by military defeat and external invasion which have been the experience of most of its continental European neighbours. Nevertheless it would be manifestly wrong to suppose that these pre-modern institutions had survived unchanged to the twentieth century and particularly absurd to think that they continued in the same power balance. Much of the essence of British statecraft from the seventeenth to the late twentieth century has consisted in adjusting the balances of an informally mixed system of government.

A consequence is that the search for political fundamentals in Britain is analogous to excavating a complex archaeological site. The investigators do not necessarily uncover neatly separable layers of habitation but old materials which have been re-used by later generations, new foundations laid across old or modern façades built to conceal earlier premises. Something of this was captured by Bagehot's famous distinction between the efficient and the dignified parts of the Constitution. The dignified parts conceal the efficient parts from view, including significant changes to the way the efficient parts operate. The population is distracted by the show, allowing the political elites to get on with the job of governing in comparative privacy. One might be tempted to go further than Bagehot and suggest that the dignified aspect becomes what is fundamental. The myth becomes a dominant discourse. As long as this is true the fundamentals can appear to be preserved while the institutions and practices are undergoing radical transformation behind the façade.

What may render this story less convincing is that we are now living in a period of disclosure, impatient of the norm of private government that has been so characteristic of Britain. The more transparent a political system becomes the less likely it is that one myth about fundamentals will convince most elites and citizens over a considerable time. What is termed fundamental is more likely to be perceived as a social construct and to be deconstructed. Fundamentals are expressed through routines which significant agents with appropriate resources seek to perpetuate and reproduce, or to challenge, in the course of social and political interaction. In this sense, just like structure and agency, fundamentals and statecraft go hand in hand, constantly affecting one another (see Chapter 9). If this is so one will not expect to identify fundamentals of British politics that are unchanging so much as practices that are sustained by elites over a period of time but are intermittently under challenge (see Chapter 10). At the same time if the suggestion is true that this is a period in which transparency has become a norm, even if not a reality, it can be expected that it will be a time when such routines are more subject to doubt. The investigation of fundamentals is thus timely as a very reflection of uncertainty.

The Commonalities of the Modern Liberal-Democratic State

With these caveats in mind any study of the construction and deconstruction of British political fundamentals needs to consider whether the proposed fundamentals are specifically British or common to the type of regime to which Britain belongs. Britain is usually described as a state, a nation state, a liberal state and a democratic state. All these have their own characteristics, sometimes in a degree of tension with one another.

The modern state is usually defined as a form of public power with a governmental apparatus that is separable from the persons who rule or administer the apparatus and which exercises monopoly jurisdiction over a given territory. The state is in part an abstraction which then has to be made concrete in law that defines the competencies of its agents, such as civil servants and judges. Some such legal framework is fundamental and in this limited sense Britain does not differ markedly from other states, except in two important respects. First this legality is not contained in or based upon a single written constitutional document. Second, the British state has not generally been conceived, as it has been in the continental European tradition, as a set of institutions that embody a sense of intrinsic public interest not fully reducible to an aggregation of private interests. The British formula of the Crown in Parliament both implied that the supreme authority was rooted, through representation, in society and, increasingly during the nineteenth century, entrusted ministers, formally 'of the Crown', with enhanced power. The effect was an expansion of government comparable to that in continental Europe even though the underlying public philosophy differed.

Another way of approaching the modern state is to regard certain of its functions as fundamental – external security, internal order, welfare provision, education. Nevertheless only the first two have been unequivocally part of state responsibilities from the earliest times. Moreover the meaning of each is contestable. Order is never complete and the provision of welfare may be minimal or extensive. Taken together, however, they have involved an expansion of state activities that is common to modern states, rather than distinctive to Britain (see Chapters 2 and 4).

A nation state is one where the governmental institutions are exercised over a population which possesses a common ancestry, history, culture and, usually, a dominant language. With the rise of nationalism in the nineteenth century, the nation state became a political ideal, as embodying the community and directing it to shared internal and external goals. Britain and France were seen as exemplars. Yet few so-called nation states are genuinely mono-cultural or based on one ethnic grouping. All are to a degree constructions and Britain is again no exception. What is important is the particular history of its construction from the components of England, Wales, Scotland and Northern Ireland and the relation of this to the British Empire, what this history may indicate about how fundamental this creation of identity is and its potential for deconstruction (see Chapter 6).

Britain is also an example of a liberal-democratic polity. Once again this no longer in itself differentiates it from the more advanced industrialized states of the period following the Second World War. The difficulty of determining what is fundamental to a liberal democracy is inbuilt into the term itself. It is a fusion of two quite different ideas. Liberalism is a theory about the appropriate limits of the scope of the state agencies. It insists on restricted obligation of the individual to the state. Democracy refers to the body of persons who legitimately exercise the powers of the state – the 'rule of the people'. Thus one part of the concept asserts the power of the people, while the other is concerned with the limits, imposed or assumed to that power. The democratic element requires minimally that there are fair and free procedures by which 'the people' can individually participate in influencing government and their views be aggregated into a collective expression of political preferences, usually by some form of election. However, modern democracies offer relatively limited opportunities for direct participation and it can plausibly be claimed that systems of representative democracy are partly designed to preserve a distance between people and government. Thus modern democracy involves both participation and exclusion, and what is regarded as fundamental to any particular democracy will depend on the balance between these which historically it has maintained (see Chapter 10).

A similar ambivalence occurs in attempting to establish what is fundamental to liberalism (see Chapter 13). The core is the idea of the state as a civil association that is basically regulative. It maintains a framework of rules that permit and enable individuals and groups to pursue their private purposes in security. It is fundamentally a legalist conception. Historically it has seemed to fit with a policy of *laissez-faire* in economics. Yet liberalism has also been seen as compatible with a more positive role for the state. If it is the task of the state to enable individuals to follow their own life-choices then it may be expected to ensure that citizens are equipped to do so by possessing the requisite educational skills, health and economic security. How one measures the liberalism of any state will depend on an estimate of the rival conceptions of negative and positive liberty and how far either of these conceptions is built into the operative procedures of the state.

British Political Fundamentals in Question

There are therefore fundamentals that are generic to the kind of state
Britain is. Even if these fundamentals are constructed and contestable
they need to be remembered as part of any understanding of what is
fundamental to the distinctive British variant of the modern liberal-
democratic, nation state. Although it has been the contention that
any account of fundamentals, particularly in Britain, has to recognise
that what has been seen as fundamental is subject to historical
evolution, the significance of examining them now is that each of
the fundamental descriptions of Britain which have been favoured
during the twentieth century is currently subject to particularly sharp
challenges, which the chapters of this volume seek to delineate. It may
turn out that one indirect measure of what is fundamental to British
arrangements is by determining which of these challenges fail to offer
alternatives on which elites and citizens can agree, and which do not
cause unpredictable and unintended repercussions for other parts of
the system.

The British State

For all its pre-modern trappings the modern British state developed
from the mid-nineteenth century. A sovereign Parliament dominated
by an executive, backed by an increasingly professional Civil Service
gradually assumed more governmental responsibilities with a massive
expansion in the twentieth century as the state moved from a minimal
state to a welfare state (see Chapters 2 and 4). The apparently
inexorable rise of the state accompanied a presumption that it was
capable of successfully solving the problems it was being given. The
textbook models of Westminster politics and Whitehall government
were widely assumed to work satisfactorily, offering a reasonably
smooth conveyor belt of electoral input, parliamentary processing
and executive output by a disinterested, public-spirited bureaucracy.
Over the last thirty years this combination of models has been
increasingly attacked as an inadequate description of reality and as
offering a complacent picture of governmental performance when
compared with the apparent relative success of other countries in
responding to international economic competition. The criticisms
were from a variety of political directions. Although apparently
centralized, the system lacked adequate coordination. The demands

and expectations of the electorate both overloaded the capacity of government to deliver solutions and simultaneously required government to expand and use up a greater share of national wealth. At the same time Parliament was accused of failing to hold the executive to account, thereby allowing ministers and civil servants too often to fail to respect individual liberties when implementing policy. The public ethic of the Civil Service was challenged, particularly by the New Right, and the provision of services was alleged to be directed to maximizing the interests of the deliverers more than those of the consumers.

The response has been a significant change in central government. Overload has been treated by offload. What were until recently perceived as quintessentially public goods, such as the railways or council housing, were privatized or contracted out. The conventional hierarchical lines of accountability familiar from the Westminster–Whitehall model have been replaced in many instances by more fragmented and complex patterns resulting from the creation of executive agencies and a growing separation between the core and the periphery of the state (see Chapter 5). The objective might be to change the central state to a regulator of service providers (not unfamiliar in the nineteenth century) but it raises three questions about fundamentals. Do the new arrangements reduce the role of the state or, rather, require that its surveillance of the agents of its policies must expand to reduce the autonomy of bodies, such as universities and the professions, which previously saw themselves as self-regulating (see Chapter 9)? Second, has something been lost in the displacement of the line of accountability from citizen to government minister in the ideal or myth of the Westminster Model or is the delivery of services to consumers the modern, more relevant version of accountability? Third, do alternative lines of accountability need to be reinforced or modified in view of the allegations of executive arbitrariness or negligence? A prominent feature of recent years has been the expansion of judicial review whereby judges within the framework of parliamentary sovereignty, may examine and declare unlawful ministerial decisions if they fail to respect procedural standards of fairness or reasonableness. The unelected judges are being propelled into a more prominent quasi-political role in the processes of accountability, with consequences for British governance that are not fully worked out (see Chapter 7).

Many of the same challenges have been mounted to the welfare function of the state (see Chapters 2 and 4). In this case, however, the challenges have so far proved less successful, even though the manner in which the welfare state may have to operate in the future remains a major issue. The entitlement to welfare as a member of a national community has become such a distinctive aspect of citizen rights that a government tampers with it at its peril. Nevertheless the long-standing issues of the universality or the selectivity of provision and of how far the state is responsible for the direct provision of services or for enabling and regulating private provision have never been fully resolved. They are likely to give rise to continuing claims and counter-claims over the supposed breaches of the foundations of the welfare state – with the financing of state pensions one of the prime test cases.

Internal and external order has always been the prime function of the state, definitive of its very purpose in defending civil rights in many political philosophies (see Chapter 8). Yet in Britain the formal policing of order has been somewhat at arm's length from the central state. With the exception of the Metropolitan Police, constabularies have been formally local bodies, headed by chief constables reporting to police authorities. This, however, conceals the reality of much greater policy direction by the centre, which does not face the kind of accountability that would follow from a national police force. The dilemma confronting central government here is that it faces an expectation that it will 'tackle crime' but is reluctant to assume direct responsibility in the face of the apparent impotence of any public authority to deal with the problem or any consensus on appropriate methods. Whether these are the conditions that are likely to lead to a reassessment of existing longstanding practices is questionable.

While external security is a fundamental responsibility of any sovereign state the consequences of this for institutions and practices are heavily dependent on statecraft in the form of foreign policy (see Chapter 12). In the case of Britain the often quoted words, uttered in 1962, of the one-time US Secretary of State Dean Acheson still have relevance – 'Great Britain has lost an Empire and has not yet found a role.' It is arguable that the country is still resting on the laurels of its distinguished stance in the Second World War. It is left with a permanent seat in the UN Security Council, a possibly misplaced faith in its 'special relationship' with the USA, membership of the G7 and a sense that it has an international status that tempts successive governments to wish the country to punch beyond its weight in foreign affairs. It does not, however, sustain this role by means of compulsory national service which, in many other states, is an aspect of national citizen identity.

Simultaneously it has an ambivalent relationship to the European Union. The end of the Cold war, along with the growing recognition of interdependence induced by a globalized economy, may impel a substantial reappraisal of British foreign policy. How many horses is Britain able to continue to ride in world affairs? Is the country to commit itself to Europe? Or will it seek to play the part of the good world citizen, supporting UN operations, in the manner of Sweden or Canada? On past evidence Britain will continue to have severe difficulties in deciding on any one role, with the consequence that it will face repeated debates over the kind of security forces it requires and over defence expenditure.

It is over its membership of the European Union that Britain faces the greatest challenge to its fundamental institutions and practices (see Chapter 12). The EU is a transnational body with no true precedent in world affairs. It has features of both a state and a conventional international organization as well as, uniquely in this sphere, possessing some democratic legitimacy through its elected Parliament. As such it poses issues for Britain as a state and as a nation, and for the way it conducts its democratic and civil procedures.

The problem for Britain has arisen because post-war British elites, and public opinion, did not regard the building of the institutions of the European Economic Community as crucial to the future of the UK itself. As a result there has been an element of drift in the manner in which Britain has moved 'from nation state to member state'. The debate in Britain has been conducted in the language of 'sovereignty', which has often been confounded with the language of independence. The European Union is the most complex response to the recognition of the interdependence of modern states. Of course no state has ever been so powerful as to be totally independent of outside pressures. Britain's very development as a world power was based on its trading position and made its economy sensitive to market conditions. Nevertheless it is arguable that globalization has made states far more vulnerable, more rapidly, to developments beyond their control. The EU represents a step further than the conventional response to vulnerability through international cooperation. Although formally British membership might be regarded as ultimately compatible with traditional sovereignty since entry was a decision of the UK Parliament, the effect of joining is to create a legal relationship which cannot readily be encompassed by the standard theory of sovereignty that has been part of the operative assumptions of British elites.

British citizens are now in effect directly subject to a multiplicity of laws and regulations that emanate from the EU. Acts of Parliament are now required not to be inconsistent with European law and if in breach of this proviso may be declared unlawful by national courts or by the European Court of Justice (see Chapter 7). In some policy areas, such as agriculture, Strasbourg and Brussels have become more significant players than Westminster and Whitehall. The extent to which this is so is becoming increasingly evident to elites and citizens alike and requires new forms of political behaviour, whether it is lobbying in Europe or appealing from British to European law or disclaiming governmental responsibility for policies on the grounds that they emanate from Brussels. New lines of accountability appear to be required. Since the EU is a construction of countries with differing conceptions of the public function of the state from that traditional in the UK its political, administrative and juridical practices are likely to reflect the continental understanding of the state (or proto-state). Accordingly Britain may appear to be institutionally programmed to be an awkward partner in Europe. Nevertheless, the question facing Britain is whether its response must be to seek to reinvent European institutions to accommodate British traditions or to reinvent the UK. The first option has repeatedly been frustrated by the hesitations of British opinion at each stage in the development of the EU up to and including joining the European Monetary Union. With departure from the EU scarcely practicable this has left the reluctant modification of the UK as the only option.

Britain as a Nation

The EU is also a factor in the UK's conception of itself as a nation. The last few decades have seen an upsurge of interest, academic and popular, in the multinational composition of the UK. 'Territorial politics' – the need to maintain the internations of the English, Welsh, Scottish and Irish components of the UK – has been seen as a fundamental feature of the polity (see Chapter 6). However, this issue scarcely featured in political analyses in the earlier parts of the century, with the exception of the problem of (Northern) Ireland. Although a sense of national identity below UK level survived and was confirmed, for example, in sporting fixtures between the nations it presented relatively few problems for the centre. To a great extent the elites and aspirants to the elite in Scotland and Wales saw their interests as bound up with either England or the Empire, and a combination of native and British identity could be maintained without excessive friction so long as those interests were being served.

The end of Empire, the continuing decline of the UK's economic and political status in the world and, after both the world wars and the cold war, the disappearance of a 'hostile other' have removed some of the incentives to elites to commit themselves to a British identity. Other nation states in Europe, even those with Napoleonic centralized systems, have combined economic success with devolved or federal government, which seemed to offer more opportunities for localized elites both to maintain a particular identity and mount a platform on which to seek access to international capital investment. The EU also offered both new avenues of influence, partially bypassing the national government, and an alternative or additional European identity to the particular and the British. The result has been that territorial politics has entered the agenda but without the dominant English nationality forming any clear strategy for new institution-building.

The response of devolved government, with differing powers, parliamentary bodies and electoral systems, to Scotland, Wales and Northern Ireland constitutes a major alteration in British practices of such long standing that they are among the major contenders for the label of fundamentals, the repercussions of which are difficult to foresee. The only example of devolution, in Northern Ireland, is not encouraging as an example of British management of such a polity, involving as it did localized exploitation, violent opposition and the regular use of military force on UK soil. Nor is it entirely relevant since the cleavages and the party system were different from those on the mainland. The uncertainty over the significance of Scottish devolution is indicated by its being welcomed by some as the safeguard against independence and by others as the major step towards it. It is equally unknown whether the effect will be to strengthen or weaken the sense of British identity.

The repercussions of this new constitutional landscape stretch further. The UK is drifting into a new quasi-federal system but without the legal framework that normally underpins a genuine and consciously created federal order and allocates clear responsibilities and sorts out demarcation disputes (see Chapters 3 and 6). There is, for example, no constitutional court which has the task of resolving such matters other than the Judicial Committee of the Privy Council – a body with little public visibility. The consequences for the distribution of seats and influence in the UK Parliament have never been resolved. No attempt has been made to address the implications for the dominant English partner, either in terms of its distinctive territorial institutions or in terms of its own national culture. Here too the EU plays a role as certain European matters fall within the remit of devolved bodies. All this might admittedly be interpreted as typical British pragmatic reform, resulting in a set of institutions which no-one would have consciously invented, and a tribute to constitutional flexibility. The outcome, nevertheless, is an irreversible transformation in governance that is likely to change the rules of the political game in the UK. It sets up new power bases and opportunity structures for elites to bargain with the centre and with the external world and requires a different set of political and constitutional conventions.

Britain as a Liberal Democracy

The British form of liberal democracy faces challenges to both its distinctive liberal and its distinctive democratic elements. The form UK democracy takes has led, particularly in the post-war era, to what critics have denigrated, but some advocates have praised, as 'adversary politics' and 'elective dictatorship'. The relative majority voting system ('first past the post') favours a choice between two competing parties and, generally but not invariably, promotes the alternation of disciplined parties in office with large enough a parliamentary majority to pass their policies into legislation.

From the 1970s onwards the accumulation of power that such elective dictatorship permitted came under attack. It was argued that governments were able to push through major changes to institutions, such as local government, without adequate consultation and consent. It was also alleged that majorities could no longer be trusted to act with restraint and sensitivity when making significant alterations to long-established rights such as membership of unions or employment rights. Even if the cynic might point out that these attacks came from the political 'outs' of each period the result was a spread among elite opinion of support for constitutional reform. Two broad sets of proposals emerged – to formalize a set of human or civil rights and to reform the parliamentary system by changing the electoral system and radically modifying the House of Lords (see Chapter 3).

Although proposals were drawn up during the 1980s by various pressure groups for a written constitution and a bill of rights for Britain along the lines of the United States, the preference of the

Labour government elected in 1997 was to incorporate the European Convention on Human Rights into ordinary UK legislation. This way of proceeding may appear traditional, but its implications challenge many of the routines of British politics. First, such rights are not to be regarded as consisting primarily and negatively in the silence of the law but as stated positively and derived from a set of abstract principles (see Chapter 11). Second, the judges will not operate on the presumption of the Constitutionality of a statute passed by a sovereign Parliament but may be asked to declare whether it is compatible with the Human Rights Act. If the court declares it incompatible, Parliament will be expected to pass 'remedial' legislation. The fiction of parliamentary sovereignty is preserved but the reality will have changed. The courts will be in the unprecedented position of exercising judicial review in this area. Moreover the judges will be expected to look not merely at the letter but the substance of the law, which may lead them into areas of policy, such as abortion rights or penal provision, that have been clearly the province of elected politicians. The potentiality exists for the judicializing of issues in American fashion with serious consequences for political accountability and debate (see Chapter 7).

The problem is further complicated by the emergence in ideological debate of ideas of group rights (see Chapter 11). Historically the idea of the state as a civil association has been predicated on the individual as the subject of law and the possessor of civil rights. The law was, ideally at least, 'indifferent to difference'. Recent years have however seen a new emphasis on the need to respect difference, to acknowledge the multiple 'identities' people have as members of groups or categories. The driving force behind the ideological change has been feminism but the call has been taken up by a variety of minorities – ethnic, sexual and cultural. It has become customary to redescribe Britain as a multi-cultural society, somewhat akin to the United States where a stress on cultural and ethnic differences, admittedly empirically much greater than in Britain, has come to displace the integrationist imagery of the 'melting pot' with that of the 'salad bowl'. The implication of identity politics is that policies and laws should at the very least not discriminate against, and should possibly help sustain, minority cultural practices. Alternatively a liberal polity might be expected not to discriminate in favour of certain traditions and behaviour merely because they are shared or even in part historically constitutive of the cultural majority. One consequence may be that the courts become involved in sensitive questions affecting the rights of minority groups in relation to established practices in areas such as education, religion or marriage. These issues affect how far British people can legitimately express through their laws a 'thick' sense of identity based on a shared history or whether, in the face of modern pluralism, unity is more appropriately sustained by a 'thinner' identity consisting in a common commitment to minimal civil order. Moreover the question whether, as in the United States, the courts (composed of unelected persons largely drawn in Britain from relatively narrow sectors of society) are the most appropriate fora for resolving such delicate issues is a difficult one to answer in the context of British democracy and its public philosophy.

Reform of the electoral system also presents a major challenge to the established processes of the British version of democracy (see Chapters 3 and 10). The argument in favour of some more proportional version of voting is justified on the basis of a conception of equal weighting of votes, which might be regarded as a basic axiom of popular rule and is notoriously denied by the system of voting in British general elections. However a truly proportional system is likely profoundly to alter the nature of two-party adversarial politics. It changes the system from one in which there are usually clear winners and losers to one in which elections result in greater or lesser party representation. The clear demarcation between the party in power and a main, formally constituted Her Majesty's Opposition may become less sustainable. It would also probably result in an increase in the representation of smaller parties in Parliament and in the likelihood of coalitions and a politics of bargaining. It is sometimes pointed out that coalitions are far from unknown in British history and hence that adversarial politics is not to be regarded as fundamental but as a particular historical construct. Nevertheless for over fifty years no governmental coalitions have been formed and the procedures of British politics have, for most of the period during which one can reasonably describe Britain as a democracy, assumed the alternation of government and opposition with coalition an exception, often in some perceived emergency.

One of the features of the electoral system at general elections is that it maintains a relationship between a single Member of Parliament and a constituency. Most proportional alternatives dilute this link and many compromises may well appear unnecessarily complicated and possibly alienating to an electorate for whom these matters are of esoteric interest. But, again, multi-member constituencies were part of normal politics in nineteenth-century Britain. They may be foreign to contemporary British democracy, but they are not totally outside the longer political tradition. Any electoral system bestows advantages and disadvantages and will reflect the intentions of its creators. The question facing Britain is whether it can long sustain the incoherences that may arise when, without any change to present arrangements and proposals, the electorate encounters a patchwork of differing systems (proportional and non-proportional) of voting within one nation state for general elections and elections to the European Parliament and the Scottish, Welsh and Northern Ireland assemblies. No clear public philosophy has yet emerged to justify or rationalize what may otherwise appear anomalies.

Proposals to reform the composition of the House of Lords illustrate the difficulty both of establishing what is fundamental to Britain and of changing it. The fact that an alteration may lead to an unpredictable and unintended chain of consequences in other parts of the system is indeed an unobtrusive measure of a fundamental. The House of Lords is by any rationalist standards an anachronistic survival into the democratic era of a pre-modern institution which has been 'modernized' in a haphazard manner. However, with the exception of the abolition of the voting rights of hereditary peers (once itself a 'fundamental' but now entirely lacking a contemporary philosophical justification), there is little consensus on its reform. The coalition of groupings in favour of change threatens to dissolve in the face of any alternative proposals as it becomes clear that they would have the effect of embedding some particular set of interests in the fabric of the Constitution. A chamber of appointees shifts the balance of the Constitution still further towards the executive. There is equally, as the US Founding Fathers saw, no point in electing a second chamber that will merely replicate the first. An elected chamber intended to represent the major regions and nations of the UK could be as divisive as it could be integrative. The representation of the major interests in the country (religious, ethnic, commercial, industrial, cultural, environmental, etc.) could 'freeze' the balance of interests as they exist at the end of the millennium (just as the inclusion of bishops of the Church of England in the House reflects the establishment of the Church at an earlier era). It also leaves open which interests might be represented – *which* religions, *which* environmental lobby – and how a franchise would be constructed. There appears a problem to every solution, arising from the fact that all reformations bring new winners and losers.

Bound up with the reform of the electoral system is the fate of the political parties. Party is the binding force in democracy, belonging both to the state and to civil society. Parties were not always so fundamental to British politics. Eighteenth- and nineteenth-century parties were looser and the bond between the state and those in society who were part of the political equation was also maintained through social class and the old estates. In the twentieth century party has permeated politics so that only in limited areas of rural local government is it unimportant. It is through party that the main features of twentieth century fundamentals have been constructed and reconstructed (see Chapter 9). Nevertheless party may be on the wane in public estimation. Party activity has declined in recent decades and, particularly among the young, political participation has been channelled through interest groups in areas as various as the environment, health and gender issues. A substantial proportion of the population are members of some kind of group or association. Membership in certain groups vastly exceeds that of the political parties. Many of these associations are connected with work or leisure, and membership often consists merely of passive payment of a subscription. Nevertheless they are the source of social capital that can lead to the development of occasional activism either spontaneous or mobilized. It is sometimes protest that is mobilized and, while one should not exaggerate either the numbers who actually engage in protest or the extent to which it might have increased, it is clear that some kinds of direct activity have become part of the accepted repertoire of political conduct in Britain. The potential exists for a political culture in which participation is relatively strong in the articulation of interests but weakened in the aggregative function performed by parties which involves the art of compromise, praised by Edmund Burke as the morality of politicians but which since the concentrated onslaught on the ethic of disinterested public service has been satirized and disdained as dirtying hands (see Chapter 5).

Some electoral systems on offer as alternatives to the first-past-the-post system, such as list systems, may enhance the power of parties. However, the more the political culture comes to favour greater citizen participation the greater the danger will be to parties in appearing to increase their ability to impose candidates upon the electorate's choice. Liberal representative democracy strikes a balance between participation and exclusion. It expects citizen involvement but only consciously mobilizes it at the intervals of general elections. Representation is a process designed to keep the people at a certain distance from politics. Their role is not to rule but to choose or cashier those who do rule. For the vast majority of British citizens political activity is confined to marking a ballot paper on a few occasions in a lifetime. Only a small minority contact MPs or local councillors or involve themselves in campaigning. Radical democrats have long hoped for a transformation into a more participatory culture. In Britain the opportunities for wider participation have been few, but this is a further situation that has been changing with the greater resort to referendums on constitutional issues such as the elected governmental arrangements for Scotland, Wales and Northern Ireland, on a multitude of local issues and promised on entry into the European Monetary Union and on changes to the electoral system. To this might be added proposals for directly elected mayors for cities, elected school governors, the election of party leaders by the members instead of by electoral colleges, the growth in single-issue groups and consumer complaint procedures for some public services.

Interest representation constitutes an alternative avenue of participation in liberal democracies and has been a basic feature of the British political style since the nineteenth century. It reflects the conception of the British state as being as much a reflector and arbiter of plural sectional interests as the embodiment of an indivisible public interest in the continental European manner. This pattern of representation also displays the balance between participation and exclusion. Interest groups are many and various, but they differ markedly in political influence. In significant areas of public policy certain groups can gain 'insider' status and are involved in regular consultations with government. Policy 'networks' form that may entail a degree of elite consensus on either the procedures of consultation or even the substance of policy. One of the tasks of interest representatives is to enter the circle of insider groups. These relationships have long been portrayed as mutually beneficial to government and the interests in obtaining sound policy which will receive the consent of the affected parties. However these somewhat cosy relationships have come under attack. The Thatcher government's anticorporatist philosophy led it to challenge the special access of notable groups, especially the trades unions, but also many professional groups whose activities were subjected to more formal regulation (see Chapter 9). In addition the greater belief in transparency has opened the activities of certain pressure groups, particularly professional lobbyists, to critical scrutiny for their alleged effects on the conduct of public life. There have been growing pressures for supervision and Parliament has been induced to concede, almost without precedent, a degree of outside regulation through the office of a Parliamentary Commissioner for Standards. These developments however are unlikely to have delegitimized either interest representation or the formation of policy networks. Both are too useful as linkage mechanisms between state and civil society, however unequal the process. The activities may become more transparent and the networks may change as new interests emerge and as the policy areas become increasingly globalized, involving once again the EU as both a player and a target for pressure.

Experience advises caution in expecting a marked change in the fundamental political culture of limited and unequal participation but the normative climate may be changing. Of more concern, to other Western democracies as well as Britain, is that there may be a growing divide between those who are part of the polity and a class who combine social with political exclusion. It has always been the case that political participants have been disproportionately drawn from the more advantaged sections of the population. These are more likely to be involved in networks of associational life and are able to convert this 'social capital' into 'political capital' by knowing whom to contact or how to find their way through the bureaucracy. There is a danger, however, of the emergence of a category of the population, poor, young, unemployed and often from ethnic minorities, whose networks do not connect to either civil society or the state and who fail even to perform the minimal activity of voting. The problem facing elites and other citizens is whether the old methods of incorporation of the disaffected can be revived (especially in a climate of low economic growth) or whether the response is to be merely one of containment (see Chapter 8). This could be the greatest task confronting the disciplinary institutions of British society, understood in the widest sense to include education, welfare and social support.

Fundamentals and Power

Political fundamentals are invariably constructions and they betray the history of that construction. In Britain, more than in a country such as the US which has had its specific moment of constitution-building, the history of construction and reconstruction has been continuous. What has appeared fundamental at one period has been drastically altered at another – with the added difficulty that the novelty may be disguised behind a façade of continuity. Fundamentals are routines that are observed by elites and citizens over a period which is seldom easily definable. All such routines involve and sustain a distribution of power. This is one reason why fundamentals appear fundamental and are difficult to shift. There are almost invariably interests that are likely to be severely and adversely affected by any change to a set pattern of arrangements by which they have gained, often without their needing any effort to do so, having been sustained by what are for everyone familiar features of the political landscape. It may be an indirect test of what is fundamental to British politics at any time that it becomes extremely difficult to discover any alternative procedure or institution on which all can agree. One effect of formalizing and codifying a constitution may be to stabilize or 'freeze' a particular prevailing balance of forces in the society. Constitutions are, among other things, power maps and it is the most difficult of political arts to draw them in such a way as to be procedurally fair to all citizens and their chosen ways of life. In any new arrangement there will be winners and losers and the more 'fundamental' the innovation comes to be, the more routine the distribution of advantage and disadvantage becomes. Fundamentals are never neutral; they have histories. Political fundamentals are invariably constructions and they betray the history of that construction. In Britain, more than in a country such as the US which has had its specific moment of constitution-building, the history of construction and reconstruction has been continuous. What has appeared fundamental at one period has been drastically altered at another – with the added difficulty that the novelty may be disguised behind a façade of continuity. Fundamentals are routines which are observed by elites and citizens over a period which is seldom easily definable. All such routines involve and sustain a distribution of power. This is one reason why fundamentals appear fundamental and are difficult to shift. There are almost invariably interests which are likely to be severely and adversely affected by any change to a set pattern of arrangements by which they have gained, often without their needing any effort to do so, having been sustained by what are for everyone familiar features of the political landscape. It may be an indirect test of what is fundamental to British politics at any time that it becomes extremely difficult to discover any alternative procedure or institution on which all can agree. One effect of formalizing and codifying a constitution may be to stabilize or 'freeze' a particular prevailing balance of forces in the society. Constitutions are, among other things, power maps and it is the most difficult of political arts to draw them in such a way as to be procedurally fair to all citizens and their chosen ways of life. In any new arrangement there will be winners and losers and the more 'fundamental' the innovation comes to be, the more routine the distribution of advantage and disadvantage becomes. Fundamentals are never neutral; they have histories.

2
State, Economy and Society

ANDREW GAMBLE

The state is one of the fundamentals of British politics. But it is not easy to define; its boundaries, its capacities, its purpose and its functions are all disputed (Dunleavy and O'Leary, 1987). A key issue is how far the state has autonomy. Is the state best understood as subordinate to society, or as dominating and controlling it, with a will and interest of its own? The distinction is a fundamental one. It underpins Michael Oakeshott's characterization of the two principal ways of understanding the state in modern Western political thought, as a *civil* association and as an *enterprise* association (Oakeshott, 1975). As a civil association the state has no specific aims of its own, confining itself to providing a framework of rules within which individuals choose the aims they wish to pursue. It promotes individual liberty and minimal government. As an enterprise association the state is organized as an enterprise, with specific objectives in view, such as economic prosperity, national security or the welfare of its citizens. All other activities have a lower priority in respect of this central purpose. The state is interventionist and developmental, seeking to shape the behaviour of its citizens to achieve certain ends.

A second issue is modernity. While some have interpreted the history of the last hundred years as the gradual erosion of the liberal character of the British state as a civil association through the rise of the collectivist and interventionist politics of democracy (Greenleaf, 1983a, 1983b, 1987), others have lamented how the British state has never become a truly modern state, capable of carrying through the modernization of its economy and society. It is a dinosaur left over from an earlier period of political development, the last *ancien régime* in Europe with its array of antiquated, pre-modern institutions like the Monarchy and the House of Lords, and a political culture which celebrates tradition, prizes status and inhibits dynamism in economy and society (Nairn, 1977; Marquand, 1988).

This chapter will begin by defining the term 'the modern state' and identifying its modes of governance. It then goes on to discuss what is fundamental about the British state; is it its liberal constitution? or is it its character as an *ancien régime*? The first emphasises the distinctiveness of the British state as a self-governing civil association, enjoying parliamentary government and freedom under the law; the second its (relative) failure to become an agent of modernization. Yet what both ignore is the extent to which the British state *has* always been much more than just a civil association. Three ways of characterizing the way in which the British state has been organised to pursue particular purposes are then explored; capitalism, empire and welfare. These perspectives do not exhaust all aspects of the British state, and are often complementary rather than competing explanations of what is fundamental to it. This is because the institutions and relationships they identify are necessary features of any modern state, and make comparison between states possible. At the same time how the different structures combine, what their precise content is, and what relative weight they carry within the whole does vary between states, and it is this that makes each particular state distinctive, with its own unique history and institutional matrix (Hall, 1986).

The Modern State

The idea of the modern state signifies above all a separation of the state of the *ruler* from the state of the *realm*. From the sixteenth century onwards the state came to be seen as a form of public power separate from both ruler and ruled and constituting the supreme political authority within a defined territory (Skinner, 1978). The key aspects of this definition are the notion of the state as a separate, freestanding public power with specific competencies and capacities, the fact that its jurisdiction is territorially bounded, and that within that territory it claims sovereignty. As an agency or set of agencies the state acquires an identity separate from the society; at the same time it comes to personify and symbolize the whole society. This is how the term, the British state, can sometimes be used to mean no more than the British government, but at other times can be used as shorthand for the ensemble of government, society and economy and its modes of governance.

'Governance' means the formal and informal institutions through which a society is governed, and is much broader than the term 'government', which is one of the organizations involved in governance. The main modes of governance are markets, hierarchies, networks, associations and communities, and its main sites are the state, civil society and the household. One of the main questions to be asked about the British state or any other state is which modes of governance are most important, and how they are combined, because this relates to issues of where power is located, how agendas get set and what determines outcomes – or who gets what, when, and how.

The Whig Interpretation of History

The state in the sense of a free-standing public power is a key component of modernity, and no society could be described as modern which had not acquired a state of this kind. At one-time no-one would have doubted that Britain was a modern state. Indeed in many respects it was in the vanguard of development. The unification of all the lands of the British Isles under one central government, the high degree of ethnic homogeneity, the clear physical boundaries of the territory, and the vigorous development of new kinds of administration and representation, made the British state a quintessential example of the new form of centralized public power, and a very successful one. Britain emerged from long wars with its European rivals in possession of the largest empire in the world, and at the same time became the pioneer of the Industrial Revolution which transformed society and economy. In the middle of the nineteenth century Britain was widely seen as the most modern society, which showed to others, as Marx put it, the image of their own future (Marx, 1976: 91). Britain was at the leading edge of the capitalist, scientific and democratic revolutions, which transformed traditional societies and provided the benchmarks for modernization.

Britain's leading role in these revolutions was so obvious to contemporaries in the nineteenth century that it gave rise to a particular narrative about Britain's development, the Whig interpretation of history, which treated British history as the story of liberty, a succession of struggles which had ended with the defeat of authoritarian and arbitrary government, and the consolidation of basic freedoms for all citizens. Parliament was the central institution in this account, and was the guarantor of British liberty and its main symbol. Some of the features of the Whig view of history, such as the notion of inevitable progress, fell out of favour in the twentieth century, but what remained was a widespread view that British political institutions had reached a state of maturity which could hardly be improved upon, and which remained the standard by which political systems in other parts of the world should be judged (Beer, 1965).

The Whig interpretation of history underpins the view that Britain is a self-governing civil association and does not possess a bureaucratic state of the European kind. But the absence of the kind of legal doctrine of the state which is found in other political systems with codified constitutions and administrative law does not mean Britain does not have a modern state, only that the state in Britain is organized somewhat differently. All modern states are both civil associations and enterprise associations in Oakeshott's sense; it is the balance between the two which varies.

The British State as a Liberal State

The Whig interpretation of history is part of a broader liberal perspective which remains the most pervasive and deeply rooted of all the views of the British state. What is fundamental to the British state in this interpretation is its character as a civil association, the provision of a framework of general rules within which individuals take responsibility for themselves and make their own decisions as to how they live and with whom they interact. The state is an association among individuals for the purpose of government, and therefore can work through many different kinds of organizations.

This classical liberal conception of the state starts from the assumption that the real dynamism of the social order resides in civil society. The state is subordinate to civil society, and exists only to advance the interests and express the values of civil society. It does not have an independent role. The essence of this conception is that the state should be limited in both its powers and functions, because as an organization the state is limited in its capacity to do good, but unlimited in its capacity to do harm by taking away the liberty of its citizens (Hayek, 1960).

There are many aspects of the British state which reflect this liberal conception. The resistance to standing armies, conscription, a national or an armed police force; the divorce between power and pomp, most marked in the relatively modest style of the British Prime Minister compared with the imperial grandeur of the Monarch; the preference for running many services and organizations through appointed boards which are at one remove from government itself and act as a buffer between the state and civil society; the emphasis on individual liberties, which although not codified, are taken as inviolate, their symbol being habeas corpus; the attitude to territorial management, which permitted varied and often anomalous constitutional arrangements to exist in different parts of the kingdom; the defence of localism and a resistance to the encroachment of central authority; and the tolerance of different religions and different political opinions (in the nineteenth century, for example, Britain was renowned for the haven it provided for political exiles of all kinds from the rest of Europe).

This liberal view of the British state has been much lauded. In a famous passage which opens his book on English History, AJP Taylor wrote:

> Until August 1914 a sensible, law-abiding Englishman could pass through life and hardly notice the existence of the state beyond the post office and the policeman. He could live where he liked and as he liked. He had no official number or identity card. He could travel abroad or leave his country for ever without a passport or any sort of official permission. He could exchange his money for any other currency without restriction or limit. . . A foreigner could spend his life in this country without permit and without informing the police. Unlike the countries of the European continent, the state did not require its citizens to perform military service. The Englishman paid taxes on a modest scale: nearly £200 million in 1913–14, or rather less than 8 per cent of the national income. . . . The state acted only to help those who could not help themselves. It left the adult citizen alone. (Taylor, 1970: 25).

Taylor was contrasting nineteenth-century liberal England with twentieth-century collectivist England. This picture of nineteenth-century liberal England is exaggerated, as many critics have pointed out. The state was far more active and intrusive than Taylor suggests, particularly in local government. But there remains a kernel of truth in Taylor's account. In the nineteenth century there was something distinctive about the way in which the British state was organized and related to its citizens which set it apart from states elsewhere. In particular the state bureaucracy was comparatively small and individual liberties, at least for those with property, were better protected.

The constitutional arrangements associated with this model are described in Chapters 3 and 5. Limited government was protected through a constitution that distributed powers between Crown, Lords, Commons, and the judiciary. The checks and balances of this constitution were never laid down in a single document like the American, and so were never entrenched. They were nonetheless real, and admired by many foreign observers from Montesquieu onwards for providing the basis for strong and effective, but limited government.

The advent of democracy saw classical liberalism fragment into conservative-liberals and social-liberals, who differed principally in their view of the legitimate roles and functions of the state.

Conservative Liberalism

For conservative liberals limited government is a supreme value, so democracy is viewed as the main threat to the fundamental character of the British state. This is because democracy encourages public policies which promote centralization and uniformity, and views the state as an enterprise with a particular goal rather than as an association with no goal other than to assist its citizens in pursuing whatever goals they choose. Rather than being fundamental to the British state, democracy has been grafted onto the structure which already existed, and if not carefully controlled threatens to subvert the conditions of liberty, by sanctioning the growth of intrusive and interventionist government, rather than respecting and maintaining the traditional framework of general rules.

For its proponents the great virtue of the British state as a liberal state lies precisely in its undefined character, because it is this which gives it its flexibility and pragmatism, its ability to respond to new interests and demands and, by making timely concessions and accommodations, to preserve its essential institutional core intact. This institutional continuity of the British state has been much commented upon, and the reason for it is firmly associated with its liberal character. The state responds to the civil society of which it is a part and takes its direction from that civil society rather than seeking to impose its own will or objectives upon it. The danger of any kind of codified constitution from this perspective is that it locks in a particular set of arrangements which may be the best available at that time, but may later be judged inappropriate and then may be very difficult to change. The British state is able to evolve more easily, since there are no such legal obstacles.

Social Liberalism

The alternative way of thinking about Britain as a liberal state is the social-liberal tradition. The importance of voluntarism and strong public institutions outside the state are still emphasised, but so too are the drawbacks of a liberal state which adopts a *laissez-faire* attitude to society and the economy. At the end of the nineteenth century and early decades of the twentieth century New Liberal thinkers like Hobhouse, Hobson and Keynes justified a more active state and a more public sphere in order to protect and promote the liberal character of British institutions. On this view the British state could only retain its liberal character if governments were prepared to intervene to tackle social evils, to counter the excesses of individualism and to maintain active communities and public institutions (Clarke, 1978). What still made such programmes liberal was the belief that the state's role was chiefly to be an enabler, and that it was not necessary or desirable for the state to become the direct provider and controller. Government had to give a lead, but the public interest would be secured through the cooperation of many different groups and organizations. This social-liberal conception of the British state is in sharp contrast to the conservative-liberal view.

An *Ancien Régime?*

The liberalism of the British state, although much celebrated, has not always been regarded as a blessing. There have been critics on right and left who have argued that British government has become both highly centralized and ineffective at managing change. The British constitution has been hollowed out, and the balance between its different elements has been destroyed. The supremacy of the Commons, the marginalization of the Lords and the Crown, and the employment of the doctrine of parliamentary sovereignty to reverse decisions in the Courts has meant the creation of an 'elective dictatorship', an executive which when backed by a working majority in the Commons has fewer checks and balances than any other executive in an established democracy (Mount, 1992).

In the 1960s and 1970s Perry Anderson and Tom Nairn mounted a wide-ranging critiques of the liberal conception of the state, and the Whig interpretation of history (Anderson, 1992; Nairn, 1977). They questioned whether the British state could be regarded as a truly modern state, arguing that it was more accurately seen as a survival of a pre-modern form of state, which had been preserved into the modern era. The external success of the British state in colonial annexation and economic development had insulated it from the kind of pressures which forced change elsewhere, and had maintained a remarkable degree of institutional continuity. Many of the traditions and institutions which derived from pre-modern, pre-capitalist periods had been preserved. The most obvious sign of this was such survivals into the twentieth century as the House of Lords, a revising legislative chamber in which the hereditary principle was still used to provide the largest part of the membership, as well as the many medieval rituals which still characterized the operation of the Crown, Parliament, the Law and many other institutions and professions in British life.

More generally, Anderson and Nairn argued that although Britain had been one of the first countries to embrace capitalism the capitalist revolution in Britain had been incomplete. First, the multinational British state had never developed into the kind of nation state which was established in the nineteenth century; it owed its origins not to any principle of national self-determination but to the policies of territorial aggrandisement and strategic alliance which were practised by the English state in the sixteenth, seventeenth and eighteenth centuries. A hybrid form of state had emerged. Second, unlike other countries Britain had failed to develop either science-led industry or an egalitarian civil society. Far from maintaining its reputation of being the workshop of the world, the British economy in the twentieth century was plagued by low investment, low productivity, inadequate skills, and backwardness in integrating technological innovation with the production process. Similarly British civil society in the twentieth century was widely seen as obsessed with tradition and status, to the detriment of enterprise opportunity, and creativity.

Anderson and Nairn argued that the survival of a pre-modern state form into the twentieth century meant that Britain lacked the kind of state which was capable of modernizing the economy and society. A key moment in the birth of the modern state was the French Revolution, and the revolutions it set in train across Europe, which ultimately destroyed the basis of the old order, and the privileges of power of landowning aristocracies, and refounded civil society on the basis of universal and equal individual rights. Britain's own 'bourgeois revolution' took place much earlier, in the seventeenth century.

The issues in that civil war concerned the powers of the Crown and the claims of religion. The bourgeoisie was notably absent. It was the 'least pure' bourgeois revolution of any of the bourgeois revolutions in Europe. The justification for calling it a bourgeois revolution at all was that the kind of state which emerged from it was very unlike the absolutist states common in many other parts of Europe. The British state was subordinate to civil society and to its commercial, financial, and later industrial interests. It legitimated the existence of capitalist relations in agriculture, and made possible their extension to industry. It put relatively few obstacles in the path of the spontaneous flowering of capitalist economic activity.

Radical movements did emerge in Britain at the time of the French Revolution, which favoured sweeping away hierarchy and rank and reconstituting British society and the British state on the kind of principles which had animated the American and French revolutions. But a policy of concession and reform on the one hand, and the fear of the propertied class of the dangers of radical revolt on the other, blunted the force of the radicals, and led eventually to the coalescence of new and old elites, with the English aristocracy continuing to pay a leading role in government and in setting the ethos and style of British public life. The subsequent challenge of democracy and the rise of the labour movement was also accommodated within the traditional structures of the British state. In the twentieth century the British state still retained therefore substantial structural characteristics of its pre-modern origins, and was as a result poorly adapted to the task of modernizing British institutions. On Anderson and Nairn's account what is fundamental about the British state is the extent to which it is not a modern state at all. Many of the most important aspects of British society reflect this fact.

The Anderson and Nairn theses have sparked a great deal of debate since they were first published, with contributions from both left and right. On the left Edward Thompson argued that they were erecting an inappropriate model of what a modern state comprised, derived predominantly from French experience, and as a result were drawing false conclusions (Thompson, 1965). They failed to perceive how despite the survival of aristocratic rituals and even personnel, the state in the nineteenth century was remade both by the Victorian professional and business class, and by radical movements from below. Change was slower and less abrupt than elsewhere, and was in line with English traditions and circumstances, but Thompson argued it was no less thorough-going. He argued that Anderson and Nairn were wrong to use a single model of development against which all other states should be judged. There are several ways in which states can be modern. The British path of development might be unique but so was the French and the German. Although there were certain commonalties each country had its own distinctive path. There was nothing backward or pre-modern about Britain. They were also wrong to see political change as the result of a hegemony orchestrated from above. He argued that they underestimated how the state was constantly being remade by the struggles and pressures from below. The great achievements of the radical movements were lost to view. Thompson shared Anderson and Nairn's emphasis on the importance of class for understanding the British state, but argued that their analysis was far too pessimistic about the possibilities for change.

On the right Jonathan Clark criticized Anderson and Nairn from a different angle. What is fundamental about the British state for conservatives like Clark are the institutions which define identity, and preserve order and authority. Like Anderson and Nairn he rejects the Whig view of history and accepts their idea that Britain had an *ancien régime* rather than a modern state. But whereas Anderson and Nairn traced the origins of this *ancien régime* back to class relationships, Clark argued that this misunderstood the fundamental character of the British state, which lay in religion as the primary source of authority and legitimacy (Clark, 1990). The period of the civil war in the seventeenth century was a brief interlude, after which the essential features of the British state were re-established. This state, Clark argues, was based on a particular relationship with the Anglican Church, and was organized to restrict liberty, not to further it. This *ancien régime* lasted intact until 1832, which for Clark introduced the first real break in continuity and set in process the democratic, collectivist and secular trends which over the next century and a half were gradually to destroy the fundamentals of the old state. For Clark the final point in this development is the subordination of British sovereignty to a new putative European sovereignty under the terms of the Treaty of Rome.

The State as an Enterprise

The debate on Britain's *ancien régime* dispelled some of the complacency that British political institutions could not be improved upon, and drew attention to the actual historical paths which had shaped

British institutions. The Whig view implied that because Britain had self-governing political institutions it had no need of an interventionist state, while Anderson and Nairn argued that it was desperately in need of such a state in order to modernize its economy and society. Their thesis was an arresting one, but underplayed the enormous transformation of economic, social and political institutions which had occurred in Britain in the previous two hundred years – which included the gaining of universal suffrage, the spread of urbanization, the creation of an industrial economy, the establishment of a welfare state, the rise to global hegemony and the subsequent withdrawal from empire. A true *ancien régime* might have been expected at some stage to have become an absolute barrier to progress. But this was not Britain's experience.

The main objection to the liberal idea of the state is that, using Oakeshott's terminology (Oakeshott, 1975), it exaggerates the character of the state as a civil association and downplays its character as an enterprise association. The basis of the latter is that the state is a legal organization which claims a monopoly of the means of violence as well as the authority to make collectively binding decisions. As such the state is both a civil association and enterprise association simultaneously. In law it is endowed with its own will and personality, able to act and assume responsibility. From this is derived its autonomy and also the notion of the state standing above or apart from civil society, controlling it, steering it, and seeking to impose its own purposes upon it.

What are fundamental to the British state as an enterprise association are the particular ways in which the state has been organized to pursue distinct purposes – economic prosperity, national security, and social welfare. These purposes have been responsible for the enormous expansion of the size and functions of the state, and have shaped the organization of the different parts of the state, the nature of its agendas and decision-making, and how it relates to other institutions and organizations in the economy and society.

None of this implies that the state is necessarily an active initiator of policy, although there is a presumption that it will be. The state can also be conceived as a more or less passive reflector of interests, relationships and structures; an arena in which conflicts originating from elsewhere are played out. But where even these conceptions differ from the concept of the state as a civil association is that the purpose of the state is seen as being substantive rather than procedural; the state is not organized in a neutral manner. It has a structural bias, which gives priority to certain objectives and interests over others, and therefore raises the question of power – in whose interests and to what ends is the coercive power of the state being exercised? In the rest of this chapter three different ways of characterizing this structural bias – capitalism, empire, and welfare – are explored.

Capitalism

The conception of the British state as a capitalist state treats the organization of the economy as fundamental for explaining the structural bias of the state. The purpose of the state is to ensure that the economy prospers, and this presupposes a strong relationship between economic power and political power. At one extreme the state can be characterized as a simple instrument in the hands of the dominant class – those who wield decisive economic power by virtue of their ownership and control of capital; at the other, the state itself is completely autonomous and pursues its own agenda for the economy, independently of class interests. More sophisticated accounts recognise the complex links between class power and political power, and how the interaction between them creates opportunities and spaces for political action as well as imposing constraints (Jessop, 1990).

In a capitalist economy the state is organized to sustain the social relationships and institutions which determine how wealth is produced and distributed. Its own existence depends on its ability to raise taxes and this in turn requires economic prosperity, so at the very least the state must not irrevocably damage the engine of wealth creation by losing the confidence and cooperation of those who own and control productive assets. This is why the overriding purpose of the state as a capitalist state is to ensure economic prosperity, the ability of the economy to reproduce itself and to grow. The ways in which the economy is reproduced and the wealth that it creates is distributed depends vitally not just on the institutions of civil society such as companies and markets, but also on households, the sphere of unpaid domestic labour. The role of the state is to remove all obstacles (whether cultural, political, or economic) in the way of faster and smoother growth, and to sustain the legitimacy of the capitalist order and its modes of governance. In this endeavour modern states have developed many different agencies and policies.

The political economy of British capitalism has revolved around two key issues; the position of the British economy within the global economy and the governance of the national economy. The bitterest and most intractable political divisions have arisen over strategic choices about Britain's relationship with the global economy; free trade versus protection in the first half of the nineteenth century; tariff reform before 1914; and European integration since the 1960s. In comparison the debate on economic governance – how the state should relate to the economy – has been more muted. It has primarily been concerned with the familiar left–right division over the extent of government intervention in the economy, particularly the boundaries of the public and private sectors, the levels of taxation, the funding of the welfare state, and the priorities for macro policy. But these issues are more susceptible to accommodation and compromise than those concerned with the global economy. The spectrum has lain between *laissez-faire* and planning, and more recently between the merits of a developmental as against a neo-liberal state (Marquand, 1988).

Decline

Discussion of economic policy in Britain and the strategic choices facing governments has often been dominated through the last hundred years by recurrent anxieties about decline and programmes to remedy it (English and Kenny, 1999). These anxieties have been fed by the steady erosion of Britain's leading role in the global economy, first as the economic hegemon and second as the possessor of the largest territorial empire. They have been intensified by the relative economic decline of the post-war period, which saw Britain record significantly lower rates of growth of output and productivity than most other leading economies, as well as suffering periodic bouts of high inflation, high unemployment and industrial unrest.

From the perspective of Britain as a capitalist state decline has been a fundamental feature of British politics in the twentieth century, determining many of the contours of British politics and the issues between the parties. British capitalism came to be perceived as dysfunctional – failing to perform as a modern capitalist economy should, and thereby imperilling all the other objectives of the government, not least its ability to be re-elected. The more apocalyptic warnings about British decline never materialized, but for a period, particularly in the 1970s, the political regime was gripped by success-ive crises, brought on by the inability of successive governments to stem the decline or get on top of the problems it created. Many different institutions and aspects were blamed, ranging from the burden of empire, the *ancien régime* and the organization of the state, to the culture of the elites, and the attitudes and behaviour of employers and workers. If any consensus emerged it was that the problem of British decline was inseparable from the nexus of state–economy relations which had evolved over a long period and was deeply embedded and resistant to change.

Three particular features of this nexus have received attention. The first is the special role which finance has occupied in Britain. The size and importance of the financial sector compared with other capitalist states has been notable ever since Britain became the centre of the global economy in the mid-nineteenth century, and provided so many of the financial, commercial, and shipping services which that economy required, with sterling the international currency linked to the gold standard. This gave a further boost to the position of London, and to a further centralization of power, population, and wealth on the capital and its surrounding region. No other leading capitalist power, not even Japan, has a metropolis which is quite so dominant as London, and one of the key factors in London's importance has been the presence of the financial businesses of the City.

The relative strength of the City contrasted with the relative weakness of many sectors of manufacturing in the twentieth century. One influential argument has been that the City had sufficient political power to set the parameters of economic governance, particularly in relation to the domestic policies needed to sustain monetary stability, and the external policies needed to preserve the openness of the British economy and the position of London as the centre of a global network of trade, investment and finance (Ingham, 1984).

A second feature of the relationships between the state and the economy has been the position of agriculture and manufacturing. Britain industrialized early, and lost the bulk of its population from the land much sooner than other capitalist states. This made Britain an urban and industrial country ahead of all others, which had a number of consequences, particularly for British democracy. One of the reasons why democracy was resisted by the property-owning classes was that it inevitably meant handing decisive electoral power to the voters in the new urban centres. There was no significant rural population which could be used as a counterweight against the towns. Although Britain was a multinational kingdom, urbanization and industrialization penetrated all parts of the British Isles, so that there was no significant centre–periphery split. Scotland for example, with its huge concentration of industry around Glasgow, participated fully in the industrial success of the economy. The prosperity which industry brought was a crucial foundation on which the stability of the state rested. The main exception to this was Ireland, the bulk of which remained agricultural, and apart from a few centres such as Belfast was shut out from the prosperity of the rest of the UK. The failure to integrate Ireland laid the basis for a fierce conflict between Irish nationalists and the British state which led ultimately to the secession of much of Ireland from the United Kingdom (see Chapter 6).

A third feature was the concentration of manufacturing in particular regions of the country which helped give rise to distinctive working-class communities and working-class culture, which were in sharp contrast to the culture of the traditional political and social elites, and made social status such an enduring feature of British society. The upper class and the working class came to constitute two very separate worlds, with only limited movement between them. One of the consequences was a highly cohesive labour movement, both organizationally, culturally and ideologically, in sharp contrast to labour movements in many other countries. The labour interest became a significant factor in the British state, represented through the trade unions and voluntary societies like the cooperatives, and through the formation of its own political party, the Labour Party.

All these features of Britain as a capitalist state reappear in the debates on decline. Marxist explanations all emphasise class. Instrumentalist accounts argue that the capitalist class has always fundamentally been in control of the British state and ascribe decline either to the interests of the dominant fractions of capital becoming detached from the interests of the British national economy, or to the political and industrial deadlock between labour and capital (Coates, 1994). Low investment and low productivity and overmanning in British industry in the first case is ascribed to rational calculation by the capitalist class that the highest returns come from their external operations, and in the second to their inability, despite their control of the state, to overcome the opposition of organized labour (at least until the Thatcher governments of the 1980s). Other Marxist accounts however do not treat the state as a simple instrument, and allow politics and ideology much greater autonomy. This allows for explanations like Tom Nairn's, which argue that it is the

particular character of the British political elite and the dominance of
the financial interest over the industrial, reinforced through the
institutions of the *ancien régime,* which created in practice an institutional consensus against modernization, whatever the rhetoric of
politicians. The economic crisis is refracted through politics and
ideology.

Institutionalist explanations give no automatic priority to class,
and are therefore much more likely to prefer explanations which
stress politics or ideology or the organization of civil society. They
look for the specific institutional pathways which have locked the
British economy into low performance, low investment and low
productivity (Elbaum and Lazonick, 1986). Industrial backwardness,
and the way in which the state has helped perpetuate it, becomes a
central theme. In this respect the contrast between a *laissez-faire* state
and a developmental state is highly pertinent. The failure of a
developmental state to emerge in Britain, despite the many attempts
to create one, is a key focus of attention in a long line of writing on
British political economy (Hutton, 1995).

Neo-liberal explanations, often associated politically with the New
Right, argue instead that the main reason that Britain has not been a
more successful capitalist economy in the twentieth century is that the
state constantly encroached too much on the market order, disrupting
its working. The public sector became overextended, and as a result
the government fell prey to numerous special interests and became
overloaded with demands and tasks (Brittan, 1977; Olson, 1982). The
deterioration of British economic performance is therefore due
directly to government interference in the economy. Were the interference removed then the economy would flourish. The essential
foundation for a stable legitimate polity is a polity that is limited
and which respects the boundaries of the economic sphere.

Empire

The conception of the British state as an imperial state treats Britain's
imperial past as fundamental for explaining the structural bias of the
state. The purpose of the state is to safeguard national security, which
is much broader than external defence, because it includes the
protection of the British way of life and the preservation of order,
authority and moral health throughout society, including key institutions such as school and family.

As an actor in the international system, with a unified will and purpose, and a specific set of interests and capacities, the state is here regarded as the highest expression of the national identity. In the case of Britain this national identity was forged through the long history of external expansion – first the territorial union which was established within the British Isles over several centuries and led to the creation of the United Kingdom in 1801, and second for the overseas territorial acquisitions over three hundred years which by the nineteenth century had turned Britain into the largest empire in the world (Seeley, 1909). This history of conquest and annexation transformed Britain from an obscure and peripheral island off the coast of a large continent into a great power and for a time the leading political, economic, and military power in the world. This had profound effects on British identity, and on British institutions. The iconography of the British state was refashioned at the height of Empire, and the effects were lasting.

In this conception the Empire is not just contingent to the nature of the British state but fundamental to it, and imparted a structural bias to the organization of the state which is still immensely important. The state was organized to facilitate expansion, and it pursued a consistent commercial and military strategy to achieve it. The state as a military organization, and an apparatus of force and coercion, looms large in this account, and therefore also the importance of the industrial–military complex which has sustained it – particularly the naval shipyards from the seventeenth century onwards, and more recently the aerospace industry (Edgerton, 1991). A certain kind of industry has been very important to this state, and the technological dynamism associated with it. In the liberal conception much play is made of the absence of a standing army in Britain in peacetime, a principle which was upheld until the twentieth century. In the imperial conception it is the military prowess of the state that is continually stressed, traditionally the navy, but also the army, and now the air force. Britain is regarded as a significant military power, and its people as a warrior people.

Such a history of expansion and conquest was crucial in defining British national identity (Colley, 1992), and in defining the British public interest. This can be seen in many different ways: the complex relationship between the sovereign nation state and the different nations which composed it; the strong ethic of public service which pervaded the armed services, the colonial service, the Civil Service; the support for public ownership of essential national services from the

Post Office to the BBC; and the organization of so many public services on military lines, with strong hierarchies, internal discipline and identification with serving the public good.

The imperial nature of the British state has always been controversial, its supporters arguing that it expressed the character of the British people and guaranteed their security and prosperity, as well as benefiting the subject nations, while its critics have seen it as responsible for many of the least desirable features of British life, such as jingoism and racism, inflicting great harm on those ruled. This argument was joined very early. In the middle of the nineteenth century many, including later orchestrators of imperialism such as Benjamin Disraeli, argued that the colonial empire had become a millstone around the neck of the British people. The idea of the empire as a burden, a drain on the energies and resources of the British people has been a constant refrain up to the present. The cause of British decline as a great power in the twentieth century has been ascribed to imperial overstretch, the inability of the British state to maintain and defend such a far-flung empire with such inadequate resources (Kennedy, 1988). The trade-offs between domestic investment, domestic consumption and military expenditure were resolved in ways that held back domestic investment. Many liberals and socialists regarded the empire as helping to preserve all that was backward, anti-democratic and anti-libertarian in the British state (Thornton, 1957).

The supporters of empire by contrast regarded it not as a burden but as providing an enlarged sphere of action for British citizens. It coloured the map red and made Britain pre-eminent in many parts of the world. It provided opportunities for soldiers, administrators, entrepreneurs and settlers. It provided new ways of conceiving British national identity, by creating the idea of a Greater Britain, a wider citizenship, and a British mission in the world, to provide good government, to extend civilization, and to preserve the international liberal order.

As an imperial state Britain reached its zenith in the second half of the nineteenth century and the first part of the twentieth. At the same time Britain came to exercise a hegemonic role in the world system as a whole. The most visible sign of this hegemony was the 'formal' empire, the colonies and dominions with direct ties to Britain, which constituted an economic sphere dominated by British companies, and a currency sphere in which the pound was the accepted master currency (Strange, 1971). But of even greater importance for Britain's wider hegemony was the informal empire which Britain ruled not in any direct administrative sense but through the superiority of British commerce, the penetration of British investment, and the acceptance of the pound as the undisputed international currency. Britain helped spread the ideas and institutions which supported a liberal economic order – free movement of goods, capital, and people – and provided many of the financial and commercial services which such an order required. There were no formal international institutions, but an informal set of rules and understandings developed for the conduct of the affairs of the global economy which helped sustain a long period of stability.

The experience of hegemony and empire created the view that Britain could only be Britain if it was at the centre of a wider network of economic and political relationships, and exercised leadership. What form this leadership should take, however, and which was the appropriate network, were always controversial. The Empire and Commonwealth, Anglo-America and the European Union have all figured at different times, often in conflict with one another. During the period of empire itself there was a long conflict between free trade imperialists and social imperialists, the former favouring the informal empire, and maintaining a liberal world order, the second favouring consolidating the formal empire, through the imposition of tariffs, abandoning *laissez-faire* and pursuing collectivist policies to increase security. Military strength was seen as depending on domestic policies and institutions which promoted economic efficiency and social solidarity (Semmel, 1960).

The loss of the formal empire after 1945 and the displacement of Britain from its former position of hegemony might seem to destroy the basis of perceiving Britain as an imperial state. But many of the structures and attitudes are still in place, and political argument still concerns the position of Britain in the global economy. What has happened however is that support for the social-imperialist position has dwindled; serious advocacy of protection, even within the EU, has become a rare position in British politics. Instead the free-trade-imperialist position has bifurcated into those who put priority on the Atlantic link and those who put it on Britain's role in Europe, as the best way of safeguarding Britain's interests and prosperity. Both of these are recognisable inheritors of the view of Britain as first and foremost an imperial state. For the Atlanticists the role of hegemon in a liberal world order was inherited by the United States from Britain, and they gave full support to the United States both in its economic and its military roles in the post-war order. Maintaining a liberal world order and maximum openness for trade and finance, and military support for the United States in policing this world order, is argued to be the priority for British policy. The Europeans by contrast give greater priority to involving Britain fully in the process of European integration, in the belief that this experiment in an open regionalism offers the best framework for prosperity and for maintaining significant influence for Britain in world politics.

Welfare

The conception of the British state as a welfare state treats the growth of collectivism and social democracy after 1885 as fundamental for explaining the structural bias of the state. The purpose of this state is to promote social welfare for its citizens, providing opportunities and limiting risks. Electoral pressure for collective provision against risks combined with the requirements of a highly urban society and industrial economy provided the momentum for the growth in the scale and scope of government in the twentieth century, the proliferation of new spending programmes and the enlarged range of powers and responsibilities assumed by government. The way it has become organized to promote the welfare of its citizens pervades everything the state does. The deep roots of this state in the municipal socialism of the nineteenth century is captured in a famous passage by Sidney Webb, which is in sharp contrast to the passage by A. J. P. Taylor quoted above:

> The Individualist Town Councillor will walk along the municipal pavement, lit by municipal gas and cleansed by municipal brooms with municipal water, and seeing by the municipal clock in the municipal market, that he is too early to meet his children coming from the municipal school hard by the county lunatic asylum and municipal hospital, will use the national telegraph system to tell them not to walk through the municipal park but to come by the municipal tramway, to meet him in the municipal reading room, by the municipal art gallery, museum, and library, where he intends to consult some of the national publications in order to prepare his next speech in the municipal town-hall, in favour of the nationa-

lization of canals and the increase of the government control over the railway system. (Webb, 1890: 116–17)

Two main views have dominated debate about the British state seen as a welfare state – selectivity versus universalism, which most recently has been a conflict between New Right and social-democratic views of welfare. The political problem has always lain in determining the level of services that should be provided and the best way of funding them. Once the argument for a strictly minimal state confined to the enforcement of laws and external defence had been lost within British Liberalism, it proved difficult to develop criteria to set limits to government and to state provision. The political limits that were eventually encountered turned out not to be ideological but practical, set by the ability to extract taxes, and by the need to preserve a profitable and dynamic private sector.

The social-democratic view of the welfare state has tended to treat welfare as a counterweight to the operation of free markets. The state needed to assume much greater responsibilities in providing welfare in order to ensure reasonable security for all its citizens from poverty, illness, old age and unemployment. Comprehensive welfare provision helped strengthen markets as a principle of social organization by removing their most serious defects, and making possible an approach to equality of opportunity. The welfare state is a state which has a social conception of citizenship as well as a political and legal one (Marshall, 1950). Every citizen has certain social rights – to education, health, and security.

What is characteristic of all conceptions of the state as a welfare state is that the state guarantees social rights for all its citizens, and this does mark it out quite strongly from a *laissez-faire* state But there has always been considerable debate as to how far the state itself should have a direct role in administering the services, and how far its role should be an enabling one, ensuring that the services are provided through the private sector and the voluntary sector, or pushed back to households. This question is closely related to the issue of whether the responsibility of the state should stop at providing a safety-net, a minimum level of welfare for all citizens, below which no citizen should fall, or whether in some instances it has a much broader responsibility in making universal provision. This debate over what is the proper preserve of government and what should be left to individuals and their families has always been at the heart of what kind of welfare state Britain is and should aspire to be.

Britain's welfare state has also been a Keynesian state, dedicated to economic management to promote full employment and economic growth. The responsibility of government to manage the national economy emerged alongside the responsibility of government to ensure the welfare of its citizens. Although both were strong Liberals and subscribed to liberal and individualist ideas of the state, the embodiment of the ideas of Keynes and Beveridge in policies and institutions were widely regarded as representing the final triumph of collectivist principles over the individualist principles which had governed public policy in the nineteenth century.

The policy regime which became established after 1945 was based on certain clear parameters defining the boundaries between the public and private sectors, the level of taxation, the role of local government (which had been such an important element of the pre-1945 welfare state) and the responsibilities for welfare (including education and health) which necessitated government spending programmes. Many of these assumptions were challenged by the New Right in the 1970s and 1980s. But despite the rhetoric of rolling back the state and restoring Victorian virtues the achievements of Conservative governments influenced by New Right ideas were modest. The fundamental character of the British state as a welfare state was not overturned. What Conservative governments did was to hold spending on the welfare state relatively constant in real terms, while in other countries it continued to rise, to promote forms of private provision and private sector delivery of services, and to force family members, usually women, to provide care. But the core of the welfare state, in particular the social security budget, the NHS and state education, remained intact (Pierson, 1994), although in comparison with many other welfare states in Europe, provision in Britain by the 1990s was substantially lower (Esping-Andersen, 1990).

Although New Right thinkers have been the strongest critics of the British welfare state many of them are also obliged to acknowledge that welfare remains a fundamental feature of this state, which the Thatcher years did not significantly change. They argue that the extended state of the Keynesian era has been responsible for most of the ills which afflict contemporary capitalist economies: the bidding up of expectations, the need to fund spending by additional taxing or borrowing, the continual pressure for more spending, and the proliferation of special interests which come to infest every stage of the policy process (Brittan, 1977).

In the 1970s there was a critical literature from the left about the welfare state and its dominance by the needs of the economy rather than human needs (Gough, 1979). Since the onslaught of the New Right, criticism from the left has become more muted, because of the perceived need to defend the welfare state from attack. But although the ideas of the New Right were in the ascendancy in the 1980s, many New Right thinkers have been pessimistic about the prospects for implementing them. This is because the New Right would like to dismantle the welfare state but its own analysis of the political process tells it that interests and structures matter more than ideas and that therefore the prospects for reform are limited. It criticized the earlier notions that the state was uniquely capable of defining and advancing the public interest because it was staffed by disinterested and enlightened individuals. The state is not omniscient and enlightened, the New Right argued, but rather is made up of politicians, bureaucrats and lobby groups, all of them pursuing their own self-interest under the cloak of the public interest. The democratic process is deeply flawed because it gives power to take decisions to state agents without any adequate accountability. In casting their votes voters have to accept the whole programme put before them; they have no means of discriminating; and they have no budget constraint. Politicians determined to maximize votes outbid one another in promising increased spending, and lower taxes. This leads to a permanent fiscal squeeze on the public sector, despite the growing wealth of the economy, because demands for public services and the costs of supplying them increase faster than the means of funding them. But no one within this system has any incentive to act in any other way, so the system perpetuates itself. The New Right view of the British state as a welfare state is therefore both that it is the cause of most of the ills of British economy and British society and also that it is virtually impossible to reform.

Some recent work on the organization of the British state has emphasised the extent to which the state has been hollowed out through the separation of policy from delivery, and the creation of many new agencies at arm's length from government and direct political control (Rhodes, 1988). Initiatives involving the private sector and the third sector in the delivery of services have also abounded, but these alter some of the organizational features of the welfare state rather than the existence of the welfare state itself. The politics of funding and managing welfare remains a defining feature of the British state at the end of the twentieth century.

Conclusion

This chapter has explored different ways of understanding what is
fundamental about the British state. There is no single answer. The
state is a highly complex, multi-layered, and multi-level institution
composed of many different agencies and organizations, often with
competing aims and priorities, and with fluctuating boundaries
between the public and the private. A basic divide which has been
identified in writing on the British state is between those approaches
which stress the liberal constitutional features of the British state as
its most fundamental characteristic, as against those which see the
state as having acquired substantive purposes which have transformed its relationship to the economy and society.

Many of the old constitutional features of the British state are still
much in evidence, particularly the uncodified constitution, the doctrine of parliamentary sovereignty, the highly centralized character of
the polity, the absence of serious checks on the executive, the
unproportional electoral system and the hereditary element in the
second chamber. Serious reform of many of these is currently under
way or under consideration. But their existence has not prevented the
state developing its capacities to pursue major purposes such as
economic prosperity, national security and social welfare. These have
come to define what a modern state is about – the agencies, funding
and programmes associated with them define the character of the
modern state. The way they are organized differs between countries;
so too does the priority given to these three objectives, and also the
modes of governance chosen to deliver them. The balance between
these purposes also shifts. For much of the twentieth century the
purposes of national security and welfare have predominated. Since
the 1970s economic prosperity has assumed centre stage. Governments are now focused on the economy and on economic success
more than on anything else. But all three purposes remain fundamental to an understanding of the British state.

3
The Constitution

NEVIL JOHNSON

This is a difficult time at which to write about the British Constitution. Constitutional reform is a major plank in the legislative programme of the Blair Labour government, making it hard to predict with any confidence which of the familiar constitutional landmarks will still be there in five years time and in what form. For two centuries at least, however, British constitutional development has been widely praised for its continuities and the Constitution may, indeed, have fundamental and enduring features which will survive the winds of change now blowing. In this situation how should we approach 'fundamentals'? It is desirable to proceed by asking some general questions. First, since there are problems in defining the British Constitution we need to start with a basic question: what is a constitution and to what species of constitution does the British belong? This leads to a further question: in what sense is the Constitution in Britain 'fundamental'? And finally there is a third question calling for more specific answers: what in fact are the fundamental features of the British Constitution however we may have defined it? We begin by tackling the first of these questions.

Constitutions, Ancient and Modern

The modern idea of a constitution is that of a written document defining the main institutions by which a country is governed – the legislative, executive and judicial powers – and setting out the rights of citizenship. This understanding has its roots both in the American War of Independence and the United States Constitution of 1787 and in the French Revolution with its proclamation of the sovereignty of the people in whom is vested a 'constituting power' or *pouvoir constituant*. But, of course, it took a long time for this view of a

45

constitution to become widely and effectively adopted. Indeed, it is only since 1945 that it has become dominant, first in the West, then more widely in the world at large.

There is, however, another and older view of a constitution which has not died out entirely. This sees the constitution as rather like a summary of how a society or nation is politically constituted or, perhaps more specifically, how its political and legal order fits together. According to this view we do not start with the formal statement of constitutional norms and then read forwards to find out how they are applied and what they mean. Instead the constitution is treated as the outcome of shared experiences and practices, the result of a common history rather than a founding declaration. Such a constitution evolves over time and is to be deduced from the ways in which a society manages its public affairs and deals with its members. It is not so much a set of instructions on how to do things as a set of precedents and notes of guidance extracted from past experience. It is clear that this kind of constitution is (or was) rarely collected into one document, even though its existence depends upon much that has been formally enacted and established as law. By virtue of its character as a summary of practice and precedent such a constitution has been resistant to formalization, and indeed there may be uncertainty about which practices and procedures are genuinely constitutional (Dicey, 1959; Maitland, 1908: section K). This kind of constitution will be called a customary constitution in contrast to one which is codified and formal.

The distinction between these two species of constitution – one eminently 'modern', the other 'ancient' at least in the sense that its roots reach back into pre-modern practices and conditions – is not at all absolute. A customary constitution is unlikely to have special rules for its amendment, chiefly because it is the outcome of adaptation and evolution in response to changing circumstances and needs. But a formal constitution will have special rules (of varying kinds) for its amendment, and may well provide the basis for a sphere of constitutional law distinct from ordinary statute law. Often enough constitutional law will be interpreted by a court whose conclusions are final and binding for the whole society. Nevertheless, a formal constitution does not dispense with the need to develop and use some elements of precedent and practice typically characteristic of a customary constitution. Formal rules have always to be supplemented by practice and convention, mainly because they can never take care of all future contingencies. There has to be room for at least some of the flexibility commonly regarded as a virtue of a customary constitutional tradition.

The British Constitution is the outstanding surviving example in the modern world of an 'ancient' or customary constitution. To talk about it is to talk about how the country is governed and what its citizens can and cannot do. But this has to be done not by reference to a consolidated formal statement indicating the powers and duties of institutions and the rights of citizens, but by referring to a continuum of laws, charters, legal precedents established by case-law in the courts, parliamentary declarations, institutional procedures, political practices and conventions, and occasionally even what so-called 'authorities' have said when writing about the Constitution. There is testimony to the validity of this account of the Constitution – or more precisely of how one sets about specifying what it is – in the fact that most treatises written on it during the past century and a half are concerned chiefly with describing British political and legal institutions and with showing how the country is governed through them. What is rarely found is constitutional dogmatics – texts offering commentaries on constitutional law and setting out the manner in which its prescriptions should be applied in the government of the country and in public life generally. Constitutional lawyers in Britain have for long enough had a raw deal, being required to make bricks with very little straw.

Fundamental in What Sense?

What has just been said leads on to the question about the sense in which the Constitution in Britain can be said to be 'fundamental'. It is fundamental because it is held to summarize and express at particular points in time an unbroken political evolution. For a short time between the execution of Charles I in 1649 and the death of Oliver Cromwell in 1658 it looked as if England might be endowed with a written constitution and a new form of government. But the Instrument of Government of 1653 barely outlived Cromwell and since the restoration of the Monarchy in 1660 there has been no radical break in institutional continuity and, therefore, no need to engage in any total reconstruction. As a result it can be said that the British Constitution is defined at any particular time by the manner in which the institutions which make-up the British state are used and understood. The Constitution is the political order itself and the rule of law it sustains. But this means that there can never be a wholly authoritative and conclusive statement of what the British Constitution amounts to. The understandings of it have usually embraced argument and dissent as well as consensus, and most significant accounts of the Constitution have generally expressed in some degree the commitment of their authors to particular political values, aspirations or fears. Indeed, much writing about the Constitution has been part of an ongoing political debate about what can properly be done and what objectives can be legitimately pursued within the framework of the traditional institutional structures and the legal rules underpinning them. In *The English Constitution* (1867) Walter Bagehot saw his account of the Cabinet as laying bare the 'efficient secret' of the Constitution, while at the same time he did not disguise his hope that the very success of Victorian parliamentary government would keep 'democracy' at bay (Bagehot, 1963). A. V. Dicey, the most influential of all writers on the Constitution, was clearly concerned in his *Introduction to the Study of the Law of the Constitution* (1885) to emphasise as fundamental those features which pointed towards a minimalist view of public powers in the interests of individual rights (his account of the rule of law) and the preservation of a unified British state (his view of parliamentary sovereignty) (Dicey, 1959). In contrast, writing about fifty years later Sir Ivor Jennings frequently qualified Dicey's analysis (though not rejecting its main elements) in order to justify a more collectivist view of the proper use of the Constitution (Jennings, 1959). And more recently, most writers on the Constitution have argued that it has lost the checks and balances it supposedly had in the past and now facilitates a dangerous accretion of power in the hands of an overweening central government. Such a view has found expression, for example, in F. Mount's *The British Constitution Now* (1992) or some years earlier in Lord Hailsham's *The Dilemma of Democracy* (1978).

Nevertheless, the fact of institutional continuity indicates that there have been dominant themes in the constitutional development of modern Britain. Foremost among these have been the following:

● There is a long and continuous tradition of parliamentary government. In modern times this has meant that political authority should be vested in elected officeholders who can, by virtue of election, be held accountable for their actions and decisions. This is at the heart of the British idea of government by consent which has for the most part meant government by and through ministers answering to Parliament.

- The exercise of public powers is subject to a rule of law which has acknowledged the supremacy of statutes approved by Parliament and is administered and interpreted by independent judges who also sustain a system of common law.
- The system of law has rested on the primacy of individual rights and claims, notably in relation to the ownership and use of property. There have been times when such rights have taken a back seat, for example during both world wars this century and in the wake of much collectivist legislation passed after 1945. But there has remained a hard core of attachment to individuals and their rights and claims which has more than anything else disqualified in British eyes the language of the state and rendered the 'state' suspect as an impersonal collective force threatening individual freedoms.
- The unity of the system of government has generally been affirmed. This has been symbolized by the Crown on whose behalf and in whose name the most important executive and judicial office-holders exercise their powers and carry out their functions. The principle of unity also found expression in the supremacy of Parliament (which is why the devolution of legislative powers remained a contentious matter), in the existence of a unified Civil Service, and in the maintenance of a unified judicial structure administering (subject to qualifications referred to below) one body of law.

To summarize, the British Constitution is essentially a political phenomenon. It is fundamental because it embodies the British view of how best to sustain a unified system of self-government through institutions and procedures which respect the rule of law, but at the same time acknowledge the claims of political democracy and discretion. The Constitution is constantly subject to change and adaptation, but so far at least there have been remarkable continuities in the principal themes expressed in it.

Fundamentals in Practice

We can now turn to the third question about the particular institutional features of the constitutional structure and procedures which, up to now at any rate, have been regarded as basic or fundamental. It is a familiar fact that even though the theory of the separation of powers was extrapolated from the British Constitution in the eighteenth century, it has never been clearly reflected in the institutional structure. Instead, the executive, the legislative and the judicial elements in the government of the country have been interwoven and in varying degrees interdependent. Nevertheless, when analysing the Constitution it is still useful to distinguish these three traditional powers in the state, beginning with the executive.

The Crown and the Executive

Britain remains a constitutional monarchy (Bogdanor, 1995), and this has important consequences for both the status and powers of Her Majesty's Government, the most familiar manifestation of the executive nowadays. Originally the monarch was, of course, the ruler and actively involved in government. While in some degree constrained by statutes even by the sixteenth century, the sphere of the royal prerogative or inherent discretion was wide and it was mainly through the exercise of prerogative powers that the monarch governed. But over the past two centuries all this changed radically and the monarch is now confined almost entirely to a symbolic role. It is symbolic in two ways. The Queen is a representative figure who represents the British state, its government and the people, on innumerable occasions at home and abroad. She stands for continuity, public duty and the integrity of British institutions. It has become natural to assume that this role requires the monarch to remain detached from political controversy and all aspects of party politics. As a consequence the monarch (and this goes too for the closest members of her family) is not expected to reveal any personal judgements which might bring her into political controversy. At the same time the monarch is generally expected to embody and express certain virtues. This is not so difficult in the case of eminently public virtues like service and dedication to the duties of the office, but in a climate of rapidly changing social and moral values it has been harder to sustain such virtues as commitment to the family.

The Monarchy is symbolic in another sense, that expressed in the term 'the Crown'. The Crown is no longer as a rule the person who wears it (Maitland, 1908). Instead, the Crown is a curious mixture of symbolism, specific institutional arrangements stemming from it like the Privy Council, and a more abstract role as the ground for so much that is done 'on behalf of the Crown' or in its name. Judges dispense justice in the Crown's courts, ministers have inherited most of the Crown's discretionary or prerogative powers, even Parliament is only complete and, therefore, sovereign when acting as 'the Crown in Parliament', something it does every time a piece of legislation is passed and receives the royal assent. The continuance of the Crown as a ground of authority for institutions which act on its behalf still has considerable practical importance. It is in effect and in part a British substitute for that legal construction often known elsewhere as the state.

What this points to is the role of the Crown as a means of holding together at least part of the complex web of public institutions which now exists and thus of maintaining some degree of coherence in the public domain, though it has to be noted that nowadays the range of public authorities and functions is far wider than crown functions as such. More narrowly, the Crown embodies the belief in a unified executive power: it is the Queen's government and is expected to speak with one voice. It is to ministers that most of the Crown's prerogative powers have been transferred and by whom a large part of the powers conferred by statute are exercised. The extent of the Crown's remaining prerogative powers is very narrow, though conceivably in some circumstances they could be of real political significance. The monarch has to invite someone to form a government after an election or in the event of a government resigning. But such a power is more theoretical than real, since as a rule the election result has made it clear who is to be Prime Minister or the majority party has itself chosen a new leader in the event of a resignation of the Prime Minister. Nevertheless, it is possible to envisage circumstances in which the monarch would have to exercise discretion in deciding who might be best able to form a government. A shift to a proportional voting system is one instance. It used to be thought that the monarch might also have discretion when deciding whether to grant a request from the Prime Minister for a dissolution of Parliament, but it is doubtful whether this is any longer so. The Queen must always act on the advice of her ministers and this applies to dissolution as to any other public act.

The monarch's retreat to a symbolic and representative role, along with the survival of the Crown as a ground of authority and as something rather like a unifying principle in the state, serve to cast into sharp relief the fact that executive power is concentrated in ministers, individually and collectively. The idea that the Crown has to have both a chief minister and a range of other advisers selected by him (or her) antedates modern political parties, though from the early stages in the development of the Cabinet it has been recognised that its members had to have the confidence of Parliament and, in particular, of the House of Commons. The evolution of the Cabinet in the twentieth century reflects the consolidation of parties and the discipline they exercise over Members of Parliament, the strengthening of the Prime Minister both as party leader and head of government, and a great increase in the executive powers and responsibilities of ministers. But there are few formal principles and precious little law governing the manner in which the Cabinet and its members should operate. All those aspects of the Constitutional position of ministers remain largely in the sphere of convention and usage, matters for domestic regulation by the Prime Minister and his or her colleagues (see Chapter 5).

The Prime Minister has virtually no statutory duties, though he normally holds the position of First Lord of the Treasury. His authority stems chiefly from convention and from his status as the party leader charged with forming a government. The Prime Minister's ability to make such appointments as he sees fit within the government is extensive and few would dream of challenging his discretionary rights in this regard. The Prime Minister controls the agenda, structure and much of the working methods of the modern Cabinet, a power which has often been used to secure a dominant position in policy decisions. The administrative apparatus at the command of a Prime Minister is small, but its quality is generally high and it occupies a crucial strategic position in relation to the wider pattern of central government departments and to the exercise of the Prime Minister's powers of patronage. It is thus easy to understand why so many writers on the British Constitution during the past fifty years or so have concluded that something like prime-ministerial government has replaced Cabinet government (Crossman, 1963; Mackintosh, 1962). Yet this represents an oversimplification of the situation.

There are at least three reasons why the Cabinet survives as a basic institution in British government. First, it represents in some degree at least a collective party leadership. The Prime Minister has great influence over all Cabinet members, but they are not simply his nominees: some at least are people of influence and reputation within his party. Second, at the formal level the Cabinet remains the final arbiter in British government and all crucial decisions are made either by it or at least in its name. A Prime Minister cannot act just like an American president, at any rate not unless he is quite sure that he has the full support of his Cabinet. Third, most executive powers are vested in ministers, and to a large extent by statute, and it is they who make most executive decisions and announce them, after reference to their colleagues in Cabinet if necessary. This is still a fact of great importance and is intimately linked with the practices of accountability and the theory of responsible government. These are matters which require further attention.

It is a fundamental principle of the British Constitution that authority to make policy and to exercise a substantial discretion in implementing it should be vested in politically accountable officeholders. At the level of the central government this generally means a minister (or secretary of state as most senior ministers are now entitled). To be politically accountable means for the most part to be a Member of Parliament and to be subject to the necessity of accounting to the House of Commons. In theory a minister responsible to the House of Commons can be censured there and forced to resign. But it is well known that ministerial responsibility to Parliament does not in the normal course of events involve such risks and the penal impact of ministerial responsibility is a rare occurrence. What is involved in accountability to Parliament is a reasonably regular public interchange between ministers and Members of Parliament. In such exchanges a minister is subject to the constraints of justifying what he has done to Parliament (usually the Commons) and to the public. Despite all their contemporary shortcomings the procedures of parliamentary accountability remain a crucial element in British constitutional practice. Accountable government means government according to procedures which require named officeholders to answer for particular actions and decisions as well as for the direction of policy. Even though in the day-to-day conduct of politics there are many ways in which ministers can blur their responsibilities and circumvent their critics, accountability procedures remain one of the most characteristic features of ministerial life and a minister who has no skill in self-defence when under attack is unlikely to enjoy much success. These procedures define how the doctrine of individual ministerial responsibility works out in practice and there can be little doubt that they still act as a discipline for ministers. In contrast, collective responsibility has a far more limited impact on their work. It emphasises the solidarity of the Cabinet and seeks to maintain the loyalty of all ministers of whatever rank to the government as a whole. And more important still, it strengthens the authority of the Prime Minister in relation to his colleagues. But in normal circumstances collective responsibility is taken largely for granted and a government with a secure majority and a united party in Parliament has little need to worry about it.

There is in Britain no unified public service. Instead there are many different public services, each employed by a particular public sector institution. The most influential branch of the public service is that employed by and owing loyalty to the Crown, the Civil Service. Nowadays, however, the link between the Crown as a focus of allegiance and civil servants who work for the government is more tenuous than it was a century ago. Effectively, and probably in law too, the government of the day now occupies the place once held by the Crown in relation to the Civil Service. Some features of the British Civil Service can, however, still be explained only by reference to its overarching relationship with the Crown. Of these the most important is the party-political neutrality of the service. The Crown, so it can be held, has an interest in ensuring that its ministers, regardless of party, receive efficient and impartial support in the carrying out of their functions. This is why the political neutrality of the Civil Service and the procedures in place to maintain this have remained fundamental to the executive arm of government in Britain.

There is, of course, something schematic about these remarks on the Civil Service. It is nowadays a highly diversified service, and both its work and its management are substantially devolved to semi-autonomous 'Next Steps' agencies. As a result the direct link with ministers has been weakened. The practice of competitive entry has almost entirely given way to dispersed recruitment by the employing institutions and this has reinforced the shift away from a unitary Civil Service. But for the most part political neutrality and even some degree of individual anonymity remain important characteristics of the British Civil Service. Constitutionally the effect of this is to emphasise the primacy of elected politicians. It is they who possess political authority and are entitled to determine policy: officials are in constitutional terms their servants and agents.

Parliament and Parliamentary Government

When we refer to Parliament nowadays we nearly always have in mind the House of Commons, the elected chamber in which most ministers sit. The second chamber, the House of Lords, has far less political significance and is of constitutional interest chiefly in relation to the structure of Parliament itself. In other words, the existence of the House of Lords maintains a bicameral Parliament, even though in the exercise of powers the Commons has long been predominant.

The procedures of the House of Commons serve both the needs of the government and the requirements of political control over government. The executive is entitled to use Parliament for the purposes of governing and will expect to secure the passage of its legislation. But equally it has to account publicly to Parliament and in turn Parliament has powers of control in relation to the government. What these relationships mean in practice is that Britain must be governed by parliamentarians, that is to say by elected politicians who have served in the House of Commons. This is the way in which the constitutional principle of representative and responsible parliamentary government (Birch, 1964) has found its embodiment in practice.

There are many ways in which the procedures of the House of Commons illustrate the dynamics of mobilizing support for a government and holding it to account. The House of Commons does, comparatively speaking, have very long working sessions of around 170 sitting days per year. The government controls the bulk of the available time which is used largely for securing the passage of its legislative proposals, together with necessary financial business. The executive does not, however, have a monopoly over the use of time. The official Opposition and the other opposition parties have a substantial allocation and there are considerable opportunities for individual or 'private' Members too. For example, they play a major part in asking Parliamentary Questions (four times a week), there is private Members' legislation which, though dependent for its effectiveness on government support, still testifies to the notion of the individual Member as law-maker, and there are short adjournment debates almost daily which are at the disposal of private Members (Griffith and Ryle, 1989: ch. 10).

These and similar procedures underline one of the ways in which the House of Commons differs from many other legislatures. The Standing Orders of the House are written by reference not to parties but to Members. This enshrines the principle of the equality of Members just as it also serves to highlight the traditional antagonism between the Crown's ministers – the front bench – and the House as a whole. This still finds expression in the distinction between private Members (or backbenchers) and those who hold office on behalf of

the Crown or aspire to do so. Even though today the control function
of private Members has greatly weakened, not least due to the growth
of disciplined parties and the formation of governments on that basis,
the survival of the principle that all Members have equal rights in the
House still confers status and dignity on them. Meanwhile, much of
their control function has in practice passed to the opposition.

The origins of something like a standing opposition, presenting
itself as an alternative government, lie far back in the eighteenth
century, long before the emergence of modern political parties. The
opposition was originally a group of private Members united in their
hostility to the government of the day and anxious to take its place.
Something like public recognition of the desirability of there being an
official opposition to the government came fairly early in the nineteenth century and since then there has been a steady consolidation in
the procedures of the House of Commons of the rights and privileges
of the opposition. The position of Leader of the Opposition received
statutory recognition in 1937, with provision for the Speaker to
resolve any dispute about which party leader is at the head of the
largest party opposed to the government. As a rule it is the electorate
which has determined which party constitutes the opposition, though
there was some ambiguity about its decision in the first election of
1974. With the provision of public funds for the opposition since the
late 1970s it became necessary to give a share to parties in opposition
other than the official opposition: thus, for example, the Liberal
Democrats have in recent years had financial support for their
activities in Parliament. Nevertheless, it is Her Majesty's Opposition
– that party which seeks to support a claim to be the alternative
government in waiting – which is the main beneficiary of the
procedural rules of the Commons designed to facilitate the task of
opposition within the British parliamentary system. All this indicates
that the institutionalization of an official opposition within the House
of Commons is one of the fundamental conditions of the British
Constitution (Johnson, 1997).

These remarks on various aspects of the procedures of the House of
Commons are intended to show that in important respects such
procedures define fundamental features of the Constitution in a
manner rarely found outside Britain. Parliament is in part a stage
for public debate, in part a means of public inquisition of the
government. These have been two essential components of parliamentary government in Britain and have owed their vitality to the
institutional framework within the House of Commons. The doctrine

of parliamentary sovereignty has to be set within this political context. Strictly speaking it is the Crown in Parliament – the fusion of executive and legislative powers – which has been regarded as legally sovereign, that is to say unlimited in what it may do by way of statutory enactment. It has followed from this proposition that Parliament may repeal any previous enactment, that entrenchment of a law may be constitutionally impossible, and that where laws conflict the courts will give precedence to the most recent statute (the idea of implied repeal). As we shall note later on, elements of the sovereignty doctrine are now subject to question. Nevertheless, it probably still holds good despite the *de facto* restrictions on its supreme authority which Parliament has accepted in recent years. The theory of parliamentary sovereignty has also had an internal as well as an external reference. Parliament has so far been sovereign in respect of the conduct of its own business and the behaviour of its Members. Parliamentary privilege, a body of rules and precedents stemming from the status of both Houses as constituting the High Court of Parliament, testifies to the autonomy of Parliament in relation to its own affairs and to its right to protect itself against any threat to the freedom of Members in the carrying out of their parliamentary functions. This too is an aspect of parliamentary sovereignty now subject to some questioning, notably through the appointment in 1995 of a Parliamentary Commissioner for Standards.

The significance of parliamentary procedures for constitutional practice can be illustrated by one more example taken from the usages of the House of Commons. This is the status and role of the Speaker (Laundy, 1979). Originally an agent of the Crown the Speaker came to be regarded more and more as the voice of the House of Commons and the protector of its privileges. By the end of the last century the office was losing its party-political colouring and during the twentieth century has been lifted out of party politics. The two major parties have in a rough and ready way taken it in turns to provide the Speaker, whose discretion in relation to the conduct of debate, the selection of participants and the determination of points of order is very wide. But what has been crucial to the office has been the ability of those chosen to behave impartially and to distance themselves from partisan considerations when discharging the duties of the Chair. What the office does is to affirm that in a partisan democracy there is a place for impartiality and detachment from party commitments as a means of preventing the complete absorption of public life by party interests and controversy. This is not a principle written down anywhere, yet it is fundamental to the manner in which the House of Commons manages its business and, therefore, to the British Constitution as a whole.

Reference has been made to the fact that Parliament consists of two Houses, the Commons and the Lords. It is necessary to consider briefly how far, if at all, the retention of two chambers is a constitutional fundamental. In modern times the House of Lords, a body of hereditary and appointed members, has become subordinate to the will of the Commons and of the government of the day. Formally it retains rights equal to those of the Commons in the passage of legislation, other than financial measures, but it exercises these subject to statutory restrictions on its power to delay (reduced from two years to one by the Parliament Act 1949) and the convention that it should not frustrate the wishes of the electorate as expressed by a majority in the Commons. The curtailment of the powers of the Lords has confined it to the functions of a revising chamber where (if time permits) detailed scrutiny and amendment of bills can take place. Such a function is certainly desirable and useful, especially as the legislative process in the House of Commons often does not allow for the careful examination of legislation. But it is rather doubtful whether the performance of such a task justifies the conclusion that the House of Lords is a 'fundamental' element in the British Parliament. Yet it survives, despite all-too-familiar criticisms of its composition. Why is this so and does it point after all to something fundamental in the Constitution?

The House of Lords has survived in part because it has adapted to changing political circumstances and has been able to perform useful tasks. But more decisive has been the difficulty of reaching agreement, even among reformers, on what kind of chamber might replace it. There are relatively few protagonists of outright abolition and a unicameral Parliament, chiefly because there is political danger in the claims of a single-chamber sovereign Parliament. For some this has meant 'elective dictatorship' (Hailsham, 1978). But if the only plausible solution were to be a wholly elected second chamber it then becomes likely that such a body would be unacceptable to the Commons. Past experience has made the latter exceedingly jealous of rivals and a second chamber claiming the legitimacy of election would inevitably be a rival, since it is hard to see any group of elected politicians being ready to exercise the remarkable restraint typical of the present House of Lords. What even a cursory consideration of the issue of Lords reform indicates is that a fundamental feature of modern parliamentary government in Britain is the political supremacy of the elected House, notwithstanding the risks of dictatorship of the majority that that carries with it. Precisely on that account it may well be that the House of Lords is likely to survive only as some kind of appointed body.

The Judicial Power

Britain has a unified judicial power and a single system of law. Qualifications have to be made to this statement to take account of a certain autonomy of Scots law and some distinctive features of the Scottish courts and judges. But the differences which exist are not such as to fracture the essential legal unity of the country. After all, Lord Mackay, the last Conservative Lord Chancellor and head of the judiciary, was a Scot, while Lord Irvine, his Labour successor, is also a Scot, practising until his appointment at the English bar.

It is usual to say that the British arrangements for the exercise of judicial functions run contrary to the notion of a separation of powers in several remarkable ways. The Lord Chancellor who is at the apex of the judiciary is a member of the Cabinet, acts as something like a Minister of Justice, though sharing some of those tasks with the Home Secretary, presides over the House of Lords and plays an active part in its proceedings. Yet he is also a judge and entitled to sit when the House of Lords is acting in its judicial capacity as the highest court of appeal. Most judicial appointments are made by the Lord Chancellor, though a few of the highest positions are filled by the Prime Minister after consultation with the Lord Chancellor. Lords of Appeal in Ordinary along with certain other senior judges sit in the House of Lords and take part in its debates. Finally, it should not be forgotten that the courts are the Queen's courts, that judges administer justice in her name and on her behalf, and that judges swear to uphold the laws as established by Parliament. For the tidy-minded all this might appear to be a strange mix-up.

However, there is a sharper separation between the judiciary on the one hand and the executive and legislative powers on the other than is sometimes apparent as a result of too narrow a focus on the points at which they intersect. The independence of High Court judges from executive interference was one of the most decisive achievements of the 'Glorious Revolution' of 1689. Subject to 'good behaviour' they hold office until retirement, and by convention (and possibly in law) can only be removed by resolution of both Houses of Parliament. The independence of the judiciary is buttressed in another way. Like civil servants, judges are appointed on the assumption of political neutrality and it has been part of their professional ethos to abstain from public involvement in controversial issues. Despite the fact that this convention is breached from time to time, the judiciary has for the most part kept out of political controversy and public party identification. This has done much to strengthen them in their official judicial role, especially when they are deciding cases involving an exercise of power by ministers or other public bodies.

The restrictive approach of the British judiciary to the interpretation of statutes has also worked in favour of judicial independence. The courts have been accustomed to interpret the law in a literal, positivist way and generally have not tried to go behind the words of the statute or well-established Common law precedents. In particular they have been cautious about superimposing their view of the values immanent in the law on what appears to be a plain reading of the relevant provisions. This method of interpretation has, of course, been congenial to Parliament and to politicians suspicious of judicial checks on what they might wish to do. In short, neutrality and independence of the judges has gone side by side with judicial restraint. Only in recent years has this situation begun to show signs of change (Johnson, 1998). The possibility of challenging the legality of executive actions has a long history, but until recently the procedures for seeking what is now called judicial review were slow and uncertain. Since 1978 they have been greatly simplified and this has resulted in easier access to the courts and a wider range for judicial review. In turn this has meant that ministers have been checked in their actions rather more often than used to happen, a trend sometimes misinterpreted as a sign that the judiciary is more often involved in politics than before. This is hardly the case. What has happened is that long-established judicial controls have been strengthened, but without a major break in the tradition of judicial autonomy and separation from executive concerns. It remains to be seen whether the forthcoming conferment on the judiciary of a responsibility for interpreting human rights legislation will bring about a major shift in the customary relationships between the judiciary and the other branches of government. At the very least there will have to be continuing judicial restraint if the judiciary's lofty independence of political influences is to be maintained.

There are certain other aspects of the legal system and how it works which perhaps have constitutional status, though it is hard to be sure. One is trial by jury, a practice of medieval origin now restricted to serious criminal cases. A second principle, closely linked to trial by jury, is the adversarial procedure followed in most court proceedings. Put briefly, it is not the function of the court to establish the truth in cases brought before it. Instead there is prosecution and defence, plaintiff and defendant, and each side is required to argue a case, often with most of the pleading offered in open court. While there have been some departures from adversarial procedures in the British legal system, it seems highly unlikely that the adversarial method of handling cases could be abandoned across the board. Moreover, it should not be forgotten that the adversarial procedure has been carried over into many spheres of social life and, not least, into politics. The popularity of the idea of debate expresses the influence of adversarial procedures in the courts. A third principle is the inviolability of the courts, expressed most concretely in the law of contempt through which they are empowered to enforce strict compliance with their procedures and requirements. Here again, the independence of the judiciary is vividly demonstrated.

The Established Churches

Britain is not unique in still having a state church, or to be more accurate two, one in Scotland and another in England. Most of the Scandinavian countries and Iceland also maintain their established Protestant churches. These arrangements reflect, of course, the conclusions reached after earlier phases of religious and constitutional dispute. In a predominantly secular age it is easy to overlook the Constitutional aspects of the establishment of religion or to conclude that the whole business should be wound up in favour of a thoroughgoing separation of church and state.

The Church of Scotland owes its establishment to different circumstances from those which produced the Church of England. The former was founded on a Presbyterian form of internal government and has maintained that character ever since. In an important sense it has, therefore, been a church of the people and this has had an impact on Scottish political life too. Though its rights and freedoms were confirmed in the Treaty of Union of 1707 its actual privileges consist less in special legal rights, material possessions and buildings than in public acknowledgement of its form of government and of its independence in matters of doctrine. This latter point was underlined by the Church of Scotland Act of 1921. The situation of the Church of England is very different. It is in England 'the Church by law established', its 'Supreme Governor' is the reigning monarch (who must be a Protestant), and it is only quite recently in 1970 that it set up forms of synodical government which go some way towards diminishing the Church's dependence on parliamentary legislation for changes in doctrine and internal structure. Diocesan bishops are appointed by the Crown on the advice of the Prime Minister, but under a concordat reached in 1976 between the Church and the then Prime Minister the latter's choice is restricted to one of two names put to him by the Crown Appointments Commission, a Church body including bishops and members of the General Synod. Should the Prime Minister not wish to propose either of the two names put forward, he may request alternatives. It is known that this happened in 1997 when an appointment had to be made to the bishopric of Liverpool. However, in return for what has been its subjection to Parliament and the Crown the Church has enjoyed substantial benefits. Twenty-six of its bishops constitute the Lords Spiritual in the House of Lords, its hierarchy plays a major part on many state occasions, and its representatives are to be found in numerous consultative bodies in the public sphere. Its lands and properties have not been sequestrated and remain substantial in scale, though the income from them has to defray the ever-rising cost of clergy stipends and the maintenance of an immense range of historic buildings. There is no doubt that disestablishment would confront both the government and society at large with major practical problems.

There is a paradox about religious establishment and that is that it has in Protestant countries often been associated with religious tolerance and the acceptance of dissent. Anglican dominance in the eighteenth century did not prevent the growth of religious dissent. It is in fact the broad and generally tolerant character of the Church of England that has enabled establishment to last for so long: the claims that the Church raises are modest and limited. But is establishment in some way a fundamental of the Constitution?

It is difficult to answer this question. For some establishment does underline the fact that Britain is a Christian country and part of a wider Christian world community. Those who wish to emphasise the Christian character of the society are, however, also exposed to the need to recognise the religious pluralism already existing and now extending far beyond the Christian denominations. Then there are the intimate links between the Monarchy and the Church (and indeed both established Churches) which are probably of more significance for the former than the latter. Through establishment and the link with the Crown the sacred aspects of monarchy itself are preserved. And there is too the maintenance in the sovereign institution of Parliament of a special voice for the Church and the beliefs and principles it stands for. Again, some would regard this as of great importance. Perhaps, therefore, the only general answer that can be given to the question posed is of a somewhat negative kind. If the Churches were to be disestablished and a complete separation of church and state effected, this would bring about imponderable qualitative changes in the manner in which many people perceive the Constitution of the United Kingdom, that is to say in the ways in which the country is politically and morally constituted. To this extent the severance of the special links between church and state would represent a change in fundamental governing conditions, though the consequences of such a step are impossible to foresee.

Checks and Balances and the Sovereign People

During the past decade and longer the most common criticism made of the British Constitution is that it has opened the door to a highly centralized pattern of government. Yet in some respects this is at odds with much of the historical experience of British government. Precisely because 'treating each case on its merits' has almost had the status of a constitutional principle there has been a tolerance of diversity and anomaly in the development of the United Kingdom which marks it off from most of its European neighbours. Measures of devolved administration in Scotland reach back to 1885 and have conferred many benefits of special treatment on that part of the United Kingdom; Wales has been a more recent beneficiary of administrative devolution; Northern Ireland did for fifty years have a large degree of political autonomy until internal disorder forced the British government in 1972 to revoke the province's home rule provisions and institute direct rule; the Channel Islands and the Isle of Man enjoy their own somewhat archaic forms of self-government rooted in a distant past; local authorities, though always dependent on statute and subject to repeated modifications to what they may do and with what resources, have generally enjoyed substantial scope for managing their own affairs and budgets; the same inclination to leave public bodies with the responsibility of operating independently within whatever conditions have been laid down for them can be found at work throughout the public sector, and reaching out to bodies like universities which are legally private corporate bodies rather than public agencies; and there are many modern examples of a willingness to leave tasks to private bodies operating in the public interest rather to set up special public organizations. This pluralism within the overall administrative structure of the country has stemmed from a constitutional preference for indirect rather than direct state (that is, central government) action. This in turn has maintained an evolving pattern of checks and balances which has often moderated the impact of the pressures for uniform services and conditions of life which have been strong for at least fifty years now.

However, institutional pluralism is not an explicit constitutional principle and its effectiveness in Britain has varied according to the prevailing political mood and configuration of social interests. Overall the political and social environment has for some considerable time been less favourable to the toleration of independent action by bodies within or linked with the central government and administration. True, the public sector has in the past twenty years been reduced in size, notably by the privatization of what were previously state-owned industries. But at the same time the powers of many public authorities have been extended and central government control or influence has been strengthened. As this has happened, so the reality of the informal checks and balances embedded in the structures of government has been eroded.

In so far as there is a constitutional explanation for this trend towards greater centralization of powers it is to be found in the underlying commitment to majoritarian popular government. More than a century ago Dicey recognised that the ultimate sovereign was the people: it was their consent which legitimized the grand claims he made on behalf of Parliament (Dicey, 1959: 73). But the consent of the electorate is conveyed through the ballot box and votes are cast for political parties which are highly disciplined and generally hostile to internal dissent. It is parties which have largely determined the agenda of political action and, through their programmes and the mandates they receive for them, driven forward the process of popular government. As a result democracy has been seen predominantly in terms of making choices between alternatives put to the people by the organized political forces in the country. They in turn have generally favoured retention of relative majority voting along with the simplification of choices which it encourages through a two-party alignment and the alternation of two parties in office. Most of the institutional practices defining the modern British Constitution are means of responding to that familiar pattern of relationships. The need for consent to government is indeed one of the enduring fundamentals which has found expression in many different ways over the centuries. The risk now may be that the people are so manifestly sovereign that the institutions which have embodied that principle no longer have that degree of stability and authority which is needed if they are to protect the sovereign people against abuses of power by the very majorities they endorse.

The Constitution Under Fire

The emphasis so far has been on explaining how the Constitution has been understood, what its guiding principles have been, and what it has meant in practice. At the same time it has been made clear that such is the nature of the British Constitution as a summary of actual political practice and relationships that it is very hard to pin down its essential elements and then to define them as fundamental. Indeed, it has to be recognised that at different times and under the influence of prevailing social values widely differing interpretations have been offered of what can properly be done under the Constitution. This has sometimes resulted in serious conflict about institutions and their powers, as happened in relation to home rule for Ireland between the 1880s and 1920, in the controversy over reforming the House of Lords shortly before 1914, and over the arguments about devolution in the 1970s. Nevertheless it has also to be noted that the institutional continuities of the British constitutional system, reaching back to the settlement of 1688–9, today find a parallel only in those of the United States. Yet while the American Constitution still commands the almost universal respect of its citizens, the British has in recent times been exposed to a great deal of criticism. Proposals to introduce major changes are now well advanced and in this concluding section we will consider briefly some of the implications of these for the fundamentals of the Constitution.

At the institutional level the attack has been focused mainly on the concentration of power in the hands of a government with a firm Commons majority. This critique was accentuated by the reforming zeal of the Thatcher governments between 1979 and 1990 which, somewhat paradoxically, combined a programme to dismantle large areas of publicly owned industry and to reduce the role of the state, with a readiness to impose on institutions previously able to claim a high degree of autonomy new centrally determined policies, for example in relation to the contracting out of public services or standards in schools. The main response to this was the call for new measures of decentralization and devolution. Then in the sphere of values and social attitudes many changes have reinforced the sympathy for institutional reform. One factor has been a rapid erosion of the respect for conventions and traditional forms of social behaviour in the wake of the widespread acceptance of highly individualistic values, a phenomenon which could not fail to have serious implications for a constitution so dependent on convention and usage as the British. All this has been congruent with a renewed emphasis on individual rights and claims and, in contrast with the traditional approach to the protection of rights, on an appeal to abstract principles and their enforceable application. Another factor contributing both to the build-up of sympathy for change and strong hostility to it has been the diffused impact over many years of Britain's membership of what is now the European Union. On the one hand this has underlined the contrasts between the 'customary' constitutional traditions of Britain and the formal written arrangements of its European neighbours, thus prompting many to argue that Britain should bring its methods into line with theirs. On the other, however, it has added force to the argument that the kind of constitution Britain has had is fundamental to the country's idea of self-government and therefore of political democracy.

This is not the place to examine the variety of proposals made nor the diversity of groups and organizations involved in the propagation of reform. Instead, reference will be made only to the schemes of reform known to be in train already or to which the present Labour Government is committed. These include:

- The passage of a Human Rights Act incorporating the European Convention on Human Rights into British law.
- The enactment of schemes for devolved assemblies in Scotland and Wales, along with a similar measure for the future government of Northern Ireland following the Good Friday 1998 agreement. Loosely linked with the policy of devolution is the plan to establish

an elected Mayor for the London conurbation alongside the existing local authorities there.

- The promise of legislation to remove the voting rights of hereditary peers in the House of Lords, but so far with no definite indication of what further changes in composition or powers might follow.
- The prospect of a Freedom of Information measure, though whether this should be regarded as a constitutional matter is open to question.
- Several changes from relative majority voting to proportionality are already in the pipeline, along with a review by the Jenkins Commission of options for changing the rules for national elections and a review by the Neill Committee on party funding.
- Inquiries are in hand by a select committee into ways in which the procedures and methods of work of the House of Commons might be 'modernized', though it is far from clear whether modernization will lead to major changes in how the House operates and in its relations with the government.
- Four referendums have been held since May 1997, at least two more have been promised, and there are signs that the present Government is generally sympathetic to such popular consultations and would welcome more regular resort to them.
- Finally there are moves towards more support for a variety of policy developments inside the European Union, some of which could in principle have important constitutional implications.

None of these proposals, actual or promised, can be discussed in detail here. All that can be done is to consider how far individually or collectively they point towards a constitution radically different from that which provided the framework for British government for most of the twentieth century. In one respect at least the reforms now in train look surprisingly 'traditional'. They are being developed and put forward piecemeal, almost entirely by the government, and there has so far been no suggestion at all that they might be brought together into something like a 'Bill of Rights' (of the kind enacted in 1689 after the removal of James II from the throne) or a new constitutional settlement. Thus they retain much of the character of pragmatic reform and adaptation, and this may allow some familiar landmarks to survive. Furthermore, it is possible that some of the proposed changes will have only limited effects. For example, if the removal of the voting rights of hereditary peers in the House of Lords is not

followed by any further changes in composition or powers then there
might be little change in the present role of the House.

Several of these impending changes do, however, seem likely to
have more far-reaching effects. Devolution has been recommended by
many of its advocates as a means of strengthening 'the Union',
despite the fact that nothing remotely like a genuine federal union
is currently on offer. Yet historical experience suggests that devolution in all its forms is likely to encourage the growth of distinctive
political cultures in the minority nations and that this process will in
turn lead to the weakening of British national political institutions
and identity. This is why there is the possibility that devolution may
eventually lead on to the break-up of the United Kingdom. Moreover, the measures so far presented seek to maintain the special
economic and political treatment long accorded to the non-English
parts of the Union. An eventual English reaction against the burdens
imposed by this policy could well have further disruptive effects.

Just as devolution in favour of three parts of the United Kingdom
threatens to weaken substantially the national political institutions –
notably Parliament and the national government – a comparable risk
arises in the case of human rights legislation. Under current plans it
will become possible to ask the courts to consider how far existing
statute law is in breach of particular provisions of the human rights
legislation and for them to issue declarations of incompatibility if they
are satisfied that this is the case. The executive will then be able to
prepare 'remedial' orders modifying the offending piece of legislation
for rapid passage through Parliament and without scope for amendment. It is possible that the courts will turn out to be very cautious
in their approach to pleas under the human rights provisions and
will seek to avoid making incompatibility declarations as far as is
possible. But even if that happens, the new legislation marks a radical
change of principle in the relationship between the courts and
Parliament, and between statute law and the higher principles contained in a human rights code written long ago with no thought that it
would ever be embodied in this way into British law. The way will be
open to a formally limited rather than a sovereign parliamentary
institution.

Then there is the possibility of the replacement of relative majority
voting and single-member constituencies by various forms of proportional voting. It could be argued that a change in the voting system is
not *ipso facto* a constitutional matter. The underlying principle is
universal suffrage and provided there is no departure from that it

might be held that a move to proportional voting would represent merely a change of method. But in the British case this is not so. Many cardinal features of the British Constitution and of the practices of the House of Commons have reflected the dynamics of relative majority voting – the tendency to a two-party competition, the practice of opposition as alternative government, single-party rule, the popularity of debate as a way of reaching conclusions, the sense that an MP has of representing all his or her constituents and so on. The abandonment of relative majority voting points to very different political conditions, namely those best summed up by two terms: the politics of bargaining and coalition rule. Proportional representation through regional lists was adopted for the 1999 European Parliament elections, the schemes for Scottish and Welsh devolution incorporate regional lists to supplement and correct the results of constituency elections, while the new Northern Ireland Assembly is elected by single transferable vote. If and when these precedents have an impact on voting for the Westminster Parliament, the way will be open for the most profound change since the Reform Act of 1832 in the character of British politics and the assumptions on which the institutions of government are based. Inevitably a large step would have been taken towards methods of government in which parties and the management of their relations with each other are the dominant factors outweighing all else. An added impulse would also be given to a more intense professionalization of political careers within party structures. Needless to say, a decision to introduce substantial public funding for political parties would confirm and accelerate this process (Johnson, 1992).

It remains to make a brief remark on the effects on the British Constitution of membership of the European Union. Notwithstanding the limitations on the autonomy of British governments and on the legislative discretion of Parliament already stemming from membership, it has so far been generally possible to avoid a sharp clash between fundamental features of the British Constitution and the demands of EU membership. The room for manoeuvre has, however, grown smaller and this looks like being the direction of future development. But apart from the narrowing of scope for independent action inherent in EU membership, there is a general aspect of how the EU works which has profound implications for character of British political life and the Constitution. This is the fact that the EU can operate and survive only on the basis of continuous (and often private) bargaining and negotiation among member states. This is very hard to reconcile with responsible government and public accountability as understood within the British political tradition.

We come back to the theme of continuity. The British people as a whole have inherited a long tradition of institutional and legal stability. While the Constitution has continually adapted and changed over the years to accommodate new needs and demands, it has retained certain fundamental features as the British version of a form of parliamentary government held to be both representative and responsible. The supremacy of this dominant tradition has made radical change difficult. There is, however, an unusual conjuncture of circumstances at the present time which appears to favour a sweeping programme of constitutional change and adaptation inspired principally by the slogans of democratization and modernization. The outcome of this process may be that it will no longer be possible to live by the old constitutional principles. If that happens, then the need will become urgent for a statement of what new principles are to replace them which is more mature and coherent than any offered so far.

4

The Growth of the State

GILLIAN PEELE

The twentieth century saw a massive expansion in the British state. By almost any measure – the volume of legislation, the level of government spending on goods and services, the percentage of the workforce employed in the public sector or the number of public bodies – the growth was dramatic. By the end of the century, despite extensive political debate about the role of government in British society and an unusually concerted effort in the last quarter of the century to trim the tentacles of Leviathan, the large state remains a fundamental feature of the political system. Instead of the limited and reactive role which it played for much of the nineteenth century, the state in the twentieth century became increasingly proactive, acquiring responsibilities for all aspects of its citizens' existence. In addition to its extensive role in the management of the economy and of welfare, the state by the year 2000 had become involved in moral issues such as *in vitro* fertilization and surrogate parenthood, extending its responsibilities, which had hitherto lain from the cradle to the grave, back to the very point of conception. It was also indicative of the wide-ranging public expectations of the state that ministers acquired responsibilities for the millennium's celebrations and the impact of its arrival on the functioning of computers.

The evidence of the state's growing involvement in all aspects of British society is the vast and varied range of governmental programmes initiated and sustained over the period since 1900 as well as the complex array of links, both personal and institutional, between the public and private sectors. Indeed, as will be argued in this chapter, the twentieth century saw not merely a significant expansion of the state but a major change in the way it operates. Not only is it more difficult now to see the state as a single actor; but many state objectives are today achieved through a complex pattern of relationships with the private sector. Models of the state which emphasised its organizational insulation and its hierarchical features have given way to models which capture the fuzziness of the borders between the

71

public and private sectors as well as the diversity of state agencies and the techniques available to promote their policy preferences (Maidment and Thompson, 1993; Ling, 1998).

The twentieth-century growth of the British state, and the subtle changes in its operation, raise fundamental questions for students of politics. How should we now define 'the state'? What are the causes of state growth? Is it possible to detect any pattern in the functions which the state has acquired over the century or in its methods of organizing and managing them? Is the big state now an inevitable feature of the British political system? If so, what is the impact on that system? Although these are not of course simple questions, this chapter will attempt to address them by looking first at the key factors in the process by which the contemporary state developed in the UK. Then it will examine some key changes in the pattern of state activity and the manner in which the state managed its responsibilities in the twentieth century. Finally, the chapter will highlight changes in the techniques used to secure accountability and responsiveness. First, however, it is necessary to provide a working definition of the state.

What is the State?

Although British political theorists have frequently used the notion of the 'state', it is not a familiar concept in English constitutional law. For the purposes of this chapter, it is not necessary to get involved in definitional disputes. Rather I shall use the term 'state' to refer to the totality of institutional structures which legitimately (that is, within the framework of existing law) make the collective decisions for the society. It is not a single organizational entity but a series of bureaucratic organizations with different powers and functions and operates at both the central and at the local level. On occasion it also operates at the supra-national level and since 1973 many decisions which were once taken by the UK have been taken within the framework of the decision-making structures of what is now the EU.

From the perspective of the members of society, the state is experienced not as an abstraction but in terms of the programmes and policies it manages. Expanding, contracting, sustaining or neglecting these programmes, and the business of managing the organizational problems presented by the enterprise as a whole, constitute the collective decisions of the society. Inevitably also the 'state' is experienced in terms of the officials who are responsible for running these services whether they are formally civil servants or fall into some other category such as local government or National Health Service employees. Given the growth in the public sector it is also experienced by many members of society as an employer as well as a provider of goods and services.

What follows from this definition is that although this chapter will inevitably devote a good deal of attention to changes in the role of central government, it must be remembered that the state is much more complex than that, encompassing such important structures as local government and health authorities.

The Growth of the Modern State

The expansive state which has been so ubiquitous and controversial a feature of the twentieth century has its roots deep in the nineteenth century (MacDonagh, 1977; Greenleaf, 1987). Although the British state performed few functions in 1800 and certainly very few of the welfare responsibilities which have come to absorb so much public energy, the processes of industrialization and urbanization generated a range of new problems which gradually changed the nation's political agenda, forcing government to intervene to correct or at least modify the forces of the free market. The transformation of Britain into a democracy over the nineteenth and early twentieth centuries through the extension of the franchise reinforced the process of agenda change, stimulating government to respond to a much wider range of interests and causes than ever before. As Ling (1998) has noted, government intervention is rarely neutral in its effect: it privileges some interests and disadvantages others. For example, in the nineteenth and early twentieth centuries government financial support for education was seen by Nonconformists as subsidizing Anglican schools at their expense. Initiatives designed to provide basic protection through the state against sickness and unemployment in the Liberal governments of 1905–15 not merely seemed to threaten the medical profession's freedom and the interests of the friendly societies but also concentrated on improving the lot of the male breadwinner rather than women and children.

The pattern of governmental intervention from the nineteenth century onwards was piecemeal and gradual, creating a tradition of incremental rather than radical or comprehensive reform. Thus for example the setting up of a National Vaccine establishment in 1808 was followed in 1853 by the introduction of *compulsory* vaccination against smallpox and then by further legislation in 1861, 1867 and 1871 to ensure that the national policy was effectively enforced. As Greenleaf notes, the pattern implicit in the smallpox example shows the state identifying a problem and a possible solution and moving in stages through permissive schemes to compulsory legislation. The pattern was repeated in numerous policy areas and by 1900 the British state exhibited a wide range of regulatory legislation involving substantial powers of enforcement as well as legislation which was permissive rather than mandatory in character, allowing local authorities to provide a service if they so wished. Thus although the state's role in housing provision was not really developed until well into the twentieth century, nineteenth century legislation (the Artisans and Labourers Acts of 1868 and 1875) provided local authorities with powers to deal with insanitary housing and these powers were used effectively by Joseph Chamberlain when Mayor of Birmingham (Greenleaf, 1983a).

Public health and poverty were perhaps the most significant areas of nineteenth-century state activity on the domestic front and both spawned new programmes and a momentum for administrative reform. The line of administrative reform was not always straight, of course. Thus Chadwick's concern for efficient public health authorities produced a degree of centralization which generated a backlash in favour of localism after his resignation from the Board of Health in 1854. Yet the dynamic of centralization reasserted itself as local authorities saw the need for expertise and as central government officials developed their own policy initiatives in response to recurring problems.

The motives for state intervention in Victorian Britain were inevitably mixed. Early forms of state provision for welfare and education contributed to the socialization of the poor and to a more efficient workforce as well to the needs of the recipients; and they supplemented, but did not replace, private philanthropy which continued to be an extremely important factor in British social policy well into the twentieth century (Owen, 1965).

Yet, although the British state's nineteenth-century expansion was patchy and unsystematic, there was no doubting the direction of change. The twentieth-century expansion of the state was thus not a new development but, to a large extent, a continuation of trends already clearly apparent in the nineteenth. Isolating the causes of the expansion of the twentieth-century state is thus an exercise fraught with methodological difficulties, not least because of the artificiality of separating nineteenth- and twentieth-century developments. Despite these caveats it is possible to identify four broad factors which contributed to the growth of the twentieth-century state.

Changes in Public Philosophy

The public philosophy was a major factor affecting the role of the state in the twentieth century. Although not all governmental growth is the result of a reflective or deliberate choice but is incremental in character, some changes in the role of the state are the product of explicit decisions to employ public power to counteract the free play of market forces. Inevitably there has been much debate about the precise role played by ideas in the process of governmental intervention. For some scholars, ideas such as utilitarianism (which in the nineteenth century suggested that the purpose of government was to advance the greatest happiness of the greatest number) or neo-liberalism (which reasserted the values of individualism and the market in the late twentieth century) were crucial triggers of policy change, prompting respectively an expansion and a contraction of the British state. For other scholars, the natural processes of governmental decision-making, not ideas, were the real causes of policy change (MacDonagh, 1977). Yet however sceptical one is about the relationship between ideas and policy-making, the intellectual assumptions prevalent in a political system at any given time are important not least because they determine the language in which policy choices are discussed and predispose policy-makers to one set of solutions rather than another.

The twentieth century saw, of course, extensive debate both about the role of state in the abstract and about the wisdom of particular approaches to specialist areas of policy such as the economy or health. The debate was conducted at various levels and was shaped by pressure groups, political parties and social movements anxious to mobilize the power of the state behind their causes as well as by politicians, policy-makers and philosophers. Within this long tradition of argument about the proper sphere of the state, two intellectual paradigms can be discerned: the *laissez-faire* model and the collectivist one. The *laissez-faire* model stressed the importance of individual rights (especially property rights) over collective benefits. It demanded a strong justification for governmental intervention in the market and preferred to see private or charitable solutions to social problems rather than governmental ones. The collectivist model by contrast urged the need to use public power to promote the collective good and subordinated considerations of individual liberty to the wider social interest. This model ascribed no particular merit to the workings of the free market and saw governmental intervention as a rational force preferable to private philanthropy (Greenleaf, 1987). Throughout the twentieth century these two models vied for supremacy, but at no point did either completely eclipse the other.

From 1900 to the end of the First World War in 1918, two political developments moved the role of the state further towards the collectivist model and away from *laissez-faire*. The first was the emergence of the 'New Liberalism' which saw a strengthening of the radical and reformist strand in the Liberal Party (represented by figures such as David Lloyd George and Christopher Addison) and the consequent championing of a much more positive governmental role in promoting the welfare of the population (Freeden, 1986). This ideological shift was reflected in the range of important reforms initiated by Liberal governments between 1906 and 1915 including the introduction of old age pensions in 1908 and national insurance and labour exchanges in 1911. The Liberal legislation of this period engaged the state much more fully than ever before in the fight against social deprivation and in many ways created the foundations of the modern welfare system. The second important development between 1900 and 1918 was the emergence of Labour as an independent party. Although the debates about the proper scope of state authority cut through the parties, the advent of Labour changed the nature of political debate. Whereas the Liberal commitment to reform through state intervention had been based very largely on a moral justification, Labour's arguments also used the newer language of class.

The First World War itself did much to transform the nature of the state and with it the assumptions of the country's governing elite. An unprecedented degree of state intervention in the economy occurred between 1914 and 1918 and novel uses of discretionary powers were tolerated. The imperatives of war also led to the modernization of the Cabinet (through the creation of the Cabinet secretariat) and of the Prime Minister's Office, so that under Lloyd George these key agencies became more efficient centres of decision-making. New ministries and boards were created to manage new government functions such as labour and munitions.

Some reformers such as Christopher Addison hoped that the power of the newly expanded state could be used for social reconstruction after the war (Morgan and Morgan, 1980). Victory however witnessed a substantial dismantling of the economic controls and a reassertion of older attitudes about the proper role of the state. Thus although the promise of a new approach to social problems had been an important part of Lloyd George's popular appeal in 1918, his postwar coalition government (which lasted from 1918 to 1922) was increasingly influenced by conservative forces demanding retrenchment. Despite savage spending cuts (the 'Geddes axe' of 1922 for example reduced benefits by 10 per cent) the state's role in the management of welfare continued to expand in the inter-war years and it developed its responsibilities in health and housing. The administration of the poor relief was reformed in 1929 by transferring responsibility from the elected Poor Law guardians to the county councils and county boroughs, a move which for some critics helped shake off the stigma of the Poor Law but for others weakened democratic control of the system (Vincent, 1991).

The crucial factor in thinking about the role of the state in the inter-war period was the economy. Recession had hit the British economy in 1920, but in 1931 Britain like the rest of Europe and the United States felt the effects of major financial collapse. This crisis of the capitalist order produced social misery and political upheaval. The collapse of the economies of the West also raised the question of whether the state should have a greater role in economic management in order to prevent such calamities. Economists on the left argued that state planning was the only corrective to market failure; on the right, defenders of classical economics argued that for the market to operate effectively it had to be freed of the distorting effects of trade union power, government intervention and concentrations of capital (Helm, 1989). A third approach which was to have an enormous long-term effect on the role of the state in Britain was that of John Maynard Keynes.

Keynes focused on the framework of economic policy in the explanation of economic dislocation and the persistence of such problems as unemployment. He pointed out that there could be economic failure – a lack of aggregate demand – at the macro level of an economy regardless of the level of efficiency displayed at the micro level. This inefficiency, he argued, could be corrected by the state which could intervene to increase demand or to restrain it. In Keynes's opinion, the degree of intervention required was limited.

The state needed to give the economy a gentle steer to adjust its course and to provide sufficient aggregate demand to produce full employment without inflation (Helm, 1989). Keynesian ideas were circulating in the inter-war period (and he contributed to the intellectual revival of the Liberal Party in that period), but they did not seriously influence government until after the Second World War. Although closely associated with the direction of policy after 1945, Keynes's idea of the proper role of the state in the economy did not entirely coincide with those of the 1945 Labour government, notably because Keynes was not unequivocally in favour of public ownership and he wanted to use monetary, not fiscal, policy to manage demand (Skidelsky, 1989).

The Second World War itself – like the first – produced massive changes in the role of the state, as government intervened to control many aspects of the national life, and there was a significant shift towards the collectivist pole in the public philosophy, as the common sacrifice made by the people strengthened arguments for using state resources to promote social justice. The Labour government elected in 1945 built on the sense of common purpose created by the war and developed a set of new policies and programmes which reflected the party's own ideology and left an important institutional and intellectual legacy for the post-war British state.

Three aspects of that institutional and intellectual legacy deserve mention here. The first was the acceptance of the idea – building on the doctrines especially of Keynes – that the state could and should play a role in managing the framework of the economy. The second was the idea – following the Beveridge report of 1942 – that the state had a major responsibility for protecting its citizens from social deprivation. The third was a visible increase in the scope of the state and its bureaucracy. Between 1945 and 1951 key industries and utilities (coal, gas, railways, electricity, water) as well as the Bank of England were taken into public ownership, bringing their employees within the public sector. In addition, the role of local government was expanded by the extension of welfare services, and important new bureaucratic structures were created in the NHS.

The outlines of the more extensive state created in the period from 1945 to 1951 were accepted by the Conservatives when they returned to power. There is now a vigorous debate about the applicability of the term 'consensus' to the period from 1945 until the mid-1970s (Addison, 1994, 1996; Jones and Kandiah, 1996). Yet whatever the Conservatives' initial doubts about many of Labour's policies, their desire for re-election kept public spending on welfare high under the Conservative governments of 1951–64 and ensured that the fundamental features of the British state's role (including its role in the economy) were not challenged until the mid-1970s.

Radical doubts about the direction of the British state emerged in the 1970s and as a result the scope of government became an important issue in political debate. The doubts were in part occasioned by a series of practical problems which affected both the UK and other advanced political systems: economic decline, fiscal crisis and governmental overload (Rose and Peters, 1979; King, 1976). There was at the same time a reassertion of interest in the ideas of libertarian and free-market thinkers as the Keynesian economic consensus collapsed (Cockett, 1995). Together these developments created a new intellectual climate in which arguments for reducing the state's role were advanced seriously and successfully. When Margaret Thatcher became leader of the Conservative Party (1975) and Prime Minister (1979) she brought to the forefront of public debate important elements of New Right thinking about the need to strengthen the market and to cut back the responsibilities of the public sector.

The period from the mid-1970s until 1997 was an unusual one in the context of the twentieth century as a whole since it saw a concerted attempt to reassess the role of the state and to pare down its functions. Trade unions were brought within a new legal framework, a series of nationalized industries were privatized, long-established state functions (such as the provision of free school meals) were limited or abolished and there was a general attempt to target welfare provision more effectively. Particularly noteworthy was the introduction for council house tenants of a right to buy their houses in the Housing Act 1980, which signalled a beginning of the state's retreat from the field of public housing. Alongside these sweeping policy changes, the state's administrative style was changed by the introduction of private-sector techniques of management and the contracting out of services by central and local government. The organizational structure of government and the culture of the Civil Service were further altered by the introduction of executive agencies designed to enhance accountability and inject a more managerial style into the public sector. Although the high point of interest in free-market economics and new public management had perhaps passed by the middle of the 1990s, one important effect of the sustained counter-collectivist mood of the 1980s was felt in the Labour Party which was forced to revise its own thinking about the role of the state. Blair's

1997 government accepted the outlines of the state restructured under Thatcher and Major and indeed signalled that in some areas, such as welfare reform, he wanted to be more radical than his Conservative predecessors. The 1997 Labour government was also committed to an ambitious programme of constitutional reform (such as devolution to Scotland and Wales) which was itself bound to have an indirect effect on the role of the state. Labour's public philosophy at the century's end was expressed in terms of a 'third way' – a synthesis of ideas employing state and market solutions and a rejection of the paradigms of both free-market individualism and collectivism (Giddens, 1998; Blair, 1998).

Changes in State Capacity

A second factor of major importance in the growth of government is state capacity. Where a state is weak it is unlikely to take on new functions; as the state's capacity grows it will increasingly be seen as the solution for new or emerging problems. The capacity of a state is determined by many factors including infrastructure, the availability of suitable personnel and communications, knowledge and leadership.

The quality of a state's infrastructure inevitably affects the quality of its policy-making and policy implementation. Administrative bodies must be available to put programmes in place on the ground and the absence of an efficient system for implementing policy will usually restrict the possibility of government intervention. (On occasion, however, policy change triggers administrative reform – as occurred in the field of health provision over the nineteenth and twentieth centuries.) Central government in Britain for much of the nineteenth century had to rely on local agencies for such basic state functions as law and order and had not the capacity for extensive service delivery. Local government in the nineteenth century itself provided little effective infrastructure since, outside the towns, it was chaotic and corrupt. Thus when Chadwick was organizing the reform of public health in the early nineteenth century, he was convinced that new special authorities needed to be created because of the administrative weaknesses of the old unreformed local government system (Finer, 1952). The expansion of the British state over the twentieth century is thus very much a story of two interconnecting processes: the elaboration of governmental responsibilities through newly devised and refined programmes and the reorganization of the administration to reflect new programmatic concerns. This interactive process of expanded intervention and administrative reform generated in the first part of the twentieth century a host of new departments (education, health, pensions, labour, agriculture) as the boards through which central control was formerly exercised proved inadequate to an expanded role and were turned into more specialized and high-profile instruments of state intervention. In the second part of the twentieth century the administrative map accordingly looked much neater until the 1980s and 1990s when the introduction of executive agencies (and other developments such as devolution) again complicated the scene.

A coherent pattern of administrative authorities is not the only important element of the state's infrastructure, however. Also vital are the interrelated resources of personnel, finance and communications. The reform of personnel was vital to the evolution of the modern British state. The framework of the Civil Service was set by the 1854 Northcote Trevelyan Report enacted in 1870; its detail was refined as the state's functions grew in the late nineteenth and early twentieth centuries. The key features of the personnel system erected for central government were that it recruited increasingly on merit not patronage, that the career at the highest levels was prestigious and therefore attracted able applicants, and that top civil servants did not change with governments. It was a highly compartmentalized system and one which separated policy generalists from subject experts such as economists and scientists. The number of civil servants increased in tandem with the expansion of the state's responsibilities. In some cases (for example with the new system of labour exchanges in 1911 and in wartime) expansions of government personnel took place outside the framework of the normal rules of recruitment. Numbers employed in local government service also grew over the twentieth century, reflecting the expansion of the role of local authorities, although the qualifications and ethos of local government service were very different from that of the Civil Service proper (Beveridge, 1953).

The capacity of the state is also constrained by its ability to raise money. Additional programmes require enhanced financial support, so that before a state can grow it must have available mechanisms for paying for governmental activity. Equally, the provision of public money (through grants and subsidies) may draw government into the general administration of a service, as occurred with education from 1833 onwards. Thereafter the state moved from grants to private bodies to provide education, to the direct provision of a complete system from nursery schooling, through to higher education. In the nineteenth century the important function of the relief of poverty was funded from a specially levied local 'rate'. As the national governmental role increased, general taxation became the primary source of funding for programmes and the number of different taxes has risen through the twentieth century. Income tax now represents a larger proportion of total revenue than it did in 1900, and the balance between central and local taxation has shifted towards the nationally as opposed to locally imposed taxes. Within the central government the Treasury has consistently exercised a constraining role in relation to government expenditure, which has frequently brought it into conflict with advocates of new policy ventures and openened it to charges of obstructionism.

The infrastructure of the state was transformed in the nineteenth century by improvements in communications. Until well into the nineteenth century poor transport facilities made local administration the norm and limited the scope of central control. But with improvements in the roads and the coming of the railways, on-the-spot inspection and more detailed monitoring of services became possible. Efficient mail services enhanced governmental capacity following the introduction of the penny post in 1840. In the twentieth century technological change made monitoring and service delivery easier and administrative distance was further reduced especially with the coming of computers and electronic mail.

A state's capacity to act is also constrained by the knowledge at its disposal. This fundamental point has a negative and a positive aspect. The negative aspect is that states will be unwilling to intervene in the absence of substantive knowledge, but equally advances in scientific knowledge create their own momentum for applications and frequently in the twentieth century such applications involved government. In the nineteenth century governmental intervention was deeply affected by the pace of scientific advance. Some gains in medical knowledge pointed the way to improving public health, although it should be noted that then as now it was often difficult to obtain agreement within the scientific community and difficult to integrate scientific findings into the policy process. By the same token the limits of medical knowledge set limits for governmental ambition in such areas as health provision.

State capacity was also limited by ignorance about the character of British society. The first census was taken in 1801 but government remained very ill-informed about many aspects of social life. The capacity of government to see a problem depended on the availability of reliable data about social conditions. The surveys of London and York produced by Booth (in 1892 and Rowntree in 1901) were important turning-points in the rediscovery of poverty in late Victorian and Edwardian England, stimulating debate about the role which government could play in coping with poverty. Sometimes however the discovery of social ills occurred accidentally, as happened when the recruitment process for the Boer war revealed the poor physical condition of much of the population. Similarly, economic management was dependent on advances in theoretical understanding of the economy. Thus the state's confidence in its ability to shape the economic framework grew when Keynesian ideas (which were extensively expounded in his *General Theory* in 1936) and the understanding of the techniques available for implementing them were widely circulated.

The growth of the state also required leadership. Although it is difficult to disagree with one authority on the evolution of British administration who noted that 'the system developed the way it did more as a result of general forces and not because of this or that Minister or managerial innovator' (Chester, 1981), individuals – politicians, civil servants and pressure group leaders – played an important part in changing the scope of the British state at different points in the twentieth century. For example, Lloyd George's personal dynamism as premier between 1916 and 1922 triggered the creation of a more formal Cabinet secretariat. The charisma and skill of Aneurin Bevan were vital in implementing the NHS in 1947–8 despite opposition from the medical profession. And Thatcher's personality clearly was a significant factor in shaping her government's neo-liberal agenda in the 1980s (Kavanagh, 1986). Among officials, a variety of individuals had a substantial individual impact in the twentieth century: witness the role of Robert Morant in relation to education and William Beveridge in relation to social security (Chester, 1953; Harris, 1977).

Crises in Public Policy

Crises may also lead to substantial changes in the role of the state, not least because they highlight administrative weaknesses and social problems. The more serious the crisis the more likely it is to shatter normal expectations about political acceptability, dissolve old alignments and create new political patterns. In the twentieth century war was the cause of major change in the British state. Although Britain did not experience military defeat in the twentieth century it came close to it – beginning with the Boer War, which shook the country's complacency. The First and Second World Wars were unlike previous wars in the extent to which they mobilized the total population and occasioned a hitherto unparalleled degree of state intervention in all aspects of society.

The First World War, although in the short term it arrested schemes of social reform being put in place by the Liberals, in the long run saw a massive extension of collectivism. It brought experience of conscription, censorship, control of industry, food production, pricing and distribution as well as experiment with executive discretion and the use of compulsory powers. 'Never before' as one authority noted, 'had the state assumed such sweeping responsibilities for directing and organizing production [in] industry' (Morgan and Morgan, 1980). An enhanced governmental role was retained after the war for a variety of reasons – inertia, support for government intervention, the difficulty of removing government controls in all areas of national life and the existence of an agenda of reconstruction. The First World War – like the Second – heightened demand for the state to address issues of social inequality and injustice. Both wars also encouraged a shift towards a more corporate style of policy-making involving the employers and the trade unions in decision-making (Middlemas, 1979). And both wars facilitated a shift in party strength. The Liberal Party was severely weakened by the first world; Labour was strengthened by its participation in Churchill's coalition government from 1940 to 1945.

War is not the only crisis which can generate substantial change in the political order and in the role of government. Severe economic crises may have the same effect – witness the impact of the Great Depression on the role of the federal government in the United States (Ackerman, 1991). In Britain the stock market collapse of 1931 brought down a Labour government which did not want to cut social benefits and precipitated the formation of a coalition government which was willing to reduce unemployment payments and impose a means test on benefits. The 1976 IMF crisis forced extensive reductions in public spending on a minority Labour government and undermined confidence in Keynesian methods of managing the economy.

Internal disorder can produce change in the role of the state. The eruption of conflict in Northern Ireland in the 1960s not only brought the end of devolved government there but led to the expansion of the military and police presence in the province.

Epidemics can also be a spur to administrative reform or simply expose weaknesses in the state policy-making machinery. Cholera in the nineteenth century was a critical factor in administrative change in the area of public health (Morris, 1976). In the late twentieth century both the AIDS epidemic and BSE exposed deficiencies in the British government's ability to address major health problems and, in the case of BSE, led the state to prohibit the sale of many meat items, such as beef on the bone.

External Pressure

A final cause of change in the role of the British state has been external pressure. The British state is a capitalist state which operates in the context of the world economy. It is therefore subject to competition and may be affected by changes in the global environment. Thus the general move towards the protection of industry after the First World War occurred because British industries were no longer able to maintain their market share in the new international environment. Similarly the government has from time to time taken steps to encourage civil research by financial grants and subsidies.

The role of the state has also changed as a result of the successful examples of policies operating in other systems. Beveridge records that Lloyd George's commitment to the introduction of sickness and invalidity insurance into the UK occurred as a result of a visit to Germany in 1908 when he was impressed by the system introduced by Bismarck in 1889 (Beveridge, 1953). More recent examples of policy transfer across national boundaries include the Child Support Agency from the United States and Australia and 'workfare' from the USA.

Britain's membership of the EU since 1973 has profoundly changed the scope of the British state. First, the UK government no longer acts alone in a number of policy areas but participates in a broader, multinational policy-making process. This change is significant because the mix of programmes and policy instruments within the EU may be very different from those which the UK acting alone would have employed. Thus for example law plays a larger role in the administrative process of the EU than it has traditionally done in the UK; and agriculture is a more important economic sector for many European countries than it is for Britain. Second, a range of new regulations affect the UK, forcing the British state to bring its policies into line with European ones, for example in relation to food production.

The Changing Pattern of Governmental Functions

A range of factors has affected the growth of the British state even in the twentieth century. That growth was experienced by the population in terms of an expansion of services and regulatory activity as well as taxation. Inevitably different classes reacted differently to the changes. As the state has expanded its reach and accumulated new functions, two questions have repeatedly arisen. The first is the extent to which it is possible to distinguish between the various functions of government on some rational principle. The second is whether it might be possible to identify some functions as crucial to the state's existence and to devolve other activities to some other agencies including the private sector. Although the process of state expansion has generally been a gradual and cumulative one, there have been some periods of reappraisal of the state's role – most notably at the end of the First World War with the Machinery of Government or Haldane Report of 1918 and in the period of neo-liberal ascendancy under the Thatcher and Major Conservative governments of 1979–97. Both of these efforts to impose some order on the multiple functions of the state (and in the case of the Conservative governments of 1979–97 a determined effort to make the state contract) underline the difficulty of setting limits on the expansion of the state or attempting to channel its activities in accordance with preordained principles of administration. Equally difficult is the question of how to classify state functions and it is even more problematic to try to distinguish between state functions in terms either of their inherent importance or the political significance attached to them by voters. What can be done here is simply to provide a sketch of the broad areas of government activity in a way which illuminates the changes in the state's role since 1900.

Core Functions of the State: Foreign Policy, Defence, Law and Order, Finance

Certain core functions exist in every modern state, although even these functions have been elaborated and refined in the twentieth century with the growth of government. Moreover, in many respects the functions have become more intertwined and interdependent. Thus, foreign policy, which for a long time was seen as a specialist function (and has been handled by a separate ministry in Britain since 1782) is now to a large extent integrated with many other aspects of government. Indeed so extensive has the transformation of the foreign policy process been, that there is a questioning of the requirement for a separate diplomatic organization and a natural tendency for governments to see cuts in the foreign policy establishment as a simple way of reducing costs. Inevitably, the significance attached to the foreign policy-making process (and the role of the Foreign Office) changed over the twentieth century as Britain's world role altered, although some critics would argue that the two are still not perfectly aligned. At the beginning of the twentieth century the UK was a major world power and the centre of a vast imperial structure. In 1900 a range of departments had important overseas responsibilities so that in addition to the Foreign Office there were the Colonial Office and the India Office, each managing the state's responsibilities for sections of the British Empire. By the end of the century Britain had to seek her security within larger multinational organizations, especially NATO, rather than enjoying great-power status in her own right.

Rapid changes in the international environment especially after 1945 affected the foreign policy process itself. Traditional notions of diplomacy gave way to the more routine notion of managing external relations and the agenda of foreign policy became more concerned with economic and trading issues than with such classical diplomatic concerns as providing a channel of communications between governments and protecting British citizens abroad. Technological change – the advent of the telephone and later e-mail – also radically changed the diplomatic world.

The broader conception of foreign policy which emerged after 1945 demanded greater economic and technical expertise and meant that departments other than the Foreign Office necessarily developed overseas responsibilities. The inclusion of civil servants from the Treasury, from the Ministry of Agriculture, Fisheries and Food and from the Department of Trade and Industry in international policy-making blurred the line between domestic and foreign policy concerns. The traditional foreign policy function in government was further changed by British membership of the EU which continued the process of giving an international dimension to many policy areas and placed added emphasis on the coordination of policy – a process which the Foreign Office and the Cabinet Office shared.

The international agenda was also reshaped by the end of the Cold war. Many of the major issues which remain on the international agenda now have an ethical dimension – for example aid and the environment. Although Liberal and Labour governments in the twentieth century have wanted to highlight the humanitarian and moral aspects of foreign policy to a greater extent than have Conservative ones, all parties now recognise the importance of humanitarian concerns in foreign policy. As a result there are extensive aid programmes which although administered separately from traditional Foreign Office concerns may be seen as part of the wider foreign policy process.

Closely related to foreign policy is the traditional function of defence. The experience of war in the twentieth century stimulated collectivism and centralization. The significance of defence as a state activity has however changed greatly over the twentieth century, reflecting the changing role of Britain in the world. Traditionally great reliance had been placed on maintaining a strong navy and comparatively little emphasis had been placed on keeping a strong army in peacetime. Rivalry between the services persisted within government and until 1964 was exacerbated by the survival of separate ministries for the five defence-related departments (War Office, Admiralty, Air Ministry, Aviation Supply and Defence). In 1964 however a radical reorganization brought all these departments into a single super-department of Defence. While this move did not entirely quell inter-service rivalries, it represented a substantial step towards integration of the services. As with the Foreign Office, the defence function is one which is vulnerable to cuts in an era when Britain's defence arrangements seem increasingly dependent on multilateral arrangements. Nevertheless the state's defence role remains significant not merely because the function itself is important but also because it gives the state massive leverage in the private sector (where defence contracts are highly lucrative) and has provided over the century an important source of employment.

The maintenance of law and order has long been seen as a core function of the state. Indeed the monopoly of the legitimate use of coercion has been seen as one of the defining characteristics of the state. The significance of order issues grew during the nineteenth century and became increasingly specialized. In the twentieth century the state's role in penal policy and in crime prevention grew. And although the state retained its pre-eminent role in this policy field, the late twentieth century saw experiments with the devolution of policing and prison functions to the private sector.

The discharge of the function of law and order remains diffused within the political system. The Lord Chancellor provides unity to the judicial system but also combines a variety of roles – legislative, executive and judicial (see Chapter 7). The task of managing the courts has become more complex over the twentieth century and the growth of the state itself (especially in the field of welfare) produced a plethora of new specialist courts and tribunals to resolve benefit disputes; and these in turn produced an increasingly developed system of administrative law and a demand for public funding for legal services.

The evolution of the policing function in the nineteenth century reflected the tradition that law and order was (outside London) primarily a *local* function. The administration of justice at the lowest levels was in origin a matter for the local lay magistrates and the lord-lieutenant of the counties. In addition to their responsibility for administering justice, magistrates exercised other administrative roles such as licensing. In the counties magistrates were part of the local political elite, and for much of the twentieth century social position together with party politics influenced the selection of magistrates.

The law-and-order functions of the state increasingly involved far more than the detection of crime and the punishment of offenders. The modern British state developed a host of specialist programmes relating to all aspects of crime and punishment – for example in relation to the management of prisons, juvenile offenders, and after-care services.

Even a state with minimal activity has to be funded but the way it is done may ease or restrict the process of growth in the role of government. In Britain, the Treasury has existed as a separate department at least since 1667. Charged primarily with the responsibility of raising the money to pay for expenditure on wars, administration and state services, its ethos in the nineteenth and twentieth centuries was often a restrictive one which urged the adoption of the most economical provision of a service if the state should provide it at all. Until the twentieth century direct taxation was generally low and the system was not seen as a way of reducing inequality. The 1909 Budget was something of a turning-point here; not only did it establish a relationship between taxation and the ability to pay but it also linked politically the ability to provide welfare services for the mass of the population with the need to obtain greater tax revenues.

With the growth of state functions the Treasury's responsibilities became more complex and the key functions of controlling public expenditure, funding government programmes and managing the Civil Service all grew in strategic importance, giving the Treasury enormous power over all aspects of government.

Beyond the Core: State Intervention in the Economy, Welfare and the Quality of Life

Although the government's commitment to comprehensive planning of the economy was not a feature of the British state until the Second World War (and even then somewhat minimal), government intervention in different aspects of the national economy had long been a feature of the society. The Board of Trade which had its origins as a Committee of the Privy Council had in the nineteenth century acquired a number of regulatory responsibilities as the nation's commercial activities expanded. Thus from the initial concern with commercial treaties and relations with overseas settlements the Board of Trade (which became a separate department in 1867) acquired functions relating to railway regulation, merchant shipping, the Companies Acts, bankruptcy and patent legislation. It also became intimately concerned with labour.

Labour issues became increasingly important to government in the late nineteenth and early twentieth century as trade unions became more powerful. Humanitarian concern with the conditions of work had already prompted a large amount of labour legislation in the nineteenth century but became more pronounced in the twentieth century. Government's right to regulate the hours and conditions of work was taken for granted by the time of the First World War. Low pay was an acknowledged problem which governments in early Edwardian England tried to tackle through such measures as the 1909 legislation which created wages boards for a number of 'sweated' trades. The need to regulate labour in the First World War led to the creation of a separate Ministry of Labour in 1916 which institutionalized the state's new role in this fundamental aspect of the economy. Although it was to be more than fifty years before it was finally implemented, there was even discussion of a minimum wage in the immediate aftermath of the war.

Closely related to labour issues was the question of employment since clearly the level of employment was the key issue determining a range of other social issues in the country. The question of unemployment relief had long troubled decision-makers but it was not until 1911 that the state made a concerted effort to provide workers with some protection against the vagaries of the employment market. Then however only a small percentage of the population was covered and important categories (such as domestic employees) were left out. The scourge of unemployment in the inter-war period made this a high-profile issue. It was not until 1944, however, that the government made its crucial commitment to a policy of full employment. The Labour government elected in 1945 was explicitly committed to the policy and employment levels were high for much of the post-war period, encouraging governments of all parties to think that they had learned how to manage the employment issue. In the 1970s however unemployment began to rise again. By this stage however there was less confidence in the ability of governments to produce full employment, given the increasing impact of the global economy on national conditions. Instead there was an emphasis on training and the transmission of market skills to increase the competitiveness of potential workers.

The state had become increasingly involved in key areas of social policy – poverty, health and education – from the nineteenth century. Education for example was one of the earliest services to attract government grants in 1833. Thereafter not merely did the grants increase but the principle of compulsory education (already implicit in the Factory Acts) was made explicit in legislation in 1870. Legislation in 1902 introduced compulsory secondary education and in 1906 legislation allowed schools to provide meals to pupils. This provision was made compulsory in 1914 and remained until legislation in 1980 removed this obligation on local authorities. Until 1988, however, when the Education Reform Act gave the government powers to set a national curriculum and require the regular testing of pupils, there was no detailed control by central government of the curriculum except in relation to religious worship.

Concern for public health and the desire to protect children led naturally to school medical inspection and ultimately to the establishment of a separate Ministry of Health in 1919. The first world war prompted government intervention in the housing market through rent and mortgage interest control and then to a series of measures (such as the Addison Housing and Town Planning Act of 1919 and the Wheatley Act of 1924 which brought central government pressure on local authorities to build new houses and clear slums).

The Second World War and the election of a Labour government in 1945 marked a new stage in the growth of the state's responsibilities in the field of welfare. A range of programmes and policies were put in place as part of an explicit commitment to social justice and a welfare state. In education the principle of free access was established in 1944; a comprehensive national health service was put in place; in the field of social security a range of programmes for children, pensioners, the unemployed and the very poor was designed to ensure that everyone had access to a basic minimum income. The broad outlines of the welfare state put in place after 1945 were accepted by both parties until the mid-1970s. Part of the debate that then emerged related to the rising cost of welfare; but part related also the extent to which welfare should be seen as an automatic right rather than a facility conditional upon some contribution to the society. On the right there were arguments about the extent to which welfare encouraged dependence while within the Labour party there was concern about the extent to which benefits should be linked to willingness to work (King, 1995).

One factor affecting the debate about the role of the state in the late twentieth century has been an increasing awareness of issues which have become more prominent as concerns about basic living standards have receded. Although concern for the environment became a high profile issue in the 1980s, the state had been increasingly involved in this field since the nineteenth century. Thus the Alkali Acts with their own inspectorate date from 1863 and bear witness to the state's determination to regulate some aspects of the environment. The state's involvement in town and country planning and slum clearance had also been there since the late nineteenth century, while interest in wildlife protection dates from before the Second World War. Increasingly also the state had become involved in quality-of-life issues as a subsidiser of libraries, museums, galleries and general culture.

The state had always structured gender relations in British society, not least through the way it developed its welfare programmes. Thus the innovative national insurance legislation of 1911 was targeted at the male breadwinner; and the 1931 Anomalies Act 1931 had the effect of discouraging married women from remaining in the labour market by disqualifying any insurance qualifications made by women before marriage. The state was involved only intermittently in efforts to produce equal pay between the sexes and to promote female equality more generally. In 1970 the Wilson Labour government passed an Equal Pay Act and this was followed in 1975 with a Sex Discrimination Act; the Equal Opportunities Commission has the responsibility of enforcing the law in this area and monitoring discrimination against women. The state has also intervened in the field of race relations since 1965 in an attempt to secure greater equality for ethnic minorities and to prevent discrimination and racial abuse in society.

The Organization of the State

It is not possible to separate the question of the growth of the state from organizational issues. In the nineteenth century, as has been seen, much had to be done locally rather than centrally and new functions frequently emerged as the result of permissive legislation. In the twentieth century, central government more frequently took the initiative to provide a service or made its provision by another agency compulsory. Central government also expanded its complex procedures of inspection and control. And, when there was a danger as in the inter-war period that some left-wing authorities such as Poplar would provide higher than average unemployment relief, Parliament passed legislation in 1921 to allow the central government to determine the scales of benefit.

An important element in the dynamic of state growth was the creation of a separate organizational structure for a function which might hitherto have been handled as one task within a ministry covering a much broader area. The struggle for a separate Ministry of Health (which ultimately came about in 1919) showed how important was a separate department for the independent development of a function (Honigsbaum, 1970).

There has been much fluidity in the precise responsibilities of various government departments (Clifford *et al.*, 1997). Yet the form of the central department has remained remarkably constant. In organizational terms, the ministry or department has been structured with a minister or secretary of state (aided by junior ministers) answerable to Parliament for all the activities of the department. Ministers have been supported by a tightly organized Civil Service structure headed by a permanent secretary who was also the accounting officer of the department.

There have been two major exceptions to this model of central governmental organization. The first occurred when the decision was taken to use a different organizational model for industries taken into public ownership after the Second World War. Then instead of using a department to manage coal, electricity and the other industries, the model of the public corporation was used. This model was designed to separate the day-to-day running of the industry from political control and to recruit staff who were not formal civil servants. The purpose of the model was to combine a limited degree of political accountability with commercial values, but it was increasingly subject to criticism for failing to satisfy either the criteria of public responsiveness or of profitability.

The second exception is more recent. As part of the wider interest in introducing private-sector norms and techniques into the public sector, it was thought that many aspects of government could be discharged by executive agencies which would be able to concentrate on the delivery of the service and might operate rather differently from the departments of which they were formally part. The focus on service delivery initially appeared to produce improvements in efficiency (at least in terms of the number of cases handled), but there remained doubts both about the ability to separate policy from day-to-day management of services such as the Child Support Agency and the Prison Service and about the accountability of these services. Although the experiment was introduced under a Conservative government, it was not reversed by the Labour government elected in 1997, so that executive agencies seem likely to be a permanent part of the state's structure.

In addition to the structures of central government proper, the state has used a range of boards, commissions and authorities to advance its purposes. Local government, although reduced in power and autonomy in the post-war period, has also continued to play a crucial role in the delivery of services. And new forms of partnership between the public and private sector – for example enterprise zones and urban development corporations – underline the fragmentation and the amorphousness of the British state at the century's end.

Conclusion

It has been argued here that, although state growth has been a fundamental feature of British politics in the twentieth century, the process of state expansion cannot be easily attributed to any single set of factors. It remains to be asked whether the process of state growth is set to continue, or – to put the question another way – is the big state a fundamental of British politics? If so, what are the consequences for political life?

A glance at twentieth-century British history suggests that a substantial reduction in the role of the state is unlikely. Different ways of delivering services may be initiated, as has occurred with privatization or the use of executive agencies; and there may be some alteration of balance between state functions. International cooperation – especially within the context of the EU – may be expected to increase. But even where the state appears to be in retreat – as in the case of privatization – on a longer view it may simply have changed its mode of operation, preferring the steering of regulatory agencies to direct control. In some areas (such as the education curriculum and the provision of higher education) it should be noted that the state has actually become more interventionist since the 1980s. Even the Labour government's dramatic renunciation of the power to set interest rates on election in 1997 may be less significant in an increasingly integrated international environment.

If the mode of state intervention has changed, the citizen has still to live under a state with extensive powers. The consequences for the country's political life of a big state are multi-faceted. Assuming that radical changes in the role of the state are unlikely then the emphasis from the perspective of those concerned for the quality of democracy must surely be on refining the formal instruments of accountability – through Parliament, the courts and other devices such as ombudsmen – and on making sure that the services delivered to consumers are what they, rather than officials, want. An extensive state and individual liberty are not necessarily incompatible; but the massive inequality of power created by the big state requires balancing mechanisms and controls if it is to be kept in check. However much movement there has been in the direction of legal control (a greater role for judicial review and the incorporation of a bill of rights), the British state retains some of its traditional features of secrecy and non-accountability. The challenge of the twenty-first century is to develop techniques which are capable of controlling the powerful state created over the course of the previous century.

5

The Institutions of Central Government

MARTIN J. SMITH

It is impossible to understand the operation of British central government without examining the philosophical and historical background of the modern core executive. Both the analysis and operation of central government has been underpinned by sets of principles that have been reinforced by historical practice. These principles – parliamentary sovereignty, ministerial and Cabinet responsibility, secrecy and the public-service ethos – are closely interlinked and mutually reinforcing. They reflect constitutional doctrine and practice and define the powers of government and how they are perceived. They have also had a significant impact on the study of government through the development of the 'Westminster Model' which defined power as being concentrated within the parliamentary system. The executive (Cabinet) made decisions but was accountable to Parliament. This chapter demonstrates how these closely linked principles have informed the operation and analysis of central government. However, it is apparent that the Constitutional focus also skewed much of the analysis of central government and resulted in political scientists examining a limited set of issues and institutions. Therefore the chapter also outlines how recent events have highlighted the weaknesses of the traditional understanding of central government and opened the way for new approaches that adopt more sophisticated forms of analysis.

The Principles of British Central Government

The nature and operation of British central government is underpinned by two paradoxes and many of the rules and institutions of government derive from attempts to resolve them. The first is the relationship between the principle of parliamentary sovereignty and the practices of ministerial government. Both concepts are central to the British state, but the idea that sovereignty lies in Parliament is threatened by the fact that ministerial departments control the majority of policy-making. The second is the conflict between popular representation and limited participation. The British system is, in principle, democratic with government elected by, and responsible to, the people. However, theories of liberal democracy, deriving from John Stuart Mill, are essentially opposed to rule by the masses, seeing them as too ill-informed or self-interested to be closely involved in government. Hence government is democratic but essentially conducted by a closed and unresponsive elite. These conflicts are permanent features of the Constitution. Therefore it is difficult to appreciate the nature of the core executive without understanding the Constitution as a force *on*, as well as *in*, politics (Dearlove, 1989) and also on the analysis of policy. Thus many of the attempts at constitutional reconciliation are concerned with adapting an ancient constitution to the requirements of modern government.

The foundation of British central government is parliamentary sovereignty. Even today ministers continually look to Parliament to legitimize decisions and the speaker remonstrates with ministers for releasing information to the media before giving it to Parliament. As Judge (1993) reminds us, the Monarchy's power was exercised through Parliament from the middle ages. However the Constitutional Settlement of 1689 limited the role of the monarch and the principle of the supremacy of Parliament became implicit: 'what was asserted and accepted in 1689 was the principle of the supremacy of Parliament, whereby Parliament secured legal supremacy among the institutions of the state' (Judge, 1993: 20).

The combination of the Constitutional settlement and specific historical practice placed parliamentary sovereignty at the centre of British government. Parliamentary government partly arose with the crystallization of the commercial classes. During the eighteenth century commercial interests became increasingly strong, exacerbating conflicts between the landed classes and commercial classes. Commerce supported an aggressive foreign policy in pursuit of raw materials and new markets, while the landed classes were not prepared to pay the extra taxes that imperialism required. At the same time, radical voices called for the overhaul of an antiquated and corrupt Parliament. By the end of the eighteenth century the landed classes had passed the zenith of their power and were finally forced to make concessions to the capitalist class with the 1832 Reform Act (Moore, 1966).

After 1832, Parliament consciously used its power. MPs were able to force governments out of office and reject budgets, for example Lord Althorp's in 1833. MPs were in control and the government could not be certain of outcomes in the division lobby. Between the 1830s and 1880s parties were amorphous organizations and MPs voted on party lines on less than 30 per cent of all issues. Consequently, legislation was made on the floor of the house and Parliament controlled its own timetable (Lenman, 1992).

Nevertheless, this period of parliamentary government was relatively short-lived. Social and economic change created pressure for greater government activism. When these forces were combined with the organization of pressure groups and the development of party discipline, there was a shift away from the parliamentary arena to the executive. Despite this rise of the executive, parliamentary government had become established as a constitutional myth that has informed the operation of government throughout the twentieth century. Consequently the rise of the modern state created a problem: the need to secure the (myth of the) supremacy of Parliament with a reality of executive domination. This became a particular problem with the development of the administrative state based on rationalized processes and regularized procedures.

The Development of the Administrative Machine

The nineteenth century saw growth of government as a response to industrialization, social dislocation and political reform and restructuring. There was, as a result, concern over how the development of bureaucracy could be reconciled with parliamentary government and popular representation. Up to the middle of the nineteenth century government departments remained very small, with officials appointed through patronage. However, this was not a very effective means of developing an efficient and bureaucratic state with the capabilities of delivering an increasing range of economic, welfare and foreign policies.

At this time, owing to the limited size of government departments, most policies were not delivered by the central state but by boards, such as the Poor Law Board, which were again based largely on patronage. They undermined notions of parliamentary sovereignty because they made and delivered policy without direct reference to Parliament. However this limited state was unable to cope with the demands of industrialization and imperial expansion. A resolution to the confict between patrimonial forms of government and the need for greater state capabilities was necessary. One solution was the development of a Bismarckian or Bonapartist authoritarian state (see Moore, 1966). However, in Britain the representative gains by the middle class and the principle of parliamentary sovereignty made this path difficult. New forms of state that could deliver a growing number of public goods had to be reconciled with a role for Parliament.

Ministerial departments were nineteenth-century creations which developed as a mechanism for fusing the requirements of increased governmental activism, representative government and parliamentary sovereignty. The two crucial elements inherent in this solution were ministerial responsibility and a meritocratic and neutral Civil Service. Before 1860 most decisions were taken either directly by ministers – who had very little in the way of bureaucratic support – indeed, Sir Robert Peel used to answer all his own letters by hand – or by boards. The use of boards was subject to widespread criticism from political thinkers such as Bentham and Mill. Bentham, demonstrating the longevity of the quango debate, wrote:

A Board, my Lord, is a screen. The lustre of good desert is obscured by it – ill desert, shrinking behind, eludes the eye of censure – wrong is covered by it with a presumption of right, stronger and stronger in proportion to the number of folds: and each member having his own circle of friends, wrong, in proportion again to the number, multiplies its protectors. (Quoted in Schaffer 1957: 63)

The problem with boards, apart from issues of corruption or patronage, was that they broke the link between Parliament and decision-making because decisions were not directly open to Parliament. Ministerial departments, on the other hand, allowed the expansion of government without threatening parliamentary sovereignty. They also ensured some popular representation because elected government ministers rather than appointees made decisions. Thus writers and thinkers such as Bentham, Mill and Bagehot called for the development of ministerial departments as the key

administrative unit because it meant ministers, who were responsible
to Parliament, and ultimately the electorate, would make decisions:

> The Ministerial department came to have certain specific features.
> It was to be headed by a single political person, at once exclusively
> responsible, the most powerful and yet the most temporary element
> in the organization. Underneath the Ministers would be certain
> senior officers reporting directly to the Permanent Head and
> appointed like him in consultation with the Prime Minister and
> the general manager of the department. As the general manager he
> would also be the accounting officer. Thence downward there
> would be a continuing hierarchy. (Schaffer, 1957: 60)

Thus the administrative fusion of ministers and parliamentary
sovereignty had important implications for the development of
British government and the distribution of power, within the core
executive. Departments became the site of the majority of policy-
making with ministers having a monopoly of control over policy
(Beattie, 1995). As a consequence, a hierarchical form of government
developed. In law, it is the minister who is responsible for the actions
of the ministry. This, combined with political accountability, means
departments are centralized and hierarchical institutions with the
minister at the top (Judge, 1993). These developments led to another
problem. If ministers are responsible for decisions, officials exist to
implement their wishes; therefore departments founded on the principle of ministerial accountability require a professional, anonymous
and neutral civil service. However, officials have to reconcile neutrality with loyalty to the minister. While officials are on one side
perceived as neutral, there can be no disunity between minister and
official because only ministers are held publicly to account. Officials
in this sense cannot act in their own right.

Ministerial responsibility was also a means of reconciling the
notion of democratic government with limited popular participation.
Parliamentary sovereignty implied that MPs had to be representatives
rather than delegates – if they were delegated then the people would
be sovereign. Therefore, it was to the representatives rather than
the people that the policy-makers were responsible. Thus the establishment of departments placed policy-making firmly in the executive
and away from electoral constraints. Ministerial responsibility created
a direct chain of accountability from ministers to MPs and

consequently only a limited role for the citizen in the process of government. A common theme of 'liberal' thinking on representative government is that only 'educated' people can realistically be involved in government and therefore representatives have to use their own judgement rather than to, in Joseph Chamberlain's phrase, 'truckle with the multitude' (quoted in Jennings, 1966: 1).

Consequently, the development of a professional Civil Service occurred coterminously with the development of departments. The Northcote–Trevelyan Report of 1854 proposed a professional, meritocratic and permanent Civil Service which had a degree of independence from their political masters (Northcote and Trevelyan, 1954). This was important. With the increasing size and responsibilities of the state, politicians were unable to make all the decisions and control all the operations of a department. They needed advisers they could trust. First, officials had to sift, organize, and provide ministers with information on key problems, and the available policy options. Second, the ministers needed high-quality staff who could take decisions independently in an increasing number of areas. Third, there was a need for the administrative machinery to implement decisions in an increasing number of areas of civil society (Cronin, 1991: 19).

Nevertheless, there was much opposition to the Northcote–Trevelyan reforms and it was not until 1870 that open competition for Civil Service posts was introduced and even then the Home Office and Foreign Office resisted reform for a number of years (Greenleaf, 1987). Moreover, the reforms were evolutionary rather than revolutionary (Hennessy, 1990) and did not undermine the night-watchman state. They did, however, establish the basis of the modern Civil Service which enabled the creation of a bureaucratic, administrative state. The aim of the reformers was not to expand the state but to make it more economical and efficient (Greenleaf, 1987; Hart, 1972). Increasing its capabilities was in a sense a side-effect. By abolishing patronage and creating a class of what later became known as policy advisers, the reforms enabled the development of a more effective Civil Service. Again the notion that officials were neutral and anonymous reinforced the principle of ministerial responsibility and parliamentary accountability. Officials did not have to be accountable, because they were implementing the minister's will. This principle was firmly established with the Haldane Report of 1918. The report recognised that 'civil servants as advisers have an indivisible relationship' with ministers (Richards, 1997: 236) and so further ensured the unity of the central state. If ministers are responsible then officials cannot be distinct actors.

Developing Collective Responsibility

Departmental government presented a further threat to the indivisibility of sovereignty by placing policy-making in distinct, autonomous departments. The development of departments required the establishment of collective mechanisms within the core executive. The growth of collective government was much more erratic and *ad hoc* than the establishment of a professional civil service. The piecemeal nature of its development accounts for many problematic and contradictory elements in the modern core executive. These changes in the Civil Service were paralleled by changes in other parts of the core executive. During this period the Cabinet became increasingly institutionalized and power relationships within it changed. From the middle of the nineteenth century 'most government tasks came to be formalized under the effective responsibilities of ministers' (Daalder, 1963a: 18). In order to coordinate the work of ministers, the Cabinet grew and became much more rule bound in its structure (Daalder, 1963b). According to Mackintosh (1977b: 143), the Cabinet was now

> the centre of political power; it was the body which determined policy. It was possible for Prime Ministers, Foreign Secretaries and even lesser Ministers to take some decisions on their own, but if there was any dispute or challenge from Parliament or the Press, the matter had to be settled in the Cabinet.

The two important factors in the development of Cabinet were the First World War and the Haldane Committee Report mentioned above.

The Cabinet system developed along side a system of Cabinet committees, the Cabinet Office and, in the period from the 1960s, the Prime Minister's Office as means of imposing collective agreement on ministerial departments. Collective responsibility resolves a problem for government. Parliamentary sovereignty and accountability mechanisms led to the establishment of ministerial departments. Strong departments threatened the unity of sovereignty and therefore required the imposition of collective government. Collective government thus reinforces the power of the central executive by imposing on departments the requirement to accept the collective decisions of government whether they were involved in or agreed with the decision. In principle it gives the Cabinet predominance over departments. This explains why so much analysis has been centred on the Cabinet rather than departments; political scientists have accepted the Constitutional precepts rather than the institutional structures as a more accurate indicator of the sources of power. Of course, it suited government to present this view because then government is seen as unified, strategic and democratically accountable. However as successive Prime Ministers have found, from Churchill's experiments with overlords to Blair's development of ministers for coordination in the Lord Chancellor and the 'Cabinet enforcer', Jack Cunningham, imposing collective government on the institutionally strong departments is extremely difficult.

As well as a system of collective government, with strong and relatively autonomous departments it was also important to develop a means of financial control. Again, as departments became stronger, the need for financial control become more important. Gladstone, in particular, created capabilities for effective control of departmental expenditure. He set up the Public Accounts Committee in 1861 and with the Exchequer and Audits Department Act 1866 he tied together the procedures of estimates, appropriations, expenditure and audit and created the office of Comptroller and Auditor General (Rosevere, 1969) and established Treasury primacy: 'By creating the first effective machinery for a retrospective, annual audit of government expenditure it put a willing Treasury on its mettle to enforce the strictest standards of financial propriety among the departments' (Rosevere, 1969: 141). For Thane (1990: 27), 'Treasury primacy was recognised in 1867 when its permanent secretary was granted seniority over the heads of other departments.' The Treasury's role was to determine the limits of government through the overall coordination of spending and policy.

Wright (1972), however, questions the extent of Treasury primacy. First, Treasury control was negative and, therefore, if a department did not demand increased money, the Treasury had very little control over its expenditure. Second, powerful Cabinet ministers need not automatically accept the decisions of the Treasury. Third, controls on Admiralty and War Office expenditure were almost non-existent. Fourth, 'the Treasury attempted nothing in the way of systematic and continuous review of either the estimates (civil and military) or expenditure generally' (Wright, 1972: 200). For Wright, the degree of Treasury control depended on the particular circumstances and relationships which existed between the Treasury and each department: 'In many respects negotiations between a department and the Treasury resemble a very formal and elaborate game, the rules of which were well known to both contestants but never openly discussed between them' (Wright, 1972: 222). The fact that departments played this game placed some restraint on what was spent. Nevertheless, the strengthening of the Treasury was to create a continual tension within the core executive between the Treasury's desire to control and departments' desire to spend.

Although the Treasury had problems exerting control, to which the dramatic increase in public expenditure at the end of the nineteenth century is testament, it did become progressively more influential towards the twentieth century. It established the basic mechanisms for assessing government expenditure and entrenched, in principle, a system for controlling the level of increase. Nevertheless the battle between the Treasury and departments was constant. During particular periods departments were in ascendancy, particularly during the First and Second World Wars and in the 1950s and 1960s as a result of welfare expansion. At other periods, in the 1920s and 1930s and in the 1980s, it was the Treasury that was dominant. The tensions and fluctuations highlight two important points – collective decision-making is largely a myth and the relationships within the central state are complex and ever-changing.

By the end of the nineteenth century the number of departments had increased to 18 and included Agriculture, Health and the Ministry of Works (Willson, 1955). Departments were also developing their own bureaucratic techniques for gathering information, raising their policy expertise and improving the machinery for implementing policy (Savage, 1996). A further paradox then emerged: departments were established to protect parliamentary accountability, but as they grew a minister was less able to control what occurred in his or her name. Consequently the professionalization and bureaucratization of departments undermined notions of ministerial responsibility. Decisions could no longer be made by individual ministers. They increasingly relied on their civil servants, which affected the balance of resources between ministers and civil servants.

The second half of the nineteenth century laid the foundations of the modern state and established some of the lines of dependence which are still present in today's core executive. Nevertheless, it was the social legislation of the early twentieth century and the First World War which established the modern core executive. Collective government, ministerial departments and a neutral Civil Service were means for resolving the contradictions of government expansion, departmental policy-making and parliamentary sovereignty. For Beattie (1995: 160):

The aim was to ensure that 'government appeared to the individual subject as a unitary and consistent set of practices, rather than as a plurality of specialised individual tasks' [Cranston, 1985: 269–72]. As long as 'the government' was ultimately controlled by ministers, the location of responsibility was clear and parliamentary control thus assured.

The problems that continually replay throughout the British core executive are the demands of a modern state for functional expertise with the Constitutional requirements for unity through parliamentary sovereignty. It is almost impossible to reconcile these contradictions and what indeed has occurred is that the political reality has been masked by constitutional myths which are themselves continually reinforced by ministers, officials and political scientists. The maintenance of these myths has been made all the easier by the final elements in preserving the integrity of the system: secrecy and the public-service ethos.

Secrecy is crucial to the British political system (Hennessy, 1990: 346). At its most prosaic level, secrecy prevents policy-makers from having to answer for why they made the decisions they did. More importantly it functions to protect the myth of collective government and Civil Service powerlessness. Moreover, secrecy reinforces the liberal and conservative notion of representative government because it excludes the people from the policy-making process. It therefore helps to resolve the several paradoxes of the core executive; it hides disunity and legitimizes democratic and limited participation. People do not know what is going on and therefore they cannot be involved in decision-making. They cannot know what is going on because they are not responsible enough to know and or to understand the complexities of government. If they were more involved they would try to persuade politicians to make poor decisions. It is a circular argument that protects elite policy-making.

Secrecy suits both ministers and officials – it means no one can be directly attributed with responsibility for decisions. Ministers only have to account for *the final* decision and not for how they came to that decision. The role of officials in decisions is largely hidden and even the new Freedom of Information Act will not reveal official advice to ministers, effectively hiding the policy process. In the view of the former Cabinet Secretary, Sir Robin Butler, secrecy is 'in the interest of good government' (*Guardian*, 5 January 1998).

Secrecy is legitimized by the public-service ethos (Richards and Smith, 1998). Despite the many treatises available, it is difficult to conceptualize what constitutes a public-service ethos. Indeed, when one former Cabinet Secretary was recently asked to provide his own definition of such an ethos he observed that, it is, at best, 'a portmanteau concept'. In fact, it is because of the very existence of the Haldane principle, which espouses the interdependent relationship between ministers and officials, that British public servants, along with their political masters, have consistently and successfully resisted outside pressure to introduce any statutory codification of the ethics which would create a more formal definition of a public-service ethos. The same former Cabinet Secretary provides a clear testimony of such a disposition:

> I think one can try to define it [a public-service ethos], try to make it articulate . . . but in the end it is going to be example that carries it through. I do not believe one can rely solely . . . on codes or guidances to do so . . . I think it would be impossible to try to prescribe in too much detail what flows from the sense of public service or the public-service ethos. (Armstrong, 1997: 7)

Despite the absence of any formal ethical code, it is possible, through the testimonies of public servants and academic writings and, by a series of conventions which inform the (un)written constitution, to compile some evidence of the various elements which constitute a British public-service ethos. In 1996, the summary section of the Nolan Committee's First Report on Standards in Public Life, pronounced that there were seven principles of public life: selflessness, integrity, objectivity, accountability, openness, honesty and leadership. These could have been the very same principles espoused by Northcote–Trevelyan 150 years earlier, and later reiterated by Haldane, Hankey and Fisher. More particularly, civil servants, through their social status, education, training and a process of socialis-ation, have been implicitly trusted to maintain and uphold these principles.

This set of principles has been shaped and informed by the various cultures of Whitehall and underpinned by a framework of ethics. O'Toole (1990) argues that these ethics derive from the ideas of the Victorian idealist, T. H. Green (1879, 1883). O'Toole contends that in the same way that the organizational framework of Whitehall was constructed by Northcote–Trevelyan, it was Green who provided the ethical framework within which civil servants developed integrity in their work. This, concomitantly, led to their ministerial masters tacitly accepting them as being politically neutral. As Massey (1993: 36) observes, O'Toole's analysis of Green provides public servants with an almost Platonic role in society.

Throughout the nineteenth and twentieth centuries, the British central bureaucracy has attached itself strongly to the principle of political neutrality. It can be argued that for British mandarins to be politically neutral they must be capable of: engaging in the mind-sets of the ministers they serve; displaying an empathy and understanding for the policy lines of the elected government; promoting the interests of that government; and, above all, showing a sympathy and loyalty to the political aims of their masters. Indeed, this approach was institutionalized by the 1918 Haldane Committee Report on the Machinery of Government. This report established that the relation-ship between ministers and officials was indivisible and should not be bound by laws or bureaucratic rules. This relationship is a key component at the heart of the Westminster/Whitehall political system if not the most fundamental one.

It is a widespread assumption that the public-service ethos is a good thing and the introduction of private sector values threatens the beneficial values which suffuse the British Civil Service. However, the public-service ethos is not a neutral code concerned with the public good, but an ideology aimed at protecting a particular con-ception of the Civil Service. The core of the public-service ethos is built on two separate, but linked, ideas: the political neutrality of officials and their pecuniary and moral integrity.

The problem with these values is that they have been constructed as: independent; normatively good; and politically neutral. The reality, of course, is that they are a set of socially constructed values which protect the interests of officials and to some extent politicians. The public sector ethos is about maintaining a particular perception of the Civil Service which both identifies and hides the nature of their power. It identifies the power of officials because it places the determination of the public good in their hands and it hides it by presuming their neutrality and the purity of their motives. Officials are working for the public good and, therefore, they have no interest in power for its own sake. Officials have integrity and can be trusted; therefore secrecy is permissible because they will make the right decisions in the public good. At the same time the ethos identifies politicians as the decision-makers and so again reveals the imprint of parliamentary sovereignty.

A crucial consequence of the public-sector ethos is to provide officials with autonomy by denying they possess power. The integrity of officials is based on the idea that they serve the will of the ministers. In this sense they lack decisional autonomy – it is the minister who makes the decision and it is left to the official to implement. This is a crucial value within Whitehall and in some ways accounts for the conflicts that occurred in the Home Office when Derek Lewis was chief executive of the Prison Service in the mid-1990s. Lewis believed that in coming from the private sector to operating in a semi-autonomous agency he could make decisions independently. The Home Secretary, Michael Howard, believed that he was a civil servant who should do as he was told.

In sum, parliamentary sovereignty and the rise of the modern state created a number of constitutional problems which were resolved through ministerial and collective responsibility, and secrecy and the public sector ethos. However, these principles also created a perception of the state that bore only passing resemblance to the reality of the policy process. Nevertheless, these constitutional myths informed both the perceptions of policy-makers and a number of analysts of the political system. The practice of the political system could not be separated from perceptions of how it should work (Judge, 1993). As a consequence much of the analysis of British central government has been sent into the cul-de-sacs of prime-ministerial versus Cabinet government and ministers versus civil servants. These debates are premised on the notion of a constitutionally bounded system of government working. The problem was, of course, that the system never did work as it should. As a result, there has in recent years been increased questioning of the Constitutional approach to central government which, combined with changes in the political system and outside world, have opened the way to new approaches to the study of central government and of understandings of where power really lies.

Undermining the Westminster Model

These precepts, perceptions and events led to the establishment and reproduction of the Westminster Model and its administrative subset, the Whitehall Model. The model resolves the contradictions outlined above. The electorate elects MPs as representatives. The largest party forms the government and the Prime Minister selects the Cabinet in which ministers make policy collectively that is debated and approved by Parliament – thus the role of Parliament is to deliberate, not make policy. Policy is then implemented by a neutral Civil Service (see Jennings, 1966). This model is replete with first-order conceptual problems and second-order empirical problems. The empirical problems concern the actual roles of Parliament, Cabinet, and the Civil Service.

The notion of the political system working in the way writers such as Jennings or Bagehot suggest has been undermined by the realities of the policy process. First, the rise of party discipline undermined parliamentary accountability. From the period from 1945 to 1979 the Commons rarely voted against the government and committee system was weak, disorganized and generally ineffective (see Robinson, 1978). Second, the process of coordination was always undermined by the weakness of the instruments at the disposal of the centre. Despite the strong constitutional need for collective government, the core executive has remained weak at the centre and strong in the departments. This weakness is created by the fact that there is no single coordination centre but at least three, the Cabinet and the Cabinet Office, the Treasury and the Prime Minister.

Third, the Cabinet system, at Cabinet level, was never very effective at making decisions. Key decisions – such as Britain's nuclear policy in the 1940s and 1950s and key elements of economic policy in the 1980s – were made without Cabinet discussion or sometimes knowledge (Hennessy, 1986; Burch, 1988). As government has become more complex, Cabinet has not been used a forum for decision-making. Increasingly, decision-making has occurred through bilateral meetings and Cabinet committees. Cabinet committees are now the focal point for collective decision-making. But they too display important weaknesses. Many issues do not get to Cabinet committee. The bypassing of committees was greater under Thatcher when decisions were either made bilaterally or in *ad hoc* and informal meetings (Hennessy, 1985; Lawson, 1992). Foster (1997) argues that the Cabinet system lost influence during the 1980s and that Thatcher effectively moved away from a system of formal Cabinet committees:

> Since 1979, every step of (the) previously standard procedure has been broken. Departmental ministers generally still initiated policies, but on occasions so did other ministers, even the Prime Minister. Announcement of policy . . . may have preceded Cabinet approval.

Moreover, as Lawson (1994: 442–3) informs us:

> when an issue comes to be collectively discussed, in a Cabinet committee where real decisions are taken, in a Cabinet committee, say, chaired by the Prime Minister of the day (as a number of them are), then a minister who is involved in some running battle with the Prime Minister over a matter where he has departmental responsibility may well feel reluctant to spend too much of his political capital, arguing a case against the Prime Minister in a field which is totally outside his departmental responsibility. It is some other Minister's baby and some other Minister's responsibility.

These problems emphasise once again the centrifugal forces of departments and the tensions that exist between the Prime Minister and the departments rather than between the Cabinet and departments.

Fourth, the role of the Treasury in coordination is also limited. While it has 'a finger in every pie' (Lawson, 1992), its ability to coordinate in any positive sense is constrained by its concentration on controlling expenditure and therefore on limiting the activities of departments. For much of the twentieth century, the Treasury has been remarkably ineffective even at controlling the expenditure of departments. Really, until the IMF crisis of 1976 and Thatcher's desire to reassert the primacy of the Treasury, there was little control over departmental expenditure. Despite prime-ministerial support, the Treasury was unable to reduce the level of public expenditure during the Thatcher administration.

The principles of parliamentary sovereignty, the public-service ethos, ministerial responsibility and collective Cabinet responsibility were not only the cornerstone of the Constitution; they were also the key principles of political analysis. They suggested that decision-making is confined within the parliamentary system – and in particular the executive – and raised questions concerning what is the relationship between ministers and the Prime Minister and between the executive and Parliament. A set of supplementary questions follow concerning whether officials are usurping the Constitutional power of ministers and whether sovereignty is being undermined. Consequently, many analysts of central government have been concerned with answering questions suggested by the Constitutional focus rather than the realities of the political process. This led to approaches that were essentially focused on individual actors, formal institutions and observable behaviour, and while authors rejected the simplicities of the Westminster Model they were still confined by the options it presented. As John Mackintosh (1977a: 31) pointed out: 'This is partly because its language is still used and misleads current observers and its maxims are still quoted either to cover up or try to accommodate current practice.'

Analysis of central government has been concerned with discovering the locus of power, seeing power as residing somewhere: with the Prime Minister, the Cabinet or the Civil Service. Consequently power was conceived as an object located in an institution or an individual rather than something deriving from relationships and constantly changing. Power – or the achievement of goals – does not reside with the Prime Minister or the Cabinet. If ministers, the Prime Minister or officials want to achieve policy goals they do not have to defeat other centres of power; instead, they need each other. Each part of the core executive has resources. According to Rhodes (1988: 42), 'The resources of an organization constitute a potential for the exercise of power.' Being a potential which is to some extent subjective, resources have to be exchanged in order for actors to achieve goals. Therefore, the policy process is about developing processes of exchange. Goals are achieved as a result of the exchange of resources that occurs in the relationships between Prime Minister, Cabinet and other actors within the core executive. Power there is dynamic and fluid and based on interdependency, not individual volition.

Third, much of the focus on central government has been on the 'heroic' institutions of the Prime Minister and the Cabinet. This has led to an over-concentration on these institutions and a tendency for many analysts to be more concerned with the personality and style of the Prime Minister than the operation of the processes of central government. Journalistic accounts have dominated perceptions of how government works and the media are more interested in personalities than in the way institutions structure relationships. Consequently it is often suggested that central government changes according to the personal preferences of key ministers.

A number of studies have attempted to get away from highly personalized accounts of central government and to question the traditional, constitutional and institutional approaches. In the 1960s and 1970s authors such as John Mackintosh started to question some of the implications of the traditional assumptions concerning Prime Minister and Cabinet. However despite innovative and interesting work by commentators such as Mackintosh (1977a), Anthony King (1985) and George Jones (1975), their terrain was still largely framed by the Constitutionally defined agenda.

However the fundamentals of both the Constitutional and analytical position have been undermined by a number of recent empirical and theoretical challenges (Smith, 1998). First, the New Right perspective on the state challenged many of the assumptions of the Westminster Model. It sees government and the Civil Service not as neutral and electorally responsive but more concerned with personal utility maximization and attending to the claims of special interests. The result is an overextended state which takes too great a share of national wealth and is inefficient at producing public goods. Consequently, parliamentary accountability is not seen as an effective mechanism for controlling the behaviour of either politicians or bureaucrats. Indeed, much of the New Right project has been concerned with introducing new forms of accountability – such as markets and managerialism – into government (see Stone, 1995).

A further important change has been the increasing 'internationalization' of government. Government is now continuously involved in making decisions in international arenas and is increasingly affected by and constrained in its actions by international events. The most obvious institution is the European Union, but this is just one of many international organizations that bind government. The postwar period has seen an exponential growth in the level of foreign trade, foreign exchange dealing and transnational companies. The 1970s and 1980s in particular saw increases in foreign exchange markets, euromarkets in credits and bonds and the number of multinational banks (Hirst and Thompson, 1995). 'Perhaps the main development of the 1980s was the growth of international markets in bonds and equities, and the growth of cross-border dealing in derivative instruments such as options, futures and swaps' (Hirst and Thompson, 1995: 39). In addition, the development of information technology and communications have greatly reduced the relationship between space and time. Whether this constitutes globalization is a relatively minor issue here, what is important is the way it undermines the sovereignty of Parliament. International organizations provide a higher authority and international factors mean many decisions occur outside the parliamentary arena.

The impact of New Right ideology and internationalization was to undermine the notion of a hermetically sealed, unified and sovereign executive. Further threats to the perception of the central state have developed with the reform of Whitehall. Since the early 1980s Whitehall has been under going a 'dynamic evolution' (Richards, 1997) with the introduction of managerialism into central government. Initially this process involved the introduction of greater efficiency into departments through the Financial Management Initiative and the privatization of many state owned industries. In 1988 the Ibbs Report, *The Next Steps,* proposed a division in departments between those who are policy advisers at the core of departments and those concerned with service delivery. This led to a rapid division between the core and the periphery of the state (Kemp, 1993). By 1995–6 there were 109 executive agencies covering 386 000 civil servants (Cm. 3579, 1996/7). The aim of the new agencies was to break the traditional uniformity of the traditional Whitehall bureaucracy, which has resulted in the introduction of open competition for posts and fixed-term contracts. These changes have impacted on the central departments with the Comprehensive Spending Reviews and the Senior Management Review cutting the core funding of departments and trying to de-layer the senior levels of the civil service so that the policy process has become more flexible.

A number of commentators have suggested that these reforms signify a changing relationship between ministers and officials (Foster and Plowden, 1997; Campbell and Wilson, 1995). Officials are seen as becoming more managerial and concerned with service delivery rather than policy-makers. Ministers, it is argued, have much more developed ideas concerning the types of policies they want and are therefore much less reliant on officials. Increasingly, policy advice is coming from think-tanks and from political advisers.

Further fragmentation has occurred with increased marketization in areas such as the National Health Service and contracting out. Increasingly government is relying on the private sector under contract and voluntary agencies to deliver public goods. These policies have important implications for the distribution of resources and the nature of relationships within the core executive. The growth of the state up to the 1970s saw the development generally of hierarchical line bureaucracies. In departments such as the Department of Social Security decisions were taken in the centre and implemented uniformly throughout the country according to a set of extremely detailed rules. In other departments such as Department of Education the process was more complicated. The departments to a large extent relied on local authorities and were in close contact with interest groups. Nevertheless, the number of actors and institutions involved in developing and implementing of policy was relatively limited. In the last fifteen years the policy process has fragmented. Ministers are increasingly likely to take advice from think-tanks and other outside bodies; and the decision and implementation process may include the department, agencies, a regulatory body, a privatized industry, local authorities, a range of quangos and a number of pressure groups. While Thatcher's intention was to limit the role of the state, the impact of the reforms is actually to extend the role of the state and to make it much more difficult to control by the core executive.

This process of fragmentation has been taken further by the growth of external constraints on the core executive. Traditionally, the key constraint on the core executive was Parliament. Throughout the twentieth century power has shifted from the parliamentary arena to a range of bodies including policy networks, sub-government, the judiciary and perhaps most importantly the EU. Not only does the EU place limits on what national governments can do in certain areas – for example agricultural policy and trade policy are almost solely determined at the European level – but it has also changed the nature of the core executive (Buller and Smith, 1998). To a certain extent this has increased the role of the Cabinet Office and the Foreign Office, which both have a role in coordinating Britain's position in Europe, but increasingly departments are developing their own European expertise. The EU is only one of a range of international organizations that limit the core executive, NATO is crucial in terms of defence policy and the World Trade Organization has a significant impact on trade policy. Moreover, while its impact is subject to much debate, it is difficult to deny that owing to the growth in international trade and the size of currency transaction, national economic policy can be developed only within the context of the world markets, which often leaves the Treasury with limited room for manoeuvre.

New Approaches to Central Government

These empirical challenges to the Westminster Model have encouraged the development of analytical approaches which try to cope with the changing context of British central government and which are critical of the Constitutional conventions. In recent years there has been a move to more analytical accounts of the core executive. One of the earliest was Bruce-Gardyne and Lawson's (1976) detailed case-studies in public policy which highlighted the complexity of the policy process below the Cabinet level. More recently Burch and Holliday (1996: 5) have developed an approach which recognises that

> Cabinet system actors operate within a series of limits which are both internal and external to that system. Internal limits comprise abiding organizational patterns and established ways of working. They shape behaviour, and provide the immediate context within which opportunities to exercise individual initiative arise. . . External limits comprise the economic, social and political context within which all Cabinet system actors operate. . . . In our way of looking at things, the role of the individual is conditioned by and secondary to these limits and constraints.

Burch and Holliday's approach is extremely useful because it emphasises the importance of institutions, rules and values in structuring the behaviour of actors within the central state and consequently it highlights the limitation of personality derived approaches.

Perhaps most influential in reassessing the approach to central government is Dunleavy and Rhodes's call for a more systematic research agenda for core executive studies (Dunleavy and Rhodes, 1990; Rhodes and Dunleavy, 1995). They suggest we can improve our understanding of the core by widening the focus of central government studies and applying a range of conceptual and theoretical approaches. The notion of the core executive can be developed into an approach to central government that is: consciously analytical;

concerned with the wider context of central government policy-making; and shows that the policy process is not about command but negotiation (Smith, 1999).

Crucially there is no point looking for a single actor or institution that has a monopoly of power, because all actors and institutions within the core executive have resources and are therefore dependent on each other to achieve their goals. Some of these resources are structurally determined – the Prime Minister has certain resources that derive from his or her position – while others vary according to particular circumstances. For example, authority is an important resource. Authority varies with the success of a minister, the degree of support he or she has in the party and, sometimes, personality.

The impact of the Prime Minister, of a Cabinet minister or of an official on policy depends on the structures of dependence linking them to other actors and the resources that each of these actors control. This structure of relationships provides the framework within which the actors of the core executive operate; it does not determine policy outcomes or who 'wins'. The effectiveness of actors within the core executive depends on the tactics, choices and strategies they adopt in using their resources. Ministers and Prime Ministers can build alliances, officials can withhold information or call on other departments to support their arguments. It is not always those with the most resources or the actors who are the least dependent who win. The choices that actors make affects the outcome of policy. Nevertheless, as Burch and Holliday indicate, these choices are made within a set of structured relationships and institutions.

Moreover the freedom of actors to use their resources will depend on the particular context. For example, after an emphatic election victory a Prime Minister is usually less dependent on his or her Cabinet than when the government is behind in the polls and the Prime Minister is an unpopular leader. Therefore we can assume that following electoral success the Prime Minister has more freedom to use resources than at other times. Nevertheless the Prime Minister is nearly always constrained by the structures of dependency. It seems that circumstances will have to change greatly for Tony Blair to sack Gordon Brown, for example. Margaret Thatcher, despite her apparently high-handed manner and clear ideological goals, never removed Peter Walker even though they had strong political differences.

Consequently, it is impossible, and indeed fruitless, to try to identify a single site of power within the core executive because, to use a fashionable post-modern notion, it is everywhere. The structures of dependency and the distribution of resources mean that all actors can have some success. No single actor can achieve what he or she wants without exchanging resources and therefore compromise is built into the structure of government. The Scott Report into the sale of arms to Iraq highlighted how officials thwarted ministers but also how officials were forced into line by ministers and demonstrated that they were often unwilling to act without ministerial cover. Thatcher, often depicted as an authoritarian Prime Minister and even as presidential (Pryce, 1997), was forced out of office (Smith, 1994). Prime Ministers may in particular circumstances ignore or override their ministers but they can do this only if the Cabinet provides them with the necessary authority. They will lose that authority if they continually act alone.

Power within the core executive does not depend on the personality of the Prime Minister. Thatcher appeared strong in 1987 and John Major appeared weak in 1997 not because Thatcher was a dominant personality and Major was a weak personality but because their circumstances were different. Major had no majority in Parliament, the government was divided and the popular perception was that his government lacked economic competence – circumstance created Major's indecisiveness; it was not indecisiveness that led to the Conservative defeat.

It is also important to remember that while relationships of dependency and the distribution of resources may be structural, they are not permanent and fixed. The resources of actors and their relationship to each other change across time. The relationship of the Treasury to departments has been in constant flux in the twentieth century and the post-war period has seen the Prime Minister accrue more resources with the development of the Prime Minister's Office. This means that while the Constitution may point to a hierarchical, unified and hermetically sealed system of government the reality is increasingly, and probably always was, very different.

The core executive has to be analysed as a set of overlapping networks which cut across government and link with the outside world. In recent years it has been suggested the state has been 'hollowed out' (Rhodes, 1994) and that power is increasingly dispersed among a range of state and non-state actors and institutions. This fragmentation is the consequence of two factors: reform and increasing external constraints.

Conclusion

The organization of central government in Britain is derived from and shaped by a set of interlinked principles emanating from the presumption of parliamentary sovereignty. Parliamentary sovereignty meant that the development of modern state had to retain a link with Parliament. This resulted in the growth of departments which were governed by ministerial responsibility. Ministerial responsibility required both processes of collective government to preserve the unity of sovereignty and a neutral Civil Service to preserve accountability to Parliament. A neutral Civil Service was legitimized by a public-service ethos which also justified a secretive policy process. This secrecy meant that the myths of the Constitution could be more easily preserved and it enabled the exclusion of the masses from policy-making.

These constitutional principles were relayed into the study of politics through the Westminster Model which was accepted by a number of authors as an accurate representation of the policy process. In the 1960s and 1970s a number of institutional and behavioural accounts questioned the simplicities of the Westminster Model but they did so largely in terms of traditional approaches, questioning the accuracy of its description but not the principles underlying its approach. However, with the emergence of a series of empirical and theoretical challenges a number of questions about the Westminster Model have been raised and more analytical approaches to the study of the core executive have been developed.

These challenges highlight the shaky foundations of the British constitution. Developments such as inter-governmentalism and Next Steps agencies have brought into question the sovereignty and accountability of the British political system. However, despite arguments over the flexibility of the British constitution, it is very difficult to change. Once one element is questioned then the others start to come under scrutiny. Consequently changes such as freedom of information or devolution have a knock-on effect throughout the political system. This appears ultimately to prevent politicians from supporting any significant reforms in how central government operates.

6
Territorial Politics

IAN HOLLIDAY

The United Kingdom is a composite state with a complex pattern of territorial politics. It is a unitary state, in that all domestic sovereignty is formally concentrated in the Westminster Parliament. Equally, it is what Rokkan and Urwin (1982: 11) have called a union state, in that it does not have a uniform political and administrative structure. Instead, some institutions created in pre-union days have been allowed to persist, and others have been established to meet specific sub-national needs. The resultant system of territorial politics is unique, though it has not always been seen as such. Some 30 years ago the conventional wisdom was that the UK was a largely homogenous state in which matters like region and religion had been stripped of political salience by the process of modernization (Pulzer, 1967). Since then, the realities of UK political life and the concerns of political scientists have moved some distance from this position. Now territory is recognised to be a critical aspect of UK politics.

In this chapter the fundamentals of UK territorial politics are examined chiefly by focusing on ways in which power relations have been managed both *between* the UK's main component parts – England, Scotland, Wales and (Northern) Ireland – and *within* each of those component parts. In recent times there has, however, been an additional dimension to UK territorial politics generated by the country's accession, in 1973, to the European Community and by its participation in the subsequent development of the European Union. It is therefore necessary to look not just at the many domestic dimensions of territorial politics, but also at the ways in which those politics are affected by EU membership.

The Making of the UK

The traditional starting point remains the best. The UK came into being through the English conquest of Wales in 1536, union of this

119

entity with Scotland in 1707, incorporation of Ireland into the union in 1801, and secession of the Irish Free State in 1921. Its most notable feature is the overwhelming dominance of England: at the turn of the millennium 83 per cent of the UK population, or five people in every six, live there. Behind this rather neat chronology of political development lies a difficult set of relationships which continues to affect UK territorial politics to this day. The most important tensions relate to the role played, or held to have been played, by a dominant England in first assembling and then managing the union.

In the Irish and Welsh cases, direct English involvement and interference stretch back across many centuries. Indeed, the Norman conquest did not stop at England, but rippled into other parts of the British Isles. It would, however, be anachronistic to claim that for the best part of a thousand years England has played a controlling part in the domestic affairs of both the Irish and Welsh states. On the one hand, it is hard to identify the political and military elite which sought to control twelfth-century Ireland and Wales as English, most of it having only recently arrived from Normandy. On the other, none of these places – not England, and particularly not Ireland or Wales – remotely resembled a state, or even an identifiable political unit, in the late middle ages. Instead, they joined the rest of the British Isles in being controlled mainly by shifting sets of warrior chieftains. It is only with hindsight that we can make out the borders which are now so familiar (Kearney, 1989).

Comparatively early union between a dominant England and an incorporated Wales ensured that Welsh political institutions developed on much the same lines as English ones. Two Acts of Union, passed in 1536 and 1543, introduced uniform legal codes and administrative structures in England and Wales. Courts of the Great Sessions applied English law to Wales. A Council of Wales oversaw administration in thirteen new shire counties, which also sent MPs to the Westminster Parliament. The Council of Wales was subsequently abolished in 1688 and the Courts of Great Sessions in 1830. In 1746 the Wales and Berwick Act stated that legislative references to England should be taken to cover Wales too (Griffiths, 1996: 46). Quite rightly, analysts of UK institutions have tended to examine English and Welsh institutions together. There never was a separate Welsh state, or for that matter an English one, in the modern sense of the word.

In Ireland, English dominance also came early, but it was not complete until the start of the seventeenth century and did not result in union until the start of the nineteenth. At the end of the twelfth century Henry II created a 'lordship' of Ireland and obliged some Gaelic chieftains to pledge submission to the English crown. In 1541 Henry VIII assumed the title King of Ireland (among others). However, throughout these years English control was limited to a part of Ireland – the Pale – with continually shifting frontiers. Only in 1603 was the whole of the island brought under effective English control. Then the protestant ascendancy sought to do in all Ireland what it had been trying for some years to do within the Pale: establish a political, legal and administrative system similar to that of England itself. By the end of the eighteenth century Ireland did have a functioning Parliament, legal system and pattern of county government. In 1800, however, identical acts of incorporation were passed by the Irish and UK Parliaments, and at the start of 1801 Ireland was formally incorporated into the union. In place of its own Parliament it was given representation at Westminster (Beckett, 1966). Uniquely, it was administered as a separate unit within the UK, with a lord-lieutenant heading Irish government and a chief secretary heading Irish administration (Kendle, 1997: 19). In 1920, in the midst of civil war, Ireland was divided by the Government of Ireland Act, and given northern and southern Parliaments, both of which remained subordinate to the Westminster Parliament. In December 1921 the Anglo-Irish Treaty gave the 26 counties of the south domestic independence and dominion status within the Empire (Quinn, 1993: 13–16). For the next fifty years Northern Ireland was governed as a semi-autonomous region of the UK, with its own Parliament at Stormont (Buckland, 1981: ch. 2). In response to the breakdown in civil order, the Stormont Parliament was abrogated in 1972 and direct rule was imposed from London.

In the Scottish case parliamentary union in 1707 was preceded by regal union in 1603 (which, in turn, was preceded by centuries of often violent conflict across what eventually became the Anglo-Scottish border). The union of 1603 had, however, very little impact on political structures. Riley (1978: xiv) writes that 'constitutionally the kingdoms were independent of each other, the sovereign of each country happening merely to be the same person. England and Scotland had little else in common'. This is something that is often forgotten, particularly by the English. The fact that James VI of Scotland became James I of England (and Wales and Ireland) did not in any sense bring a separate Scottish state to an end. Even after 1707, when the two Parliaments passed Acts of Union and were fused in

Westminster, Scotland retained a number of distinctive institutions, notably its legal, religious and educational systems. It was, however, given representation in the Westminster Parliament and its administrative structures were gradually assimilated to English. Although a Scottish Secretary of State was created in the first post-union government, the position was dispensed with in 1745 and responsibility for Scotland passed to the Home Secretary, though most effective political power was exercised by the Lord Advocate (Scottish Office, 1997).

The UK was, then, a long time in the making, and the means by which it was brought together were often very haphazard. An analysis of the British Isles in the seventeenth century would reveal that one king ruled all four UK sub-nations. However, the institutions of only two of those sub-nations, England and Wales, had been fused. The other two, Scotland and Ireland, retained their own political and administrative structures. The result was three separate kingdoms with three separate Parliaments, privy councils, churches and national aristocracies. On this information alone it comes as no surprise to learn that Charles I lost control of all three kingdoms in the years 1637–42 (Brown, 1992: 7–8). In mid-century Cromwell fused some of these national institutions, but this initiative did not survive his death in 1658 and the restoration in 1660. The Anglo-Scottish union of 1707 did simplify things considerably. Only, however, in 1801 were a single kingdom and single Parliament created in the British Isles. This settlement survived for 120 years.

Analysing the UK

What all this amounts to, so far as the territorial politics of the UK state are concerned, has been the subject of much debate. In large part that debate has been run by historians, who in telling the story of the UK's construction have also advanced claims about its territorial politics. However, political scientists have also had things to say (Griffiths, 1996: ch. 1).

The traditional view is the Whig interpretation of history which dominated Victorian historiography (Butterfield, 1931). This holds that the English have a genius for governing and that the spread of their political institutions first throughout the British Isles and second across much of the globe (by means of imperial advance) was one of their great gifts to humankind. It is a striking feature of this literature that although it surfaced in a multinational state it told the story of only one of its constituent nations, England. Equally striking is that this type of history continues to be written in the late twentieth century when English political genius is nothing like as evident as it once was (Cannadine, 1995: 14–17). In political science the related perspective is the homogeneity thesis, which maintains that UK politics are largely uniform and modelled on an English pattern of class politics (Budge and Urwin, 1966: 48–52). The territorial relationships outlined by proponents of this view are essentially benign. The virtues of English government that they identify are the common law tradition, parliamentary democracy and a talent for pragmatism and gradualist change. A good deal of local variation and indeed autonomy can be built into such accounts, both within England and in the other constituent nations of the UK.

The Whig interpretation has faced a number of challenges. One of the most hostile came from Michael Hechter, whose Marxist analysis *Internal Colonialism* also painted England as an expansionist state, but held that England's imperialist drive into the Celtic fringe of the British Isles was malign, and resulted in alien political structures being imposed on Gaelic peoples. For Hechter, economic development in the Celtic fringe was driven by the needs of English capital, with elite positions being taken by the English rather than by indigenous people (Hechter, 1975). Little of this stands up to historical scrutiny, but its political message has nevertheless been quite powerful in recent years. A more nuanced Marxist account was developed by Tom Nairn in *The Break-up of Britain?*, which argued that peripheral elites in the 1970s were mobilizing nationalist forces to disengage from a UK in terminal decline (Nairn, 1977). Nairn's was, though, a less critical account of UK territorial politics. More neutral still is the analysis of historians who hold that English expansionism was a consequence of defensive measures taken to prevent Catholic encirclement of England.

A more fundamental critique has been developed by historians who hold that the state-building experiences of the British Isles cannot be understood by focusing on a single dominant nation. Instead, they must be interpreted as the interactions of all the nations which people those isles. Although histories of each of the nations found in the British Isles were written in the eighteenth and earlier centuries, the recent revival of interest in this kind of approach may be traced to the mid-1970s, when J. G. A. Pocock published 'British History: A Plea for a New Subject' (Pocock, 1975a). In the past twenty-five years historians have explored three main avenues of inquiry. One focuses on Scotland as a major player alongside England in the construction of the UK, and places great emphasis on the degree of political autonomy the Scots were able to preserve on entering the UK. A second engages in explicit 'four nations' history (Kearney, 1989), and highlights the contingencies which marked each stage in UK territorial political development. A third analyses the forging of a genuinely British nation in the decades after Anglo-Scottish union in 1707 (Colley, 1992), and comes close to endorsing the UK homogeneity thesis.

The Primacy of EC Law

Given all that has just been said about historians' and political scientists' disputes over the emergence and nature of the UK, it may seem strange to list the primacy of EC law as the first principle of its territorial politics. However, the final chapter in any full historical analysis, and the first in any advanced by a political scientist, must acknowledge that the UK took a critical step when it joined the EC in 1973 (Geddes, 1999). The primacy of EC law is now the most fundamental principle of its territorial politics. Within the EC this principle was established as early as 1964 in the case of Costa v. ENEL. In English law it was confirmed in 1973 *by Aero Zipp Fasteners* v. *YKK Fasteners (UK) Ltd* (Nicoll and Salmon, 1994: 98–9). Its territorial consequences are that some sovereignty, or political power, no longer resides in the UK but has instead been transferred to the EU institutions located in Brussels, Luxembourg and Strasbourg. The important issue is which elements of sovereignty are implicated in this change.

Only a few points can be made here. One is that the UK's supreme court in areas covered by EC law is now the European Court of Justice, which sits in Luxembourg. There is one UK judge among the fifteen current members of the ECJ, but that judge does not in any sense act as a representative of the UK government or as a proponent of UK interests. A second point is that some important political decisions affecting the UK are taken in the political arenas of the EU. Pre-eminent among these is the Council of the EU, as the Council of Ministers has been known since ratification of the (Maastricht) Treaty on European Union. In this forum the UK's veto, along with that of all other member states, exists only when qualified majority voting is not in operation. In the increasing number of spheres in which this procedure has operated since the Single European Act came into force in July 1987, the UK cannot block political initiatives on its own. Since the Treaty of Maastricht and the introduction of the co-decision procedure, the European Parliament has also gained some policy-making powers when deadlock triggers conciliation. The UK elects 87 members to the 626-member Parliament and again, there-fore, does not have anything like a majority voice. A third point is that some administration has shifted to the European Commission, where the UK has two Commissioners who are bound to look first and foremost to the interests of the EU as a whole (Nugent, 1999).

UK membership of the EU is, then, a territorial political change of the first magnitude. It has caused some political power to flow out of the UK to EU institutions. Many key decisions affecting the UK are no longer taken on UK soil, but in European forums. As the process of European integration continues apace in the future, this outflow is certain to increase.

Parliamentary Sovereignty

Domestically, it is a commonplace that the core constitutional principle is parliamentary sovereignty. What is striking, in a constitu-tion that is still uncodified, is not that this principle stands at the heart of classic analyses – such as A. V. Dicey's set of lectures published in 1885 as *The Law of the Constitution* (Dicey, 1959) – but that it is scarcely challenged by any others. Even in books written in times when 'constitutional ways of thinking' were more developed than is the case today (Johnson, 1977: x), there is very little dissent from either the fact or the desirability of this core principle (Kendle, 1997: 172). It must now be understood in the context of EU membership, but that is a different issue.

The centrality of this principle is evident in the very creation of the UK. Fusion of Parliaments is what marks development of the union. Today, those parts of the globe which elect representatives to the Westminster Parliament *are* the UK (Rose, 1982: 46). Thus, England, Scotland, Wales and Northern Ireland are in. Places like the Channel Islands and the Isle of Man are out. They are direct dependencies of the Crown, with their own legislative and tax systems (Hunter, 1995: 1305). At the end of the nineteenth and start of the twentieth centuries, so great was the belief in Parliament as the ultimate political arena that projects were seriously advanced for giving all the white settler dominions of the Empire representation in it (Kendle, 1997: ch. 3). Even today, Parliament retains a strong symbolic power as the focal point of national political life.

The doctrine of parliamentary sovereignty states that the writ of Parliament runs throughout the UK, and is subject neither to a higher law nor to the countervailing regional powers that are found in a country like Germany. Although Britain's accession to the EC in 1973 changed things somewhat, and its incorporation of the European Convention on Human Rights into UK law by means of the Human Rights Act 1998 changed things further (see Chapter 7), this principle remains central to the analysis of territorial political relations within the UK. It means that, ultimately, all power can be centralized in the Westminster Parliament. The extent to which this has or has not in fact happened is analysed later. Alongside this principle of political centralization lies a series of countervailing principles.

Territorial Representation

The first principle is territorial representation in the Westminster Parliament. It is sometimes forgotten that both the House of Commons and the House of Lords are chambers of territorial representation (or the House of Lords traditionally has been one). When Wales, Scotland and Ireland were incorporated into the union, a central element of the settlement was representation at Westminster. In the negotiated union of 1707, for example, Anglo-Welsh and Scottish representation in the new Parliament of Great Britain was calculated on the basis of population (5:1) and fiscal capacity (36:1), with the result that England and Wales sent 190 peers and 513 commoners to Westminster and Scotland sent 16 peers and 45 commoners (Mackie, 1978: 261). Ever since, the principle of territorial representation has been a fundamental of UK politics. To this day Scotland, Wales and Northern Ireland are over-represented at Westminster. The key question, however, is the extent to which the salience of this principle has changed over time.

Before the coming of democracy, its significance was that Parliament was the place where the great territorial magnates congregated to discuss matters of common interest or concern. This was also true of those national Parliaments which were suppressed as the union increased its territorial reach. In no instance prior to 1832 was territorial representation equal or just, chiefly because of pocket boroughs and corrupt practices more generally. Nevertheless, in a UK polity which until well into the nineteenth century was structured chiefly by territory, the ability of distinct parts of the country to have a say in Parliament was highly valued. One important consequence was that throughout the eighteenth century and for much of the nineteenth the local act, by means of which localities petitioned Parliament for permission to build roads, canals and railways, levy tolls, deal with specific problems and so on, constituted its main business.

In the course of the nineteenth century the principle of territorial representation was fully respected by those who sought to modernize the UK constitution. Although democratic reformers were concerned to correct both abuses and the territorial imbalances generated by industrialization and urbanization, they did not take the chance to set the UK electoral system on an entirely new, non-territorial, footing. Instead, they reaffirmed the constituency base of UK politics. However, one development triggered by reform did start to undermine the importance of territorial representation. The rise of disciplined parties, notably in the wake of the second great Reform Act, of 1867, increasingly meant that what mattered in Parliament was not constituency, but party affiliation. It would be wrong to say that party has wholly undermined territory, for in many parts of the UK territory at least partly structures the vote. The Conservative, Labour and Liberal-democratic parties all have territorial strongholds. This is yet more obviously true of the Scottish National Party and Plaid Cymru. At the extreme, voters in Northern Ireland have for many years only been able to vote for Northern Irish parties. However, territory has certainly diminished in influence during the past 130 years or so.

In the twentieth century some small moves have also been made to depart from a strict territorial linkage in UK electoral politics. In Irish elections in 1919, Stormont elections until 1929, Northern Irish elections to the European Parliament since 1979 (Mount, 1992: 169), elections to each of the devolved assemblies set up by the Blair government after 1997, and UK-wide elections to the European Parliament since 1999 some form of proportional representation has been used. Against this, a central part of the brief given to the 1997–8 Jenkins Commission on electoral reform was to 'keep the link' between MPs and geographical constituencies. Moreover, the British version of the additional member system used for elections to the

Scottish, Welsh and London assemblies and proposed by Jenkins for elections to the Westminster Parliament is characterized by a majority of constituency representatives (and a minority of top-ups). Jenkins's small top-up areas are also a reflection of the importance of the local constituency in British (though not necessarily Irish) politics.

How fundamental, then, is territorial representation today? In large part answers to this question depend on assessments of the importance of Parliament itself. For constitutional romantics like Tony Benn, Parliament remains the great forum in which representatives of the people come together to discuss the great issues of the day, and territorial representation is still valuable. For others, Parliament is slipping from sight and territorial representation with it. There is much to be said for this competing viewpoint. As recently as the inter-war years, Prime Ministers spent hours in the House of Commons, in part because they were usually also Leader of the House. Churchill finally ended this practice in 1940, and at the same time changed for all time the relationship between the premier and the legislature: 'before 1940 Prime Ministers were often multi-faceted parliamentary performers . . . in the modern period Prime Ministers have tended to attend the Commons only for a set and specific purpose'. In the 1980s Margaret Thatcher was a very reclusive figure, 'far and away the least active Prime Minister in the Commons for the last hundred and twenty years' (Dunleavy *et al.*, 1990: 136–7). Nevertheless, she was still something of a parliamentary figure, in 1983–4 voting in about 33 per cent of all divisions. In the late 1990s, Tony Blair had cut his attendance to the bare minimum. In 1997–8, his first year as Prime Minister, he voted in about 5 per cent of divisions (Riddell, 1998). As the executive engages with the public in ever more direct ways – from focus groups to referenda – territorial representation in a sovereign Parliament becomes less and less fundamental to UK politics.

Local Government

The second principle which has always counterbalanced political centralization in a sovereign Parliament is local government. Again, the extent to which this principle is fundamental has changed substantially over time.

In the pre-modern era politics in all the UK sub-nations was predominantly local, and comprised some form of aristocratic government exercised by nobles and chieftains. This form of government was challenged from two main directions. At the local level the emergence of merchants in towns prompted the development of a system of elected councils. Far more importantly, at the national level the rise of the modern state generated a substantial challenge to aristocratic government. Indeed, through control of Parliament the executive part of the state is now able to impose many of its wishes on local councils.

When the aristocracy was the dominant force in the land, it was precisely those individuals who controlled local affairs who also met in Parliament, whether in Westminster or in a pre-union sub-national capital. In Wales the nobility was Anglicized from an early stage. In Ireland it was increasingly dominated by the English colonial ascendancy. In Scotland it was mainly native until 1707 (Brown, 1992: 47), but then became increasingly Anglocentric. Even when a system of county and municipal government began to spread across the whole of the UK, it continued to be run by local economic and social elites. As these were often exactly the same people who had seats in Parliament, it is difficult to say with any precision where local government ended and central government began. At this time the extent of elite integration in the UK was substantial.

Possibly the purest form of local government was witnessed in England and Wales in the 150 to 200 years following the Glorious Revolution of 1688 and the Act of Union of 1707. Sidney and Beatrice Webb (1963: xviii) write of the period 1689–1835 that 'For the first, and perhaps the last, time in English History, the National Government abstained from intervention in local affairs, practically leaving all the various kinds of local governing bodies to carry out their several administrations as they chose, without central supervision or central control.' Similarly, Fraser (1979: 1) states of England that it was governed mainly at the local level for at least two centuries, from the late seventeenth to the late nineteenth centuries.

This real local government was often underpinned by functioning local societies. It would be wrong to romanticize, but in rural Britain the county was not the more or less arbitrary territorial unit which exists today. 'With its own head, the Lord-Lieutenant, its own ecclesiastical organization, its own courts, its own foxhounds and beagles, it was a self-contained society' (Hanham, 1978: 3). Sometimes, of course, it was several self-contained societies, for divisions within counties were certainly not unknown. In urban Britain municipal corporations jealously guarded their powers and freedoms, and an 'urban squirearchy' (Garrard, 1983: 13) emerged to control towns.

These were, then, not only real local societies; they were also headed by a 'natural' and in many ways unified and self-confident governing class, the gentry that many observers (perhaps most famously de Tocqueville) have celebrated. This local government was not democratic. 'County government by country gentlemen', writes Lee (1963: 4), 'was perhaps the purest example of oligarchy to be seen in England'. But it was local, and it did give Britain – though not Ireland – a very diverse pattern of control.

The key county institution was the quarter session, the arena in which justices of the peace (JPs) operated. JPs had not only judicial functions but also administrative and legislative ones, for they were required to interpret the laws made in Westminster. In pre-democratic times, then, they were part of a vast network of territorial institutions focused on Parliament. At the genuinely local level, the parish was the central unit of organization and administration, and its officers – constables, overseers of the poor, church wardens and surveyors – were significant political figures (Webb and Webb, 1963: 15). These various individuals managed the affairs of county and parish, oversaw administration of the Poor Law, and operated as a channel of views to and from Parliament. Municipal corporations performed many of the same functions in towns.

Although the UK's tradition of local autonomy came to be severely challenged as the nineteenth and twentieth centuries progressed, it was never entirely lost. At the level of principle, it retained adherents on both left and right. In the mid-nineteenth century, Joshua Toulmin Smith published books which extolled the virtues of real local government at the level of the parish. Maybe he was justifiably dismissed as a 'constitutional romanticist' by the great German commentator on English local government, Josef Redlich. More realistic was the 'civic gospel' spread by Joseph Chamberlain as mayor of Birmingham in the mid-1870s, which called for local intervention in the spheres of education and public health. This was to develop into 'gas and water socialism' and a vibrant left-wing tradition of municipal enterprise. In the 1980s it spawned assertive Labour councils in London and the metropolitan counties, and a broad movement of the new urban left. At every stage this tradition provoked local right-wing reaction, in the guise of 'apolitical' forms of conservatism such as independence and ratepayerism. Often, these movements were also committed to real local government.

More important to the maintenance of local government were, however, pragmatic decisions taken by governing elites in London.

Bulpitt has argued that in the first half of the twentieth century a 'dual polity' existed in which London government took control of 'high' politics and contracted out to collaborative local elites those 'low' politics in which it took little interest. The dual polity, with its system of indirect rule, was deconstructed only when overarching concerns to drive efficiency into all parts of the British state emerged in the 1960s (Bulpitt, 1983).

Administrative Decentralization

A third counterbalance to political centralization has been administrative decentralization, or deconcentration as it is sometimes called. This form of decentralization is not to be confused with the transfer of functions to elected local government. Instead, this is a case of functions remaining strictly within the structures of the central state. The most important instances of administrative decentralization have taken place in Scotland, Wales and Northern Ireland.

The Scottish Office was the first territorial department to be created, in 1885. Until the First World War, the office was relatively insignificant. The Scottish Secretary did not have a seat in Cabinet – his office was based exclusively in Dover House, London, and much Scottish administration was fed through a series of 'autonomous' boards. All this started to change in the inter-war years. In 1919 a second minister was appointed to the Scottish Office. In 1926 the Scottish Secretary was made a member of the Cabinet (Scottish Office, 1997). In 1928 the various boards became departments of state within the Scottish Office, though they still had a certain degree of independence. In 1937 they were placed firmly under the control of the Secretary of State. In 1939 a Scottish Office was created in St Andrew's House, Edinburgh, to take many functions from Dover House, London. Further growth took place after the Second World War, as more ministerial posts were created and increasing numbers of civil servants were recruited (Hutchison, 1996). In 1999 the Scottish Office, based mainly in Edinburgh but also retaining an office in London, comprised five main departments dealing with agriculture and the environment, education and industry, housing and local government, home affairs, and health. It had a ministerial team of six and in April 1997 employed 5108 officials in its core departments. A further 8249 officials worked for the Scottish Office, chiefly in the Scottish Prison Service (Cabinet Office, 1998: table 1D). In Tony

Blair's first government, the Scottish Office was represented on 13 out of 19 standing ministerial committees of the Cabinet (Cabinet Office, 1997).

The Welsh Office is a more recent invention. Wales slowly developed an administrative identity from the closing years of the nineteenth century. Separate legislation was conceded in the Sunday Closing Act 1881 and the Welsh Intermediate Education Act 1889. A Welsh Board of the Department of Education was created in 1907, a Welsh National Insurance Commission in 1911, and Welsh Boards of Health and Agriculture in 1919. In 1951 the Home Secretary was also named Minister for Welsh Affairs. In 1957 this responsibility transferred to the Minister for Housing and Local Government. Finally, in 1964, the Welsh Office was created under its own Secretary of State and gradually increased the range of functions over which it presided (Griffiths, 1996: ch. 3; Welsh Office, 1997). In 1999, the Welsh Office, based mainly in Cardiff but with a small office in London, had a ministerial team of three. In April 1997 it employed 2290 officials (Cabinet Office, 1998: table 1D), and in Blair's first government was represented on 13 out of 19 ministerial standing committees (Cabinet Office, 1997). The Welsh Office remains something of a shadow of its Scottish counterpart.

The Northern Ireland Office has a very different history. It was created in the midst of crisis in 1972 when civil rights protests turned violent, the structures of devolved government centred on the Stormont Parliament were suppressed, and direct rule was imposed from London. It took on functions formerly exercised in both Belfast and London. In 1999, the Northern Ireland Office had a ministerial team of five. In April 1997 it employed 212 officials in London (Cabinet Office, 1998: table 1D). The Northern Ireland Civil Service, which staffs government offices in the province, is separate from the British Civil Service. In Blair's first government the Northern Ireland Office was represented on 14 out of 19 ministerial standing committees (Cabinet Office, 1997).

No equivalent English office has ever existed, and England has never been directly represented as a territorial unit in the structures of UK government. Here, individual departments have tended to develop territorial offices within regions on an *ad hoc* basis. The regional boundaries adopted by the different ministries have never been consistent. One result is that no sense of regional deconcentration has ever existed in England. This did, however, start to change in April 1994, when the Major government created a series of Government Offices of the Regions intended to implement a new single regional budget and to generate precisely the regional focus that had hitherto been lacking. Even this initiative did not make all UK government department regions within England consistent, but it did go a long way down that road (Hogwood, 1995). This is the foundation on which regional development agencies were developed by the Blair government. These could, in turn, form the basis for elected regional government.

The single exception to the general lack of regional focus which characterizes state administration in England is London. In the 1990s both Conservative and Labour governments had a Minister for London as well as a standing ministerial committee of the Cabinet on London. In the Blair government this committee was chaired by the Deputy Prime Minister, John Prescott.

Central Supervision and Control

Cutting across these varied countervailing powers has been a tradition of central supervision and control deriving from the core constitutional principle of parliamentary sovereignty. Application of this principle has been different in distinct parts of the UK. At one extreme, in Ireland, it has been the product of an effectively colonial relationship. For many years central control, often brutally applied, was the only means by which an unwilling province could be subjected to rule from London. At the other extreme, it has not been an expression of force and repression, but instead the result of a series of drives which paralleled or were consequent on the spread of democracy in the UK.

It is fair to say that in the Irish case local government was never a major part of the governing tradition. Here, in fact, local government for a period increased over time as London administrations first grew tired of the Irish question, and then came to believe they had solved it through partition and devolution of some functions to the Stormont parliament. Although some local government was granted to Northern Ireland in the half-century from 1921 to 1972, it nevertheless operated on a very fragile basis, as suppression of Stormont proved. Only in 1998 was some measure of local government returned to Northern Ireland, on a progressive basis, following the Good Friday Agreement and the June elections to a devolved assembly.

In the rest of the UK – that is, in Britain – local government succumbed to central control not as the result of an overt power play, but as the result of a changing public philosophy on the part of governing elites. One relevant factor was the decline of all those elements which had underpinned real local government in the seventeenth, eighteenth and nineteenth centuries. The demise of a powerful provincial press in the past century is merely one indication of this change. But there were also positive drives in the direction of central control.

The first centralizing force was the aspiration towards uniform standards of public provision which developed at much the same time as democratic ideals began to spread across the UK. This aspiration was initially evident in the first two classic Royal Commission reports, on the Poor Law in 1834 and on the municipal corporations in 1835. From this point forwards, the search for uniformity in public provision was conducted with great purpose. Its intellectual inspiration was Jeremy Bentham, whose advocacy of 'inspectability' in the Constitutional Code became a key theme of central–local relations. These ideas were taken to the heart of the reform process by Edwin Chadwick and Nassau Senior, both friends of Bentham who became dominant members of the Royal Commission on the Poor Law (Keith-Lucas, 1952: 5). They ensured that a central board of Poor Law Commissioners was created to oversee its operation in all parts of the country. The path from here to extensive central control of local government business was by no means short or straight. But in time central government did seek to ensure that its conception of necessary standards was realised throughout the UK. The key steps on this path were the introduction of minimum standards in the 1830s, and the shift towards uniform standards later in the century. The Public Health Acts 1848 and 1872 are often held to be important in this regard. The Local Government Act 1858 was also key. A single clause in the Sanitary Act 1866 is held by some to have marked the real shift from permissive legislation to compulsion (Prest, 1990: 209). In the twentieth century central control of local affairs, by means of legislation, directive and exhortation, has been extensive. It was given a major boost by creation of the welfare state, which saw many previously local responsibilities, notably in health care, taken into the realm of central government.

The spread of democracy also had serious implications for local government, though this was not immediately apparent in the 1830s. Often local elections were not contested on rigid party lines, and even when they were they remained essentially local affairs with different variants of the main national parties contesting elections in different parts of the country. In time, however, party became a major instrument of central control, as local elections became seen by party managers as critical to national party fortunes. As is more generally the case, party was a real force for centralization in UK territorial politics.

A third centralizing force has been financial control, for alongside central aspiration to uniform standards has been a real concern to control public expenditure, including that which is formally decided at the local level. This centralizing strand reached its zenith in the years after Britain's fiscal crisis of the state first seriously developed in the mid-1970s. In the final quarter of the twentieth century UK sub-central government has been subjected to extensive financial control.

A fourth factor has been centrally inspired efficiency drives, most prominent in the years since about 1960. Towards the end of the long period of Conservative government which stretched from 1951 to 1964, modernization became the watchword of political elites. The reasons for this are several, but chief among them was a concern that the UK economy, though growing, was failing to exhibit the dynamism shown by its major competitors, notably in western Europe. With regard to local government, this obsession with efficiency, shared by Conservative and Labour governments in the 1960s and early 1970s, prompted root-and-branch reform by means of the London Government Act 1963, which totally altered local government in the capital, and the Local Government Act 1972, which did precisely the same thing in the rest of the UK. The point has often been made that such a thorough structural reorganization in peacetime conditions is inconceivable in almost any other developed country, reflecting one major consequence of the UK's anomalous lack of a codified constitution (cf. Ashford, 1982, 1989).

A final factor has been straightforward political advantage. It can of course be argued that this has played a part in all central intervention in local government matters. Structural reorganization in both the nineteenth and twentieth centuries has certainly been seen in this way, and as most of the big changes have been enacted by Conservative governments it is Conservative political advantage that is uniformly held to be one of their leading motivations. Abolition of the Greater London Council and the six metropolitan counties by means of the Local Government Act 1985 is often seen as the paradigm case of politically inspired central intervention. It would be foolish to deny that this has been relevant.

Union Maintenance

Putting all these various factors together – and coming up with a union in which regional and local autonomy have often been sacrificed to central control – it has to be asked what other aspects of territorial politics there have been that have helped to maintain the union and keep the show on the road. These have come in a number of forms, from selective incentives to identity-building.

It is important not to overstate the scale of the task here. In some ways, the UK has been a difficult territorial construct to keep together. Periodic troubles in Ireland are sufficient evidence of this. Nevertheless, one striking feature of the UK is in fact the limited extent of sub-national tension within it. It must immediately be said again that Ireland is in many ways a case apart. Scotland and Wales have, however, been relatively easy to govern from London. From time to time concessions have had to be made, but on the whole their places in the union have been taken for granted by both centre and periphery alike. Indeed, when Bernard Crick (1996: 262) writes that 'we are a multinational state and the main business of politics has been, since the Act and Treaty of Union in 1707, holding it together', it can only be said that he is wrong. The main business of politics has usually been elsewhere: in imperial affairs, in wars with foreign powers, in construction of a welfare state, in management of the economy.

Selective incentives have played some part in union maintenance. Given what has just been said, it would be hard to argue that there has always been a conscious strategy here, but there has, at any rate, been something of a reliance on instrumental gains for all. For England, these have taken the form of secure boundaries to the west (Wales, Ireland) and north (Scotland), and of an extension of London government to, at one stage, all corners of the British Isles. For non-English parts of the union they have taken the form of spin-off benefits from England's early industrialization, participation in the imperial adventure, membership of a comprehensive welfare state and receipt of direct cash injections. Since the late 1970s the Barnett formula has ensured that all parts of the UK outside England are given a more than proportionate share of public spending.

Besides this, promotion of a British identity has been important, chiefly through demonization of non-British elements. In particular, the French have frequently served as an 'Other' in opposition to which a British identity could be forged (Colley, 1992).

Finally, containment of the Irish problem has played a part, in the dual sense of minimization of its extent within Ireland and limitation of its spread to other parts of the UK. The fact that Ireland has been in many ways an offshore problem has made this policy more effective. It has also been reinforced by the development of a British identity and by instrumentalism. At least until recently, both Scotland and Wales were characterized by some degree of British feeling. Perhaps more importantly, neither nation had much to gain from leaving the union, with the result that neither sought to exploit the Irish problem for its own ends.

Nationalist Challenges to the Fundamentals of UK Territorial Politics

The principles which have underpinned UK territorial politics have been by no means uncontested; the most dramatic challenges have come from nationalist groups in the UK sub-nations. In the second half of the nineteenth century in Ireland, and in the second half of the twentieth century in Northern Ireland, Scotland and Wales, such challenges have been substantial and have in each case prompted change in UK territorial politics.

The basis for nationalist challenges has been a disjuncture between state-building and nation-building. As has been seen, the UK state was assembled in a series of stages marked by precise dates of incorporation and secession. Nation-building was not a simultaneous process, by which is meant that the people who came with the territories did not immediately assume a UK identity. Instead, they retained the wide series of identities they had had prior to state-building, and only slowly changed, if at all.

In the early stages of nation-building those identities were often predominantly local. The UK as late as the eighteenth century and even the nineteenth was a highly textured place where territory, not class, was the main political cleavage. Leading politicians like Tory Prime Ministers George Canning (in the 1820s) and Benjamin Disraeli (in the 1860s and 1870s) had precisely this understanding of the political nation, believing the politics of, say, Yorkshire to be fundamentally different from that of Essex (Hill, 1929: vi). With industrialization and urbanization this slowly changed, such that over time individuals began to place less emphasis on the local identities that had been passed down the generations and to identify with a rather larger social unit. Increased social mobility clearly facilitated this change. However, it was by no means a UK identity that individuals assumed. Instead, alongside national identities such as English, Irish, Scottish and Welsh, it was British that became the key overarching identity for UK people. The way in which this 'imagined political community' (Anderson, 1991) was constructed had, and still has, critical implications for UK territorial politics.

Linda Colley (1992) argues that the forging of the British nation took place chiefly, though by no means uniquely, in the years between the Act of Union with Scotland in 1707 and the formal dawning of the Victorian age in 1837. Her contention is that British identity was shaped mainly in opposition to a 'hostile Other'. Above all, this Other was France, against which Britain fought a long series of wars from 1689 to 1815, but it was also to some extent peoples encountered through imperial expansion. 'Not so much consensus or homogeneity or centralisation at home, as a strong sense of dissimilarity from those without who proved to be the essential cement' (Colley, 1992: 17). As such, British identity became militantly Protestant (in opposition to French Catholicism). It also came to celebrate those aspects of British politics held to mark it out, such as a dominant Parliament and a system of free trade, both within and, increasingly, without. Further-more, it came to be identified with success. Whereas England, Scotland and Wales had been rather peripheral European nations before 1688, Britain after 1707 was an increasingly important European power. It was also increasingly wealthy.

The implications of this analysis are many. One is obvious: that, despite Catholic emancipation in 1829, the Irish could never be fully incorporated into the union. Another, equally obvious and linked to this, is that the UK is a place where state and nation have never been – and, it is safe to say, never will be – coterminous. Today at least six 'national' identities exist within the four sub-nations that make-up the UK. They are English, Scottish, Welsh, the two main identities to be found in Northern Ireland and, stretching over all these identities and having a by no means easy relationship with any of them, British (Rose, 1982: 15). A third implication is that British identity, and therefore the underpinnings of the UK state, were certain to come under strain when the factors promoting it – notably a hostile Other and success – declined in significance. The loss of UK economic and political power, and the (consequent) entry of the UK into the EU, have placed great strain on the UK state.

Conclusion

The fundamentals of UK territorial politics have traditionally been a sovereign Parliament counterbalanced chiefly by territorial representation, local government and administrative decentralization. It is clear that the ways in which these fundamental principles interact has changed markedly in the course of the past century and more. Many factors have provoked that change, but central to them has been the rise of party. A disciplined party system undercut territorial representation and was a major element in the decline of local government. Party-political considerations also played some part in the administrative decentralization that has been witnessed in recent years, for the rise of nationalist parties outside the UK's English core has forced metropolitan elites to make concessions.

Indeed, party politics lie at the heart of the shift in territorial fundamentals witnessed in the UK. This is, moreover, a factor to which insufficient attention is paid in the debate about the UK analysed earlier in this chapter. The centralization witnessed in the UK in the twentieth century is different from that classically associated with France. There the prefectoral system, which embodies metropolitan power and control, was put in place at the very start of the nineteenth century. Mercantilism, linked with Colbert, came even earlier. In France, the *étatiste* tradition made centralization a fundamental aspect of the state's ethos and operational principles. Traditionally this was not the case in the UK, which was always held to contain multiple centres of power, as is clear from the writings of Burke and Disraeli (Blake, 1985: 123). Here, centralization came comparatively late, and it came as much as anything else through the rise of party, which generated a certain degree of homogeneity (Pulzer, 1967) as well as a large amount of centralization.

Party is also a key element in any explanation of the territorial pressures which now face the UK state. It is true that removal of a hostile Other (through EU membership) and lack of success (in relative economic decline) have contributed to those pressures. However, party has long been the main mediating force in UK politics, and it is both a failure and a triumph of party that has contributed to the current situation. The failure has been sustained by those parties of national integration which no longer have much purchase in peripheral parts of the UK. It is hard to believe that as recently as the 1955 general election the Conservatives polled 50 per cent of the Scottish vote and secured 50 per cent of Scottish seats. In 1997 their poll was 18 per cent and their seat count zero. The Tories were also written out of Northern Irish politics when Unionists broke away in the early 1970s. They have never been strong in Wales. On the other side, while Labour remains a potent force in both Scotland and Wales, it has not been able to eliminate the challenge posed by the Scottish National Party and Plaid Cymru. The triumph can be claimed by these two parties, notably the SNP, which genuinely have changed the nature of UK politics in the past thirty years. This achievement has not been conjured out of thin air – the fact that it patently could not have been secured in Yorkshire (which in terms of population is bigger than either Scotland or Wales) makes it clear that the pre-history is critical – but it has not been effortless either.

The territorial challenge to UK politics is now substantial. In Scotland by the middle of 1998, more than 50 per cent of respondents said that they were in favour of independence, and a real sense of difference had developed. 'English manners, once respected or at least regarded with some awe, now simply grate' (Lloyd, 1998: 11). While there was always a lot of grumbling about England, it is only recently that Scots have lost their traditional deference to English authority. This is a shift of the first magnitude, and suggests that radical change is very much on the agenda. In this light, the Scottish Constitutional Convention of the mid-1990s becomes a critical event in UK politics. It might seem that John Major was right all along. Famously, at the close of the 1992 general election campaign, he issued a dramatic warning about the dangers devolution posed to the UK: 'Wake up, my fellow countrymen. Wake up *now* before it is too late' (Baker, 1993: 37). In Major's view, there are certain issues that are just too dangerous to be raised. Devolution is certainly one, and the slippery slope is very much in sight. Yet it is not clear that this issue could have been stopped in its tracks by the time the 1990s had come around.

The final question is the impact on UK fundamentals that devolution and a possible break-up might have. The obvious answer is that this impact will be huge, which on the whole is correct. However, it is worth noting that change in Northern Ireland, if contained, is not likely to alter territorial fundamentals very much. This was certainly the case in the 1920s and is equally likely to be the case now, for this union has never been a central part of the UK political tradition. The

Anglo-Scottish and Anglo-Welsh unions are, however, very different matters. These genuinely are fundamental, and any major change here would transform UK politics. It could be argued that England is simply so dominant in the union and has determined so many of its political and institutional features that its polity could survive even change of this kind largely unscathed. It seems more likely, however, that the political and psychological shocks would be so vast that not only Scotland and Wales but also England itself would be taken into a very new era governed by distinct political and institutional principles.

7

Law and Politics

ROBERT THOMAS

Perhaps the most striking characteristic of the relationship between law and politics in the British state is the marked separation between the two. Politicians do not wish to be seen to undermine respect for the law, and lawyers generally have little desire to interfere in the processes of political decision-making. This is largely the result of the unusual degree of continuity in British political institutions and the evolutionary character of the British constitutional tradition (see Chapter 2). While other states have experienced decisive breaks and have been compelled to redefine the relationship between law and politics, the British state has demonstrated a remarkable ability to adapt in response to changing circumstances. This chapter will first examine the history of the relationship between law and politics and then consider the extent to which this relationship is challenged generally by recent trends such as the upsurge in the numbers of applications for judicial review of governmental decisions and the increasing impact of EC law and the European Convention on Human Rights (ECHR), together with the Labour government's programme of constitutional reform.

Law and Politics in Britain

The dominant tradition of law and politics in Britain stems from the nineteenth century. While this tradition had been developing since the Glorious Revolution of 1688 it was only in Victorian times that it came to be recognised. Its central characteristic is that the relationship between law and politics is not defined by a formal constitutional structure but is the product of the accumulated experience and wisdom of its participants. From this perspective the British polity is viewed as the climax of political achievement in which great statesmen, having been educated within the traditions of the ruling class, contribute to the conversation of mankind (Bagehot, 1963).

This tradition of law and politics was informed by the customary practices and tacit understandings concerning how government was to be conducted. While this club style of British government is frequently recognised, it is often overlooked that the practices of the law have also been informed by a similar cultural orientation. The entire corpus of the law has been developed by lawyers who received their training in the spirit and traditions of the common law. Rather than viewing the common law, and the common law should be viewed not as an objective set of rules but rather as a range of values which the judges serve to protect.

The common law derives from ancient custom, which provides a prescriptive wisdom handed down from generation to generation. By contrast, the continental civilian legal tradition informed by Roman law, which was never influential in Britain, has a more formalized and rational structure whereby law is viewed as being specifically made for certain purposes. While the common law is a product of English courts it also forms the basis of the legal system in Northern Ireland. As for Wales, its legal system has always been joined with the English one. Scottish law is heavily influenced by the Roman law tradition, but as regards the relationship between law and politics Scotland has formed part of the United Kingdom since the Act of Union in 1707 (see Chapter 6).

Statute law is law laid down by an Act of Parliament, whereas the common law is a product of custom and the applied reasoning of lawyers during attempts to resolve constructively and rationally disputes between the individual and the state. Statute law has been consciously made for specific purposes whereas the common law has the appearance of law which has existed since 'time immemorial'. In reality the common law is every bit as consciously made by individuals, but the common law tradition seems to include reverence for the antiquity of the law through reliance upon decided cases or 'precedents'. Just as politicians have evolved customary practices and understandings through their experience, lawyers have drawn upon precedents to guide them in the resolution of disputes. In this sense the British constitution based upon practices and traditional manners of behaviour is a product of the common law method of drawing upon precedent and reasoning by analogy. When viewed side by side the parallels between the styles and cultures of political and legal practices can be clearly seen.

An important factor in the make-up of this tradition has been the education of those who belong to it. Politicians and lawyers were overwhelmingly drawn from the same ruling class in society. After a liberal education at the ancient universities young gentlemen joined the close-knit worlds of the Bar, the Civil Service or Parliament. The club style of British government has not been restricted solely to politics but informs the traditions of the law also. Being drawn from the same social background both lawyers and politicians have been educated to understand the subtle relationship between law and politics through unspoken assumptions, and the delicate constitutional balance between their respective roles in the polity. Throughout the nineteenth century the relationship between lawyers and politicians was largely harmonious because, with the small franchise, the political world was largely the reserve of the ruling class. Consequently the mutual respect between law and politics could operate without any friction at all. However, following the extension of the franchise in the Great Reform Act of 1867, the power to expand the size of the state to include wider social purposes was increased. The seeds of potential tension between the law and politics were sown although it took a few generations before the first conflicts came to the surface. One upshot of the dominant tradition was that lawyers were overwhelmingly conservative-minded and opposed to the increasingly collectivist measures of the state. In response to social legislation lawyers would prefer traditional common law rules such as privity of contract and property rights which protected individualistic values. It was against these background assumptions that Dicey articulated his orthodox theory of British constitutionalism and law (Dicey, 1959).

Dicey's work was a remarkably successful and influential attempt to reduce the complex practices and culture of the Constitution to the three basic principles: the sovereignty of Parliament, the rule of law and the practice of constitutional conventions. For Dicey the sovereignty of the Crown in Parliament was the dominant characteristic of British political institutions. This doctrine means that whatever Parliament (consisting of the House of Commons, House of Lords and the Crown) decrees is law. Although it was recognised that this could be used as an instrument for social despotism, at the time it was tacitly assumed that Parliament would observe self-restraint and legislate only upon certain matters. In other words, Dicey's doctrine of sovereignty should be viewed as a Victorian response to the Hobbesian need to recognise a permanent sovereign power in society rather than a means by which the state could democratically identify which social purposes were to be achieved. Just as Hobbes reasoned that if a number of competing wills existed, society would collapse into a state of nature, a war of all against all, Dicey reaffirmed the need for a single, omnipotent, sovereign power and located this within Parliament (Hobbes, 1996). For Dicey it was implicit that Parliament would limit its law-making power and not pass laws which would extend the size and role of the state.

The doctrine of the rule of law was predicated upon certain assumptions. Thus the courts should resolve disputes between individuals and the state by drawing upon the ordinary law of the land; the notion that the state could constructively develop a law to meet the changing needs of public administration was inconsistent with the established constitutional traditions. Dicey also went so far as to state that the idea of the rule of law was inconsistent with an expanded role for public administration and sought to criticize the growth in social legislation by drawing upon the customary practices of the common law.

The third doctrine, of constitutional conventions, concerned those customary practices which politicians use in the business of government. For instance, the practice concerning the formation of a government is a constitutional convention to be found only in the experience of the participants.

The period in which Dicey wrote was characterized by huge social and economic changes which rebounded upon the style of politics. As Dicey's whole conceptual structure rested upon a limited conception of the state it came to be superseded by the growth in the scale and complexity of modern government. The impact of such developments upon constitutional thought can be demonstrated by the change in Dicey's views. When his book was first published in 1885 Dicey celebrated the rule of law to be the true foundation of the British polity and a distinctive feature of British law. However, only thirty years later in an extended introduction to his work Dicey mourned the marked decline in the ancient veneration for the rule of law which he considered to have arisen because of the increase in legislation influenced by socialistic ideas (Dicey, 1915). Dicey's account still provided the dominant framework of the role of law in politics. However, because this model was never designed to resolve the new problems created by the growth of the state, law came to be displaced as a mechanism for controlling and structuring governmental activity. Britain has developed a political constitution in which the law has come to play a marginal role (see Chapter 3). Unlike continental states where a written constitution sets out the purposes of the state and a constitutional court adjudicates on disputes concerning the Constitution, the British polity lacks an articulated set of objectives which the state exists to fulfil. Instead at the heart of the British state there is that mysterious entity, the Crown, which the law has traditionally viewed as non-justiciable (that is, not subject to legal supervision).

While the Victorian tradition of law and politics rested upon certain assumptions as to how governance was to be carried out both through law and politics, the central presupposition concerning the limited size and role of the state was set aside by democratically elected politicians. The response of lawyers, such as Dicey, was to criticize this development as incompatible with the customary values of the law rather than to modify their approach in light of such changes. In other words, with the development towards a more ideological style of politics the old understandings and assumptions between law and politics became strained. Overall the result of this has been the increasingly marginal role of law in politics. However, at times the law wanted to strike back at state intervention, which it viewed as arbitrary social despotism. For instance, in 1925 the House of Lords held that the policy of the Poplar Borough Council to pay a minimum wage to its employees was unlawful as it was guided 'by some eccentric principles of socialistic philanthropy, or by a feminist ambition to secure equality of the sexes in the world of wages' (*Roberts* v. *Hopwood* [1925] AC 578, 594). In regard to social legislation enacted to improve housing conditions the courts placed obstacles in the path of local authorities (Griffith, 1993). With the election of the first Labour government in 1924 the tension between law and politics became more apparent. In order to take on a wider role in the social sphere government had to make more laws. However, as the procedure of legislation was slow and cumbersome, it was necessary to pass legislation which delegated greater powers to government departments. Non-judicial tribunals which offered speed and technical knowledge in the resolution of disputes when compared with the courts also became a common feature at this time. While this method of delegated legislation could help the government to achieve its objectives, it also notably drew attacks from members of the legal profession. The Lord Chief Justice at the time, Lord Hewart, was particularly vocal in his criticism of this practice, viewing it as a new despotism (Hewart, 1929).

In response to Dicey and Hewart other writers argued that the legal profession should respond positively to the change in politics and contribute towards the achievement of the collectivist ends of the state. Jennings argued that Dicey's account of the Constitution was overwhelmingly influenced by his Whig attitudes and could only be understood against these background ideas (Jennings, 1959). Robson argued that the state needed to establish a new set of administrative courts which would positively advance the purposes of the state when resolving disputes between the state and individuals (Robson, 1951). What these writers developed was a perspective which emphasised the functions of public authorities and viewed administrative discretion and delegated legislation as signs of the developing functions of the state and the democratization of society rather than of despotic power. However, this view failed to exert much influence with the majority of the legal profession who preferred to work within the established tradition of law and politics. Lawyers considered politicians to have upset the old set of constitutional checks and balances and to have devalued the wisdom and tradition accumulated over time. From the perspective of politicians elected on a mandate of state intervention, the law seemed a highly conservative-minded profession which had no legitimate role in the obstruction of public functions selected through the process of democratic will-formation.

The essential difference between Dicey and Hewart on the one hand and Robson and Jennings on the other was a political one: what is the proper sphere of state intervention? The discussion between various public lawyers could be viewed as highly specialized and technical debates over politically contentious issues. For Dicey and Hewart the individualism of Victorian England constituted the appropriate scope of the state. For instance, Dicey was positively opposed to the introduction of old-age pensions because it was part of a social and collectivist programme which tended to weaken the moral fibre of the nation. Similarly Dicey was a vigorous opponent of Irish Home Rule because, in his opinion, it would destroy the sovereignty of Parliament.

On the other hand Robson argued that there was no ideal conception of the state which could serve as a permanent model of constitutional development. If the state was developing it was because of basic social and political changes. Rather than clinging to some outmoded conception of what the Constitution should be, Robson argued that lawyers should be alive to such changes and seek to develop new ideas and institutions to deal with contemporary challenges. For Robson to opt for the alternative with Dicey and Hewart was 'to display symptoms of chronic nostalgia which are unlikely to be of much help in solving the problems of our own time' (Robson, 1948: 16–17). On this perspective Dicey's views on law and the Constitution simply became out of date because of the fundamental changes in politics and society.

These views suggest that the connection between law and politics is a dynamic one because the latter is always changing and law needs to respond to such changes. This underlying connection was well captured by C. T. Carr speaking of administrative law:

> [t]hose who dislike the statutory delegation of legislative power or the creation of a non-judicial tribunal will often be those who dislike the policy behind the statute and seek to fight it at every stage. On the one side are those who want to step on the accelerator, on the other those who want to apply the brake. (Carr, 1941: 11)

Perhaps part of the difficulty between law and politics is that lawyers themselves have only frequently alluded to the political nature of public law and have preferred to work within the established boundaries of their discipline and not venture too far into uncharted territory. At the same time students of political science have viewed lawyers as bound up within their own legal world dominated by the artificial reasoning style of the common law and therefore having little to offer the study of politics.

The Development of Judicial Review

During the Second World War the law necessarily took an extremely deferential approach to political decision-making which carried over for a generation. The problem was that the growth in public administration needed to carry out the complex tasks of the welfare state had created a new relationship between the individual and the state. Instead of its nineteenth-century *laissez-faire* roles the state was given distinct purposes to achieve and needed to interfere with the private liberty of individuals in order to achieve them. The increased intervention of the state raised the need for an administrative law to deal with the issues arising from them. As Dicey had denied the very possibility of an administrative law in Britain because it would be fundamentally inconsistent with the common law values which he saw underpinning the rule of law, this prevented the resolution of the problem. Also the courts used the doctrine of parliamentary sovereignty to justify their refusals to intervene in disputes between the individual and the state. The legal system was caught between the aim of providing protection for individuals and that of maintaining faith with orthodox constitutional theory. It had become a victim of the adherence to past and outmoded doctrines and unable to meet constructively the challenge presented to it by the growth in state activity. By the 1950s leading judges were doubtful of the ability of the common law to offer sufficient protection for the individual against the state.

However, throughout the post-war period corresponding forces developed which began to compel the judiciary to rethink their approach. First, the exposure of administrative failings in the Crichel Down affair in 1954, where the government purchased farm land for military purposes but later refused to sell it back to the former owner, caused the judges to voice a loss of confidence in public administrators (Nicolson, 1986). Second, the huge increase in governmental powers created fears that public power was capable of being exercised in an arbitrary manner, especially in regard to widely drafted discretionary powers which were not subject to legislative scrutiny or to the processes of political accountability. Third, the judiciary recognised that Parliament was becoming increasingly incapable of controlling the executive. The doctrine of parliamentary sovereignty was becoming a cover for 'elective dictatorship' (Hailsham, 1978). The judges feared that Parliament was not subjecting the executive to sufficient accountability and thereby allowing the standard of executive action to fall below what could be expected. The concern of the judiciary over the inability of Parliament to hold the executive to account became most pronounced during the last years of Conservative government in the 1990s. The judiciary's response to this was to develop the law relating to judicial review of administrative action.

Judicial review is the procedure by which individuals can ask a court to review the legality of governmental decisions. If an individual is affected by an administrative decision which they think may be unlawful then they have the ability to go to the High Court to seek to have it overturned. Judicial review forms a central aspect of what is today known as public law. The law of judicial review has developed to a stage today where the courts review, public decisions under three tests or grounds of review: first, legality (or lawfulness), which concerns whether the exercise of power was within the limits set for it; second, procedural fairness, which is related to whether the decision-making procedure paid sufficient regard to the individual by affording him a fair hearing; and third, reasonableness which tests whether the decision was irrational or wholly unreasonable. This process has involved the judges engaging in a more intensive review of governmental decision-making. In the words of a leading judge, in this area 'the barely fictional Sir Humphrey Appleby, a servant and scourge of ministers, began to find his power trumped by a more potent constitutional actor, the judiciary' (Sedley, 1994: 41). The work the judiciary has put into judicial review has been considerable. It amounts to a recognition that politicians should observe basic standards when making decisions affecting individuals. The judges have elaborated the values of lawfulness, fairness and reasonableness across a broad range of administrative programmes. However, the judges have not merely been more willing to take a hard look at governmental decisions – they have also extended the range of applicants who have the ability to challenge public decisions. The courts have not restricted challenges to just those individuals directly affected by a decision but have allowed pressure groups to apply for judicial review in certain conditions. Groups such as Greenpeace and Friends of the Earth have been allowed to apply for judicial review not because they have been directly affected by the decision but because they act for a body of people concerned that public decisions are legal.

In this way the judges have been responding to claims that Parliament can no longer offer an effective means of holding politicians to account, and therefore the scope of legal accountability has been expanded. In a high-profile case concerning the ability of the Home Secretary to introduce a new scheme for calculating the amount of compensation to be awarded to victims of crime Lord Mustill expressed these concerns:

> In recent years . . . the employment in practice of . . . specifically parliamentary remedies [of redress against the executive] . . . has on occasion been perceived as falling short, and sometimes well short, of what was needed to bring the performance of the executive into line with the law. . . . To avoid a vacuum in which the citizen would be left without protection against a misuse of executive powers the courts have had no option but to occupy the dead ground in a manner, and in areas of public life, which could not have been foreseen thirty years ago. (*R.* v. *Secretary of State for the*

Home Department ex parte Fire Brigades Union [1995] 2 WLR 464, 488)

As this quotation suggests, areas of politics and administration have been opened up to judicial scrutiny which only twenty or thirty years ago were thought to be the exclusive preserve of politicians and civil servants. The judges for their part view this development as nothing short of a refashioning of the British constitution. However, opinions in the political and media worlds have criticized the judges for interfering too far in political issues and not maintaining the traditional deference and respect they should show for politicians. Certainly the use of judicial review has brought judges into direct conflict with politicians (Le Sueur, 1996; Rozenberg, 1997). But have the judges been seeking to overrule politicians just because they disagree with their policies, or because they feel obliged to uphold basic minimum standards in a polity where traditional forms of accountability such as Parliament are weak?

By its very name judicial review suggests that the courts do not undertake an appeal on the merits of the administrative decision under review. Courts will overrule a decision only when it is unlawful, when the decision-making process was unfair or when it was so unreasonable that no reasonable authority could every have arrived at it. While in cases decided earlier this century judges may have been quite hostile to government policies, in modern Britain the state is an established feature of life, so that many of the judges hearing cases challenging administrative decisions have actually spent considerable time advising the government and local authorities before they became judges. Thus the long-term policy of the courts has not been to set up a substitute form of government but to improve the quality of the present one as well as remembering that while judicial review is a powerful weapon in their hands, it has limits which must be observed. For instance, in the case concerning the removal of social security benefits for asylum-seekers by the Major government in 1995, the Court of Appeal held that the Government could only achieve this 'sorry state of affairs' by an Act of Parliament and not by delegated legislation. This decision was subsequently reversed by Parliament in the Asylum and Immigration Act 1996, although asylum-seekers may ask local authorities for some assistance. The Court of Appeal clearly considered that the government was not treating people seeking asylum fairly because their exclusion from receiving benefits placed them in a dilemma between applying for asylum in Britain and living in destitution or remaining in their home country and being persecuted for their beliefs. This case shows how the courts view their role as upholding minimum values or standards in protecting people against government decisions and also how if the government is determined to achieve its objectives it can usually push legislation through Parliament.

While the judges have been commended by some for protecting the public against abuses of power by the government they have also been criticized by others for not appreciating the practicalities of how government operates and for imposing unreasonable burdens upon administrators. Consequently some commentators have stated that judicial review ought to be strictly limited. However, much of the law has been expressly sanctioned by Parliament. For instance, if a court defines the limits of a statutory power possessed by a public authority it is only enforcing the will of Parliament. Furthermore, while the implementation of the Human Rights Act 1998, considered below, will add another ground of judicial review, namely the breach of fundamental human rights, it has in fact been passed by Parliament.

Perhaps the remarkable characteristic of the extension of judicial review is that the judges have largely sought to present their achievement as the necessary consequence of law established for centuries. For instance, Sedley states that

> [m]uch of the apparent growth in the grounds of judicial review has been a discovery of long-established principles. But what has changed, without doubt, is the readiness of the courts to take tenable challenges seriously and to exact high standards of fairness and legality in public administration. (Sedley, 1997: 11)

Courts, unlike politicians, cannot directly appeal to politics and therefore must use legal fictions like 'the justice of the common law' to justify their role in judicial review. A further reason why the courts have developed the law by drawing upon old undeveloped law is that they do not have the benefit of a written constitution. Unlike the US Supreme Court and the Constitutional courts of continental Europe, British courts do not have a written text which can be used to justify the exercise of judicial review. The courts have had to adopt a slow, incremental approach whereby they build upon and develop established principles over time without offending the democratic arm of government. When this fact is taken into account, the development of judicial review by the British courts seems a remarkably bold project which the courts are continually refining.

The Politics of the Judiciary

Legal ideology presents the processes of law as formal, objective and value-neutral with everybody treated equally and without prejudice. In particular, judges jealously guard their much-prized independence from political influence as a fundamental aspect of the rule of law. While some lawyers may still swallow these myths (other lawyers such as Griffith have refused to do so for a long time), for a political observer this is impossible. The processes of legal development are inextricably bound up with the implicit political views of the participants. On a basic level this may mean the party-political views of the judges, most clearly demonstrated in the Poplar Borough Council case of *Roberts* v. *Hopwood* referred to above. The argument that the judiciary is a largely conservative-minded group of people has long been trailed by some academic lawyers (Griffith, 1997).

In the late 1990s a demonstration of the political affiliations of judges was presented by the case of General Pinochet. The original decision of the House of Lords that the Home Secretary had the power to extradite the former Chilean dictator to Spain to face charges of genocide was later overruled because of the appearance of bias. One of the Law Lords, Lord Hoffman, who had voted in favour of the decision, had been associated with Amnesty International which had campaigned for the trial of Pinochet and had also made representations to the House of Lords in the case. Other Law Lords later ruled that Lord Hoffman was disqualified from hearing the original case because of his association with the human rights group Amnesty International. While Hoffman may not have allowed this association to have influenced his decision, the very appearance of bias aroused suspicion and therefore damaged the credibility of the English legal system in a very high-profile case. This case demonstrates that while some judges have more liberal attitudes than their predecessors, the law requires high standards to ensure that there is no question of any impropriety.

While direct political bias in judicial decision-making is certainly not unknown, neither is it particularly frequent. Political influence is more likely to be of a more subtle kind. For instance, consider the 'political' issues raised by the following questions. What definition should be given to the right to free speech? Should a judgment favour the free exchange of ideas in a modern democratic society or should it protect the need for official secrecy? How should concepts such as 'rights', 'equality' or 'liberty' be defined? Should they reflect the principles of justice advocated by Rawls (1972) or by a New Right market philosophy as exemplified by Nozick (1974)? Which theory best fits the type of society which exists in Britain? What is liberty? Is it a negative concept which requires the absence of all restraints or is it a positive concept which requires the state to intervene actively in areas of social life (Berlin, 1969)?

The resolution of such questions raises political issues in the widest sense upon which deep political and philosophical disagreement exists and for which there is no 'objective' or 'neutral' answer. On this view every decision by a judge in a public law dispute is underpinned by some implicit background political theory. Whether the judge consciously intends to promote some political viewpoint or not, the decision will require coming down in favour of one set of values over another. For instance, in a dispute over where to place a bypass the judge will not be able to substitute his opinion for that of the Minister for Transport but the values at stake here (the need for an effective transport system against the protection of the environment) will influence the decision taken. Should the Minister consult those affected more extensively before deciding where to place the bypass? If so, then the judge will be favouring the values of environmental protection by requiring greater democratic involvement in such decisions. Public law concerns the role of law in politics, and as legal decisions take place within a political context judges will inevitably be influenced by the underlying political issues at stake. The processes of public law are inevitably tangled up with political issues and can only be understood as such.

A much-criticized decision by the House of Lords demonstrates how judges can easily find themselves caught up in such issues which they are ill-prepared to handle (*Bromley London Borough Council v. Greater London Council* [1982] 1 AC 768). In 1981 the Labour-led former Greater London Council (GLC) adopted a 'Fare's Fair' policy whereby the local authorities in London would have to pay a greater amount in rates in order to reduce the costs of public transport by 25 per cent. This policy was challenged by the Conservative-led borough of Bromley as unlawful. The relevant Act of Parliament stated that the duty of the GLC was to provide 'integrated, efficient and economic transport facilities'. However, what did 'economic' mean? Did it mean that the transport system should be run on 'business principles' in order to make a profit or did it mean 'making the most effective use of resources in the context of an integrated system'? If the first definition was adopted then the policy would be unlawful because the purpose of the supplementary rate was to subsidize public transport and not to increase profit. Alternatively, the second definition was more favourable to the GLC because it took account of the efficient use of resources within the context of the whole system of public transport. A majority of the Law Lords found that the obligation on the GLC was to run the transport on ordinary business principles and the policy breached this because of the reduction in fairs.

At the time the decision aroused considerable political controversy and the Law Lords were criticized for their bias against the policy of the GLC. However, can it realistically be contended that the case did not raise political issues in a wider sense? The precise definition given to the word 'economic' surely presented the Law Lords with a choice between different competing political theories as to public expenditure and taxation. Not surprisingly, some commentators viewed the decision as a case where the judges were prepared to substitute their view of the public interest for that of a democratically elected body and then hide this overtly political decision under a cover of legal formalism and objectivity (Griffith, 1997).

Fusion of Powers

One consequence of the profound changes in governmental structures over the last century has been that traditional constitutional doctrines have turned into clichés and no longer seem to accurately represent reality. This is clearly demonstrated in relation to the doctrine of the separation of powers and the role of the Lord Chancellor, which provides that the three forms of power in the state – legislative, executive and judicial – should be exercised by separate personnel. It was thought that by so dividing the exercise of power each would hold the other to account. However, this was always a formal cover for the reality of government. Indeed that shrewd political commentator on the nineteenth-century constitution Walter Bagehot identified the 'close union, the nearly complete fusion, of the executive and legislative powers' as the efficient secret of the Constitution (Bagehot,

1963: 65). It is indicative of the informal processes of the British constitution that the separation of powers should be breached by the position of the Lord Chancellor. The Lord Chancellor is a member of the Cabinet and heads his own department, the Lord Chancellor's Department. In this role he exercises considerable executive power concerning the administration of justice. At the same time, the Lord Chancellor is the head of the judiciary in England and Wales but not Scotland (where the Lord President holds that office) and acts as a judge when he sits as a Law Lord on the Judicial Committee of the House of Lords. The Lord Chancellor also has considerable power 'behind the scenes', for instance in recommending certain lawyers for promotion to the bench.

The tension in the varied roles of the office of Lord Chancellor is that the holder may compromise the need to preserve the independence of the judiciary with his role as a spokesman for the government. The tension between a government in pursuit of economy and judges in pursuit of justice has been reflected in the office of Lord Chancellor and criticism has been voiced from close quarters. Recently, a Law Lord, Lord Steyn, has argued that 'the proposition that a Cabinet minister must be head of our judiciary in England is no longer sustainable on either constitutional or pragmatic grounds' (Steyn, 1997: 91).

The legal implications of devolution can be briefly mentioned here. The setting up of a Scottish Parliament and assemblies in Wales and Northern Ireland will create alternative bases of power to the Westminster Parliament. The extent of devolved power is limited through the Acts of Parliament which have set out the obligations and restrictions upon the new institutions. In order to effect the division of legislative power between the Westminster Parliament and the new institutions, the courts will inevitably be called upon to adjudicate between competing claims of legislative competences. The courts are going to have to enter into constitutional adjudication of this kind because resort to the law may be the only way of arriving at a division of power which is acceptable to both national and regional levels of government. Rather than bowing down at the altar of parliamentary sovereignty, the courts will have to get involved directly in adjudicating upon claims of constitutional power. The forces unleashed by devolution will therefore contribute further towards the accommodation of greater legal involvement in political processes. The Judicial Committee of the Privy Council, being the Law Lords who sit in the House of Lords under a different name, will effectively have to act as a constitutional court deciding upon competing claims between the regional assemblies and Westminster.

The Impact of EC Law

The impact of EC law on the relationship between law and politics in Britain has been profound. The first point to note is that the EU is informed by constitutional traditions and legal ideas that differ from the British constitution. In contrast with the unwritten informal nature of the British constitution, the Treaties underpinning the EU specify the purposes for which it exists. Second, the European Court of Justice (ECJ) sees its role as actively contributing to the tasks of European integration. A principal objective of the ECJ has been to ensure the effectiveness of EC law. This is an important point. The EU has various means of ensuring that its objectives are achieved and has at its disposal various methods of translating its political decisions into law. The ECJ has held that certain provisions of the Treaties themselves give enforceable rights to individuals. For instance the Treaty provisions ensuring free movement of goods are enforceable by individuals before the national courts of the member states because the ECJ has held that such provisions have direct effect. The use of this concept of directly enforceable rights in EC law has two consequences. First, the national courts of the member state come to play an important role in ensuring the effectiveness of EC law and therefore the purposes of European integration. Second, the direct effectiveness of such provisions means that an individual does not have to wait until the member state transposes the provisions into national law; they are effective solely because of their status in EC law. This gives the EU a unique position compared with other international organizations, because it alone confers upon the citizens of its member countries the ability to protect their rights, and the courts of each member state are under a duty to ensure the effective protection of such rights. Furthermore, the EU has a law-making power under the Treaties which enables it to make various kinds of legal instruments known as regulations, directives and decisions which can also have direct effectiveness in certain circumstances.

Perhaps the greatest psychological impact of EC law has been that Acts of Parliament are no longer sovereign but can be overruled if they incompatible with European laws. European law has therefore dramatically changed one of the main characteristics of the British tradition of law and politics. British courts have been compelled to adopt a constitutional role in determining the legality of Acts of Parliament, something which they have refrained from doing since the seventeenth century.

The role of the British courts operating under EC law has made other demands beyond their more typically deferential approach under British law. For instance, European law requires the courts to go beyond a merely literal approach to reading statutes and adopt a purposive interpretation which may require them to add words to the statutory text. The British courts are also required to operate doctrines under European law such as the principle of compensation for unlawful administrative action which does not find an equivalent in British law. Large sums of money can be tied up in such litigation, making politicians extremely concerned about the outcome of cases. This has required changes not only in the approach of the judiciary but in the mind-set of politicians also.

The Human Rights Act 1998

The Members of the Council of Europe affirmed the European Convention on Human Rights in 1950. Drafted in the aftermath of the Second World War, the Convention sought to set out basic minimum conditions of liberal democracy (Harris *et al.*, 1995; Jacobs and White, 1996). The ECHR sets out rights which individuals can claim, if necessary, before the European Court of Human Rights. (The distinction between the ECJ sitting in Luxembourg which is concerned with EC law and the European Court of Human Rights in Strasbourg which is concerned with violations of the ECHR is an important one which is frequently overlooked by the British press and even some politicians.) The ECHR provides for the right to life, prohibitions against torture, slavery and forced labour, rights to liberty and security, to a fair trial, to respect for private and family life. The convention also provides for the freedoms of thought, conscience and religion, expression, assembly and association. While the convention provides for the existence of such rights they are not absolute. For instance, article 10 states that everyone has the right to freedom of expression but continues to state that since this right carries with it duties and responsibilities, it may be subject to such restrictions as are necessary in a democratic society in the interests of national security, public safety, for the prevention of disorder or crime, the protection of health, morals, the rights of others and the independence of the judiciary. The European Court of Human Rights has developed a considerable amount of case-law in adjudicating upon the extent of the convention rights and whether any limitations are justified.

The status afforded to the ECHR in British law has changed remarkably since its inception. To begin with the ECHR had the same status as any other unincorporated Treaty. As Parliament is sovereign and the Convention was not ratified by Parliament the courts were under no obligation to give effect to the rights under it. This suited British lawyers. According to the then Lord Chancellor, Lord Jowitt, Britain wanted nothing to do with what he described as 'some half-baked scheme to be administered by some unknown court'. It was only in 1965 that the government allowed individuals to take cases to the European Court of Human Rights, a long process which can take up to seven years and for which legal aid is unavailable. However, the ECHR gained greater prominence because of the number of judgments against the UK government (Farran, 1996). Up to the end of 1996 the European Court of Human Rights had ruled on 71 cases involving Britain and found some breach of the ECHR in 44 of them. In particular the Conservative government of the 1980s and 1990s was found to be in breach of the ECHR on several occasions. For instance, the shooting dead of IRA suspects by the SAS on Gibraltar in 1988 was found to be in breach of the right to life. This judgment and others clearly angered members of the Conservative government and it was rumoured that it was considering suspending the right of individuals to take cases to the European Court of Human Rights. During the same period some British judges were suggesting that the common law should be developed in order to give effect to the same rights which existed under the ECHR (Laws, 1993; Hunt, 1997). The situation seemed to be developing that the judiciary were becoming impatient with the demands of a government which had been in power for over a decade. The tension here was caused by an unelected judiciary attempting to restrain a government which, in the opinion of at least some judges, was evading full accountability for its actions. In any event the tension was left unresolved by the election of the Labour government in May 1997 which promised to incorporate the ECHR into domestic law. The Blair Government issued the White Paper *Rights Brought Home* six months after it took office (Home Office, 1997) and Parliament subsequently enacted the Human Rights Act 1998.

The format of the incorporation of the ECHR taken by the Human Rights Act 1998 is a compromise between the British constitutional tradition of parliamentary sovereignty and the desire to give further effect to the rights under the ECHR. The Act places the British courts under a duty so far as it is possible to do so to give effect to British laws in a way which is compatible with the rights under the ECHR. All British laws whether in the form of ordinary common law rules or in Acts of Parliament have to be interpreted, if possible, in the light of the rights granted under the ECHR. For instance, under section 18 of the Public Order Act 1986 it is an offence to use threatening, abusive or insulting words or material and intend thereby to stir up racial hatred. If a court is dealing with a prosecution under this section it will be under a duty to interpret the offence so in light of the rights guaranteed under the ECHR; in this case article 10 regarding freedom of speech will be particularly important. However, if it is not possible for the courts to interpret Acts of Parliament in line with those rights then the courts cannot declare that Act to be unlawful but can issue a 'declaration of incompatibility' to the effect that the Act is not compliant with the ECHR. This does not affect the legality of the Act because Parliament still retains the sovereignty to state what the law is. Although a declaration of incompatibility will not change the law it will be an important statement and might prompt the government to change the offending Act of Parliament. The government has changed the procedure for amending Acts of Parliament to make it easier for Parliament to comply with a declaration of incompatibility. However, the Human Rights Act will still allow the government to breach fundamental rights by means of an Act of Parliament and not provide an effective remedy if it chooses to do so. While the Human Rights Act seeks to establish a balance between sovereignty and the protection of fundamental rights, it may be argued that it still allows Parliament, controlled by the government, considerable ability to infringe fundamental rights if it wishes to do so. On the other hand, the Act gives the courts the power to declare lesser forms of law such as delegated legislation to be unlawful if they are incompatible with the Convention rights.

A further issue concerning the protection of Convention rights is whether the British judiciary will be able adequately to fulfil the different role which the Human Rights Act demands of them. Adjudication under the ECHR requires courts to adopt a different approach from that of determining what a specific rule of law means to realising certain values in often highly contentious situations.

Determining the extent of a right under the ECHR will require judges to address more openly than before questions which can only be resolved by taking certain political and philosophical positions regarding the relationship between the individual and the state. While the Human Rights Act 1998 does not attempt full incorporation of the ECHR it provides a strong force for further politicization of the judiciary.

Conclusion

Over the last century social and economic changes in Britain have impacted upon both law and politics and the relationship between the two. The style of politics has become more ideological and rationalistic. The scale of state intervention has transformed our understanding of what the state exists for and what it can successfully achieve. As society has become more complex and differentiated so have the demands placed upon politics and law. The increase in public administration has meant that more decisions are taken by civil servants in government departments and Parliament has become increasingly unable to exercise sufficient oversight or accountability. To these basic changes in the mode of governance has been added the shift towards greater regulation (Loughlin and Scott, 1997). However, the further step of constructing an appropriate new relationship between law and politics has not been taken.

The dominant British tradition of law and politics remains rooted in the informal approach. One upshot of this inheritance is that Britain does not have a coherent and fully developed system of administrative law, and indeed the role of law in public administration is still largely marginal. The disadvantage of this has been that law can provide little assistance with regard to the structuring, evaluating and guiding of public administration. However, contemporary developments present major challenges to the dominant tradition. The growth in judicial review seems likely to continue. The impact of EC law is constantly increasing. Parliament is no longer sovereign but is limited by EC law. The Human Rights Act 1998 has incorporated the ECHR in British law. The government's programme of constitutional reform is being enacted (Brazier, 1998). These are powerful forces towards the greater judicialization of politics; politics is becoming subject to greater legal controls.

Such challenges bring risks and uncertainty to the law. Can the law provide an appropriate framework in which to manage the greater legalization of politics? Can it develop a juridical response which can contribute to good government? The risk is not that politics is becoming more judicialized but that the style of judicialization may not be appropriate to the tasks and functions of contemporary government. In order to construct an appropriate relationship between law and politics, lawyers should recognise that politics enables the communication of ideas within the polity and that the legitimacy of state action is rooted in democratic will-formation. Any contribution the law can make is an understanding of the values and objectives which are selected by politicians. The law should not act as an independent force against political purposes but should accept such purposes as legitimate and seek means of effectively contributing towards them and affording individuals sufficient protection in the process.

8
Order and Discipline

ROBERT REINER

Order and discipline are among the most vexed issues in social and political theory. How can complex, divided and rapidly changing modern societies, which – since the Enlightenment at least – have increasingly questioned authority of all kinds, possibly survive? This problem is usually code for conservative anxiety about the breakdown of order. But there is also a long tradition of radical, liberal and anarchist theory with the opposite concern, in which order *is* the problem (Wrong, 1994).

The British have long been regarded as peculiar in relation to order, although the character of this supposed distinctiveness has shifted. In the eighteenth century the British were often depicted as an 'ungovernable people' (Brewer and Styles, 1980). Then, during the mid-Victorian period, the national image became one of unflappable self-discipline and orderliness in public and everyday life. This was symbolized by institutions like the queue, or the imperturbably stiff-upper-lipped gentleman. In the last thirty years, however, the image has again shifted, and a succession of law-and-order panics, from football hooligans to urban and then rural rioters, has stimulated endless Jeremiahs to agonise about vanished virtues.

This chapter considers first the thorny problem of defining order. It then surveys the historical trends in crime and disorder in Britain. It argues that there have been several long-term cycles in lawlessness and disorder over the last five hundred years, with corresponding changes in modes of control, reflecting broader trends in political economy and culture. The chapter then looks at the main institutions of social control and their effectiveness. It suggests that the economy is of at least equal importance for order and discipline as formal or informal control processes such as policing, punishment, or education. The conclusion draws out the fundamental aspects of order and discipline in the UK, and discusses the current vexed state of order and control. At the start of the twenty-first century the UK is undergoing a profound change in the social order, comparable to those watersheds which generated major transformations of crime, control and discipline in the past. Most analysts have assumed that all societies require a high level of order and discipline, maintained by a varying blend of coercive and ideological processes of power. However in late modernity it may be that a 'good enough' level of order can be maintained by the mundane pressures for minimal cooperation and conformity generated by a complex global division of labour. Whether this will suffice to avert the catastrophic risks which have been manufactured by modernity itself (Beck, 1992; Giddens, 1994), or be compatible with any notions of social justice, remains a moot point.

What is Order?

Order is notoriously hard to define. Most attempts involve both circularity and conservatism. 'Order' may be hard to pinpoint, but all right-thinking people know when it's not there. Order itself cannot be perceived, but disorder is manifested in all-too-tangible ways: broken windows, broken bodies, broken expectations. The central problem is that one person's order is often another person's oppression. The cosily consensual connotations of order as harmony and regularity beg the nagging questions 'whose law, what order?'. Order is intimately related to the social, political and legal power to define 'normality', and what counts as a threat to it. We can distinguish at least four different dimensions of order: legal, political, social, and what I shall call 'degree zero' order.

Legal Order

During the past sixty years a particular set of criminal offences have become designated as violations of 'public order'. The terminology itself only entered legal discourse in 1936, with the passage of the first Public Order Act. Before that the more overtly political connotations of 'public order' had been shrouded in a more euphemistic discourse of 'keeping the peace' through 'the rule of law' (Townshend, 1993: 4–5).

The formal specification of public order offences is evidently less objective than most other areas of criminal law. The behaviours they encompass are vaguely worded, and often involve explicitly subjective, inchoate and tautologous elements (Lacey and Wells, 1998: ch. 2). In effect they provide all-purpose resources for legal authorities, above all the police and prosecutors, to criminalize a wide array of actions at their virtually unfettered discretion. Although 'law and order' are eternally wedded in popular discourse, they are a very odd couple indeed. Order implies the possibility of a vast and amorphous array of behaviours which might threaten it, not the specified prohibitions of criminal law.

Public order is usually conceptualized as a sub-category of criminal law in legal texts, but the relationship is really the reverse. The set of substantive criminal laws represents a variety of specific behaviours which those with the power to make law have over the centuries designated as liable to prosecution (Lacey and Wells, 1998: ch. 1). 'Public order' offences are the residual category: a graduated hierarchy of powers subjecting to legal sanctions behaviour perceived as threatening or harmful by law enforcement agents or those with the social power to enlist their support. Public order offences run the gamut from low-level nuisances – such as the 'anti-social behaviour' newly criminalized in the Blair government's Crime and Disorder Act 1999 – to large-scale conflicts with a manifest political dimension. Even 'riot', the most serious public order offence, is described partly in vague and subjective terms. From the early eighteenth century to the present, the essence of the offence has been collective behaviour 'such as would cause a person of reasonable firmness present at the scene to fear for his personal safety' (Public Order Act 1986 s. 1).

The legal definition of 'order' empowers those with the social capacity and credibility to make their anxieties appear 'reasonable' to enlist the sanctioning capacities of the criminal justice process against others whose behaviour they experience as threatening, even when it does not fall under the more specifically designated categories of substantive criminal law such as theft or homicide. Legal conceptions of order are clearly linked to political and social control, behind the apparently neutral discourse of common sense.

Political Order

The preservation of a particular set of political institutions is often what is meant by the maintenance of order. In the context of liberal democracies this supposedly means not the protection of specific incumbents of political office, but of the overall system for political decision-making. The Security Service Act 1989, for example, placed MI5 on a statutory basis for the first time, charged with 'the protection of national security and, in particular, its protection against threats from espionage, terrorism and sabotage, from the activities of agents of foreign powers and from actions intended to overthrow or undermine parliamentary democracy by political, industrial or violent means.'

Protection of the political order rather than a partisan interest within it is often a very fine distinction. A long history of scandals – from the notorious Zinoviev letter plot which helped to destroy the first Labour government's re-election prospects in 1924 to the *Spycatcher* revelations about security service attempts to destabilize the Wilson Labour government in the mid-1970s (Wright, 1987) – demonstrates a propensity to elide the interests of national security and of the Conservative Party. This is not limited to the explicitly political branches of policing. During the 1984–5 miners' strike, for example, the 'neutral' preservation of order by the police blended into the accomplishment of the Conservative government's industrial strategy (Reiner, 1991: 8).

Social Order

Many aspects of social structure have been seen from particular points of view as coterminous with social order *per se*. These include modes of economic organization, forms of social hierarchy, patterns of family life and sexuality, or particular religious faiths.

The preservation of such patterns is often regarded as equivalent to the protection of social order *per se*. Debates about such issues are the stuff of political and social controversy in democracies, sometimes amounting to veritable culture wars. The disciplinary processes of education and informal social control are largely concerned with the reproduction of the social patterns regarded as 'normal', such as the policing of particular forms of family life (Donzelot, 1980). Formal social control agencies only become involved in the protection of such patterns when they are criminalized.

'Degree Zero' Order

Lurking behind most discussions of order is the spectre of social meltdown: failure to maintain 'degree zero' order – the minimal survival conditions of any social existence at all. A vivid illustration is provided by Dahrendorf's portrayal of Berlin in April 1945 in the hiatus between the collapse of the Nazi regime and the Soviet authorities seizing control. 'Suddenly, it became clear that there was no authority left, none at all' (Dahrendorf, 1985: 1). It is this nightmare vision of degree zero order, where nothing can be relied upon, everyone and everything is completely unpredictable, which gives plausibility to the common view that some order, however oppressive, must be better than none.

It can be debated whether a condition of absolute disorder or disorganization is in fact possible. 'Sociologists are generally ill-disposed to the term, believing it connotes a want of understanding and perception on the part of the observer . . . They would hold that, even in Beirut, Bosnia, or Burundi at their most devastated, people were able to sustain a measure of organization within disorganization' (Rock, 1997: 238).

Nonetheless, in the contemporary world it seems there are increasingly common cases of almost complete social breakdown. In many places 'lawlessness and crime have so destroyed the social fabric that the State itself has withdrawn' (Cohen, 1997: 234), or agents of the state themselves routinely engage in terrorist atrocities. Traditional distinctions between crime, disorder and war are eroded as 'low intensity warfare runs into high intensity crime' (Cohen, 1997: 243). Hobsbawm speaks of a new 'barbarism' involving

> the collapse of political order as represented by functioning states – *any* effective state which stands watch against the descent into Hobbesian anarchy – and the crumbling of the old frameworks of social relations over a large part of the world – *any* framework which stands guard against Durkheimian anomie. (Hobsbawm, 1994: 53)

Ambiguities of Order

Degree zero order – where almost any order would be generally preferable – is increasingly a possibility in some parts of the world. Nonetheless, most societies, including contemporary Britain, are characterized by more ambiguous forms of order, combining consensual and conflictual elements.

Most social and political orders rest on a combination of organized cooperation that secures the survival of the population, together with a hierarchical distribution of power and advantage from which some benefit more than others. The state and its disciplinary agencies simultaneously reproduce the conditions of existence of any coordinated life at all, and the hierarchically structured form it typically takes. 'Parking tickets *and* class repression' are simultaneously emblematic of most policing systems (Marenin, 1983).

In Britain as elsewhere, order is maintained to varying extents by the operation of power, which reproduces the conditions of social survival *and* of conflict. Three fundamental sources of power can be distinguished: coercive, ideological and utilitarian (that is, economic or organizational) (Weber, 1964; Mann, 1986: ch. 1; Mann, 1993: chs. 1, 2). Power may be exercised by the manipulation of physical force, by persuading others of the rightness of particular forms of behaviour, or by providing practical advantages for their cooperation.

Waves of Order

Crime and disorder are harder to measure than most social phenomena, above all because of their essentially contested character. Crimes and disorderly behaviour do not simply occur and leave records. They are socially constructed in conflict between those who designate particular behaviours as 'criminal' or 'disorderly' and those who perpetrate them. Crime and disorder are inherently political phenomena: they depend upon the power of some to criminalize – label and punish – the activities of others. A further problem in assessing *trends* in crime and disorder is the perennially pessimistic flavour of middle-aged, middle-brow opinion. As Pearson's history of 'respectable fears' demonstrates (Pearson, 1983), each generation tends to view its successor as lacking the standards of morality it had, and worries about a shocking growth of deviance and disorder. Since the early nineteenth century official statistics have given an apparently firm foundation to the measurement of trends in crime and disorder. However, these statistics are bedevilled by the so-called 'dark figure' of unrecorded crime (Reiner, 1996; Maguire, 1997). It has long been recognised that many crimes never come to official attention of any kind. It is only in the last three decades that criminologists have been able to get some understanding of the processes which underlie the transition of offences from the unrecorded 'dark figure' to the official statistics. This is mainly through the development of victim surveys (notably the British Crime Surveys conducted regularly by the Home Office since 1982), self-report studies of offenders, and observational studies of how the police and other criminal justice agents exercise their discretion in dealing with offences. Unfortunately for the validity of the official crime statistics, we now know that the majority of offences do *not* get recorded. This all makes the interpretation of trends in crime and disorder extremely problematic. When statistics go up or down it is never possible to know with certainty whether this reflects a change in offending behaviour, recording practices, or both.

Trends in Order in Britain

The long-term fluctuations in crime in Britain seem to be related to wider patterns of social dislocation or instability. This is most plausibly due both to the changing behaviour of people labelled as criminal *and* to shifting cultural sensibilities and modes of control. A comprehensive review of research on crime in early modern England concludes there was an overall trajectory of long-term rise followed by stabilization and then decline in the two centuries between 1550 and 1750. Prosecution and punishment records point to increasing criminalization, in the century from the late Elizabethan period up to the Constitutional settlement of the late seventeenth century, but diminishing thereafter. 'England was a far more stable country in the early eighteenth century than it was in the late sixteenth' (Sharpe, 1984: 70–1). Despite this, eighteenth-century England experienced several 'moral panics' about crime and disorder, producing the Black Act of 1723 and its multiplication of capital offences related to protecting game in the royal forests, as well as the other legislation producing the notorious 'Bloody Code' of the eighteenth century (Thompson, 1975).

The pattern of change in crime and disorder from the late eighteenth to the mid-twentieth century is broadly curvilinear, mirroring the trend in the early modern period. Crime, especially property crime, increased steadily in the late eighteenth century, accelerating in the early 1800s up to the 1850s. Thereafter, the overall extent of crime, particularly for most forms of theft and violence, levels out and then declines up to the First World War (Gatrell, 1980; Gurr, 1981; Emsley, 1996b: ch. 2; Emsley, 1997: 58–61). In the inter-war years there began a steady rise in recorded crime, which was halted during the Second World War. Since the mid-1950s there has been an almost continuous rise in recorded crime (Reiner, 1996; Maguire, 1997).

Trends in political and industrial disorder follow a similar U-shaped trajectory, in terms of frequency, scale, and the levels and forms of violence used by protesters or the state. The first half of the nineteenth century was a period of escalating political and industrial conflict, at times viewed by many (with hope or fear) as heralding a revolutionary transformation of the social order. Gradually during the later nineteenth century a process of institutionalization and regularization of conflict began, although many violent struggles continued to occur. The years immediately before and after the First World War in particular witnessed intensified industrial and political turmoil and violence (Morgan, 1987; Weinberger, 1991). The inter-war years saw numerous industrial and political conflicts, with the long years of depression (in many parts of the country from the early 1920s) and the rise of fascism. However, by comparison with other European countries (most of which experienced civil war, revolutions, or near-revolutions, of both left and right) England was remarkable for its low levels of violence in political conflict (Stevenson and Cook, 1977). After the Second World War there was a quarter of a century of remarkably low levels of political and industrial conflict or disorder. Even when political protest developed during the 1960s, around the issues of nuclear disarmament and the Vietnam War, the conduct of demonstrators and the police were celebrated as demon-strating the 'conquest of violence' (Critchley, 1970). Looking at the period from the mid-nineteenth to the mid-twentieth century as a whole it was possible to represent the trajectory of disorder and political or industrial conflict as moving from a war to a sporting model (Geary, 1985). This has altered fundamentally since the mid-1970s. Industrial, political and other forms of conflict intensified, and were accompanied by increasing levels of violence by and against the police. Police tactics were visibly and controversially militarized, although attempts were made to legitimate this as a proportionate response to the increasing violence they faced (Scarman, 1981; Waddington, 1990, 1994; Jefferson, 1990; Waddington, 1993; Critch-er and Waddington, 1996).

Formal and Informal Control

Social control is a complex and much debated concept (Hudson, 1997; Sumner, 1997). Originating in American conservative function-alist sociology early in the twentieth century, the term was adopted by radical criminology in the late 1960s, reversing the political connota-tions (Cohen and Scull, 1983; Cohen, 1985). *Formal* control processes are those which have a manifest objective of social control: criminal law and justice, policing, penality. They can be contrasted with *informal* control processes, which perform control functions although this is not their overt purpose: family, education, religion, mass media, the economy, the interactions of everyday life (gossip, ridicule, ostracism, praise).

Formal Social Control

Policing is a much broader concept than its specialized institutional form, the police (Reiner, 1997a). *Policing* is a set of processes with specific social functions, which are arguably a prerequisite of any social order. The *police* as a specialized institution are primarily a phenomenon of modern societies. In late modernity there appears to be occurring a dispersion of the policing function, with other institutions and processes (notably the private sector and citizen volunteers) increasingly supplementing or displacing the specialized police of the state (Shearing and Stenning, 1983; Johnston, 1992; Hoogenboom, 1991; Newburn and Jones, 1998).

The establishment of the British police in the nineteenth century was a fiercely controversial and bitterly contested development (Reiner, 1992: ch. 1). During the eighteenth century a variety of voices began to call for the establishment of a full-time, professional state-financed police. Pitt's abortive 1785 Police Bill aimed to establish such a force, in the wake of the Gordon Riots. This Bill, like several other attempts in the next four decades, was defeated by a host of opposition in Parliament, reflecting wider divisions of interest and ideology. In the nineteenth century Peel and the other champions of the police countered by constructing a model which was distanced as far as possible from reviled European forces. They emphasized its local, unmilitary, apolitical, civilian character, and its roots in the common law and ancient (largely mythical) traditions of communal self-policing. It was the police of the people, not the state. Once established in 1829 the police won round most middle- and upper-class opinion fairly rapidly. Working-class opposition continued to be expressed through anti-police violence and rioting as the 'plague of blue locusts' spread through the country in the 1840s and 1850s (Storch, 1975). However, the strategy pioneered by Peel of representing the police as embodiments of impartial, minimal-force discipline, itself subject to strict legal regulation, began to win gradual acceptance further down the class structure (Reiner, 1992: ch. 2).

A key facet of British police ideology, crucial to their legitimation, has been that they represent the community not the government, and are 'the most accountable and therefore the most acceptable police in the world' (Mark, 1977: 56). This is supposedly embodied in the common law doctrine of constabulary independence. As articulated in a long line of cases, constables are office holders under the Crown, required to exercise independent judgement in using their powers subject only to the rule of law. They cannot be directed in this by government, central or local. The courts have also declared a kind of self-denying ordinance: they will not intervene in the professional judgement of professional police officers unless it amounts to a complete abnegation of their law enforcement responsibilities, which to date they have never found (Lustgarten, 1986). Accountability to the law is thus something of a hollow shell.

The doctrine of constabulary independence has acted as a shield against local authority attempts to make the police accountable to them for policy decisions, despite their nominally local formation. Apart from the Metropolitan Police, which since 1829 has had only the Home Secretary as its police authority, British police forces were established during the nineteenth century by Parliament requiring local bodies (watch committees in the towns, justices in rural areas) to form constabularies. The Police Act 1964 consolidated the current 'tripartite system', whereby provincial forces (now 41 in number), are governed by chief constables, police authorities (which until 1994 consisted primarily of local councillors, with a minority of magistrates) and the Home Secretary. The meaning and acceptability of this system have been fiercely contested in academic and political controversy. However, by the early 1990s it was clear that the tripartite system was a sham. Local authorities had no effective independent power at all in any disgreement with chief constables or the Home Office. This has been shown in every single conflict since 1964. A centralizing trajectory has been evident throughout the history of British policing (Gatrell, 1990).

Legitimation of the police has, however, been successfully managed in many periods of British history. By the middle of the twentieth century the police had come to be a widely popular, almost sacred, totem of national pride in Britain (Reiner, 1992: 57–60). The fictional character Dixon of Dock Green, popular in the 1949 film *The Blue Lamp* and a long-running TV series beginning in 1956, is often taken as symbolizing this. The legend had it that Scotland Yard always got its man, and that the British had 'the best police in the world' (Weinberger, 1996). Since the development of empirical research on policing in the 1960s, however, a substantial body of evidence has underlined the limited capacity of the police to control crime rates

(Reiner, 1992: ch. 4; Bayley, 1994; Morgan and Newburn, 1997). Moreover, by the 1970s policing, law and order had become major political issues (Reiner, 1992: ch. 2; Downes and Morgan, 1997). In a less deferential society, police malpractice of all kinds came to light increasingly, and there was less automatic trust in the police. Police effectiveness was called into question by the remorseless rise in crime rates. Police tactics became more coercive and militaristic in a counterproductive bid to control crime and disorder.

There was a clear crisis of public confidence, with 1989 marking a nadir in police opinion poll ratings as several older miscarriages of justice were acknowledged by the Court of Appeal, notably the Guildford Four and Birmingham Six cases. In the 1990s the police struggled to find new ways of religitimating themselves, pursuing a variety of fashions from community policing to zero tolerance. These efforts were hampered by sudden policy U-turns by successive Home Secretaries, and by their failure to tackle the broader sources of rising crime and disorder.

The other major aspect of formal control is *penality* – 'the complex of laws, processes, discourses, and institutions which are involved in . . . legal punishment' (Garland, 1990: 10). The trajectory of penality has been shaped by the same long-term social and cultural developments as policing. Between the late eighteenth and the twentieth centuries, they shifted from processes 'which were essentially local, personal and, since constables, thief-takers, justices and gaolers took fees from clients and charges, entrepreneurial, to crime control institutions which were bureaucratic, largely impersonal, and increasingly centralized' (Emsley, 1997: 82).

During the late eighteenth and early nineteenth centuries several factors converged to make imprisonment the principal sanction for serious crimes. Critics such as Beccaria, Bentham, John Howard and Sir Samuel Romilly railed against the inhumanity and irrationality of a 'Bloody Code' whose nominal severity was so out of line with popular sentiment that capital punishment was frequently commuted. Utilitarianism and Evangelical Christianity combined to generate a growing movement for penal reform. This not only sought to substitute imprisonment for capital punishment and transportation on grounds of justice and compassion, but to make the prison into an instrument for transformation of offenders into reformed, law-abiding, productive citizens. Debates about penality focused on techniques for disciplining and 'normalizing' convicts, such as the 'separate' system (based on solitary confinement as the spur to repentance) and the 'silent' system (with a regime of strict silence as the source of salvation). Practical exigencies also fostered the rise of the prison. Transportation to the American colonies ended with the Revolutionary War. Shipment to the new destination, Australia, was hampered by the Revolutionary and the Napoleonic Wars. With the end of transportation as a judicial sentence in 1857, prison finally became the ultimate sanction for most offences.

The rehabilitative ideal was the dominant ideology of penality throughout the first half of the twentieth century, especially for younger convicts, who were always the majority (Bailey, 1987). Despite the tensions of a rising crime rate and 'moral panics' about the new youth cultures after the mid-1950s, rehabilitation remained the dominant discourse of penality up to the Children and Young Persons Act 1969, the last stand of the welfarist approach (Newburn, 1997: 639–43).

In the 1970s the Conservatives under Margaret Thatcher, backed by the police and prison services, began to campaign for tougher approaches to policing and punishment. Criminal justice ceased to be a non-partisan area of policy. The Conservatives attacked the 'soft' policies, attributed to Labour and the Liberals, which had supposedly encouraged crime and disorder (Reiner and Cross, 1991; Downes and Morgan, 1997).

During the Thatcherite 1980s rhetoric and policy remained tough. However, beneath the surface there was also emerging a more pragmatic approach, informed particularly by research on the effectiveness of alternative approaches by Home Office civil servants. This culminated in the Criminal Justice Act 1991, which emphasized crime prevention rather than after-the-event punitiveness, and diversion of offenders into community penalties wherever possible rather than prison (inspired partly by Thatcherite concern with fiscal parsimony).

Pragmatism was soon reversed by a return to the fundamentalist belief that toughness and prison 'works', under the last two Conservative Home Secretaries, Kenneth Clarke and Michael Howard. It remains to be seen what the long-term consequences of the 1997 Labour victory will be.

Informal Social Control

'Informal social control' refers to processes and institutions which have significant consequences for the preservation of social order, although this is not their overt primary purpose. The concept recognises that social order is reproduced not only by the formal control institutions of codes, courts and constables, but also by religion, family, education, peer groups, and the mass media. These are all agencies of informal socialization into a common or dominant culture, whatever their apparent purposes might be.

In addition to their overt cognitive or other content, *schools and other educational institutions* have a 'hidden curriculum': teaching children that they are obliged 'to know their place and to sit still in it' (Illich, 1973). Whatever else is taught, there are certain values which are tacitly communicated by the very nature of formal instruction. Hierarchy and authority are key: some people or texts know more and better than others, and only their knowledge carries weight. The role of the student is to learn from these authorities, and to be assessed relative to others by their incorporation of approved ideas. Sharing knowledge with others at the student's level is in many contexts regarded as 'cheating'. Individual achievement is what is usually assessed. In short, formal education teaches deference, individualism, and competitiveness alongside the three Rs.

Official policy towards education in Britain has been informed by a mixture of overt concerns: economic worries about ensuring a skilled and trained workforce, cultural preservation, moral improvement, and even at times social justice. Different interests have often prioritized or interpreted these in conflicting ways, and educational policy has usually been controversial – a sequence of 'great debates' about the future direction of culture and society. In the nineteenth century, ruling-class opinion was divided between those who saw education primarily in terms of the preservation and transmission of elite culture and values, and those who wanted it geared to industrial needs (Williams, 1961). Both had profound implications for the education of the upper classes as well as the masses. Similar divisions existed among the working class. Some saw education as the means of incorporation into full citizenship, but radicals like the Chartists feared state schooling as ideological invasion. The 1870 Education Act provided for compulsory free schooling for all children up to the age of eleven. The motivation for this was a complex blend of instrumental concern about industrial competitiveness, and worries about the moral and cultural standards of the masses – especially as after 1867 they began gradually to receive the right to vote.

During and after the Second World War, policy became increasingly concerned with equal opportunities. This was not only due to greater receptivity to social justice arguments among Labour ministers. Throughout post-war educational debate there was at least equal concern with the waste of 'human capital' resources if able poorer people could not realise their potential. Education was also seen as the key to solving social problems of all kinds, including delinquency and crime, partly by increasing employment and economic prospects, but also by civilising the masses into a shared national culture. The result was a veritable educational explosion in the post-war decades. The 1944 Education Act entitled all children for the first time to a secondary education, with the minimum school-leaving age raised to fifteen in 1947 (extended to sixteen from 1973). In the late 1950s and 1960s there was a huge expansion of higher and further education, especially following the Robbins Report.

Since the mid-1970s the nature of educational debate has fundamentally altered. The underlying source of this was the same transformation of the political economy which shifted debates about policing and penality towards the discourse of 'law and order'. Instead of being dominated by the mission of incorporating the mass of the population into full citizenship, for a blend of economic and moral motives, concern shifted to the burden of public educational expenditure at a time of increasing international competitive pressures and unemployment. Education – like all other public services – became dominated by concerns for 'value for money', especially after Thatcher's victory in 1979. Education dropped from 6.3 to 5 per cent of public expenditure between the mid-1970s and the 1990s. Policy debate focused increasingly on the restoration of 'standards', in terms of both technical achievement and social discipline, which were seen as undermined by 'progressive' methods and radical ideals introduced in the 1960s. The consumerist rhetoric made this critique of the alleged domination of education by radicals in local government and the teaching profession appeal to working-class parents. Many justifiably felt their children were relatively excluded from opportunities for educational success.

Despite the Conservatives' arguments about consumer choice, competition, and 'rolling back the state', however, the curriculum of schools was brought increasingly under central government control. The 1988 Education Reform Act was the culmination of this process. It specified a core curriculum for state schools, with centrally prescribed attainment targets and testing. Education became explicitly a vehicle for the Conservative agenda of a return 'back to basics' – not only in cognitive skills for economic competitiveness, but by reinvigorating traditional 'Victorian' values.

There is a long tradition of conservative fears about the subversive consequences of *mass media* representations. A succession of 'moral entrepreneurs' have campaigned against the alleged injection of subversive images into the minds of children by dime novels, horror comics, cinema, television, video, satellite and now the internet. Polar-opposite anxieties about media representations characterize the left of the political spectrum. A key theme of radical criminology is that the media manufactured 'moral panics' about successive varieties of 'folk devils' (Cohen, 1972; Cohen and Young, 1973), legitimating authoritarian populist styles of 'policing the crisis' (Hall *et al.*, 1978).

In the field of media studies it has been claimed on the basis of regular 'violence profiles' that television produces a 'mainstreaming' of America: a clustering of opinion around shared beliefs and values derived from the media rather than direct experience (Gerbner, 1995). Disproportionate representation of criminal violence exaggerates fears of crime drawn from 'television's mean and dangerous world', and cultivates support for authoritarian 'law and order' politics (Signorielli, 1990). Recent comprehensive reviews of the literature conclude that media representations do have small effects overall on behaviour and attitudes, in the direction of the conventionally understood meaning of the text (Wartella, 1995; Livingstone, 1996). Interestingly the few studies which have been concerned to assess the consequences of 'prosocial' images find stronger effects (Livingstone, 1996: 309), possibly because these are reinforced by other socialising agencies. The media are doubtless significant for the reproduction of order. However, their consequences are complex and interact with other factors over time, rather than being the clearly discernible immediate 'effects' which much research has tried to identify. They are part of the 'social construction of reality', and operate together with much broader enculturation processes in forming social identities and patterns of behaviour (Livingstone, 1996: 31–2).

The media are also important in the images they present of crime, criminal justice and social order (Reiner, 1997b). Typically they present a very positive image of the success and integrity of the police and criminal justice (Chibnall, 1977; Reiner, 1994; Schlesinger and Tumber, 1994). Most crimes are cleared up, because of effective policing – a very different picture from the official statistical pattern, which shows that only 3 per cent of known offences result in a conviction or caution (Home Office, 1995). Within this general pattern of representation of crime and justice there have been significant changes. These are congruent with the developments in policing, penality and education which have already been discussed. Between 1945 and the early 1960s the predominant representation was consensual. Crime was evil, police were virtuous, and justice was invariably done – the (literally as well as metaphorically) black and white world of *Dixon of Dock Green* and *Dragnet*. Order was benign and widely accepted, although clearly hierarchical. From the mid-1960s to the late 1970s this was challenged by increasingly critical questioning – from both ends of the political spectrum – of the justice and effectiveness of the police, and the legal and social systems more generally, developed. Since the early 1980s this critical stance has been replaced by a growing bifurcation of media representations. On the one hand there are counter-critical narratives, seeking a nostalgic return to the values and norms of the previous consensus, exemplified by *Heartbeat*. On the other hand, there are post-critical representations, embodying a Nietzschean world 'beyond good and evil' in which police and other authorities are not so much criticized as absent, irrelevant or placed on the same amoral plane as deviants. Post-modern reflexivity, irony and cool à la Tarantino are the only criteria of judgement.

Overall a fundamental shift in underlying discourse is discernible in changing media representations of crime and criminal justice. There is a demystification of law and authority. Crime moves from being something which must be controlled *ipso facto* because the law defines it thus, to a contested category. Criminality is less an offence against sacred and absolute norms than a mundane aspect of interpersonal relationships – just one individual harming another. The majority of media narratives continue to justify in the end the criminal justice viewpoint, although this has now to be achieved by demonstrating particular harm to identifiable individual victims. In this sense the media continue to reproduce order and to function as sources of social control. However they also represent increasingly the individualism and pragmatism of a less deferential culture (Allen, Livingstone and Reiner, 1998).

Beyond Order? From Repression to Reflexivity

Whether regarded positively as harmony and tranquillity, or negatively as unjust hierarchy and repression, order has always been a pivotal concern of social and political thought. This chapter has considered a variety of conceptualizations of order and how it is achieved in the UK.

There appear to have been long-term cycles in disorder and criminalization, although the evidence on this has to be interpreted with caution. Criminalization seems to intensify in periods when a system of production and rule is developing. This is partly because the dislocation of social relations generates increasing pressure towards crime and disorder on the 'dangerous classes' at the bottom of the social hierarchy. It is also because the meaning of this becomes more threatening to the precariously emerging elite. Consequently the 'demand for order' increases, and disciplinary processes are transformed to supply it. As structures of production and power become consolidated, however, strategies of governance shift towards cooption and incorporation by a combination of economic, political, social and ideological processes. The form this took in the later nineteenth and first half of the twentieth centuries has been designated as 'the social': 'an order of collective being and collective responsibilities and obligations' (Rose, 1996: 333).

Explanations of the maintenance and reproduction of order, whether of the right or the left, tend to emphasise the salience of informal social control or of ideological processes. It is generally assumed that without any effective apparatuses for the achievement of order chaos – earlier referred to as order degree zero – would result. While in periods of emerging rule the formal control or repressive apparatuses are of prime importance, stable systems rely more on incorporation into a common culture or dominant ideology, with formal control mechanisms increasingly having a symbolic or dramaturgical function more than an instrumental one.

This 'dominant ideology thesis' has been shown to be questionable on both empirical and theoretical grounds (Abercrombie *et al.*, 1980). In both medieval and modern societies there is little evidence of anything more than grudging *de facto* acceptance of supposedly dominant ideologies by the mass of the population. The ruling ideas were internalized more by the ruling class than by the subordinate ones. The power of the coercive machinery of the state was also significant, especially in periods of transition or threat.

Neglected by most theories which emphasise either ideology or coercion is what Marx called 'the dull compulsion of economic relations'. Most theories have emphasised the coercive and/or the ideological faces of power, neglecting the utilitarian bases of order and discipline. However, 'the non-normative aspect of system integration provides a basis of a society's coherence, irrespective of whether or not there are common values' (Abercrombie *et al.*, 1980: 168).

This argument has become more evidently important in the last three decades. On the one hand, the current period is especially characterized by a predominance of relativism and lack of consensus about the foundations of knowledge and ethics, as the currently dominant theorizations of post-modernity or reflexive modernization imply (Bauman, 1988, 1997; Giddens, 1990, 1994; Beck, 1992). Although the relativity of knowledge and ethics was inscribed in the modernist project from the start (MacIntyre, 1985), this was largely suppressed for two centuries by the confidence in progress generated by the huge transformation of material life, despite the temporary shocks of periodic slump and two World Wars. But 'the embryo of nihilism started to form in the womb of modernity' with the chimerical Enlightenment idea of 'sovereign reason' (Lyon, 1994: 5).

Perhaps a key index of this is the way that political and social elites have much less capacity to shelter behind a veil of ignorance about their activities, because of the huge explosion of mass media. While media analysis normally emphasises how they contribute to the reproduction of order by circulating dominant ideology, and by providing means of surveillance by elites of masses (for example by the growing use of technologies like CCTV), there are important reverse processes.

It has been argued that Foucault's analysis of Bentham's Panopticon as the model of modern control – the few observing the many – should be extended (Mathiesen, 1997). The mass media act as a Synopticon: they also provide means for the masses to see the few. Clearly the media provide a highly unbalanced reciprocal process of surveillance to the elite and the mass. However as the plethora of recent scandals demonstrates they undoubtedly strip away most forms of traditional legitimation from elites, who are commonly revealed as deviant or even criminal. Paradoxically this may enhance the media's disciplinary function, by providing people with a sense of power through knowledge over individual members of the elite, while leaving the structure intact. It is possible 'that the control and discipline of the "soul", that is, the creation of human beings who control themselves through self-control and thus fit neatly into a so-called democratic capitalist society, is a task which is actually fulfilled by modern Synopticon' (Mathiesen, 1997: 215).

At the same time, popular and official confidence in the capacity of the coercive machinery of the state to deal with crime and disorder effectively has dwindled, as has the self-confidence of criminal justice professionals. Although tough talk and action on crime is *de rigeur*, as much for 'new' Labour or Clinton Democrats as for the Conservatives, this can plausibly be interpreted as a motivated by unconscious denial of governmental impotence (Garland, 1996: 462–3).

The weight of crime control policy is now directed towards measures to bolster self-protection activity by potential victims of crime, and mitigate their suffering. This implies a *de facto* acceptance of high rates of crime as inevitable, while simultaneously denying this by ever more vigorous 'crackdowns' on a few offenders who act as symbolic scapegoats.

What has all but disappeared is the optimistic modernist project which flourished from the late nineteenth century to the 1960s of substantially reducing crime by social incorporation and rehabilitation of individual deviants with particular pathologies. Instead recourse is had increasingly to a 'new feudalism' (Shearing and Stenning, 1983), in which strategies of containment separate the ghettos of the dangerous classes from the castles of consumerism in which the more privileged live, work and play. Policing becomes a function of border patrol between these areas, and a variety of technological, private and self-help measures – post-modern pick 'n' - mix policing (Reiner, 1997a: 1039).

In parts of the contemporary world degree zero order is a real threat (Hobsbawm, 1994; Cohen, 1997: 242–5). However, in most industrial societies, especially established liberal democracies like the UK, it is not, despite the erosion of the coercive and cultural controls which supposedly provide the necessary underpinning of order. This suggests the possibility that in contemporary multicultural and economically decentred societies the 'demand for order' is less than in the modern era of centralized mass production systems, which required more regimented and unified populations. Much greater diversity of values and lifestyles can be tolerated as long as there is a minimal degree of cooperation and coordination of practical economic activity. Marx's 'dull compulsion of economic relations' at present carries the burden of providing a 'good enough' level of order with only vestigial support from coercive or ideological control apparatuses.

9

Estates, Classes and Interests

MICHAEL MORAN

Examining estates, classes and interests takes us right to the 'fundamentals' of British politics and raises questions about the political significance of those fundamentals. Britain's economic and social history created some brute social facts that politicians have to accommodate. The United Kingdom led the world into the Industrial Revolution, which created a powerful class of industrial capitalists and a large industrial proletariat. Peasants were destroyed as a significant social force and the economic place of agriculture was marginalized; in the process many powerful traditional interests and institutions characteristic of an agrarian society were eliminated. In short, the fundamentals in British politics for most of this century have been the fundamentals created by industrial capitalism.

Politics in a democracy must reflect those deep-seated features of the economic and social structure: the point of democratic competition is that political life should express the conflicting social and economic forces in the community. Yet the innocent image of 'reflection' misleads. Images of reflection picture politicians only as mirrors of social and economic forces. They are not. Politicians have resources and they can use those resources creatively to shape social and economic life – to shape classes and interests, in other words. Democratic politicians do indeed have to work under the influence of social and economic forces which are in some respects as uncontrollable as the weather. In Britain these elemental social influences include: the fact that the social structure was irredeemably shaped by Britain's pioneering role as the first industrial nation; the fact that the character of this pioneering role, especially as a trading and imperial nation, made Britain especially vulnerable to wider changes in the structure of the global economy; the fact that the social structure has in the last generation been reshaped by economic forces that have cut the size of the manual work force, and therefore of the traditional working class; and the fact that early industrialization bequeathed to successive British governments a problem which has still not been solved – how to reverse the decline of the economy from its early position of eminence.

This is a summary of part of the social 'climate' within which politicians in Britain have to live, and it may justly be considered part of the fundamentals. But what turns politicians into something more than 'reflectors' of the fundamentals is that, inheriting social division, they make choices, and these choices in turn both shape the political expression given to social divisions and reshape those very divisions. The choices made by politicians affect the social and economic fundamentals because politicians in Britain have resources. In government they control a state machine that can compel, expropriate and redistribute; and both in an out of office, if they have the gift of expression, they can shape the perceived significance of the social and economic 'fundamentals'. Rhetoric is the heart of the democratic politician's art. Rhetoric is in part – to quote Cowling – 'a form of exemplary utterance', an effort to persuade social actors of their interests (Cowling, 1971: 5). But it is also reflexive: the act of speaking, either in public or private, shapes the politician's own perception of the social and economic fundamentals. Politicians not only speak to persuade others; they also speak to persuade themselves.

The complicated connection between political practice and the social and economic fundamentals can be explored through the imagery of statecraft. *Statecraft* is what governing elites do. It involves using the resources of the state for strategic objectives (for an early usage see Bulpitt, 1986). Social outcomes – like changes in class equality – are in part the product of forces which are beyond the short-term control of governing elites. But the resources of the modern state, and the skill of governing elites, mean that they need not be helpless in the face of social forces. They can manoeuvre within the constraints of particular historical circumstances, and in manoeuvring they can even alter the shape of those constraints.

Statecraft has many elements, but in modern Britain three particular matters have demanded strategic choice. The first is what to do about the legacy of Britain's Industrial Revolution, especially about Britain's historically poor industrial performance. The alternatives have been to intervene using state power to protect and reorganise British industry, or allow competitive forces, including international forces, to sort out the efficient from the inefficient. The second strategic issue has been how to ensure social peace in a country with great class inequalities. The choice has been about the mix between coercion and conciliation. The coercive power of the state has always been needed, for instance to keep the most industrially militant sections of the working class under control. But since Britain is a society where civil liberties are widely respected, coercion has limited uses, and governing elites are obliged to practice class conciliation. The strategic choice facing elites concerns the appropriate mix between coercion and conciliation. All governing elites in Britain have faced these two strategic choices, but a third has been special to Conservatives, who have been forced by the shape of the class structure to solve a problem that defeated many parties of the business class in other nations: how to attract a sufficient proportion of the working class vote to ensure electoral victory under a universal franchise. (Labour too had its problem of electoral statecraft: how to attract the middle class voter. But it is Conservative electoral state-craft which dominates this chapter because, as I show, it was Conservative statecraft that shaped the fundamentals in the two critical decades identified here, the 1920s and the 1980s.)

These three elements constitute *industrial*, *social* and *electoral* statecraft. This conception of statecraft as the act of strategic choice in managing social and economic fundamentals explains why so much of what follows concerns the Conservative Party. In modern British politics the crucial choices have been made in two decades, the 1920s and the 1980s. These decades are crucial because they saw turning-points in the way the political elites managed classes and interests – saw, in other words, major innovations in statecraft. In both the key choices were made by the Conservative Party. Nor is that surprising. As the issue of electoral statecraft shows, any party of business in a capitalist democracy faces a stark choice: be creative or die.

What follows is this. I begin by describing the statecraft that crystallized the modern system of class politics, especially in the 1920s. I show how this endured for nearly half a century, and how its exhaustion provoked the great crisis of state and economy in the mid-1970s. I then describe how a new statecraft reshaped interests, especially in the Thatcher years. Finally, I show some of the problems created by this reshaped relationship between politics and the 'funda-mentals'.

The Creation of Class Politics

The Industrial Revolution laid the social foundations for a party system based on class, but the system was only built on the economic base after a long historical delay. At the beginning of the First World War the structure of interests in British politics still resembled what any observer of the political system over the preceding half century could have recognised. It was marked by a politics of estates and interests, rather than a politics of class. The key difference between estates and classes was that estates were defined legally and politically rather than economically. The three traditional estates in England were the Church, the landed aristocracy and the Commons. They had specific privileges and duties, and the right to representation in the English Parliament. The survival of the old structure of these political estates into the modern era owed much to the continuing strength of the aristocracy, and its ability to delay the advent of democracy. Despite the impact of the Industrial Revolution, the emergence of the labour movement, the gradual extension of the suffrage, and the conflicts between manufacturers and landowners over issues like the Corn Laws, non-class issues and non-class organizations remained central to British political life in the nineteenth century.

Two obvious instances are provided by religion and territory. The churches remained powerful influences in the political system. Issues of church organization were important. One concerned the connection between churches and secular power: the legal entitlements of the Church of England and, more contentious still, the official position of the Church of England's sister denominations in Wales and in Ireland. Some important political questions – notably to do with control of the drink trade – were also proxies for religious differences (Bradley, 1979: 99–122). High levels of religious observance – at least by the standards of the late twentieth century – meant that church leaders of a wide range of denominations were important public figures. The dominant party of the left, the Liberals, did indeed use the language of class, but in a way suggesting that classes were just one form of social gradation. Birch puts it well. Liberals

did not believe that these divisions were barriers, and they did not think that there was anything in the nature of an irreconcilable conflict between one class and another. In the language of modern sociology, they thought of classes as status groups which graded individuals according to their rank in society (Birch, 1964: 84).

Territory was important as both a base of political organization and a line of political division. It is well established that part of the line of support dividing Liberalism and Conservatism was territorial. That was recognised in the positions the parties took up on the Constitutional ambitions of the various component parts of the United Kingdom, with the Conservatives the party of the Union and the Liberals the party sympathetic to Home Rule. The most dramatic example of that division was the great crisis about Irish Home Rule on the eve of the First World War. (True, viewed through the lens of Empire, Ireland was only a colony. But it was a special sort of colony, because of geographical proximity, cultural integration with England and the fact of political representation in the Westminster Parliament.)

The way the great class interests created by the Industrial Revolution – capital and labour – were represented in politics is particularly striking viewed at this historical distance. Before the First World War neither the Liberal Party nor the Conservative Party was a truly cohesive national institution. They had national organizations to help fight election campaigns, and within the parliamentary elite they formed caucuses centred on Westminster, but in essence they were loose alliances of local and regional bodies, in which local connection remained very important. They were a national patchwork of local and regional institutions (McKenzie, 1963). *Neither was a distinctively class party*. They were both parties of the employing class – but, to the extent that history and local connection allowed, they represented different sections of that employing class. And, electorally, they were both parties of the working class; again, to the extent that history and local connection allowed, drawing support from different sections of the working class. Perkin summarises it well: 'Both [parties] were primarily constitutional and religious rather than economic and social institutions' (Perkin, 1969: 376).

The way capitalist interests were represented in the political system at this period was particularly significant. There was very little formal representation at all. Some individual employers' associations were formed in the later decades of the nineteenth century, but capital had nothing to match, for instance, either the Trades Union Congress or the close institutional connection between unions and the Labour Party. (Grant and Marsh, 1977: 15–30). Of course the most important reason business did not match the formal organization of the working class was that it did not need to. It was already a hegemonic interest in British society. The terms of the hegemony are well shown by the case of the City of London. In an era when the existence of an open international financial system and adherence to the Gold Standard made financial markets critical in determining economic outcomes, the 'manager' of the Gold Standard, and of the City as a whole, was the Bank of England. The Bank was a privately owned institution controlled by the City elite, owing no accountability to the state, and with little operational connection even to the central economic departments of state, like the Treasury, let alone to the wider parliamentary class.

Now contrast the world of 1914 with that of 1929. (The date is chosen because the return of a Labour government in the latter year may be said finally to have confirmed Labour's position as the main opponent of the Conservatives, extinguishing any last hope of a Liberal revival.) A system of class politics had been created. 'Creation' is advisedly chosen, because what happened showed the complex interaction between structural change and strategic choice. Politicians were faced with great social changes not of their making (such as those arising from the impact of the First World War) but the political outcomes were the result of choices made by elites in response to those changes.

Three major alterations in the landscape of interests are visible. First, many of the organizations and interests that were central in 1914 now either had disappeared or had declined to marginal significance. The most obvious changes concern religion and territory. In the 1920s there were still, admitted, important connections between religion and politics: between Catholicism and Scottish Labour Politics, for instance, and between Anglicanism and Conservatism (on the former, see Howell, 1986). Issues of church government could still cause anguish – witness the crisis over the Prayer Book in 1927 and rural unrest over tithes in the 1930s – but they mostly caused anguish to churchmen, not to anyone else (Norman, 1976: 279–363). Religious cleavages still divided the social base of the parties; but except in particular cases, like the Orange base of working class Conservatism in Glasgow, the parties did not seriously engage in arguments about either religious organization or church government. Territorial issues, likewise, had by the end of the 1920s gone underground in British politics. The Labour Party made no attempt to disturb the Protestant/Unionist domination in Northern Ireland, and by the end of the decade had left behind its old interests in Home Rule to become a resolutely unionist institution as far as the wider UK constitution was concerned. As Howell puts it: 'From some point in the 1920s, most Socialists within Britain were also British Socialists.' (Howell, 1986: 7) A curious historical inversion had occurred. In his study of the Victorian constitution Le May remarks of political division early in the nineteenth century that 'Whigs and Tories were not divided by class interests, but by a different way of looking at the Constitution' (Le May, 1979: 170). By the 1930s the two great parties were divided by class but united by their view of the Constitution.

A second major alteration involved changes in the organization of capitalist interests in the political system. There was more formality. The first peak association for industrial capital, the Federation of British Industries, was founded in the First World War. Change in the City and in the role of the Bank of England is the most striking instance of the new formality. The Bank remained throughout the inter-war years a privately owned institution, but under its great Governor, Montagu Norman, it began to professionalize itself: to 'manage' the interests of the City in a formal way; to organize financial markets, chiefly to create or strengthen cartels; and, through its developing relations with the Treasury, systematically to represent the interests of the financial sector in Whitehall.

The third change is the best known because the most obvious. The structure of interests represented in the party-political arena altered. By the end of the 1920s there were no longer two parties of capital. Of course, as the behaviour of Labour in office showed, whatever rhetoric might be used on occasions by its leaders, the party was devoted to the peaceful coexistence of capital and labour. But Labour's own connections with the business community were nothing like those that had existed between Liberalism and business. The Party leadership, at both national and local level, was dominated by bourgeois professionals and upwardly mobile working men. There was now only one party of business, and that was the Conservative Party.

Understanding why all these momentous changes came over British politics in the decade and a half or so from the eve of the First World War has occupied the energies of generations of historians, and is the subject of numerous controversies. Nevertheless, two broadly distinct forces are agreed to have been at work: fundamental social and economic change and the influence of individual agency. On the one hand, changes took place in the wider society, partly as a result of long-established trends associated with industrialization and urbanization, partly to do with the impact of the First World War in British society. The 'nationalization' of political communication and debate was hastened by changed technologies of mass communication. The most obvious sign is the central place in national life already occupied at the end of the 1920s by the BBC, a corporation which was in style and content closely attuned to the culture of the metropolis (see Briggs, 1961: 327–84 for the creation of the BBC monopoly). The process of secularization, already well established in 1914, also continued. These social changes were of course accompanied by institutional changes, the most important of which was the widening of the franchise. The last election before the outbreak of war, in 1910, had been fought on a franchise which excluded all women and a substantial section, mostly the poorest, of the male working class. The 1918 election was fought on something close to universal male adult suffrage and suffrage for all women over the age of 30; in 1928 the qualifying age for women was reduced to 21, the same as for men.

Changes in social and economic fundamentals help make sense of the crystallization of class politics, but that crystallization depended also on individual agency. The situation by the end of the 1920s was neither the product of some grand strategy to develop class politics, nor the mechanical outcome of impersonal social forces. It was shaped and mediated by the interventions of political actors. Of these, the most important were the leaders of the Conservative Party, simply because in the aftermath of the First World War the party's main historical rival, the Liberal Party, was mortally wounded. It was during the early period of Stanley Baldwin's leadership of the party (it spanned in total the years 1923–37) that the Conservatives fashioned the components of the statecraft that were to endure for half a century. With the demise of the Liberals the Conservatives were landed with the role of defending the social order, at least as far as the order of capitalism was concerned. The role of politicians was to fashion a distinctive Conservative statecraft designed to do the job of defence – the elements of which lasted for nearly half a century, finally coming to grief under Edward Heath's premiership (1970–4). Cowling's great study (1971) explores the two creative manoeuvres that established modern British politics: the Conservative decision to position the party as the defender of the social order; and the linked decision to install Labour as the party's opponents.

The burst of creative statecraft in the early 1920s needs explaining. What concentrated the Conservative mind so powerfully? Surely there can be only one candidate: the Russian Revolution. The Revolution created in the east the frightening spectre of expansionist militant Marxism. The wave of working-class unrest that swept over western European nations in the wake of 1917 showed the fragility of the capitalist order. The emergence of Conservative and Labour dominance created both a defender of the propertied classes and, in Labour, a means to channel opposition into peaceful parliamentary institutions.

Although the details of policy changed in response to contingencies, the core components of Conservative statecraft were already established by the end of the 1920s. They were highly 'Baldwinesque'. Economically, they prescribed an active industrial role for the state: it is well known that until the Labour governments of 1945–51 the Conservatives had a stronger record of extending public ownership than had the Labour Party. After its defeat in the General Election at the end of 1923 the Conservative Party edged towards interventionism, a shift that culminated in the imposition of protective tariffs in 1932 and active support for industrial rationalization and industrial cartels in the 1930s (Beer, 1969: 278–87.) Socially, notwithstanding the assault on the unions in the Trades Disputes Act 1927, the leadership used conciliatory language in dealing with class opponents. Electorally, the strategy involved maximizing the cross-class support for the party – something that proved particularly successful in the stunning landslide victory of 1931, achieved in part by incorporating elements of the Labour elite and fighting under a 'national' flag. The electoral strategy was of course partly a straightforward calculation of what was needed to win control of the state under universal suffrage in a country with a large industrial proletariat. But it also rested on something more fundamental: the party's own conception of the significance of class division. As Beer puts it:

> The Socialist theory of representation . . . is a theory of class. So also is the Tory theory of representation, although for Toryism, ancient or modern, class has a different meaning and function. Both the Tory and the Socialist conceive of society as divided into different strata and each recognizes that social stratification has an impact on and importance for politics. But while, for the Socialist, social stratification is a force dividing society and separating parties, for the Tory it is a force uniting one level of society with others and the leadership of a party with its followers. One sees, and approves, horizontal division. The other sees, and approves, vertical integration (Beer, 1969: 92).

The Crisis of the Governing Order

The social 'fundamentals' that confronted governing elites in the half century up to the middle of the 1970s amounted to: an economy declining from its historic international pre-eminence; a society with great class inequalities; and an occupational structure dominated numerically by an industrial proletariat. The period was marked by a fundamental unity of statecraft: industrially, by a collectivist strategy to try to cope with decline; socially, by policies designed to alleviate inequalities and secure peace between unequal classes; and, especially in the case of the Conservative Party, electorally by a strategy designed to build up a broad base of support across the electorate.

These three elements were interconnected, and it was the increasingly obvious failure of industrial statecraft which finally destroyed the lot. The most immediate manifestation of crisis was the catastrophic collapse of the Heath government in 1974. The attempt after 1972 to manage the economy by full-blown collectivism, especially through detailed controls of prices and incomes, produced a bruising conflict with the one of the best organized sections of the working class, the miners. The attempt in February 1974 to secure an electoral mandate for the Conservatives in their conflict with the miners led instead to the party's loss of office. Industrial collectivism, social conciliation and electoral appeals across classes all suffered simultaneous blows.

The difficulties for Conservatism were only part of a wider crisis of the governing order established half a century before. The signs of that wider crisis are well known. By the 1970s the two-party hegemony of Conservative and Labour was being challenged by third parties (see Chapter 10). Some of these, such as the Nationalists in Scotland, were dissenters from the 'unionist' constitutional order on which the two dominant parties had agreed for half a century. In a more dramatic way the challenge of territorial separatism, repressed since the 1920s, also resurfaced: the Northern Ireland troubles revived territorial conflict and greatly damaged the authority of both the Heath government and its Labour successor.

At the root of everything lay a crisis of economic management. The decline of the British economy, which had helped destroy Heath's government, accelerated after his departure from office. 1975 was a year of economic chaos. 1976 brought a humiliating financial rescue by the International Monetary Fund (IMF), at the price of a sharp change in economic policy imposed by the Fund. More important than the IMF-imposed measures, however, was what the crisis did to the governing elite. 1976 may be considered as great a crisis for the governing elite as 1940: the moment when a whole way of governing was discredited, and a governing class lost confidence in itself. 'Crisis' here is used advisedly. It was a revolutionary turning-point – but, as the next two decades were to show, the revolution came, not from below, but from the top.

In this revolution the most important agents were, in the first instance, not those who occupied governing office. It is true that 1976, rather than the return to office of the Conservatives in 1979, marked the decisive shift away from the Keynesian economic policies of the post-war years. But it was the Conservatives, rather than Labour or the Civil Service elite, which provided both the intellectual challenge and the political will to reshape interests during the 1980s – in the face, indeed, of opposition from Labour and from large sections of the Civil Service elite. Throughout the period policy creativity lay with the Conservatives. The creativity of the Labour leadership, especially after the great electoral defeat of 1983, lay in refashioning the Party so as successfully to accommodate the policy innovations of its opponents.

To understand why this happened, we must comprehend the extent to which the great crisis of the mid-1970s created both problems and opportunities for politicians. The problems were encapsulated in the circumstances of Heath's downfall: neither the economic statecraft, nor the social statecraft, nor the electoral statecraft of traditional Conservatism were any longer viable. But the way long-term social change had affected interests and alliances in the wider society also created the space which allowed the Conservatives to redesign interests. It happens that the Conservatives, faced with the choice between creativity and extinction, seized those opportunities.

Four important, long-term social changes helped create a space for political manoeuvre. First, there had been alterations in economic structure and social structure which undermined electoral strategies based on appeals to class interests. On the side of the working class these have been rehearsed *ad nauseam* by psephologists: they turn on the way changes in industrial structure cut the size of the working class employed in traditional industries and the way changes in lifestyle altered the consumption patterns of workers. (The most obvious instance of the latter was the way the spread of car ownership and home ownership reduced reliance on two key sources of collective consumption, public transport and public-sector housing.) But these structural changes were not only affecting the working class. The structure of the middle class also altered, notably because of the impact of the welfare state and the middle-class public sector employment this created. By the middle of the 1970s there existed a large public-sector middle class with interests very different from those in the private sector: the most obvious point of conflict lay in the extent to which this public-sector middle class depended on high levels of public spending and the taxes to fund that spending. The stable class base of two party politics was fragmenting (Denver, 1994).

With these changes in class structure were occurring more subtle changes in cultural patterns. The changes made a big difference in particular to the relations between the Conservative Party and the working class. The Conservatives' long-term strategy of class conciliation – of picturing the party as 'the' national party – was itself closely tied to the existence of deference in parts of the working class: to the notion that the Conservatives could be considered something more than a sectional interest because they represented part of an elite that was naturally fitted to rule. The strategy of class conciliation thus depended in part on the existence of an ideology of self-subordination in some traditional sections of the working class. But by the 1970s this deference was dying out – in many cases literally, since it was concentrated among older electors. If Conservatism was to be revived as an electoral force, some other appeal had to be found to a section of the working class, since otherwise, under the rules of electoral competition, the party could never hope to return to office. One alternative strategy – English nationalism based on racist hostility to immigrants – had been decisively rejected by Heath when he dismissed Enoch Powell from the Shadow Cabinet in 1968 for a speech which employed precisely that strategy. Some more instrumental means – either by appealing to or by refashioning working-class interests – was needed.

The changes summarized so far have to do with changes at the level of the wider society. The remaining two of our four, however, impinge more directly on the structure of the Conservative Party. The social order that the Conservatives decided to defend in the 1920s was constituted of many things, some of which by the 1970s had declined greatly in importance. Two of the most obvious instances of decline are organized religion, especially Anglicanism, and the Monarchy. But profound changes had also taken place in the structure of those parts of the established social order which had endured. The most important changes were in the business community. Not only was British business much less significant internationally in the 1970s than in the 1920s; domestic capital was also being incorporated into a wider, often globally, organized international economic system. The most marked change was in the City of the London, which by the 1970s had re-emerged as a great international financial centre, but mostly as the centre of operations for foreign financial institutions trading on a global scale. The City mattered globally as a centre for trading and commercial service; but the firms that mattered in the City were mostly foreign. The distinctiveness and the significance of *British* capital, a key historic ally of the Conservative Party, had greatly declined. The changed structure of capital, and the way its culture altered with scale, had much to do with the uneasy relations that existed between the Heath government and the business community in the years after 1970 – culminating in his famous attack on the 'unacceptable face of capitalism'. That outburst was provoked by a tax-avoidance scheme dreamed up for some of the executives in one of the buccaneering multinational conglomerates of the period. Heath's Conservative government found it easy to work with the sort of bureaucratic corporations that dominated the Confederation of British Industry (CBI); it had a more tense relationship with ungentlemanly, entrepreneurial capitalism. (For an exploration of deeper issues, see Clarke, 1981.)

The political effects of these structural changes in the nature of business were amplified by changes in the institutional relations between the party and the business community. In the 1920s these relations were primarily organic. The interests of business were represented less by any formal system of representation than by the presence of many great capitalists in the higher reaches of the Conservative Party, and by the way the lives of leading figures in business and those of leading Conservatives were intertwined. By the 1970s this sort of organic connection still largely endured between small business and the Conservative Party at local level, but it had been greatly weakened at the apex of the party. As both business life and political life became more professional and more demanding, it became increasingly difficult to combine any extensive activity in party politics with a committed business career. The most successful politicians, of whom Heath was the archetype, were by the 1970s professional politicians whose adult life and career had been dominated by political involvement (on business, Stanworth and Giddens, 1974: on politics, King, 1981).

As the life of politics and the life of (big) business separated, so business also began increasingly to organize itself as an interest independently of the Conservatives. As far as the City was concerned, the Bank of England from the early 1970s became increasingly an institution of the state rather than an institution of the markets: it was subject to growing parliamentary scrutiny, more and more integrated in its operations with the other key department of state concerned with economic policy, and was starting to take on more public duties as a supervisor. It became less the voice of the City in government, and more the voice of government in the City. Partly as result, the interests in the City began formally to organize themselves independently of government. In short, the City moved more explicitly into the world of pressure group politics.

The transformed scale of capitalism also encouraged these developments. By the 1970s many of the key institutions in the business community were such large and complex corporations, with such a spread of interests across the globe, that they amounted to complex systems of interests internally. They needed something more than the delegation of interest representation to an outside body; they had both to work out what their interests were in particular circumstances, and to control the way those interests were defended. The scale of the corporations meant that they had no difficulty investing resources in these activities. By the 1970s many of the biggest corporations were doing the job of interest representation 'in house', using their own legal and public relations departments, and in some cases even establishing their own government relations departments (Grant, 1993: 84–103). This specialization of function was also evident at the wider level of the business community. The 1970s were the golden years of the CBI, which had been formed in the mid-1960s to try to unify and professionalize business representation.

Four changes are summarized here: the fragmentation of the class 'blocks' which had been the foundation of the party system since the 1920s; the decline of deference which was forcing a different, more instrumental approach to the management of working-class electors; the incorporation of the most important sections of British business into a wider global order; and the increasing divergence, due to specialization of function, between the political elite and the business elite.

These changes, combined with the wider crisis created by the events of the mid-1970s, amount to both the problem and the opportunity for the Conservatives: the relations with interests established since the

1920s were no longer viable; the decay of many of the established connections made possible the policies reshaping interests. Combined, they help explain why the Conservatives after 1979 were the great creative force in reshaping interests and producing a more unequal Britain.

Reshaping Interests

After 1975 the Conservatives had to refashion all three components of statecraft – economic, social and electoral. Some of the changes were the result of consciously thoughtout policy addressed precisely to the problems of statecraft created by the crisis of the mid-1970s. But, as every analyst of Margaret Thatcher's governments soon discovers, much that was done, including much of the most important part of what was done, was not the result of a conscious strategy fashioned in opposition – nor, indeed, of any coherent strategy at all. The government reacted to 'situational necessity', often only half-realising, or even not realising at all, the implications of what it was doing. Policy creativity of this kind is a key to understanding the connection between fundamental structural forces and policy outcomes. The creativity of politicians is not always fully conscious; the most creative sometimes 'sleepwalk' their way to strategic solutions.

Here I examine the reshaping of interests under three headings: the reshaping of working-class interests; the reshaping of middle-class professional interests; and the reshaping of the interests of capital. All these three impinged on the problems of recreating a viable statecraft – economic, social and electoral.

Working-class interests were reshaped partly by attacking directly some of the key institutions of working-class militancy and partly by reconfiguring some key markets, notably the labour market and the housing market. The attack on the institutions took a variety of forms. The Conservatives came to office in 1979 committed to legislation which would prevent unions inflicting the sort of damage on governments and employers seen in the crisis-ridden closing months of the Heath government. Initial forecasts suggested that they would not succeed, a forecast partly based on the failure of the Heath trade union reforms of 1971, and partly on the fact that Thatcher was forced to accept as employment spokesman James Prior, a survivor of the old 'conciliatory' Conservatism (Moran, 1979). These forecasts were wrong (Marsh, 1992). The Government after 1979 proved to have learnt a great deal from the failure of the Heath attempt at reform. The traditional conciliator Prior was soon replaced by Norman Tebbit, the Conservative politician with the clearest strategic sense of what the new statecraft demanded. The government also directly attacked some of the most militant working-class institutions, and used proxies to attack others. In the category of the former we can place the landmark struggle with miners in the mid-1980s. There is some debate as to how far this confrontation was the product of a strategy originally elaborated some years earlier in opposition. That debate has no chance of being settled until we have better access than at present to the historical archives of both party and government for the period. But the consequences are not in dispute. The defeat of the miners had a powerful 'demonstration' effect: it defeated the group that had played a central role in destroying the Heath government and it cleared the way for the contraction and privatization of the mining industry, thus by the late 1990s eliminating miners as a significant social group or political force in Britain. The most important use of proxies occurred in the great disputes in the printing industry, especially that involving *The Times*. This dispute used state power (including coercion) to support a foreign-owned multinational in destroying, utterly, the power of an industrial group once thought invincible. Victory in the dispute allowed the introduction of new technology into the industry, showing the great gains in productivity and profitability which could be made by defeating militant unions.

Direct confrontation in spectacular industrial disputes was reinforced by wider economic policies. These hastened changes in the structure of the working class which had already been happening through the decline of heavy manufacturing industry. The decline of heavy industries like coal and steel, and the expansion of service sector employment, had many class consequences: it reduced greatly the employment opportunities for working class men, and expanded, in some areas, employment for women; it displaced jobs in highly unionized sectors by jobs in service sectors with little tradition of unionization; and it shifted employment from areas of the UK where class organization was historically strong to areas where it was much weaker. A simple but striking index of the cumulative effect of all these changes is the decline which took place in union membership: in 1980, 53 per cent of the civilian workforce were union members; by 1994 the figure was 34 per cent (Office for National Statistics, 1997: 82).

A more conscious strategic reshaping of working-class interests took place in the housing market. Public-sector housing had been an important foundation of working-class solidarity in the post-war years: both the culture of large public-sector housing estates and the objective interests of tenants helped foster that solidarity. An index of this is the powerful correlation between public sector housing and Labour voting. In the years after 1979 the Conservatives 'privatized' large sections of the housing market. Since the original right-to-buy legislation was enacted in 1980, about 2.2 million local authority dwellings have been sold or otherwise transferred to private ownership. The strategy had both cultural and instrumental objectives: to break up the homogeneity of public-sector estates; and to reshape the interests of residents, away from a concern with public-sector rents to a concern with mortgage markets and with the health of the markets in house sales.

The above is intended to give no more than a sketch of how by a mixture of conscious strategic choices, and the more unintended outcome of economic processes, working-class interests were reshaped under the Conservatives. These changes can probably be communicated in a sketch because they have been pretty exhaustively described. Less widely discussed are the reshaping of other interests in the years since 1979.

After the death of Liberalism as a major electoral force the Conservatives were the natural party of the professions in Britain; that was part and parcel of their role as the defender of the social order. But after 1979 the relationship between the party and the professions became much more fractious. The source of that fractiousness was the breakdown of the agreed structures of representation. These structures had allowed professions to function as independent corporate interests, governing themselves with little intervention by the state. Changes in the fortunes of three groups after 1979 illustrate the scale of change: the medical profession, the universities and the legal profession.

After 1979 there were three sources of tension with the medical profession: incursions by the state into the traditional autonomy of the profession's own regulatory institutions, notably the General Medical Council; the introduction after 1983 of a stratum of general managers into the NHS whose explicit purpose was to challenge the hitherto hegemonic role of clinicians in making decisions about the allocations of resources; and finally, after 1990, the introduction, in the face of large-scale opposition from the medical profession, of major institutional changes into the NHS which greatly altered the role of the general practitioners in the delivery of primary care, changed the status and authority of hospital consultants, and exposed the whole health care system both to competitive forces and to much more transparent budgeting than had hitherto been the case.

A comparison of the university sector in 1979 with that left by the Conservatives on their departure from office in 1997 shows an even more extraordinary change. In 1979 the university sector was small, elitist, stable and largely self-governing. Most of the expansion that had taken place in higher education in the 1970s had occurred in the public (polytechnic) sector. The University Grants Committee (UGC) functioned as a 'buffer' between the universities and the central state, and the UGC itself mostly distributed resources in large block grants to universities, allowing them to allocate resources internally at their own discretion. Constitutionally, the universities were self-governing bodies operating under Royal Charter, their staff subject virtually to no scrutiny of either teaching or research. By the late 1990s this world had vanished. A single, large university sector had been created by integrating the old independently-governed universities with the former polytechnics. This new unified sector was subject to detailed control by Higher Education Funding Councils, themselves much more closely integrated into the central state than had been the old UGC. There now occur regular, highly-publicized reviews of the research and teaching performance of university teachers. The universities have been transformed from independent self-governing corporations into state-controlled institutions. The substantive significance of this change of course cannot match in importance the great class victory over the miners. Nevertheless, it has great symbolic significance. The Conservatives had now so adapted to the governing crisis of the 1970s that they were prepared to attack a quintessentially petit-bourgeois group like university teachers.

Why was this surprising attack on petit-bourgeois interests mounted by a party with roots deep in that social stratum? The most important reason was the pressure on the party in government to reshape domestic interests so as to accommodate international competitive forces. This is made particularly clear by the treatment of the third professional group identified here, the lawyers. The changes here are given an added significance because this was a profession with a historically secure alliance with the Conservative Party. Under the Lord Chancellorship of Lord Mackay there occurred radical changes in court procedure, in the internal governing structures of both solicitors and barristers, in their occupational structures and training arrangements, and in their competitive practices. An important reason for this change was the competitive position of commercial law firms, especially those operating in the City of London. The changes were designed to help City firms compete more effectively in the international commercial law market, and to strengthen the position of London as a centre for the provision of international legal services.

There are close connections between this legal services market and London's more general position as an international financial centre. Thus the changes in the legal profession were closely connected to a centrepiece of economic strategy after 1979: building the economy of the South-East around London's position in the global financial system. After returning to office in 1979 the Conservatives allied themselves with the reformers in the City of London who were pressing for major changes in the organization of financial markets and for changes in ownership rules. The object was to promote the City's position as a leading international financial centre. Those changes were inaugurated in an agreement between the Chairman of the Stock Exchange (Nicholas Goodison) and the Secretary of State for Industry (Cecil Parkinson) in 1983. The Goodison–Parkinson Agreement led to changes which revolutionized both trading practices and the relationship between the City and the state. In trading, there was a bonfire of restrictive practices, especially over pricing. The lifting of restrictions on ownership swept away traditional partnerships and transferred ownership to large multinational financial conglomerates, many of them foreign. Under the Financial Services Act 1986 the independence of the City's own self-regulatory bodies was greatly diminished by the creation of a comprehensive legal structure headed by a regulatory institution (the Securities and Investments Board) with extensive legal powers.

The Goodison–Parkinson Agreement has some claims to be the central event in interest representation after 1979, for it was a defining moment in the history of the relationship between Government and the business community. The Conservative Party that elected to defend the established order in the 1920s defined that established order to include the manufacturing industries created by the Industrial Revolution. The connection between the party and domestic manufacturing capital was symbolized by the fact that the two dominating figures in inter-war Conservatism, Baldwin and (Neville) Chamberlain were members of families whose wealth was based on the iron foundry industries of the West Midlands. The Goodison–Parkinson Agreement not only signalled a rift between the party and the traditional interests that had controlled the City; it was part of a wider shift in strategy that diminished government commitment to manufacturing. The recession at the start of the 1980s inflicted great damage on much of the domestically owned manufacturing sector. The remaking of the economy was partly based on enticing non-EU foreign multinationals to use the UK as an entrepot economy, providing access to the markets of Europe, and partly on using the City Revolution to develop a dynamic commercial economy in the South-East. During the decade the government's relations with the representatives of manufacturing industry were often highly acrimonious: as early as 1980 Terence Beckett, the Director General of the CBI, promised a 'bare knuckle fight' with the new Thatcher Government (Grant, 1993: 114). The CBI, the main voice of manufacturing capital, saw a sharp decline in its influence by comparison with golden years of the 1970s.

Revisiting the Fundamentals

'Statecraft' has been central to the discussion in this chapter because it helps give an account of a subtle, tortuous relationship: that between the 'situational necessity' presented by deep-rooted economic and social structures and the individual agency of creative, manoeuvring political leaders. The statecraft of the last twenty years, in summary, simultaneously increased class inequality and weakened class organization. (By contrast, gender inequality and, probably, racial inequality both diminished during the years of Conservative rule.) The growth of class inequality, especially at the extremes, is one of the most striking achievements of the Conservative years. A mixture of public policies (such as changes in taxation levels) and changes in the structure of labour markets greatly increased the rewards of the very best paid, while cutting the real standard of living of the poorest in the community. After eighteen years of Conservative rule the very rich were fabulously richer and the very poor were significantly poorer than at the start of the Thatcher era. Working-class organization was weakened by the processes described in the preceding pages: by the twin effects of public policies which were designed, successfully, to restrict trade union power through law, and by economic policies which almost wiped out industries where class organization was strong, like coal, and expanded sectors where unions were weak.

Weakened working-class organization is well documented. The decline of business representation is less commonly noticed. It is obscured because the historically dominant *political* voice of business, the Conservative Party, also dominated British politics after 1979. But while the party dominated as a source of policy innovation, and controlled the state machine, its social and economic foundations were rotting away. The mass membership – once the greatest of any party – had by the 1990s shrunk to an elderly, dying core. Over large parts of the UK constituency organization virtually ceased to function. In short, at local level the party ceased to perform one its key historic roles – representing petit-bourgeois interests in British politics. Meanwhile, at elite level the pressures of government increased the long-term trend for the professionalization of politics. After years in office the party was totally dominated by professional politicians with weak links to the business community. The organic connection that had existed between big business and the Conservatives was dissolving. One sign of the Conservatives' decline as the voice of great interests is the recent history of party finance. At the height of the party's success as a mass organization, the sources of party finance were healthily diversified: large amounts came from the constituency organizations, supplemented by a stable flow of donations from big business (Pinto-Duschinsky, 1981). Although the party's secrecy about money makes generalization difficult, it seems that by the 1990s it was scavenging almost anywhere for finance. Anecdotal evidence suggests that it had become heavily reliant on donations from foreign entrepreneurs, especially from the Far East.

By the 1990s the Conservative Party had become disconnected from its historic class allies, its policies increasingly driven by internal forces – clashes between ideological factions and between factions led by competing leadership contenders. These facts help explain one of most striking features of modern British politics: that the Conservatives policies on Europe, especially on the issue of monetary unification, are now at odds with the views of their historic allies in big business, both in the City and in the manufacturing sector. The party is opposed to monetary unification; big business overwhelmingly in favour.

The way the Conservatives reshaped the class 'fundamentals' in the 1980s and 1990s presented many problems for their political opponents. But it also created opportunities. 'New Labour' has seized those opportunities. The weakening of working-class organization, especially of unions, created the space for the Labour leadership to loosen the historic link between the party and the unions. As the Conservatives in office became increasingly distant from the business community, Labour cultivated business interests, both for money and for legitimacy. In economic and social policy the Conservatives were the great creative force. The leadership of New Labour has nevertheless shown strategic acumen in accepting most of the Conservative reforms and aligning the party with the social forces that benefited from them. But Labour has also shown policy creativity in addressing one area of the fundamentals neglected by the Conservatives – the national structure of the United Kingdom (see Chapter 6). The Conservatives' electoral statecraft after 1979 was of a piece with their industrial statecraft. It involved taking advantage of the peculiarities of the electoral system to win by targeting key strata of voters in the South of England. This neglect of the party's historic 'one nation' electoral strategy led to the catastrophe of the 1997 election when it disappeared as a parliamentary force in Wales and Scotland. The Labour Party has emerged as the voice of those nations and regions which felt dispossessed by the social impact of the years of Conservative rule; this is what lies behind the Labour Government's radical devolution policies, especially for Scotland. When combined with New Labour's willingness to press forward more enthusiastically than its Conservative predecessors over European unification, the Constitutional changes promise to reshape the British state as fundamentally as the Conservatives after 1979 reshaped the social structure. For the moment, the spirit of policy creativity – the means by which individual agency can work upon 'situational necessity' – has passed from Conservatism to Labour. Whether Labour will turn out to be the dominant creative force in British politics for the next two decades, as the Conservatives were from the late 1970s, is something only time will tell us.

Acknowledgements

I am grateful to the editors, and to Steven Kennedy, for many helpful comments on earlier versions of this chapter. I also owe a particular debt to my colleague David Coates for his many perceptive comments, a debt doubled because much of what is written here he will disagree with.

10
Electoral Representation and Accountability: The Legacy of Empire

PATRICK DUNLEAVY

Throughout most of the twentieth century, the fundamental British conceptions of how liberal democracy should link citizens to their governments and political representatives have been limited, impoverished and unresponsive to wider patterns of social and political change. Political representation and accountability to citizens have been interpreted in a minimal way, crystallized in the 'Westminster Model'. This 'primitive' conception of the scope of accountability and the meaning of citizens' representatives has survived intact for virtually the whole century – despite the transformative impacts of two world wars, massive economic and social class changes, and the shift from Fordist and patriarchal social structures to 'post-modern' patterns of social life.

Answering questions about why these patterns originated and then persisted occupies the first part of the chapter. After a quick review of the 'Westminster Model' assumptions, I point to four key pillars which sustained it, little changed, for so long:

- the schizoid development of British democracy inside the broader shell of the world's most powerful and successful modern imperialist state;
- the collusive 'club ethos' which bound together Conservative and Labour elites in a joint cartel which minimized political elites' transactions costs;
- '*trahison des clercs*', the subversion of independent critique from intellectuals or from the mass media by strong partisan attachments and a pervasive 'system bias' in framing issues; and
- the willingness of a compliant but still resisting British public opinion to accept arrangements which penalized or diverted some of their preferences.

The second part of the chapter looks at when, and the reasons why, a degree of lagged change in public attitudes came about at the century's end, triggering an institutional transformation equivalent to a refounding of the British constitutional settlement.

The Westminster Model and Why it Endured

The conventional justification of accountability processes in the British constitutional settlement throughout the twentieth century had several key elements, covering voting, parties, political communications, the behaviour of representatives and control over governments.

Voting was simple. People could choose to support any party or individual standing in their local constituency. Their votes would be fairly counted and whoever got most votes in their area would win a seat, irrespective of whether they had majority support. No mechanism was provided to ensure the least degree of balance between parties' vote shares and their seat shares, nationally or regionally. Votes for a party which ran only second or third everywhere would be 'wasted' – all that mattered for winning was to come first in some local areas. The system was very easy to participate in and it was relatively easy for citizens to understand how seats were allocated. Most seats were 'safe' for one party most of the time. Elections were decided by small groups of floating voters in marginal constituencies.

Parties were seen as completely private bodies, rooted in 'civil society' but not partaking of the powers of the state. Parties did not have to be registered, nor were they subject to any special public law regulation in their internal operations. Parties could organize their own affairs as they liked, selecting candidates for Parliamentary constituencies at the local level and choosing a leadership at the national level in ways that did not have to be democratic. Similarly party policy could be determined as parties saw fit. All they needed to do was to publish a rule book and stick to it, just like any other body regulated by civil law. Members with a grievance could turn to the ordinary civil courts to seek redress. Parties did not receive state funding, but could raise political finance privately in any way they liked. They did not have to declare donations and could spend as much as they wanted on national election campaigns or general advertising (that is, spending not focused on a particular local contest). A partial exception to the non-regulation of political finance was that certain kinds of donors – trade unions and publicly quoted companies – did have to declare donations to parties under the law covering *their* normal operations. But individuals, private law companies, interest groups or front organizations could choose to donate as much as they wanted to parties, and could keep their actions completely secret, and so could foreign citizens or governments. A minimal set of laws on election expenses regulated constituency contests, however. Parties or individuals could stand easily and for nothing in local elections, but from 1918 a minimum financial deposit was required for standing at Parliamentary elections, returned if the party won a certain proportion of the vote. Initially the deposit was low while the threshold to get it back was high (one-eighth of votes cast), but towards the end of the century the financial limit was raised and the vote threshold was lowered (Blackburn, 1995: 223–31).

Political communications were virtually unregulated at the start of the century, and press advertising or commentary have continued to be. Newspapers operated under a 'free-press' regime. They could allocate coverage and make political commitments or not, solely as their market imperatives and patterns of proprietorial control dictated. Broadcasting was different, however, partly because of initial fears of its persuasive powers. First radio (from the 1920s) and later TV broadcasting and advertising (from the 1950s) were closely regulated. Under 'bi-partisanship' rules broadcasters were required to giving equal time to the top two parties, and a ration of time very approximately reflecting votes shares to other parties. Parties were allocated a fixed number of state-financed TV and radio advertising slots on the same basis, and all other broadcast advertising of politics was banned.

The behaviour of representatives was guided chiefly by the party requirement that winning MPs should rigidly support their leadership in Parliament on all confidence votes and virtually all legislation. This position was justified by the mandate doctrine that all promises pledged by a party in its election manifesto must be implemented – for anything else would be a betrayal of voters' trust. Party cohesion scores (measuring how much of the time MPs voted in line with their party in the Commons) ran at 95 per cent or above for virtually the whole century. MPs were permitted to vote freely only on 'conscience issues' where their party (and usually its main opponents as well) had withdrawn from adopting a manifesto position. MPs also claimed to represent all their local constituents on individual grievances or problems (irrespective of partisan loyalties) – although this was obviously impossible on strong partisan issues where a majority or a large minority of constituents held views opposed to those of their MP. MPs might also transmit constituents' general views upwards inside their party to Commons whips or the leadership, in so far as MPs could discern what these views were from their assorted personal contacts with constituents or with their local party membership.

Control over governments was secured only by periodic elections of what were expected to be single-party governments, which began work within hours of a national result emerging. Such governments controlled unrivalled executive action powers under Crown prerogative, and with a secure majority enjoyed complete dominance in the Commons. They were constrained in the interim only by the public relations impact of criticism by the main opposition party in the Commons, by the possibility that the weak House of Lords might vote against some minor legislative provisions (not covered in the winning party's manifesto), and by the cross-currents of opinion among MPs within the governing party itself – to the very limited extent that Parliamentary disciplines allowed such cross-currents to emerge publicly. At the end of a Parliament voters would know clearly which party had been in government and had originated all policies, and could choose either to reward them or to swing their support to the main opposition party if they were dissatisfied.

There was no codified statement of *citizens' rights*, let alone independent constitutional protection for them. Instead rights could be altered at will by a government with a Commons majority, because statute law over-rode all other sources of law (the 'sovereignty of Parliament' doctrine), and a current Commons majority could overturn any previous decision ('Parliament cannot bind itself'). Fundamental safeguards of civil liberties were provided only by the fact that elections took place regularly, and that infringements of civil liberties *might* lose the governing party votes – always assuming that opposition parties involved the issue in party competition, rather than agreeing to the infringements themselves.

This conception of liberal democracy was severely limited in several key respects. Although the importance of public opinion and voting in conditioning government policies were central to the model, there was no expectation that any fine-grained control of public policies would be vested with citizens, nor that the discretionary behaviour of political parties would be constrained by any procedural controls on them. Voters had strictly limited choices and options, and many citizens' ballots were effectively screwed up as soon as they were cast and could not influence the selection of representatives. Election results could be severely disproportional at a national level, typically with the largest party in terms of votes receiving a strongly exaggerated share of Commons seats (the 'leader's bias effect'), while third- or fourth-placed parties accumulated significant votes shares nationally but won few or no seats. Across whole regions of the country it was common for the leading party to win virtually all seats, creating 'electoral deserts' for its opponents, a trend that grew sharply worse after the mid-1970s with increasing regionalization of alignments. The information environment and political finance aspects of elections could become severely unbalanced, with the Conservatives always far outspending their rivals or enjoying a highly favourable print media advantage, with only the restrictions on broadcasting to act as counterweight.

The electorate could (normally) expect that the less unpopular of the two major parties would form a single majority government with a Commons majority. But the combination of plurality rule elections and the manifesto doctrine meant that there was no guarantee that the virtually unscrutinized policies enacted by the controlling party's MPs on auto-pilot would enjoy majority support in any individual policy area. Citizens could have more differentiated local or individual influence with MPs only on issues *outside* the scope of main party commitments, or on administrative and implementation concerns. Executive action by the government could commit the country to wars and foreign engagements without prior approval by Parliament or citizens, and legislative and public consultation processes were controlled throughout by the government. Interactions in public policy-making were severely limited and there were few effective checks and balances. With no decentralized centres of legislative or executive power above a weak local government level, policy-making in mainland Britain operated on a much larger scale than in most other liberal democracies (Dunleavy, 1995).

Completely missing from this picture were some of the 'normal' postulates of either European liberal democracies (notably, that seat shares in the legislature should accurately reflect the balance of preferences expressed by voters) or of the United States approach (notably, that citizens' rights should be specified in an invariant form and protected by strong institutions insulated from control by this year's legislative majority). This version of the Westminster Model lasted into the last quarter of the twentieth century, with only minor changes and adaptations, despite being subject to some stresses and strains. Its reverberations were accurately diagnosed by Miliband who declared that: 'By far the most important institution in the British political system is the House of Commons' (Miliband, 1984: 20). He roundly blamed what he saw as the illusory ideology of 'Parliamentarism' (the belief that a Commons majority can enact fundamental change) for sustaining 'the containment of pressure from below' and stabilizing the British social formation as a whole. But his analysis is *flawed* by a critique of liberal democracy as a whole, instead of focusing sufficiently on the unique features of the British case.

The Marriage of Democracy and Empire

In explaining the persistence of the Westminster Model the most important (and often least remembered) fact to bear in mind is that the development of liberal democracy internally in the British Isles coincided with the heyday of the Empire externally. The easiest way out of the intellectual bind of explaining how a liberal democracy could not only run an Empire, but also be so enthusiastically in favour of active imperialism for so long, was typically to deny in subtle and civilised ways the reality of a repressive imperial state run from and created by a conscious policy of expansion. The pervasive liberal myths, sustained unchallenged by most British historians (Elton, 1945: 522), all stress that the empire was an accidental creation, acquired reluctantly, almost in a fit of absent-mindedness, against the will of distracted British statesmen. It was also of course administered in a devolved, conscientious and basically decent way by dispassionate and racially unbigoted personnel, almost out of a spirit of (as we can now see, misguided) altruism. And this 'effortless rule' was maintained not by the massed force of Britain's navy, military and colonial police forces but either with the tacit consent of the subject peoples, or reflecting the innate moral superiority of (white) British officialdom when confronted with (it goes without saying) disorganized native populations (Subrahmanyam, 1995). Stokes (1959) summed up the resulting liberal authoritarianism as: 'the belief that political power tended constantly to deposit itself in the hands of a natural aristocracy, that power so deposited was morally valid, and that it was not to be tamely surrendered before the claims of abstract democratic ideals, but was to be asserted and exercised with justice and mercy'. In 1908 an Anglophile American political scientist Lowell (1908, volume I: 422) claimed that: 'The government of India is really in the hands of about eleven hundred Englishmen, of whom a couple of hundred are military officers or uncovenant civilians, while all the rest belong to the great corps of the Civil Service'. Untouched by decades of critique of occidentalism, but with marginally more realistic statistics, these views live on (Harrison, 1996). Only a few matters seem to have escaped attention here – such as, overwhelming Western administrative and military technological superiority; a well-organized and funded Indian state apparatus of over 2.5 million personnel (quite a high state/civil society ratio for a developing country); a military force of 312 000 men in 1914 (Jenks, 1923: 95), plus equivalent police forces (Anderson and Killingray, 1991); divide and rule methods of ethnic group management; and a developed system of alliances with feudal indigenous rulers.

We need to make a different move to resolve the intellectual contradictions of how a liberal democracy could run an empire for at least thirty years at full throttle (1918–47), within a longer period marked by liberal constitutionalism without full domestic democracy at one end (1868–1917) and decolonization at the other (1948–68). And this step is not to deny the realities of the coercive and despotic British empire, but instead to recognize the extraordinary limitations which it imposed on the operations of liberal democracy within Britain itself. To develop a democratic state while controlling a coercive empire the British solution was to institutionalize three separate spheres of power – a domestic, welfare-orientated 'island state' financed by British taxes; a colonial state in each overseas territory, locally financed and run; and bridging between the two an 'imperial state' focused on the defence forces, the colonial departments (India Office, Colonial Office and Foreign Office) and the intelligence services. Imperial administration, defence policy and foreign affairs were very extensively insulated from the House of Commons and from party politics, so that the coercive management needed to maintain Empire rule could operate within the accumulated British tradition of not specifying rights, relying on administrative self-restraint and the socialization of officials to ensure that excesses were avoided (Beattie and Dunleavy, 1995).

This stance *required* that liberal democracy in Britain was more or less frozen in a late-nineteenth-century mould. Civil liberties and human rights in the mainland state could never be given any codified legal protection, for fear of the spillover into the imperial realms. Even after the late-1950s when Britain signed up to the European Convention on Human Rights, Labour and Tory governments alike refused for the next 40 years to incorporate it into British law, partly for fear of its colonial implications, and partly because of the realization that its terms would indeed bind British 'parliamentary sovereignty' within the island state itself. In the event, only after surrendering the last substantial imperial possession (Hong Kong) in 1997 did a Labour administration move to domesticate the ECHR. Crown prerogative powers remained the basis for military policies, intelligence service operations, imperial administration and the conduct of foreign affairs. Government at the top in Britain remained famously 'flexible', a zone of discretionary executive action which covered all the intelligence services, critical areas of budgeting (for example, none of the secret services budgets were declared to Parliament), and the operations of the cabinet government system. A pall of official secrecy and parliamentary non-scrutiny was extended not just over the imperial domain but also across massive areas of domestic politics.

The Club Ethos of Partisan Elites

The social basis for this unusual, sustained deformation of liberal democracy was a concordat between the Conservatives, Britain's 'natural party of government' in power with secure majorities for three-quarters of the twentieth century, and their nearest rivals – successively the Liberals in the pre-1918 era, and the Labour party thereafter. The basis for this deal was to admit the opposition leadership into co-direction of the giant imperial state, so long as they played by the rules of limited domestic democracy (Miliband, 1984: 29–32). However strongly first left-Liberals and later Labour partisans abhorred the maintenance of coercive rule in the Empire, they had to confront the inescapable task of demonstrating their own credibility as governors of an apparatus that visibly could not be lightly or quickly dismantled. A key audience shaping the response of the 'island state' electorate was the powerful 'establishment' of officialdom and its related military–industrial complex (Holland, 1985: ch. 9). Labour's left maintained a constant criticism, and its leadership enunciated vaguely democratic principles: but in opposition in the 1950s the party was 'seldom if ever able to force dramatic and visible changes in government policy' on the Empire (Goldsworthy, 1971: 359). By the 1960s the military–industrial complex had moved away from maintaining colonies (see below), but by a strange

inversion the Labour leadership stoutly defended the remnants of
Empire (Holland, 1985: 276).

The central basis for binding first Liberal and then Labour leaders
and MPs into complicity in the maintenance of limited democracy
was the creation of a bi-partisan 'club ethos'. Once they accepted
these rules of the game, and agreed to suppress elements in their
parties demanding wider democratization, the leaders of the non-
Tory parties were incorporated into 'the establishment' and gained
access to a dazzling range of patronage powers, the ability to cut deals
and to secure their own political futures with the electorate and with
the personnel who controlled the government machine. The maintenance of first-past-the-post, more properly called plurality-rule
elections, was a critical basis for common agreement. It designated
at first a Conservative–Liberal duopoly of power, where plurality
rule's exaggerated rewards to the leading party provided the only
viable hope for a majority government in the period before the First
World War. At that time the ever-present threat of a unified group of
Irish MPs holding the balance of power in the Westminster Parliament filled imperial decision-makers with perennial dread. After the
Liberals split between the Lloyd George and Asquith factions in 1916,
and Labour soared to second-party status in the 1918 election, the
maintenance of plurality rule was a critical bargaining counter
persuading Labour leaders and MPs, plus huge numbers of union
and constituency activists, to buy into the re-establishment and
maintenance of the 'club ethos' on Tory–Labour lines. The long-
delayed 1945 election victory and Labour's first access to single-party
majority-government powers consolidated the party's acceptance of
limited democracy into an article of faith for successive Labour
generations.

The foundation of the club ethos was a kind of sectional but
consociational deal between the behemoths of British politics, an
agreement to co-exist and not to call into question each other's very
existence. First Conservatives and Liberals, and then the Tories and
Labour groped their way to a limited 'hands-off' agreement. The
Tory–Liberal deal broke down over the House of Lords' obstruction
of the 1909 budget. Thereafter on the Tory side it was disintegrating
so fast over Irish home rule in the run-up to 1914 that Tuchman
(1966) among others points to a real risk of civil war, with army
dissension against Liberal ministers' orders being stoked up by the
Leader of the Opposition. Restored fragmentarily by the First World
War, the Tory–Liberal deal vanished in a puff of smoke when the

Liberal split left them vulnerable to a concerted push to destroy them. Thereafter a Tory–Labour deal was central, and it endured with only minor perturbations for over sixty years. Its key elements included joint defence of plurality rule, abstention from interference in the other party's finances (only very partially abandoned by the Conservatives after the 1926 general strike), and a hands-off policy towards the other party's key institutions. In particular, Labour left the Lords and the monarchy unreformed, while the Tories accepted an *ad hoc* legal compromise that defined all strikes as technically breaches of contract but exempted trade unions from paying damages for causing them.

Yet there were two key transition points where this historical evolution was not pre-programmed, where subsequent political history might have turned in radically different directions. Both concerned reform of the voting system. In 1917, during the debates on the Representation of the People Act, the Conservatives and Liberals visibly hesitated about maintaining plurality-rule elections, while the few Labour MPs were pushing for reform (Hart, 1992). The Commons witnessed some unusually open and fluid debates, as the shadow of the first Russian revolution stretched across Europe and the rising industrial militancy at home presaged a growth of the Labour vote. Many Conservatives and Liberals wavered towards following their European counterparts further down the road to proportional representation, fearing an emergent social-democratic majority in the new mass electorate. Despite opposition from the Asquithian Liberals the Commons twice voted to adopt the Alternative Vote, a system which kept local constitutencies but where voters number their preferences 1, 2, 3 in order, and where the winning candidate must be elected with majority support in their locality. Each time their changes were blocked by Conservative peers in the Lords who inserted instead gerrymandering provisions for using the single transferrable vote (STV) in multi-member constituencies in the major cities (a move designed to improve the Tories' chances of seats in industrial areas, while preserving their single-seat hegemony in rural areas). With the Commons and peers deadlocked, and the Liberals internally divided on the issue, Lloyd George eventually accepted the Bill without any clauses changing the electoral system from the *status quo*.

A decade later, the reunited and now endangered Liberals made changing the voting system a condition for their legislative support of the 1929–31 Labour government. Despite Labour leaders' extreme reluctance to accept any reforms, the Alternative Vote system was again the compromise that emerged. Once more it was passed through the Commons only to be blocked by the Lords – with the Tory peers this time united behind plurality rule. MacDonald's administration fell over the currency crisis before the Commons could revote the Bill over the Lords' opposition. For historians who hold the 'two-party' system to be a 'natural' feature of British politics (Harrison, 1996), the 1917 and 1931 events were untypical aberrations.

The Absence of Critique

The historians' attitude reflected a much wider and complacent simplification of British experience by groups who dominated public debates – including intellectuals and the national news media. For the vast majority of lawyers, political scientists, historians and social commentators, no matter how unacceptable they found the maintenance of Empire, it became an article of faith that the British system of limited accountability and erratic representation of votes, operating within an unwritten constitution, was pretty near perfect, and not to be disturbed by formalistic critiques. Writing as late as 1977, the liberal Conservative thinker Ian Gilmour could still unblushingly affirm the century's conventional wisdom: 'In my view, a two-party system and an unfixed constitution is the highest form of political development yet seen' (Gilmour, 1977: 226). Such convictions could allow only of the most impoverished development of political debates about liberal democracy, such as the sterile 'Whig' versus 'Tory' views celebrated by commentators like Birch (1964) and Amery (1947). 'Whigs' believed only that in some vestigial sense the actions of the executive should be controlled by a popular will expressed via elections, while 'Tories' in this debate believed that the Queen's government must above all be carried on, uninterrupted and giving power-holders a permanent benefit of the doubt (Beattie, 1995).

The protection given by the intellectuals and the media to the operations of the voting system and the party system was virtually complete, and political commentators in particular developed a mythical idea of a 'two-party system' as the foundation stone of democratic choice and electoral accountability (Harrison, 1996). Only a few, more radical, historians commonly dissent from this myth (Taylor, 1965: 195). Yet the statistics tell a different story if we insist on precision about how we should define a two-party system in electoral terms (rather than in terms of Commons representation, *after* plurality rule elections have done their work in distorting a large chunk of voters' preferences). One approximate benchmark might be to demand of a designated 'two-party system' that the duopoly of major parties should attract 90 per cent of the votes, as they do consistently in US legislative elections, while a looser criterion might be that the major parties attract 85 or 80 per cent of the UK vote. Figure 10.1 shows that across the century's 26 general elections only six clearly pass the 90 per cent test (1902, 1906, 1935, 1951, 1955 and 1959). If we broaden out to an 85 per cent vote share we can add in the two 1910 elections (despite the Irish holding the balance), plus 1931 and 1945, the two 1960s elections and 1970. If we go further down to the 80 per cent level, the effect is inconsequential, adding in by the narrowest of margins only two obvious outliers (1924 and 1979), both isolated results amidst sustained periods of multi-party politics. Sticking with an 85 per cent share of the vote as the criterion of a 'two-party system' we can conclude that barely half of Britain's elections in the twentieth century qualify, while 47 per cent do not.

The ability to see two-party dominance where it did not exist electorally was a persistent and not an idiosyncratic feature of commentary, reflecting the tendency for media and academic analysts alike to assign unwarranted legitimacy to the constituency outcomes reflected in the Commons. With very large numbers of votes chewed into ineffectiveness by plurality-rule elections, the pattern of Commons representation none the less could often effectively disguise the local, experienced disproportionality of plurality rule, by apparently 'balancing' Labour over-representation in industrial cities against Conservative over-representation in suburban and countryside areas.

A further essential feature of the two-party club ethos was that the Conservatives and Labour cheerfully aided and abetted each other in using Parliamentary procedure to marginalize all other parties, to sideline their motions, to push their speakers down the agenda of debates, and to agree a timetable of mutual convenience. From the 1920s onwards Tory and Labour politicians at national level both portrayed politics in ding-dong terms, despite the existence of other patterns, for instance, anti-Labour alliances of Tory, Liberal and Independent councillors in local government. The centrality of Parliamentary government in British democracy meant that these cartellizing tactics were picked up and magnified by an increasingly partisan-polarized press. While Liberal or non-aligned newspapers lingered on quite influentially until the late 1950s, and were reborn in a minor way in the 1980s, the media's duopolistic approach was given

FIGURE 10.1 *Four periods in the predominance of the two main parties*

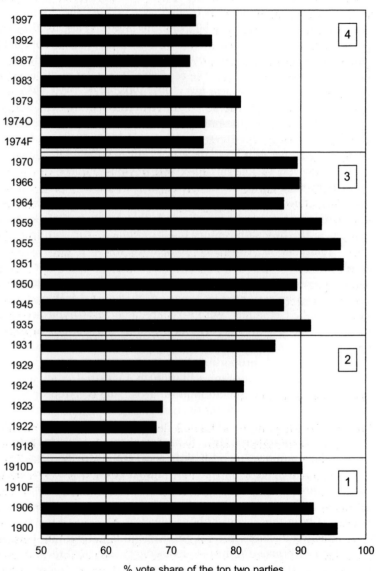

% vote share of the top two parties

a perverse boost by the growth of broadcast coverage from the 1950s – with balance being interpreted there as a 'plague on both your houses', but not multiple houses.

The most intellectually respectable defences of the two-party system pulled all these strands together, to argue that a 'two-party system' is not just to be determined in terms of vote shares, but must also make reference to parties' presence in the legislature, the extent to which the top two parties polarize and colonize the key ideological debates in public life, and of course the degree to which they monopolize government. The founding father of this post-war political-science orthodoxy was Joseph Schumpeter, whose book *Capitalism, Socialism and Democracy* provided three decades of intellectual cover for the British establishment. His revisionist model of democracy attacked unrealistic and dated 'classical' models of an active and involved citizenry, initiating policy debates autonomously and directly willing policy changes. Instead he posited a minimalist model in which two or more party elites competed for endorsement, with the elites monopolizing the production of the political agenda, and the mass of voters reduced to adjudicating between the heavily-packaged options pre-set for them. Writing in 1944 Schumpeter also managed to mis-characterize the inter-war years of the British system as a two-party system conforming to his model, and he explicitly disparaged any effort at a proportional reflection of voters' views (Schumpeter, 1992).

The Compliant Electorate

For the British pattern of limited democracy to survive, an elite consensus to 'contain pressure from below' (in Miliband's phrase) was not sufficient. Citizens, too, had to go along with the deal. They had to comply with it – which is not to say they did not extensively resist it, for in dealing with public officials (the ensemble of elected politicians and senior administrators) voters are subject to power relations which constrain their choices. In his discussion of the autonomy of the democratic state, Nordlinger famously distinguished three levels of power which public officials (politicians and civil servants) could possess. The simplest, Type I power, arises when the electorate and other civil-society interests want the same things as public officials – but public officials carry out these preferred policies for their own, not the electorate's, reasons.

In the British case, why should large numbers or a majority of voters have an interest in limiting the development of liberal democracy? Strong Tory and Labour partisans among voters may have shared some of their leaders' club ethos, looking forward to periods of single-party government in a 'We are the masters now' mode. One particular group of voters with an interest in the maintenance of the *status quo* were those implicated in the continuation of the Empire, which clearly required limited internal democracy and accountability inside Britain itself. Hundreds of thousands of British people either served in the Empire territories, or had family or service personnel there, while thousands more were involved in commercial activities, especially as British trade came to focus more and more within the Empire from the 1900s up to the 1940s. Before the end of the Second World War any government which endangered any aspect of British rule was destined for instant electoral obliteration. Despite the Labour party's ideological and rhetorical commitment to decolonization, the party's leaders who gained power in the 1920s (and the Liberal administration before the First World War) were only too well aware that their credibility in handling imperial issues was critical for their ability to survive as a viable party of government. Maintaining limited democracy inside the island state, protecting strong and relatively uncontrolled executive-action capabilities, was seen by large sectors of the electorate as critical for defending these broader interests.

Nordlinger's second type of state power occurs when public officials can successfully persuade voters to change their minds where their initial preferences ran against the state's preferences. Assailed by strong and unanimous elite messages stressing the policy orthodoxy, citizens with no or few other sources of political information adapt, revise and tone down their views, until eventually they accept that the wishes of leading state personnel are also theirs'. The club ethos ensured that for most of the twentieth century, whenever voters chose to support third or fourth parties, the leaderships of the major parties could simply maintain support for plurality rule and wait for voters to see sense. Duverger pointed out that the 'mechanical effect' of plurality rule was to ignore the ballot papers of the errant minority, but that experience of this process would also create a 'psychological effect', insistently urging those dissenting citizens trying to broaden their options not to waste their vote, to face up to political realities and to accept two-party hegemony in Parliament, the media and London political life. For a time, especially in the period from 1950 to

1970, the electorate seemed to have bought the message. But even here odd little wobbles of dissent kept cropping up.

Nordlinger's third type of state power exists where the preferences of public officials diverge from those of civil society, but public officials can just do what they want to do anyway, whatever the electorate signals. By maintaining plurality-rule elections long after the combined third- and fourth-party vote share pushed above 20 per cent from the late 1970s onwards, Britain's political and administrative elites entered into a dangerous and probably unsustainable phase – a growing and apparently permanent mismatch between the number of parties in citizens' votes and the effective number of parties winning any significant representation in parliament. The conventional political science method for measuring this divergence is called 'deviation from proportionality' or the DV score. It is simple to calculate: subtract parties' percentage shares of seats in the Commons from their percentage shares of votes in the election, ignore the plus or minus signs on the resulting deviations, add up the resulting figures, and then divide by two (to avoid double-counting). The DV score shows what proportion of MPs sitting in the House of Commons represent parties which are not entitled to those seats by their share of the votes. Figure 10.2 shows the actual DV scores for every general election since 1900, together with a trend line (showing the median smoothed DV score) which allows us to distinguish between one-off fluctuations and real changes of trends. Apart from the seven elections from 1950 to 1970 the base level for the smoothed DV score was around 17 per cent throughout the century, with another smaller dip in the two 1910 elections. When we bear in mind that a reasonably proportional electoral system should achieve results in the range between 4 and 8 per cent, it is apparent that the British system has always imposed a high level of misfit between voters' preferences and parliamentary representation, except in the 1950s.

British voters throughout the period have undoubtedly accepted general election results – they have complied with them, and seen them as legitimate enough. But they have also always resisted the imposition of two-party dominance. Even in the Second World War, with all the major parties united in the Churchill coalition, there was a measure of popular dissent – with a string of by-election victories for independents, the strange wartime party Commonwealth, and the Scottish Nationalists. The end of the 1950s' and 1960s' hegemony of the two-party system was pre-signalled by a famous Liberal by-election victory at Orpington in 1962, which pushed the third party's

FIGURE 10.2   *DV scores (%) at British general elections since 1900*

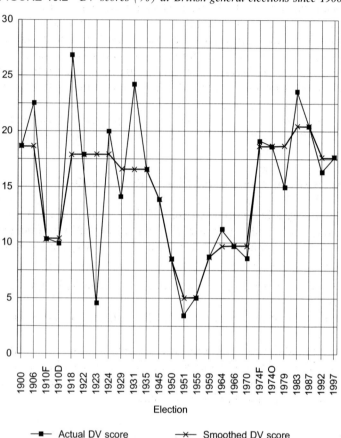

opinion poll support above 22 per cent for three months, and required strenuous two-party efforts to marginalize Liberal support again (pushing it down to half this level by the time of the 1964 election).

There is a final dimension to citizens' compliance – the power which parties could directly dispose of in their dealings with many voters. For most of the century the Conservatives were clearly the permanent party of power nationally, able to draw into their orbit many business and professional people who were anxious to extend their influence within civil society into the state apparatus. In the big cities, local Labour parties also acquired a great deal of control over the allocation of important welfare benefits, especially access to council housing (Hindess, 1971). In the enormously coercive process of slum clearance and rehousing which ran throughout the 1930s, and from 1945 until 1970, very extensive powers over local citizens were available to chiefly local Labour machines. The rehousing process and local party politics were both run in a way which crushed various kinds of political dissent – especially citizens' resistance to clearance and to rehousing in high flats (Dunleavy, 1981). Just as much as in the American 'boss' system, British citizens' compliance with two-party dominance often reflected an accurate *realpolitik* view of the possibilities open to them.

The Origins of a Modernized View of Representation

Four changes in the last quarter of the twentieth century brought about a major shift away from the limited conceptions of democracy which had dominated earlier British elite thinking and maintained voters' compliance:

- a critical realignment of electoral forces accomplished in the early 1970s;
- the apparent collapse of the two-party club ethos under Margaret Thatcher;
- the end of the cold war and Europeanization, which brought about subtle shifts in British public attitudes and party alignments;
- the growth of social diversity, which cross-cut the class bases for Conservative and Labour alignments.

The 1972 Revolution in Alignments

When by-elections are discussed in British political science they are often dismissed as evanescent in effect (Norris, 1990). But on 26 October 1972 when the Liberals won the Rochdale seat from Labour a change began whose implications are still working out in British public life. The Liberals' Gallup poll rating doubled to above 11 per cent in November 1972 and stayed in double figures for the next year until the party achieved over 19 per cent of the vote in the February 1974 general election, and consolidated an 18 per cent vote share in the follow-on October 1974 elections. Britain's third party has exceeded or kept this level of support ever since (apart from a small dip in 1979). At the same time, Scottish National Party fortunes revived north of the border, and the Welsh nationalist Plaid Cymru began to be a more consistent performer – between them the two parties took 2.6 per cent of the vote in October 1974. Not only have these important fourth parties consolidated a permanent presence, but in 1997 a record-breaking 4.4 per cent of the vote even went to short-lived fifth and sixth parties (such as the Referendum Party and the UK Independence Party). Equally in Northern Ireland the revocation of devolved powers from the Stormont Parliament in 1972 began the process of separating out a distinctive party system with no connection at all to the mainland British party system – taking a further 2.3 per cent of the vote out of reach of the major parties. The previous umbilical connection between Conservatives and Unionists has been completely severed, and in the 1998 Assembly elections held under proportional representation 12 parties obtained significant vote shares.

The coincidence of all these changes makes the 1972–74 period the second critical realignment of twentieth-century British politics, equivalent in importance to the 1918 election but much more mysterious and barely analysed, or even noticed, by most political historians. In 1918 the Liberals' relative decline and Labour's rise can be plausibly explained in terms of both the Lloyd George/Asquith split on the one hand, and the enfranchisement for the first time of 40 per cent of the adult male population. But the 1972–74 changes came out of a blue sky, for no equivalent apparent reason. However, they did follow on from the May 1968 'events' which occurred across Europe, and the shifts in alignment within Britain do have parallels elsewhere. Across Scandinavian countries the same period saw the numbers of significant political parties expand radically from four to six, again a once-and-for-all change that has endured.

Since the 1972 realignment there have been seven general elections in which the share of the third, fourth and further parties has never dipped below 20 per cent (the nadir being 1979), and has risen at times as high as 31 per cent (in 1983, when the Social Democratic and Liberal Alliance gained over a quarter of the UK vote). There have been three European Parliament elections where the third and subsequent party share of the vote exceeded 22 per cent, with a dip down to 16 per cent in 1979. In the 1989 Euro election a temporary surge of environmentalist opinion produced a Green vote share of 15 per cent, and a vote share for the non-major parties of 28 per cent. Local and by-elections have also seen high vote shares for third and subsequent parties.

For Harrison (1995: 206) all these unprecedented phenomena indicate only 'the seventh phase in the history of Britain's two-party system'. But more detached and statistically-minded observers have noted from Figure 10.1 that the two-party share of the vote has now been less than 80 per cent for nearly three decades, and from Figure 10.2 that the post-1972 period represents a qualitative increase in the deviation from proportionality score. In fact since 1972, the national DV score has increasingly concealed regional-level DV scores which are much higher, because one-party regional bastions for the Conservatives and Labour strengthened. The complete elimination of Conservative MPs from Scotland, Wales and most English metropolitan areas outside London was achieved at the 1997 general election, while Labour was excluded from almost all representation in much of southern England outside London for most of the 1980s. These twin regional polarization trends offset each other to keep national DV scores artificially low, but the underlying unfairness of the electoral system strengthened massively. In 1992, for instance, the Conservatives won 97 per cent of the seats in the huge South-East region on the basis of just 55 per cent of the votes, giving a regional DV score of 43 per cent, which was more than twice the national average of 17 per cent (Dunleavy and Margetts, 1992, 1997). In fact this particular regional performance lies at the limits of what we could regard as any kind of liberal-democratic result. The maximum possible DV score under liberal democracy in the South-East in 1992 would have been 45 per cent, so the actual score achieved was 95 per cent of the way to being completely undemocratic. At a local government level, maximally unproportional results have occurred frequently. For instance, in Newham in 1994 and 1998 Labour won just over half the votes but gained all of the 60 council seats or all but one, respectively. Such results incidentally make a nonsense of the claim that plurality rule gives voters a clear choice, since in Newham there could be no organized opposition party at all. By 1997 one in five of all local authorities was controlled by a party holding 80 per cent or more of council seats, virtually all Labour.

How long can a liberal democracy go on chewing up such huge proportions of the vote and according no representation in return but still remain basically legitimate? The Conservative and Labour leaderships made a sustained effort to find out throughout the 1970s and 1980s, somehow proclaiming their conviction that nothing was wrong. Perhaps voters would revert to the voting patterns of the golden age in the 1950s, they felt. But even if they did not, nothing had changed, and no one had any substantial grounds for complaining at the treatment of their votes. The British club-ethos argument was that since Labour and the Conservatives between them exhaustively polarized the available ideological space, and since the Liberal Democrats always sat in between the 'majors', there could be no 'real' loss from the policy agenda if third or fourth party votes were discarded, or if the two-party cartel's monopoly of the organization of Parliamentary time were maintained.

Thatcher and the Breaching of the Club Ethos

The rupturing of this elite consensus was one of Margaret Thatcher's most enduring achievements in the period from early 1982 to 1990. Buoyed by the 17 per cent boost in public opinion support created by British victory in the Falklands War, massive media backing, and fragmentation of the majority opposition vote between a failing Labour party and an insurgent Liberal–Social Democrat Alliance, Thatcher achieved a landslide victory for the Conservatives at the 1983 election. At the subsequent 1987 election a small part of the press imbalance was redressed, but previous Civil Service controls on ministers' behaviour during election campaigns lapsed. Although the Conservative party campaign attracted only slightly more TV coverage time than the campaigns for other opposition parties, leading Conservatives also gained as much coverage in their 'non-party' ministerial roles during the election period, effectively doubling the attention paid to them when compared with Labour (Miller, 1989). The Conservatives also breached previously-implied bargains between the two major parties not to interfere in each other's political finances. For the first time since the Edwardian era in most cases, a 1984 Act required trade unions to ballot periodically on maintaining their political funds – Labour's financial life-blood. These breaches of the two-party ethos, plus their party's flagging vote shares, persuaded many Labour activists to embrace proportional representation. The Thatcher experience sowed unprecedented doubts even among Labour leaders about the advantages that their traditional cooperation in working the machine still offered them, and about the time that would elapse before they might seek to redress the balance in Labour's favour.

Nor did the Conservatives in the 1980s stop at re-rigging the basis for two-party competition in their favour. They also used state finance in an unprecedented way to push through 'preference-shaping' changes which tended to build their support base and erode the opposition's vote: selling off British Telecom and British Gas in the mid-1980s for much less than their post-sale values (equivalent to offering £10 notes for £5 in the first Telecom sale); forcing (mainly Labour) councils to sell houses at huge discounts to tenants; abolishing key centres of Labour's local government power, such as the GLC; and pushing through a massive centralization of powers which radically reduced the value of Labour's support bases in local councils (Dunleavy, 1991: ch. 5). 'Thatcherism' became a hegemonic project, especially on privatization, which continued extensively under Major. Massive public-asset sales and contracting-out of public services constantly threatened to outdate Labour's policy programmes, which for more than a decade and a half were dragged unavailingly along in the wake of Tory innovations, each one pushing further back the frontiers of what was feasible in the two-party heyday of the 1950s and 1960s. Only when Thatcher over-reached herself, by forcing through a 'big bang' reform of local government finance in the poll tax, did Labour gain some assurance that sustainable limits could still be set to Conservative government actions (Butler *et al.*, 1993).

This policy climate, along with the need to have a defensible Labour strategy in Scotland, produced the most fundamental re-commitment by Labour to constitutional change since the party's early days. Devolution for Scotland was redesigned in a multi-partisan way in the Scottish Constitutional Convention in the mid-1980s, entailing a commitment to proportional representation, and the same approach was later generalized to cover Wales. With Hong Kong about to be restored to China, Labour accepted after a forty-year wait that the European Convention on Human Rights should be incorporated into British law. Promises to bring in Freedom of Information, to alter the voting system for European Parliament elections, to bring back metropolitan government in London, and to reform the House of Lords (in a tit-for-tat with previous Tory excesses) completed a mini-revolution in Labour attitudes. The whole package (known as the Cook–Maclennan pact) was launched at a joint Labour/Liberal Democrat press conference six weeks before the 1997 general election. The concertation of the two parties' positions helped produce a high level of anti-Conservative tactical cross-voting among their supporters, doubling the number of Liberal Democrat MPs to 45 (despite a decline in their vote share), and vesting Labour with an unprecedented majority (67 per cent of Commons seats for 44 per cent of the British vote). Little wonder that as late as the election night itself, Blair was contemplating a final breach in the two-party club ethos, by offering the Liberal Democrats' leader a Cabinet place in the new Labour government, instead of the eventual deal of a joint Cabinet committee.

The End of the Cold War and 'Europeanization'

A broader background change, also little noticed by British commentators, helped to bring about another transition in party attitudes. The collapse of the Berlin Wall in 1989 and the splitting-up of the Soviet Union in 1991 ushered in a new era of international relations, with significant implications for many liberal democracies' internal politics. These shifts undermined the previously predominant attitude among liberal democracies that their own political systems must be accepted, warts and all, since they were at least superior to those of the communist bloc (Dunleavy and Margetts, 1995). In Italy this reconsideration brought an end to decades of Christian Democrat hegemony in government formation, stimulated public support for an end to party-based corruption, triggered a fundamental change in the voting system in 1991 from List PR to a mixed system, and led to the disappearance of the Christian Democrat and Socialist parties. In Japan the Liberal Democrats also lost sole control of government for the first time as a result of splits, and a new mixed electoral system was brought in as part of a push to curb clientelism and corruption in parties and MPs' behaviour. In New Zealand citizens became so disaffected with the previous two-party alternation in government that a large majority voted to scrap plurality-rule elections and introduce a fully proportional system in 1992 and 1993 referenda. The first election under the new system in 1996 saw six parties winning significant votes and seats.

The foundations for a similar liberation of internal reflection on democratic practices would be easy to miss in British politics, unless we notice a key linkage between the decline of Empire and the salience of the independent nuclear deterrent. The post-imperial idea of a great power status (and a seat on the UN Security Council) founded on nuclear weapons had for a long time sustained the notion that Britain must maintain a strong executive action capability, still insulated from detailed democratic control because of its international obligations. The nuclear focus provided a means by which this small European 'island state' could continue to 'punch above its weight' in international diplomacy. The secrecy and unrestricted executive capabilities inherent in maintaining a nuclear arsenal also continued to sustain the 'club ethos' that bound most Labour leaders into a united establishment against radical left forces and 'woolly liberals' alike, notably in the Labour party's internal wars of the early 1980s.

The media's earlier attitude of 'the British constitution: love it or leave it' also began to be modified. By the mid-1990s the accumulation of major political problems labelled as 'sleaze' and a number of enormously costly policy disasters (such as the under-selling of privatized assets, the BSE crisis in farming, the poll-tax debacle, and Trident) all contributed to a perception of serious structural problems in the British way of public policy-making (Dunleavy, 1995). The possible benefits of curtailing the UK's 'fastest law in the West' approach to legislation and bringing in a more interactive, consensual and multi-stage pattern of policy-making began to be appreciated. The notions of introducing more legal checks and balances to constrain government action and of making major changes to offset the over-centralization of powers in Whitehall acquired widespread support.

The 'Europeanization' of British politics had multiple concurrent effects. Pro- and anti-European issue attitudes cross-cut the Conservative and Labour ideological divide, usually with what Poulantzas aptly described as a cross-party leadership 'bloc'. It first mainly left-Labour opposition to the EEC at the 1975 referendum, then crushed Labour's manifesto pledge to withdraw from the EC in 1983, and then in the late 1980s and early 1990s constrained the forces of Euroscepticism inside the Tory party – including the dumping of Thatcher from the Conservative leadership in 1990. A critical turning point for the bi-partisan bloc mode of management came in 1993, when the Major government could neither command sufficient Tory MPs to enact the Maastricht Treaty through the House of Commons, nor rely on the club ethos to bind the Labour leadership into abstention instead of opposition. In the end Maastricht was implemented solely because the Liberal Democrats supported European integration so much that they had to rescue the government.

British public opinion settled into a normal 'resting state' of being apathetically hostile to the European project, but resigned to its likely further development. Whenever voters had a clear opportunity to withdraw from Europe, as in 1975 and again at the 1983 election, public opinion actually swung round into a pro-European configuration for a few months, only to reassume its previous configuration thereafter. At the same time 'EuroBrit' attitudes gradually became more commonplace from the late 1980s onwards, and they accelerated in the 1990s with increased interaction by British citizens with EU neighbours in industry, the professions, education and tourism. Around a quarter of British citizens began to espouse systematically pro-European attitudes, extending to an appreciation of more 'modern' and constitutionally codified systems of government – views that were more marked among younger age cohorts and least well-supported by the elderly.

The Growth of Social Diversity

The social foundation of the two-party system in its heyday was a situation in which class was the basis of British politics (Pulzer, 1967). By the late 1960s that dominant social cleavage began to be thoroughly undermined by numerous forces. Shifts occurred in the balance of social classes, with manual worker jobs decreasing. From 1970 both manual and non-manual groups reduced their levels of support for their allegedly 'natural' class parties, partly because of the growth of third- or subsequent-party support, but partly because of a 'blurring' of the two parties' traditional support-bases in social terms. The growth of ethnic minority populations progressively changed the Labour party's support-bases in many major city areas, and reactions to that change among some white electors also cross-cut social class lines. In the 1980s also there were temporarily significant efforts to politicize sexual-orientation elements, with some 'loony left' Labour-party activists in city areas advocating a 'rainbow coalition' strategy for their party.

State growth itself had a major impact on party competition. Public-sector unions became more important in Labour's power structure, and Labour candidates and policy positions were increasingly differentiated from the Tories by a commitment to expanding the welfare state, rather than by any class-based policies. The Tories, especially under Thatcher, found fertile ground in broadening their appeal among anti-statist working-class voters. The Liberal Democrats found a good deal of their support among those social groups 'cross-pressured' by their social class and sectoral positions, especially the public-sector middle class.

In Scotland and Wales the social appeal of nationalist parties became progressively more fixed as their long-term viability became assured, and as cross-generational transfers of nationalist alignments from parents to children became feasible. Liberal Democrat support, once famously resistant to characterization in social class terms, became less of a 'hotel party' with people checking in and out for single elections, and more fixed by multiple social cues. Liberal Democrat supporters are most distinctive in having higher levels of education; not reading partisan newspapers; and living in areas of the party's relative strength – which are often built up via local council victories, and span some 'dissenting' rural areas, some professional suburban areas, and one or two inner-city seats.

The cumulative impacts of these changes were traceable in the Conservatives' inability to broaden their support-base under Thatcher. Despite its enormous political advantage in terms of partisan uses of state power, political finance and mass media predominance, the governing party was unable to secure more than 43 per cent support in either 1983 or 1987 – chiefly because the Tories seemed to aggravate or threaten too many diverse groups. In its fightback from its nadir in 1983 Labour too found it hard to extend its appeal in a more complex and pluralistic social structure. Some of its constitutional proposals, notably the adoption of proportional representation for the new metropolitan government of London (now a 25 per cent black and Asian city), reflected the party's recognition that social diversity had to be better reflected in political life and constitutional structures.

Conclusions: Political Representation in Britain

At the end of the twentieth century Britain stands at a 'defining moment' (Barnett, 1997). The long-lived public and elite acceptance of very limited and partial liberal-democratic controls on government has gone. Most citizens and, in their hearts, a majority of national policy elites no longer believe in an uncodified constitution where large numbers of votes can be discounted in awarding representation, nor that the protection of civil rights and political diversity is best left to the 'good sense' of the governing classes. These are critical changes, whose consequences have already mapped into radical institutional shifts, notably the implementation of voting by proportional representation in five different contexts (Scotland, Wales, Northern Ireland, Greater London and the European elections), a radical extension of legal protection for civil rights, reform of core institutions such as the House of Lords, and the recognition of political parties as public law bodies, whose finances must be scrutinized by the state. Current indications suggest that there is little prospect of the Conservatives reversing any of these policies should they regain government in the future.

This fundamental change should create a gestalt shift in intellectual attitudes, throwing into sharp relief the conventional assumptions that somehow a 'two-party system' is bedded down naturally and ineluctably in British public opinion and elite psyche. Informed by the knowledge of what has now happened, we can begin to track back through the history of elite manipulations and public compliance to ask why this change came so much later than in other modern liberal democracies. At the same time important possible reforms remain unimplemented – as attested by Labour's fierce internal debates and perhaps inaction over implementing reform of Westminster elections on the lines recommended by the Jenkins Commission, along with the failure to modernize the Commons legislative procedures significantly, and the predominance of 'democratic centralism' in Tony Blair's mode of government. The pluralization of British constitutional arrangements may yet be halted, and political regressions to a 'club ethos' mode of operating the party system may once again occur. But these ebbs and flows will not now qualify a fundamental underlying change of stance. Britain has become a 'normal' democracy, instead of a special case.

11
Citizenship and Identity

ELIZABETH MEEHAN

A chapter on citizenship, if less so in respect of identity, may be thought to sit oddly in a book called *Fundamentals in British Politics*, for it can be argued that citizenship is far from fundamental to British political praxis. Citizenship as a status replacing subjecthood came into being only in 1948 and more consequentially in 1983 (when the 1981 British Nationality Act came into force) (Gardner, 1997: 5). Moreover the legal foundations of citizens' rights are variable in the different parts of the United Kingdom and, in general, complex. This can be construed positively, as it is by John Patten (Mount, 1992: 33–4), on grounds of adaptability, or negatively because of the fragility and uncertainty of rights (Klug *et al.*, 1996; Gardner, 1997).

Defects in citizenship as a practice were intensely debated at the turn of the nineteenth and twentieth centuries and a 'lively debate' continued until about 1950. The debate 'dried up' then, possibly because the welfare state 'made it possible for all individuals to feel that they were fully respected members of society' (Oliver and Heater, 1994: 1). Achieving the right kind of citizenship only re-emerged as a common concern crossing different political parties in the 1980s (Phillips, 1993, ch. 4; Miller, 1995: 433). Questions about identity and difference have always animated disputes over women's citizenship but assumed a new importance from the 1980s (Phillips, 1993; Lister, 1997). This peak coincided with the new interest in citizenship and its development took place alongside other kinds of 'identity politics' arising, from the 1950s onwards, out of decolonization, immigration, Scottish and Welsh nationalism and attitudes to European integration (Parekh, 1994: 493), to which could be added the intensification of conflict in Northern Ireland (Oliver and Heater, 1994: 2).

The relationship between 'difference' in the politics of identity and 'citizenship' is problematic. On the one hand, awareness that different identities give rise to unequal citizenship is a spur to renewed ambitions to transform the 'false universalism' of citizenship (Lister,

1997) into a real experience of equality. On the other, citizenship as 'a unifying force in a divided world' (Miller, 1995: 433), or 'a concept that deliberately abstracts from those things that are particular and specific' (Phillips, 1993: 81), seems to compel us to leave behind 'our local identities and concerns'. Exploring these apparent contradictions is bringing about a new language of citizenship similar to that which Lister (1997: 90, 115, 167, 197) calls 'differentiated universalism'.

This chapter starts with the main British debates about citizenship; that is: negative liberties versus positive rights; and various versions of active versus passive citizenship. Whether the formal universalism of citizenship can accommodate class differences is integral to these debates. The next section of the chapter considers other groups whose members identify themselves by reference to their difference – social, ethnic or national – and who argue that difference needs to be taken into account in the arrangement of politics. In dealing with the multinational character of the UK, the chapter indicates the possibility that parts of it are better equipped – or feel the need more intensely – than others to respond positively to European developments. In conclusion, it is suggested that all these themes and debates about them are adding up to a new language of citizenship and identity in the UK.

British Debates about Citizenship

Despite the ambiguity of UK citizenship rights, British political figures have contributed significantly to how people think about citizenship. The principal debates have focused on positive rights versus negative liberties and active or passive citizenship.

Britain's Contribution to the Idea of Rights but its Preference for Liberties

Many people believe that Britain has made a unique contribution to the idea of rights and the democratization of power. The English Magna Carta, in affording medieval barons rights against the exercise of absolute rule by the king, still resonates – since 'from it derive the concepts of natural justice and trial by jury which characterize the English legal system to this day' (Klug *et al.*, 1996: 4). And the 1689

Bill of Rights gave legal rights to the propertied subjects of the king which remain with us in the prohibition of excessive or cruel punishment. E. P. Thompson (1980: 153) tells us that 'the gentry [who] emerged as the rulers of England and (more selectively) of Scotland and Wales . . . wished to be left free to govern in their own way in their own spheres of influence'. Although this was far from democratic, 'it did afford shelter for libertarian modes of thought . . . and . . . vigorous resistance to the . . . absolutism . . . [of] continental monarchies'.

Revolutions in France and America and their respective Declaration of the rights of Man and Bill of Rights were inspired by two English theorists, John Locke and Thomas Paine (Klug *et al.*, 1996: 4–5). Many English-speaking commentators on today's centre-left see the French Revolution as a definitive inauguration of a new social order. It is seen as displacing the divine right of kingly rule by increasingly democratic governments and universal liberty and equality through which people could shape their own social worlds (Twine, 1994: 23) – though it should be noted that its promise for a new world for women quickly reverted under Napoleon to what had been traditional.

During this revolutionary era, however, Paine was indicted for seditious libel, domestic demands for popular sovereignty were repressed (Klug *et al.*, 1996: 5) and Edmund Burke's view that 'natural rights' were meaningless abstractions was more influential. His belief that rights and customs should not stem from reason but emerge gradually in an organic, ordered society often cause this Anglo-Irish thinker and MP to be called the father of English conservatism. But, such has been his influence on the fundamentals of political thinking that he may be more the philosopher of 'British political life from Right to Left' (Richard Crossman, quoted in Klug *et al.*, 1996: 5).

Burke's ridicule of natural rights was shared by nineteenth-century Utilitarians and by Alfred Venn Dicey. The work of Dicey – a defender of Irish unionism and opponent of female suffrage – became and remained 'the rock upon which' British governments continue to adhere to the negative tradition that 'every subject is free to do that which is not forbidden by law' instead of the idea of positive rights, as in written constitutions and international instruments (Mount, 1992: 47–60).

Libertarian approaches to citizenship continue in the twentieth century but the political culture of opposition to codified documents is on the point of change. The uncodified system of rights was able to coexist with 1948 United Nations Declaration on Human Rights because the latter is, more or less, merely declaratory. Individual access by British citizens to the European Court of Human Rights, set up by the Convention – whose preamble links individual freedoms with democracy and the protection of human rights – involved, hitherto, a long-winded process. But the Labour government elected in 1997 incorporated the Convention into British law by means of the Human Rights Act 1998, making its provisions accessible in the domestic courts. The codification of rights is also a key component of the 1998 Agreement on the future of Northern Ireland. The Amsterdam Treaty, signed on 2 October 1997, announces that EC law will embody the principles of the Convention and its jurisprudence. EC law is more than declaratory; once agreed by the member states, it is binding, applicable in domestic courts and justiciable in the European Court of Justice.

The twentieth-century version of libertarian approaches to citizenship is ascribed by Miller (1995: 440–3) to the New Right. Miller suggests that, from the New Right point of view, there is no need to value citizenship for its own sake – since people have, or may have, 'radically different conceptions of the good life' and their needs are best satisfied through private and voluntary activity or exchanges. A 'common framework' (constitutional or merely statutory) is necessary only 'if desired goods . . . cannot be obtained in these ways'. However, 'paring down' the rights of citizenship may be self-defeating, eroding the core of commonality necessary to the even temper of everyday life. This, he feels, ultimately pulls the New Right back to the centre-right which, like the centre-left, now espouses 'active citizenship'.

Active and Passive Citizenship

The idea that citizenship could be 'a unifying force in a divided world' (Miller, 1995: 433) has been adopted by both centre-right and centre-left; but for different reasons. For conservatives, the welfare state had engendered a 'passive citizenship', entitlements having become more important than the achievement of personal independence or autonomy. Moreover, as the New Right suggested, the means of meeting such entitlements through taxation and paternalistic bureaucracies could be construed as coercive (Ignatieff, 1991: 26, 27). But cutting back the role of the state has adverse consequences; as Miller (1995: 433) points out, loss of a sense of responsibility for others, lack of alternative forms of assistance in the absence of state support, and even increased criminality of both the 'ordinary' and 'white-collar' type. Emphasising citizenship as activism on behalf of others through charitable and community service could be a means of reasserting moral values and social responsibility in the context of a less statist society.

Miller explains the centre-left's espousal of active citizenship by reference to its need to transcend the dissolution of the working class which removed the majority basis of social-democratic politics. Citizenship came to be seen as a way of appealing to an 'array' of new social groups; through general principles which could 'harmonize the demands of the residual working class, welfare claimants, ethnic minorities and radicalized women'. As he and Marquand (1997: 38) point out, this left–right convergence of enthusiasm for citizenship is reflected in the cross-party Commission on Citizenship which recommends education on citizenship and voluntary service as an avenue for the practice of citizenship

The modern distinction of active versus passive citizenship has both similarities to and differences from past debates. The argument about whether, historically, the British enjoyed active or passive citizenship has two dimensions. One is primarily about legal and political citizenship and the manner of its universalization. The other focuses on the social dimension and whether or not an activist civil society indicates the presence of a vigorous citizenship praxis.

The first of these two debates rests on a claim that extensions of citizenship – either to new people or covering more areas of activity – which are 'handed down' from those in power may be intended as a means of social control (Turner, 1990). This makes citizenship less 'real' or democratic than extensions of rights which are struggled for by ordinary people. Under the first understanding, extending the franchise, introducing trade union rights, developing social security systems, adopting anti-discrimination legislation, and so on, serve a number of instrumental purposes: for example, to secure acceptance of industrial change; to induce national loyalties and fitness for war; or to ensure that working class men and, later, women and minority groups did not rebel against arrangements meeting the needs of economic and political elites. The claim that British citizenship is 'top down', reinforcing 'subjecthood' to the Crown in Parliament, may be seen as corroborated by more modern evidence; for example, in Almond and Verba's (1963) account of deference in British political culture and, perhaps, in Parry *et al.* (1992) who found few examples, beyond local government, of activism in political arenas.

This understanding of the origins of citizenship is echoed partly by
E. P. Thompson (1980: 245–5) in the claim that a 'manufactured
consensus' had displaced a political culture of dissent and debate.
However, he does not accept a wholesale version of the 'top down'
understanding of British citizenship, arguing that rights were not
'handed down' without struggle. New proposals were resisted by the
bourgeoisie and seized, often rebelliously, by the poor and unemployed (Thompson, 1980: 39–41; see also Ascherson, 1988: 47–8).
Contrary to the idea that class dominance is always inevitable,
Thompson (1980: 155) does not accept that it is a foregone conclusion
'that ordinary people will lose every contest with power'. While the
extension of liberties in Britain may have tempered violence, positive
responses from the authorities did not pre-empt trouble, were 'greatly
disliked' and created 'intense difficulties' (Thompson, 1980: 205).
According to the British Household Survey (Heath and Topf,
1988), British people remain cynical of politicians and willing to
contemplate direct action – instead of making formal representations
– when they think that something is wrong. Lister (1997, chs 7, 8),
too, points out that women are much more active – formally and
informally – at the local level than is revealed by mass surveys.

The second of the two debates is expressed in a pair of related
dichotomies; 'civic republican' and the 'citizenship of contribution'
versus 'liberal-individualism' and the 'citizenship of entitlement'.

Modern liberal-individualist citizenship descends from Thomas
Hobbes and Edmund Burke. In its Hobbesian origin and Burkean
development, individuals traded subjection and obedience for protection by the state and, possibly, some political rights (Clarke, 1996:
46). The Burkean legacy of negative liberty (see above) means that
liberal-individualist citizenship is about the: 'rights of the individual
against the community to enable the pursuit of private affairs without
interference from society or other citizens' (Marquand, 1997: 45). A
modern version of this approach accommodates social entitlements as
well as legal and political rights on the ground that, without them,
individuals will be impeded from exercising legal and political rights.

The civic-republican approach rests on a different view of human
nature. Here, individuals are human only by virtue of their membership of a community. Thus, there can be no private interests – since
the interests of individual human beings lie in the promotion of the
collective well-being of society (Jordan, 1989). Twine (1994: 11)
argues that the 'self' is damaged in a system which excludes others.
And, according to Clarke (1996: 85–6), where active citizenship is

absent, humanity is depoliticized – particularly in systems where citizens and humans are understood as different categories, as in the case of guestworkers and illegal immigrants, who may (or may not) enjoy social protection but who are unlikely to be able to participate in formal politics.

The principal, classic British advocates of the establishment of arrangements for the expression of positive, ethical relationships among individuals and between them and the state were the turn-of-the-century English humanists and idealists (Vincent and Plant, 1984; Clarke, 1996: 45) and 'New Liberals' – a term used by Finlayson (1994) which embraces the former and a similar tradition in Scotland. Of more modern thinkers, T. H. Marshall (1950) – influential beyond the shores of the UK – may be read as either in the tradition of socially oriented liberal individualism or as seeking to promote a more positive status in collective life for the least well-off. The civic republican or 'citizenship as contribution' tradition is echoed in the focusing of the centre-right, centre-left and the Commission on Citizenship on voluntary activities.

However, voluntarism as an avenue for the practice of citizenship can be viewed ambivalently. Marquand (1997: 48) argues that the tradition of voluntarism upon which the centre-right draws is not that of civic republicanism but one of monarchical service; that is, not participation in self-governing associations but acceptance of public duties, the contours of which are determined by the state. In the past, voluntarism was sometimes a means of social control. Burke's *Reflections on the Revolution in France,* Finlayson argues (1994: 51–3, 75–7), inspired a quasi-feudal and authoritarian streak in philanthropy; good works could be a way of upholding law and order, protecting property, defending the established social order and socializing the working class – not to mention the personal gratification as a result of doing good works. Service rather than self-government is more characteristic of the modern devolution of responsibilities that is occurring with the 'hollowing-out' of the state' (Rhodes, 1995; Meehan, 1995).

But the voluntary tradition is manifold, including not only philanthropy but also self-governing associations and mutual aid (Finlayson, 1994). Contributing to one's own or other people's well-being is part of Michael Walzer's (1992: 99) claim that civil activism in society can shape the larger polity and economy. This is why it can be adopted by not only philanthropists but also social-democrats – though not uncritically. In interacting with dissent, voluntarism has contributed to 'bottom up' extensions of citizenship of entitlement and contribution.

Finlayson (1994: 121–3) suggests that the emergence of Chartism helped to put socio-economic aspects of citizenship on the political agenda. Friendly societies were at first viewed suspiciously by governments as subversive and only later as useful in distracting the working class from radical and reforming activity (Finlayson, 1994: 83–4). The ideas of the idealists and 'New Liberals' between the 1880s and 1920s, while adaptable and adapted to benevolent conservatism, were principally concerned with democratizing personal and political autonomy (Finlayson, 1994: 159–63 on T. H. Green and others, including women suffragists; Marquand, 1997: 143 on Hobhouse).

Problems of resources and effectiveness, together with notions of human dignity, motivated growing demands for state-sponsored rights and services (Finlayson, 1994: 159–63; Marquand, 1997: 143). But the optimism of the 1950s and 1960s that the state had become an effective guarantor of rights and provider of the material basis of equal citizenship (overcoming, for example, the 'stigmatizing' means-tested benefits of the 1930s) was short-lived. In the 1970s, Richard Crossman abandoned his 1930s view of voluntarism – that it was 'odious' (Finlayson, 1994: 249–50, 255, 318–19) – when he saw how alienating to users was the welfare state and how heavily it depended on volunteering. In the 1980s, voluntarism was construed as a positive virtue by David Blunkett who, in supporting proposals by the Prince of Wales in the 1980s to encourage young people to undertake voluntary work, likened them to 'something that goes back to the very origins of the Labour movement. It's built on an acceptance of our obligations to others' (Finlayson, 1994: 374). This transformation coincided with the emergence of the New Right (see above) and the centre-right's shared concern to reduce state intervention without eroding the core of social cohesion. Hence, the similarity of expositions of voluntarism by, for example, Douglas Hurd (Miller, 1995: 433) and John Patten (Mount, 1992: 33–4).

Perhaps in order to harness the best of 'active citizenship' – emancipation, participation, influencing the shape of one's world – while eliminating its being a means of control and of devolving predetermined duties, British people are developing a new language of citizenship. This is discussed in the conclusion. Before that, it is necessary to discuss another feature which is contributing to this new language – the interaction between senses of citizenship and senses of identity.

Citizenship and Identity

The relationship between citizenship and identities is problematic on two counts which have come to the surface in the UK over the last thirty years. These two difficulties relate to social or cultural identities and national identities, which are increasingly the bases of political mobilization.

On the one hand, feminist analysis suggests that the universalistic language of citizenship disguises assumptions of difference between men and women and between public and private virtues and activities, which together mean that, by definition, the identity of 'woman' renders women incapable of being citizens. The assertion by women that their difference should be acknowledged positively and taken into account in political arrangements has some counterpart in assertions of cultural identities among ethnic minority communities. The situation of ethnic minority communities also overlaps with the second question about citizenship and identities – that of nationality.

The words 'citizenship' and 'nationality' are often used coterminously. This overlap stems from the rise of nation states in the eighteenth and nineteenth centuries in which developing the commonalities of citizenship served the purposes of nation-building within state borders and of controlling who could traverse frontiers with other states. Because of this, the overlap between citizenship and nationality can be said to be a matter of historical contingency rather than analytic necessity (Heater, 1990). Indeed, a modern survey of eleven western European countries shows inconsistencies between the possession of the nationality of a state and access to citizens' rights conferred by it (Gardner, 1994). Nevertheless, the link between citizenship and national identity has had a powerful psychological hold which is only now fraying with migration and European integration.

In contrast to the prospect of a looser link between nationality and citizenship raised by migration and integration, it has been argued that their overlap serves a useful purpose. That the universalization of citizenship involves extending rights and power and, except in the strong libertarian case, the redistribution of resources raises the question of why people accept these consequences. Miller (1993) argues that it is a common sense of nationality that enables them to do so. But, as an overarching identity, 'Britishness' on its own is weak, both among ethnic minority communities and among the pre-British nationalities inhabiting the territory of the UK.

The Assertion of Social and Cultural Identities

Sometimes similarly and sometimes in different ways, neither ethnic minority communities nor women, whatever their origins, share the same material basis of equal citizenship or the same political opportunities as men of the majority community – despite domestic anti-discrimination legislation and, in the case of women, the additional protection of EU laws.

Social disadvantage is not exclusive to minority communities but falls disproportionately upon them and the criminal justice system often treats them differently and to their detriment (Klug *et al.*, 1996: 111, 250–1). Ethnic minority communities experience cultural marginalization as a result of immigration being treated as a threat (Parekh, 1991) and in efforts to insist on assimilation, as in the former Conservative minister Norman Tebbit's 'cricket test' of allegiance, which set support for the England team as a criterion of national identity (Andrews, 1991: 13).

Female members of ethnic minority communities can find themselves facing a multiplicity of identity hurdles. They may be doubly marginalized by public authorities and employers as minorities and women; they may be criticised by male members of their own community if they emphasise matters arising from their identities as women; yet, they often find that feminist analyses and action originating in the majority community overlooked differences relating to the interaction of ethnic minority and female identities. Indeed, in making this apparent, women in ethnic minority communities (as well as the deconstruction of overarching identities in post-modernism) have contributed greatly to the incorporation of difference into feminism. As Lister (1997) also shows, comparable issues arise in situations of disability and sexual orientation.

On the other hand, women from a variety of ethnic backgrounds are actively engaged in the community politics of civil society which, as Walzer (1992: 99) puts it, 'stands outside the republic of citizens, as it is currently conceived'. The defining out of 'citizenship' of what women do and the marginalization of them and minorities from the mainstream practice of politics and policy-making has led to interest in 'identity politics' or the 'politics of difference'. One fundamental starting point for women is the work of Carole Pateman (1988, 1989) who argues that they were incorporated into liberal society, not in their own right, but as the legal dependents of men. She also argues that, notwithstanding universal suffrage, the assumption that women properly inhabit the private sphere in relationships of dependency was built into the modern welfare state and taxation systems. Pateman's purpose is to analyse, not to prescribe; but another influential thinker, Iris Marion Young (whose various works are discussed by Phillips, 1993; Miller, 1995; and Lister, 1997) goes further and also considers other excluded groups as well as women.

Young notes that, in nineteenth-century discourse in the USA, women, Native Americans, Blacks, Jews and homosexuals were used interchangeably as examples of 'uncultivated passion' and 'wild nature' which sat in opposition to 'civilised republican life' (see Lister, 1997: 72). She also argues that the impartiality of republican life imposes a homogeneity which suppresses group differences in the public sphere (Lister, 1997: 30). This leads her to propose that there should be a politics of group assertion articulated through separate organizations and that political arrangements should provide mechanisms for the expression of distinct voices (Lister, 1997: 78–9), including veto powers (Phillips, 1993: 93).

British thinkers and activists who are persuaded by Young's analysis of the suppression of differences are not always convinced by her case for separate mechanisms of representation. Phillips (1993: 93–9), for example, suggests that she underestimates problems in how to identify groups (and who does so), how they can be judged to be representative and be held accountable and the risk of 'freezing what are multiple and shifting identities'. Lister (1997: 210–11) gives an example which encapsulates all three difficulties when she reminds us of 'a letter to the *Guardian* (22 July, 1989) from Southall Black Sisters and the Brent Asian Women's Refuge' attacking the 'Labour Party's support for separate Muslim Schools as delivering them into "the hands of male, conservative and religious forces within our communities, who deny us our right to live as we please"'. In arguing that identities are influenced – and shift accordingly – by historical and political circumstance, Hall (1992) argues that minority and majority ethnic identities interact to give rise to 'cultures of hybridity'.

Several writers draw attention to the identification of 'woman' with 'mother' and the advantages and drawbacks of this (Dietz, 1992; Phillips, 1993: 82–4, 86; Lister, 1997: 149–52). They agree that celebrating motherhood, or even merely insisting it be treated as a normal 'difference' routinely taken into account in policy-making (Bacchi, 1990), is a welcome counter-balance to its use, as in the hands of the anti-suffragists, as a detriment to women – regardless of whether they were mothers or not. On the other hand, they argue that motherhood and citizenship are different; being a good mother is not the same as being a good citizen, even though identification with other mothers may be one of the social associations that Walzer (1992) sees as a possible source of influence upon the wider polity. A good citizen enters into dialogue and negotiation with others to ensure that all legitimate voices have a place on the public agenda – in a society or polity, which in coping with tensions between liberty and equality, is able to distinguish fairly between differences which matter and those that do not (Mouffe, 1992).

The connection between the two forms of identity and activity is captured in Nira Yuval-Davis's idea (discussed in Lister, 1997: 82) of 'transversal' politics in which actors remain 'rooted' in their own identities and values but are willing to 'shift' their views in dialogue with other people with other identities and values. Lister (1997: 82–3), acknowledges Yuval-Davis' point that not all conflicting interests can be resolved through dialogue. But she provides examples, involving both ethnic and women's identities, of positive outcomes in situations of severe conflict – including Northern Ireland where, despite a specially difficult relationship between women's citizenship and ethnicity or nationalism, there are potential, if fragile, opportunities for a more 'woman friendly' polity (Wilford, 1996).

In terms of political activism in Britain, there are some separatist approaches similar to Young's which may have a unifying potential for the group in question; for example, mobilization around a perceived need for a Muslim parliament. Conversely, the rise of 'difference politics' has been accompanied by a certain fragmentation of the English women's movement, or, perhaps, localization and concentration upon protest politics (Byrne, 1996). Fragmentation has not happened in Scotland, partly because of the Constitutional debate and links between consciousness of women's interests and Scottish identity (Brown, 1996; and Mackay, 1996, on local government). The Scottish experience, however, is reflected in general approaches to increasing women's participation in party politics and influencing public policy. Here, activist ethnic minority communities and women of minority and majority communities accept that successful mobilization depends on working on the basis of difference and commonality.

Successful women's strategies are dualistic: working through women's and 'male' organizations and seeking to persuade men that it is in their interests to see it as of universal value to acknowledge women's needs and skills (Lovenduski and Norris, 1993). The large increase in the number of successful women candidates, particularly in the Labour Party, in the 1997 election is a notable result of this approach. While failure to acknowledge relevant differences among ethnic minority communities has caused widespread alienation, leading in the 1980s to violence, Parekh (1991) draws attention to ways in which different ethnic minority communities are cohering and asserting a new political consciousness. He sees hope in this – and in aspects of the justice system which can apply general principles flexibly to specific situations – for the promotion of a form of integration in which equality does not mean uniformity but unity and diversity. Lister (1997) makes a persuasive case that a truly inclusive practice of citizenship must combine even more fully what is different and what is universal.

If immigration and migration have compelled calls for 'unity in diversity' in respect of the mutual accommodation of ethnic identities within the British state, migration is also a factor in the identity politics of trans-state regulatory regimes. As Lister (1997: 44) points out, it is increasingly difficult to disguise the existence of female migration under the assumption that migrants are male and, hence, to ignore the gendered character of immigration rules. Equally, there are concerns about racism in the common rules of the EU, in terms of entry to it from 'third countries', over the treatment of such migrants once inside the common borders, and the risk of discrimination against nationals of member states – particularly those with an imperial past – whose ethnic minority background may be taken by officials to mean that they could be immigrants. It remains to be seen whether the provisions on immigration and resident or national ethnic minorities in the Amsterdam Treaty will satisfy such concerns. Women, including minority and majority British women, are increasingly mobilizing around international human rights organizations, a development that shows an impact on the EU in its understanding of women and politics (Hoskyns, 1996). If mobilization based on national versions of cultural identities is escaping the confines of nation state borders, questions about the political consequences of national identity are also occurring below the level of the UK state – where people may also look beyond the UK for part of their resolution.

The Reassertion of Politics Based on Pre-British Identities

In 1962, Hugh Gaitskell told the Labour Party Conference that UK accession to the European Communities would mean 'the end of a thousand years of history'. In the early 1990s in a television debate on the future of the Monarchy, Baroness Warnock, also invoking a thousand years, referred to English history. No-one appeared to notice how she had qualified her remark or that this very qualification might be a reason for questioning whether the Monarchy united, as she thought it did, the UK culturally and constitutionally. In contrast to conflating a millennium of English and British history, Marquand (1997: 192) argues that the British state is more fragile than people assume. The union of Scottish and English Parliaments in 1707, under a monarchy joined by inheritance a century before, was not the consequence of shared national feeling but the creator of common loyalties, established to overcome past animosities. That 'Britishness' is a weak form of identification is also demonstrated by Brown *et al.* (1996, ch. 9).

As Brown *et al.* (1996: 11) argue, it has been an enduring feature of Scottish life that, to be a true nationalist, it is necessary to be a unionist – to promote Scottish interests in England and further afield, particularly in the Empire. But, equally, to be a true unionist, it is necessary to be a nationalist – since, in the absence of assertions of Scottishness, the union would degenerate into a takeover (see also Devine, 1994, ch. 2). A self-conscious conservation of a pre-British identity – a reconstitution of Celtic traditions as the heritage of all Scots – was facilitated by the terms of the Union, which left intact the institutions of Scottish civil society. Three hundred years later, between two-thirds and three-quarters of Scots (Catholic and Protestant) identify themselves primarily as Scottish and about a quarter as equally Scottish and British (Brown *et al.*, 1996: 198).

The figures are almost as striking for Wales, incorporated into England about 500 years ago, where about 50 per cent prioritise their Welshness and 30 per cent identify themselves as equally Welsh and British (Brown *et al.*, 1996: 203). About one quarter of people living in England identify themselves as only English or more English than British and nearly half see themselves as equally English and British. In all cases, albeit that the figures vary in different surveys, very few English, Welsh or Scots people see themselves as exclusively British or more so than anything else. The exception is Northern Ireland, where two-thirds to three-quarters of Protestants define themselves primarily as British, with only 2 per cent describing themselves as Irish (Gallagher, 1995: 17), the latter figure having fallen during the last thirty years of conflict. Conversely, about 60 per cent of Catholics define themselves as Irish and between 8 and 12 per cent as British. About a quarter of Catholics describe themselves as primarily Northern Irish and a quarter of Protestants are divided over whether they are Northern Irish or men and women of Ulster.

If, as Hall (1992) argues, identities vary according to political context, political developments themselves seem also to change direction as a result of people's interpretation of themselves and others. Pre-British identities in Scotland, Wales and, though differently, Northern Ireland, now imbued with factors arising from European integration, are providing the bases for constitutional reform, leaving the English-British and, possibly, ethnic minority communities in all parts of the UK with something of a problem.

In Scotland and Wales, many people 'increasingly feel frustrated by comparison with their counterparts in regions in other European states which allow regions a much greater opportunity to participate' (Paterson, 1994: 8). Because of this, subsidiarity defined as decisions being taken as close as possible to the people (as in the Preamble to the Maastricht Treaty) is popular in the component parts of the UK. However, subsidiarity as defined in article 3B of the Treaty is read by the UK government as protecting central state powers *vis-à-vis* common institutions. Herein lies a twist – for the Scots are 'much more likely than people in the South of England to think that the best level of decision-making might be above the nation state' (Paterson, 1994: 4), thereby 'squeezing out' the authority of the British state as currently constituted. Indeed, debate in Scotland about its place in Europe is intimately linked with debate about its place in the UK, Europe being 'an alternative site for Scottish aspirations' (Paterson, 1994: 4) – just as the union of 1707 once was. This is perhaps reflected in the 10 per cent of people who see themselves as Scottish and European and the 11 per cent who see themselves as Scottish, British and European (Brown *et al.*, 1996: 211). These indices of identification with Europe are higher than in Northern Ireland, though people there are more likely than in Great Britain to favour UK membership of the EU and even closer integration (Smith and Corrigan, 1995: 87, 90). The overall higher Northern Irish approval disguises significant differences within Northern Ireland.

Northern Irish attitudes to Europe, as with national identification, are complicated by the partition of Ireland and the continuing conflict arising from that (Meehan, forthcoming). Before UK accession to the then EEC, nationalists and republicans – as all nationalist parties in the UK – saw integration as a threat to the possibility of independent statehood. Traditional unionists, though divided, were, on the whole, pragmatically favourable. What might be called 'conditional' unionists (union for as long as people want it), the Alliance Party, have been strongly in favour of European integration since the inception of the party in the early 1970s.

The first years of UK membership coincided with renewed violent conflict in Northern Ireland and the imposition of direct rule from Westminster. During this time nationalists began to look to European integration as a model for conflict resolution with lessons for the island of Ireland. This was reinforced by acknowledgement of interdependence and notions of 'post-nationalist' or post-modern nationalism. The 'Europeanization' of the Republic of Ireland caused northern republicans grudgingly to accept that European integration might have something to offer (Cox, 1997). In reaction to nationalists' espousal of the idea that integration could transcend the competition between old Irish and British nationalisms and as integration increasingly implied the permeability of borders, traditional unionists became more suspicious of the EU with its policy principles of partnership within borders and cross-border schemes for economic development.

Nowadays, however, Euroscepticism among young people from a traditional unionist background is much lower, their attitudes being much closer to their Alliance and nationalist counterparts (Smith and Corrigan, 1995: 98). And it can be argued that the experience of European issues has helped contribute to there being a new language with which to discuss the internal, north–south and east–west components of the Good Friday Agreement which was endorsed in the referendum of 22 May 1998. Though unionists of all generations have reservations that the EU could encourage 'rolling devolution' into a reunited Ireland, they share Welsh and Scottish concerns that their interests can be different from those of England and may be imperfectly protected in the Westminster system (Bew and Meehan, 1994). Constitutional reform in all three places includes special arrangements to ensure that their distinctive voices are heard in the EU Council of Ministers.

While the pre-British status of Scotland, Wales and Northern Ireland are now the bases of devolved forms of government, the loosening of relative constitutional uniformity creates problems for

England. The comparatively weak priority given to Englishness by the English coexists with a diminution of the meaning of the British-ness with which almost half of them doubly identify themselves (see above). Except among Northern Irish unionists, components of Britishness – protestantism, parliamentary sovereignty, empire, mon-archy – are disappearing or being challenged (Lee, 1995; Eatwell, 1997). It is not easy to see what can be reconstituted or how, since there seems to be a difficulty in understanding what Englishness means outside its overlap with Britishness.

According to Marquand (1997: 175), 'the state is British but its identity English'. But that still leaves open the question of what 'English' means. Marquand (1997: 154, 174) argues that very few intellectuals, except George Orwell and A. J. P. Taylor, feel comfor-table with English nationalism. This may arise from abhorrence of the colonization by the far right and 'little Englanders' of British imperial symbols and distaste for the nostalgia of 'the heritage industry'. But England's social and economic geography makes it very difficult to identify a single 'imagined community' that could be shared by all. When John Major adapted George Orwell's words about 'old maids cycling to evensong' he detached them from the noisy northern connotations given to them by Orwell and linked them, instead, to southern images of cricket and warm beer (Lee, 1995).

Whether the EU can have similar effects in England to those in other parts of the UK is questionable. Elsewhere in the UK, 'pooling sovereignty' in the EU is seen as an opportunity for the enhancement of autonomy; the experiences of smaller European states such as the Benelux countries and Ireland are taken as examples. In contrast, many Parliamentarians at the time saw UK accession to the EU as less of an opportunity than a final recognition of defeat – a stream of thought that remains among English conservatives, notwithstanding a prevailing cross-party consensus to the contrary. However, the varied social geography of England again comes into play. To Paterson's reference above to Scottish and Welsh envy of other European regions could be added non-central English regions and localities which, as Paterson also says of the Scots, may see oppor-tunities above the level of the state. One doubt about local govern-ment reform in the early 1990s was that the new units of government would be too small to exploit European opportunities. The local authorities making up Merseyside – which is now an Objective One Region in the EU – have come together to ensure that local and regional definitions of needs prevail in the structural plan over central government ideas about what those interests should be. In other words, local policy-makers are behaving similarly to those in regions which are able to identify themselves on a national basis. It seems unlikely, therefore, that constitutional changes elsewhere will remain self-contained. Indeed, from 2000 London is to have an elected mayor and the Agreement on Northern Ireland envisages a network of bi- and multilateral linkages between Ireland, Northern Ireland, Wales, Scotland, the Isle of Man, the Channel Islands and, if they are established, devolved institutions elsewhere in the UK.

However, despite the exclusionary purposes for which the far right uses British symbols, a diminution of the meaning of Britishness may have difficult implications for some ethnic minority communities. A descendant of Jewish immigrants from Lithuania told me that her community prefers the more universalistic label of 'British-Jew' to that of 'English-Jew', on the ground that 'British' indicates a legal commonality while 'English-Jew' is a pair of incommensurate ethnic identifications. If this is a widespread view, similar considerations might apply to other religious–ethnic groups and arise in other parts of the UK. The question of how to accommodate various sorts of identities within a general commonality is leading to a new language of citizenship.

A New Language of Citizenship which Incorporates Diverse Identities

In many ways, the recent search for new expressions of citizenship is proactive, as in the case of parts of the women's movement, the more cohesive ethnic minority communities and the smaller nations of the UK. In some senses, it seems reactive. What Richard Crossman observed (see above) about bureaucracy and public services was also identified by Margaret Thatcher. Both recognized that 'new social citizens probably did not feel they controlled popular institutions – the doctor's waiting room, the playground, the schools, etc.' (Marquand, 1997: 152).

But Marquand also argues that Thatcher did not transform 'our subject culture', as witnessed by her 'abhorrence of the French Revolution', and by implication the Declaration of the rights of Man. Even Major's transformation of citizens from electors to consumers did not make them active participants in policy formation (Stewart *et al.*, 1994: 3). And, as Lister (1990) points out, New Right policies effectively reinforce a state of unequal citizenship, those who are self-reliant being full citizens and those in poverty seen as dependent and, as such, subjects.

Thus, despite support for issues on the agenda of the Constitutional campaign group Charter 88 and assertions of national and regional identities, the new voices are somewhat incoherent (Marquand, 1997: 81–2). Nevertheless, they reflect what Miller observes about the New Right's having to pull back to the centre-right position on citizenship (see above) and the beginnings of a more civic republican or communitarian approach. Young's claim that civic republicanism cannot accommodate pluralism notwithstanding, the emerging approach is based upon the proposition that solidarity and common citizenship require reform of the British state and recognition of the coexistence of diversity and commonality (Miller, 1995; Marquand, 1997: 85–6; Lister, 1997).

One of the most important aspects of a state which fosters civic republicanism is the need for scope within which permitted activities make a significant difference to the way people lead their lives (Clarke, 1996: 50). In making this claim, Clarke argues that representative democracy tends to institutionalize second-class citizenship because it denies widespread opportunities to participate (Clarke, 1996: 54–5). This is similar to John Stuart Mill's justification for healthy local democracy and democracy in the work-place. It is also reflected in the demands of devolutionists (in English regions, too) and of new, radical democrats who call for a properly constituted public realm in which people can discuss each others' opinions and needs as a basis for determining together what are reasonable arrangements for their community (Mouffe, 1992).

The need for space seems to be felt by 'ordinary people' too. In the sphere of local government, where voting turnouts in formal politics are low, people undertake other political activities more frequently than in connection with Parliament (Parry *et al.*, 1992). There is evidence that participation can be, and is being, made more significant at the local level in terms of numbers and impact. Local authorities can build, and some are building, the habits of citizenship by changing themselves and adopting new forms of negotiation with the public. A growth of interest in deliberative opinion polls, consensus conferences, citizens' juries, panels and forums (Stewart *et al.*, 1994) perhaps substantiates E. P. Thompson's (1980: 169) claim that legal juries are not a product of bourgeois democracy 'but a stubbornly maintained democratic practice' – which may flourish in their new form in a revitalised democracy. The Agreement on Northern

Ireland introduces into the formal constitution, for the first time in the UK, a Civic Forum of voluntary and community participants which will sit alongside the Assembly of conventionally elected representatives – and the possibility that a similar body may operate in tandem with the North–South Ministerial Council.

Given that the new voices express the need to recognise diversities of gender, ethnic identification and nationality as much as the need for equal treatment to bring about social and political inclusion, it is perhaps fitting to end with a reminder of Ruth Lister's (1997) appeal for 'differentiated universalism' and Bhikhu Parekh's (1991: 202–3) observation that being British *does not* mean resisting change, *does* mean recognizing the different accents in which a common language of politics is spoken *and needs* 'a new spirit of partnership – what the Romans called civic friendship'.

Acknowledgements

The author would like to thank Simon Lee of Hull University for comments on an earlier draft. He, of course, bears no responsibility for remaining mistakes or misrepresentations.

12
Sovereignty and Interdependence

JOHN PETERSON

To argue that Britain is unique among nation states is to invite the obvious riposte that all nation states are unique in their political histories, traditions and institutions. Yet, Britain may legitimately claim the titles of the world's first truly modern nation state, its first industrialized economy and first global power. Leaving aside Denmark, Britain's monarchy has reigned without interruption for longer than any other in the world. Its legislature deserves to be called the 'the mother of all Parliaments', even if the label is often used derisively.

The longevity of Britain's institutions both reflects and contributes to the uniqueness of its people. British exceptionalism has been proclaimed as much by foreigners, such as Voltaire and Tocqueville, as by natives, including Churchill and Orwell (Morgan, 1984). The British nation has exceptionally deep roots and its national identity is profoundly shaped by tradition. John Major's 'back to basics' campaign showed that the idea of Britishness is a powerful one even when, as in Major's case, attempts to use it 'as a substitute for new political ideas' fall flat (Eatwell, 1997: 50). Nearly 70 per cent of modern British citizens say they 'take pride in the fact that Britain once had a great empire' despite the disputed political correctness of such sentiments (Gallup Poll in *The Economist* 28 March 1998).

The idea that British people were somehow uniquely placed – even destined – to wield influence globally was nourished by Britain's emergence as the world's first global power. Subsequently, Britain's institutions, language and traditions were adopted or adapted internationally in a way unmatched by those of any other nation. An important legacy of Britain's status as the world's first global power was an engrained attachment, among both its political class and ordinary citizens, to British sovereignty and 'independence'.

Arguably, the very ideas of sovereignty and independence have ceased to have much more than symbolic meaning in the modern world. The British commitment to these values has been, in terms of strength and durability, extraordinary by international standards. Furthermore, Britain's political class has tended to assume that sovereignty and independence are interchangeable synonyms (Wallace, 1986). This assumption has fundamentally shaped post-war British foreign policy, particularly by skewing judgements when choices have had to be made about how best to achieve British objectives in a world where all states have found themselves with progressively less control over their destinies. Two of the most important and fundamental legacies of British government in the late 1990s are likely to be the end of foreign policy which aims to preserve British sovereignty at all costs, and the beginning of an overdue process of modernizing British institutions.

What Price Interdependence?

At first glance, the meaning of sovereignty seems quite straightforward: ultimate jurisdiction over a body politic with freedom from external control. In British political discourse 'sovereignty is an emotive concept, associated as it is with the notions of power, authority, independence and the exercise of will. It has several meanings, none of which in any definitive sense are right or wrong' (Nugent, 1996: 3). To illustrate the point, Geoffrey Howe (1990: 676), a former Foreign Secretary with long experience of defending both British interests abroad and Britain's global role domestically, defines sovereignty as 'a nation's practical capacity to maximize its influence in the world'. For Howe and many other post-war British policy-makers, sovereignty may be conflated with 'influence', or even 'power'.

Part of the problem, of course, is that Britain's experience of sovereignty has been unique. Since at least the eighteenth century, Britain sovereign authority has clearly and unequivocally rested with the Queen or King in Parliament. 'Parliamentary sovereignty', or the idea that Parliament enjoys unfettered power and faces no constitutional limitations, remains at the heart of the British constitution. Constitutional development has been a far more continuous process in Britain than elsewhere, including in other 'centralized, unitary, colonizing states like France and Spain' (Howe, 1990: 678). France's Fifth Republic dates only to 1958. Post-Franco Spain set out upon the path of democracy only in late 1975.

Students of British political culture argue that 'belief in the superiority of the British Parliament, symbol of liberty' has been and remains an essential element of 'Britishness' (Eatwell, 1997: 52). Yet, parliamentary sovereignty has become an idealized and even outdated notion. If for no other reason, it has been compromised by British membership of the European Union (EU, known before 1993 as the European Community). In legal terms, membership means accepting that European law is superior to national law, and inviolable by any Act of Parliament. In political terms, European integration tends to be viewed as a zero-sum process in Britain: each time the EU gains new powers they are lost to Britain.

As William Wallace (1986) argues, British attitudes towards the more informal process of rising interdependence have been far more relaxed. Simply put, interdependence means mutual dependence. An interdependent world is one in which 'events occurring in any given part . . . of a world system affect (either physically or perceptually) events taking place in each of the other parts' (Young, 1969: 726). Britain clearly has been an important force in promoting interdependence: spreading its institutions, culture and language across the world, embracing global free trade as a doctrine, and championing leading collective security organizations such as NATO (the North Atlantic Treaty Organization). Britain's economy is highly interdependent with those of its EU partners. Over half of British trade is directed towards the rest of the Union. EU membership means that the British market (of 56 million consumers) is subsumed within the world's largest single capitalist market (of 370 million consumers). Still, interdependence is a relative concept and 'measuring' it is difficult.

In contrast, sovereignty is clear and measurable in the formal or legal sense of 'recognition by internal and external actors that the state has the exclusive authority to intervene coercively in activities within its territory' (Thomson, 1995: 219). Thus, the British Parliament remains 'sovereign' in that it is the ultimate political authority in Britain. No foreign power can circumscribe its will. In the end, it could choose at any time to withdraw Britain from the European Union. In theory, Parliament could refuse to provide more than token support to a NATO ally that faced a military threat. Despite Howe's

(1990: 679) protests to the contrary, in principle (if not practice) sovereignty is like virginity: it is black or white, all or nothing, and absolute.

Yet, independence (like interdependence) is fundamentally different: it involves a state's practical power to exercise its sovereign rights in pursuit of its national values and interests. When states perform this exercise, they act with varying degrees of independence: some (such as the United States) can pursue their national goals fettered by relatively few international constraints and while paying relatively little heed to the actions of other states. Many states (for example, Luxembourg) cannot. Independence and interdependence thus form a kind of continuum.

Interdependence naturally gives rise to attempts by governments to manage it. Historically, highly interdependent states have not always sought peaceful relations with each other. In fact, the most influential school of thought in the study of international relations, the 'realist' (later 'neo-realist') school, assumes that all states naturally seek maximum independence, which is assumed to equate to maximum power. Thus, states do not form permanent alliances. All are 'egoistic value maximizers' (Baldwin, 1993: 9). International relations are a dangerous, competitive, Hobbesian 'war of all against all' (figuratively, at least) even during times of peace.

At the end of the twentieth century, realist assumptions began to seem anachronistic. Specifically, they seemed incongruous with a 'system in which economic interdependence is compelling, where the network of common rules and institutions is dense, where the utility of force has decreased both because of the nuclear danger and because of the irrelevance of war to many of the conflicts economic interdependence breeds' (Hoffmann, 1995b: x–xi). After the end of the cold war, war seemed mainly a domestic matter between rival political, religious or ethnic groups in poor and undeveloped states. Liberal states did not make war with each other: they created a 'separate peace', as they had throughout history (Doyle, 1997). They competed in economic terms for wealth and investment, but virtually all states embraced free trade and open markets.

The intellectual rationale for unfettered 'free trade' is the most powerful idea in the history of the study of economics: comparative advantage. Simply stated, it teaches that the more states trade with each other, provided they specialize in the products they are 'best' at producing (most cheaply or of the highest quality), the richer all states become. Stability in the global system thus becomes viewed as a common good because instability, ultimately leading to war, disrupts economic exchange and negates its wealth-creating effects. In political terms, open global commerce fosters heightened interdependence. The logical method for managing interdependence is developing international organizations that can enforce rules which promote free trade. If governments decide that co-operation is in their interests, they have incentives to construct institutions which facilitate ongoing negotiations or even enforce the terms of bargains that are struck. Otherwise, international agreements become voluntary: states may renege on them when circumstances – especially, governments – change.

The EU represents the most developed modern experiment to ensure that agreements between sovereign states are enforced. Compared with other international organizations, the Union is vested with far wider and deeper powers. By the mid-1990s, EU member states found that one-third to one-half of all new domestic laws originated from EU legislation. The Union exercised considerable 'supra-national' powers, or powers which transcended national boundaries, authorities or interests.

The goal of forging 'an ever closer Union among the peoples of Europe', as stated in article 1 of the EU's governing Treaties, suggests that the EU exists to make European states ever more interdependent, by voluntarily embracing economic and political integration. Integration implies forming, coordinating and blending national economies and polities into unified and functioning wholes. The assumption that ever closer integration makes Europe richer and more powerful remains widely supported by political elites across Europe. The argument that 'European interests' are best defended by political solidarity is frequently made in EU politics, even when common interests are disputed or hazy.

An ironclad law of realism remains that each individual state pursues its national interest: 'having examined its security requirements, it tries to meet them' (Waltz, 1979: 134). Particularly on matters of 'hard' security, or the defence of national territory and citizens from military threat, all governments are reluctant to integrate or create supra-national institutions. In a classic work from 1960 on the limits to interdependence, Hoffmann (1995a) distinguishes between the 'high politics' of foreign policy and defence, where 'political integration' is unlikely to proceed very far, and the 'low politics' of trade, agriculture and so on, where considerable 'economic integration' may be possible. While the distinction may be far fuzzier in a post-cold-war world, it is clear that 'in areas of key importance to the national interest', such as defence and foreign policy, 'nations prefer the self-controlled uncertainty of national self-reliance, to the uncontrolled certainty of the blending process' (Hoffmann, 1995a: 84). Thus NATO is a collective security organization, but it has no supra-national powers.

Even in other, less dramatic areas of 'low politics', national and supra-national interests may come into conflict. States may make the choice to bind themselves to international cooperation by 'pooling' sovereignty within international organizations, but later find that cooperation does not solve problems effectively because problems are not shared uniformly by all members. In the case of the EU, the point is particularly salient given the Union's likely enlargement in the early twenty-first century to become a far larger and more diverse collection of member states.

Nonetheless, sovereignty is not the same as independence. In important respects, the UK and other EU member states would become less independent if they withdrew from past commitments and annulled their membership of the Union. In or out, they would remain highly dependent on EU policies concerning basic questions of money, food and trade, over which non-members have no formal power and often little influence. Given a high level of economic interdependence in Europe, decisions taken within the EU often narrow drastically the parameters of national policies for both members and non-members. As such, the 11 applicants which sought EU membership by 1997 faced a sort of imperialism: Poland, Hungary and others were effectively forced to adopt EU standards and 'shadow' Union legislation even though the Union did not (yet) offer them a 'seat at the table'. They enjoyed national sovereignty, but little independence. Clearly, it was in their national interest to pool sovereignty in selected policy sectors at the EU level.

The very notion of national interests highlights British exceptionalism. In the UK more than elsewhere, policy-makers have tended to operate on strict realist assumptions. British national interests have been assumed to be 'eternal and enduring', as they were famously described by Lord Palmerston in 1848. Perhaps because the statement came at a time when British global power was near its apogee, Palmerston's claim Britain had 'no permanent allies or enemies, only permanent interests' had a lasting, powerful resonance.

Of course, all states have permanent, core interests in ensuring their security and promoting their prosperity. National interests are always defined in a cultural context, which usually changes slowly. Britain's national identity always shapes and colours any British government's choices about which national interests matter most and how they should be defended. When a government is replaced – even by one of different political complexion – more often than not the new government will fight for most of the same policies in international organizations as did its predecessor. Thus, in negotiations on the EU's 1997 Amsterdam Treaty, the Blair government insisted as staunchly its Conservative predecessors had done – that NATO should retain primacy among European security organizations.

Yet, Palmerston's doctrine obscures a fundamental point: national interests never exist in any abstract or objective sense. They are defined by particular governments at particular times. Increasingly, in a post-cold-war context, national interests are based on party-political calculations. For example, after the EU's Social Chapter was fought tooth-and-nail by the Major government, the Blair government made signing up to it one of its first acts after taking office in 1997.

In short, 'national interests' are malleable, politicized and increasingly subject to change, but are still often presented by governments as timeless and enduring. Usually, the intent is to stymie debate about the policy choices made by governments. The time-honoured British aversion to 'permanent alliances' has often led to the assumption that arresting or even disrupting European integration was in the British 'national interest'. Relatively little thought was given to how the EU could best work as a platform for the expression of Britain's voice internationally or how further European integration might actually serve British interests.

Any discussion of Britain, sovereignty and interdependence must highlight the fundamental differences between being a member state of the European Union and a nation state in the traditional sense. EU membership imposes obligations, some of them onerous. It also helps reduce the price of interdependence by facilitating collective action by European states, which usually are far more powerful when they act together than when each acts independently. Britain has long been a global trading power, and has welcomed and even nurtured economic interdependence. But European integration has posed special problems for long-established states such as Britain and France. In Britain's case, the most fundamental problem is the perception that European integration threatens national sovereignty, and that sovereignty and independence are the same things. Britain clearly retains its

sovereignty, even in areas where it has pooled it with those of its EU
partners. That does not mean that the UK is independent.

The Legacy of Empire

Britain's preoccupation with preserving its sovereignty and its aloof-
ness from the European continent are perhaps natural consequences
of Britain's long state tradition and unparalleled national 'reach'. A
good starting point for understanding these impulses is 1648, when
the Treaty of Westphalia 'set the ground plan of the international
order in central Europe for the next century and more' (Davies, 1996:
565). It brought together nearly all powerful state actors in Europe to
partake in a comprehensive and (mostly) peaceful carve-up of territory following the Thirty Years' War. The Treaty also certified a
religious settlement between Protestantism and Catholicism, thus
dashing hopes for a universal Christendom and tipping the power
balance away from church towards state. The Westphalian state
system was thus created: 'the organization of the world into territorially exclusive, sovereign nation states, each with an internal monopoly of legitimate violence . . . [and] alike in that they are juridical
equals and are sovereign over their territories' (Caporaso, 1996: 34).

Most European states were still at an early stage of development in
1648. However, Britain quickly became the first truly successful
Westphalian state. Within less than 60 years, mainland Britain was
territorially 'complete' (after the 1707 Act of Union with Scotland)
with a central administration capable of tax collection and law
enforcement. Not until much later, in the nineteenth century, did
other major European states such as Germany or Italy become stable
Westphalian states.

Britain's national identity was forged primarily (and quickly) in the
eighteenth and early nineteenth centuries (Colley, 1992). As military
conflicts raged on the European continent, Britain mainly avoided
involvement, instead offering aid to coalitions assembled first against
revolutionary France and then against Napoleon. Meanwhile, the
British hold on India was bolstered. The Dutch East Indies, through
Britain's control of Singapore, became British-dominated and Ceylon
(later Sri Lanka) was conquered. Egypt became subject to a British
claim and South Africa was essentially taken over from the Dutch, as
were (more informally) the former colonies of Latin America from
Spain.

The Napoleonic wars of the early nineteenth century laid much of the essential groundwork for European unity in the late twentieth century. Trafalgar and Waterloo were stunning victories for Britain, but by 1815 Napoleon's conquests already had cast much of Europe in a French mould: the laws, administration, measurements and customs of France became generalized across Europe. For its part, Britain lost much of the European vocation it had prior to 1789, when Adam Smith and David Hume were as renowned and at home in Paris as in Edinburgh, and maybe more so than in London (Harvie, 1984: 436). The map of Europe and the institutions of nearly all its major states were radically transformed, while British borders remained inviolable. British institutions remained mostly unchanged until the Reform Act of 1832.

Meanwhile, Britain avoided European commitments while advancing its sphere of influence through limited military campaigns in India and China. After 1814, efforts led by Tsar Nicholas I of Russia to promote cooperation between the great powers in the Congress of Europe clashed with Palmerstonian doctrine, which decreed that Britain should act as a 'balancer', which would switch sides if necessary to ensure equilibrium in a European 'balance of power'. The idea was that no state (including Russia) or alliance of states should be allowed to become strong enough to threaten another. Palmerston dominated the British Foreign Office for over thirty years, after becoming Foreign Secretary at the age of 46 in 1830. During his long reign, 'Palmerston personified the bombastic self-confidence of Britain as the only world power, and succeeded in being simultaneously an aristocrat, a reformer, a free-trader, an internationalist, and a chauvinist' (Matthew, 1984: 465).

The force of British chauvinism was illustrated throughout the period from the Irish crises of the 1830s to the Boer wars of the 1890s. An almost miraculous economic boom reinforced the force of free trade as a doctrine after 1850. The link between the removal of tariff barriers and the mid-century boom was indirect and even tenuous, but the belief that market forces were the solution to nearly all economic problems became pervasive in Britain. Meanwhile, vast swathes of land were annexed in Africa, the Far East and Pacific, but not because 'trade followed the flag' (Matthew, 1984: 505–7). On the contrary, Britain became a nation of urbanized, outward-looking and entrepreneurial people who pushed the state to extend the empire ever further. The British nation led and the British state followed as the empire expanded.

Britain's decline began in the aftermath of the Crimean War of the 1850s (Davies, 1996: 870–96). Turkey – a British client state in lower Asia – became gradually more feeble and vulnerable to Russian-inspired disintegration. The collapse of the old Ottoman Empire left Egypt more self-reliant, but unstable. The Suez Canal, after being opened in 1870, became a vital British concern as a point of access to India. When Egypt approached bankruptcy and a military coup loomed, the liberal government of Gladstone invaded (reluctantly) in 1875. Turkey's degeneration induced the UK to extend the empire to the eastern Mediterranean and North Africa, even as the Boer War posed huge costs on the British Treasury and sparked domestic protests in Britain.

By 1900, Britain still possessed the largest empire in history, which extended to around a quarter of the world's population. It also had a sort of 'informal empire' extending to most of the underdeveloped world, even as Canada, Australia, New Zealand and other more modern British territories were making the transition to self-govern-ance and then independence (Hobsbawm, 1969). However, the under-pinnings of Britain's global power were eroding. The spread of industrialization meant that British goods began to be priced out of markets in North America and Europe, where domestic producers were often protected by high tariff walls. British industry was mean-while weakened by rising imports into its unprotected home market. Britain's declining economic performance eventually was reflected in a shifting military balance.

In particular, Germany began to challenge both Britain's naval power and doctrine of 'splendid isolation' in the early twentieth century. Slowly, Britain drifted towards the Franco-Russian alliance as tensions mounted. But British influence over continental affairs weakened as the Liberal Party tore itself apart over foreign policy and the Concert of Europe disintegrated in a wave of nationalistic aggression. The continental land war that broke out in 1914 found the UK woefully unprepared in military terms. The strength of Britain's national identity, spurred by the popular portrayal of Germany as an evil and dangerous threat, led huge numbers of ordinary Britons to volunteer to fight in an abominable war. The sacrifices made were distributed quite evenly across classes, thus giving further foundation to the relatively homogenous and tightly bound, if still 'imagined community', called Britain (Eatwell, 1997: 54; see also Anderson, 1991). Yet, the war marked the definitive end of the 'British century', and proved that the success of Britain's 'remarkable public experiment in liberal, capitalist democracy . . . was premised on free trade and world peace' (Matthew, 1984: 522).

British victory in the First World War was crucially abetted by American intervention, thus planting the seeds of the 'special relationship'. After the war, as the US drifted towards isolationism, Lloyd George's predisposition to act as a peacemaker in Europe became unpopular domestically. His political opponents urged a more familiar policy of withdrawal from Europe and reverence for the empire. Britain turned inwards, particularly when working-class revolt culminated in the General Strike of 1926. After Hitler came to power in Germany, there was little practical alternative to appeasement, leaving aside the option of a rapid, expensive and unpopular military build-up.

By this time, Britain had undergone a sort of 'revolution' (Rhodes James, 1977). In the previous sixty years, its enormous Victorian wealth and power had leaked away to the point where it was left struggling, at times desperately, for survival. In economic terms, Britain's decline has been 'one of the most investigated issues in economic history' (Kennedy, 1988: 294), but its central cause was the erosion of special historical circumstances that made Britain far richer, far sooner than other states. In political terms, Britain's decline was abetted by a range of sources, including 'the Boer farmers, the Irish nationalists, the followers of Arabi in Egypt, of Gandhi in India, of Kemal in Turkey, of Lenin in Russia and of Hitler in Germany' (Rhodes James, 1977: xii). Palmerstonian doctrine clearly had failed to guarantee Britain's 'independence'.

Nevertheless, victory over Germany in the Second World War, again with indispensable American support, gave British exceptionalism fresh life. Most post-war European governments were joined by one of the most influential of twentieth-century political scientists, E. H. Carr (1945), as well as successive US administrations, in believing a selective pooling of sovereignty was the key to European peace. Most of the British political class dismissed European institution-building as impractical and inappropriate for Britain. In 1946, Churchill (1994) boldly called for a 'United States of Europe', but also insisted that Britain could retain its global role by asserting its influence where three 'concentric circles' merged: the 'English-speaking world', the empire (soon to become the Commonwealth) and Europe. However, the Americans were unchallenged in the first domain, as revealed during the Suez crisis in 1956 when the US essentially vetoed a British foreign policy decision. The Empire underwent profound political upheaval, even as Britain remained economically focused on imperial markets which were unchallenging, and offered few incentives to modernize. Meanwhile, Europe was building new institutions that freed trade, sharpened industrial competitiveness, and reconciled France and Germany.

In short, the legacy of the Empire was to sustain British exceptionalism, perhaps past its sell-by date, while discouraging Britain from developing a European vocation. Britain retained a relationship with the US that was as 'special' as any bilateral alliance in existence, but also marked by a huge asymmetry in power. Vestiges of the Empire, particularly Britain's interests in Asia, helped sustain her claim to be a global trading power. The export of British institutions, as well as expatriates, helped uphold Britain's status as a major diplomatic power, while also discouraging domestic political reform. But surely one of the Empire's most important effects on British political life was to encourage a fundamental confusion about the meanings of sovereignty and independence.

Britain and the European Project

In one sense, Britain's experience of Empire was one of dispersing its sovereignty, often under primitive conditions. In contrast, the 'European project', to create a peaceful and unified Europe, involves an obverse process: 'the recombination of national sovereignty for more effective partnership under modern conditions' (Howe, 1990: 693). A prominent theme of scholarship on post-war British foreign policy – especially in contributions by practitioners (Ball, 1968; Denman, 1996; Renwick, 1996; Craddock, 1997) – has been the contrast between Britain's record in Europe and its record nearly everywhere else. Difficult transitions from colonialism to independence were coaxed along by skilful British diplomacy throughout much of the former Empire. In contrast, Britain's 'European policy' failed almost entirely to shape the course of European integration to suit British preferences. One of Margaret Thatcher's foreign policy advisers offers a simple explanation for Britain's isolation in Europe: 'we did not even know what we wanted' (Cradock, 1997: 210). Political classes on the European continent, particularly those of the original six EEC member states, tended to be much clearer about what they wanted: an 'ever closer union', or even something resembling a federal Europe.

Explaining this gap in perceptions and preferences starts by noting that the UK is a European state, but hardly a typical one. Compared with other regions of the world, the continent of Europe has a very large number of small and densely populated states that occupy a relatively small landmass. One effect is to encourage expressions of nationalism so that European peoples can differentiate themselves as Dutch or German, French or Belgian, Scots or English. But another is that European states have little choice but to cooperate if they wish to prosper, or even survive (Dogan, 1994). For many reasons – geographical, historical, cultural, and psychological – such cooperation has come more naturally to continental European states than to Britain.

The EU grew out of attempts to institutionalize cooperation that Western Europe clearly needed to prosper (even survive) in the 1950s. European integration as a process subsequently led to the gradual pooling of sovereignty by EU member states in selected areas of policy, such as trade, competition and agriculture. The methodology employed was functionalism (or, in its more recent academic permutation, neo-functionalism). Functionalist integration happens almost by itself, step by step, as integrated policies in one area create pressures for integrated policies in other, related areas. Thus, advocates of Economic and Monetary Union (EMU) argue that the EU can never have a truly a single market without a single currency.

The functional approach is almost instinctive for many German elites. After all, the first step towards the (original) unification of Germany in the nineteenth century was the Zollverein, or the formation of a customs union (a forerunner to a 'single German market') between Germanic regions and city-states. In key respects, the pattern of German state formation followed economic function.

In contrast, the British attachment to sovereignty and independence, and the tendency to equate one with the other, breeds an almost primordial scepticism about functional integration. Britain has consistently either misjudged other European states' will to make the EU succeed or else has made it a national priority to curb their ambitions. Often, the effect has been to redouble the efforts of continental leaders to push European integration forward, while offering relatively few concessions to Britain.

At each turn, there has been no shortage of reasoned, pragmatic justifications for British reluctance. For example, the post-1945 Labour government, which had nationalized Britain's coal industry, was narrowly re-elected in 1950 on a platform to complete the nationalization of British steel as well. As such, the Labour government could claim that it had little choice but to refuse to join the European Coal and Steel Community (ECSC), the first institutional prototype for the EU. The decision may have marked a 'missed chance' at leadership at a time when Britain could have established itself as the political leader of Europe 'for a song' (Denman, 1996: 2). However, in the early post-war period, as in the nineteenth century, leadership of Europe was not a priority of the British government.

Britain's failure to take seriously the subsequent negotiations on the Treaty of Rome, the original birth certificate of the EU, was perhaps less excusable. The construction in 1960 of the European Free Trade Association (EFTA), with Britain in the lead, yielded 'a remarkably successful organization' (Vasey, 1986: 612). But nearly all of EFTA's founding members eventually abandoned it for the more tangible privileges of EU membership, thus highlighting the lack of continental support for the 'British vision' of Europe. Britain itself was ready to bail out of EFTA to join the Common Market, as the EC was then commonly known, as early as 1961. The Macmillan and Wilson governments' half-hearted commitments to European unity, their dogged devotion to the 'special relationship' with America, and the complex motives of France's President, Charles de Gaulle, led to French vetoes of the first two British attempts to join the Community. Only in 1973, at the worst possible time in the global economic cycle and after the expensive and wasteful Common Agricultural Policy (CAP) was fully constructed, was Britain finally admitted.

Arguably, Britain's ambivalence towards European integration was a product less of habit or history, than of a fundamental lack of leadership on the part of its political class. Both Labour and Conservative governments had enormous difficulties maintaining a broad consensus within their own parties on the need for Britain to be a constructive, adaptable EU partner. The post-1974 Labour governments had the temerity to demand that the terms of Britain's (late and unenthusiastic) entry into the Community be renegotiated, then to put British membership of the Community to a popular referendum (which produced a resounding two-thirds of the votes cast in favour). The governments of Margaret Thatcher (1979–90) and John Major (1990–7) both fell (under decidedly different circumstances) primarily due to divisions within the Conservative Party over European integration. It was easy to see why the Blair government treads carefully on most European questions. Still, Blair struck a far more pro-European stance than his predecessors, unveiling a 'changeover plan' in 1999 to facilitate Britain's future membership of the euro and effectively signalling an intention to join monetary union (after a referendum) if re-elected to a second term.

The electoral dangers of ignoring the ingrained 'Euroscepticism' which pervades British public opinion seem clear. Yet, British public opinion was decidedly less 'Eurosceptic' than Austrian or Swedish opinion by the late 1990s (Peterson, 1997a: 28). Most British voters seemed pragmatic, if not idealistic about European integration: about half thought Europe was 'most important to Britain', while only about a quarter chose America and less than a fifth cited the Commonwealth (Gallup Poll in *The Economist*, 28 March 1998). The Blair government's case for a constructive, if reserved, British policy on monetary union seemed to have shifted public attitudes significantly towards the euro, within a year of Labour's election (*Economist*, 1998; MORI, 1998). More generally, there was little evidence to suggest that 'EU-bashing' retained 'clear electoral attractions' (Eatwell, 1997: 63) in any permanent or inalterable way.

Compared with their European counterparts, British citizens show little enthusiasm for the 'European project'. Most continue to resist adding a new 'European layer' to their identity. Even so, the EU has become the logical and central foil for the modernization of British policies to deal with thorny issues such as environmental protection, organized crime and immigration. As Jack Straw, the Blair government's Home Secretary, pursued cooperation on the problem of football hooliganism with his continental counterparts in advance of the 1998 World Cup football championship, he complained that 'we have nineteenth century procedures to pursue twenty-first century criminals' (quoted in *Financial Times*, 29 December 1997).

A plausible vision of the EU of the twenty-first century is one of a German-led (if not dominated) federation with a centre of gravity far to the east of its traditional borders. This vision assumes that the logic of functionalism remains sacrosanct. For example, creating a single currency will create powerful pressures to create a sort of 'economic government' and enhanced EU powers to tax and spend.

This European future is clouded, if not proscribed, by three caveats. First, the successes of post-war European integration have required political leadership. In nearly all important instances, France and Germany have provided that leadership jointly. Before 1990, the Franco-German alliance was a partnership of rough equals. Afterwards, Germany's population was more than 30 per cent larger than that of France. The German economy was 40 per cent bigger than the

French economy and about the size of the British and French economies combined (Messerlin, 1996). In terms of both political acceptability and sheer force of habit, the rest of the EU remained far more predisposed to leadership by the French and Germans acting together than by the Germans acting alone. But the durability of the Franco-German axis seemed uncertain.

Second, new questions emerged in the late 1990s about the depth of German commitment to the European project. Public scepticism about the euro in Germany was less surprising than unprecedented complaints about Germany's very large (and longstanding) net contribution to the EU's central budget. The German budgetary concerns were easy to understand given the very high cost of unification, stubbornly high rates of German unemployment, and, above all, a jockeying for position both ahead of and after the 1998 German domestic election. They nevertheless caused a frisson in Brussels, where it was taken for granted that the Germans would always be willing paymasters of the European project.

Third, the EU's enlargement to incorporate the new democracies in Central and Eastern Europe was inevitable by the late 1990s. Nonetheless, even the 6 (of 12) applicant states which began accession negotiations in 1998 Cyprus, the Czech Republic, Estonia, Hungary, Poland and Slovenia were about one-quarter as wealthy as the EU (as a group per capita), with three times more farm workers. The CAP and the EU's regional development policies were clearly incompatible, in their present forms, with enlargement. It was possible to imagine a future EU of as many as 25 or 30 member states extending from the Atlantic to the Asian steppes. It was impossible to imagine an EU as cohesive or politically unified as the Union often was after the mid 1980s, given the very wide disparities of wealth, power and vocation which characterized its future membership. Blair's Foreign Secretary, Robin Cook, confidently asserted that the 'high tide of integration ha[d] passed' (quoted in *The Economist*, 1998).

Such glibness recalls the blithe assumptions of early post-war British governments about the impracticality of European institution-building. Debates about whether the EU is (or is becoming) a 'state' seem a dubious investment of academic time and energy (see Peterson, 1997b). However, just as Europe is unlike any other region of the world, the EU clearly is unlike any other international organization. As Ludlow (1997: 16) argues, 'The management of interdependence, whether it be within states or between states, requires a bedrock in strong institutions and mutual confidence, which the EU has already begun to provide, but which no global or inter-regional organizations can hope to replicate for a very long time to come'. No other international organization has a system of law that is 'superior' to the law of its member states. None has a directly elected legislature comparable to the European Parliament (EP). As such, the European Court of Justice (ECJ), the EP and the European Commission (the EU's hybrid executive/Civil Service) are supranational institutions, which often assert their own interests and agendas as political agents. Disputes rage between scholars about how powerful the EU's institutions are *vis-à-vis* the national governments of its member states. Realists dismiss them as weak and unimportant, yet, the EU's institutions have jealously defended their independence from national influence and become a stimulus, in their own right, for closer European cooperation.

At the same time, scope for the expression of national interests in EU policy-making has always been wide. In concrete terms, there is surprisingly little about the EU that is 'supra-national', in the sense that outcomes are imposed on member states. Even the CAP, one of the EU's only truly 'common' policies, gives considerable leeway to member states (Grant, 1997). Despite the creation of a 'Common Foreign and Security Policy' (CFSP) by the Maastricht Treaty of 1993, European cooperation remains no more than a reference point – albeit a central one – for national foreign policies (Peterson and Sjursen, 1998). National EU governments continue to engage in considerable unilateralism on matters of 'high politics' such as Bosnia or Algeria. The EU remains a very long way from the vision, widely held in the early 1990s, whereby the Union would become a sort of 'suzerain' power which controlled the foreign relations of its member states while allowing them 'sovereign authority' in most of their internal affairs.

Perhaps above all the EU remains plagued by a generally low level of democratic legitimacy (Shackleton, 1997). European integration has not yet resolved the problem that 'democracy and democratic institutions are firmly wedded to the territorial state' (Cooper, 1996: 28). Regardless, the EU has become a sort of 'post-Westphalian' polity, in that modern European states have given over to it slices of their previously territorially exclusive sovereignty.

Looking towards the future, it is clear that the euro is the true wild card in the EU's prospective development. Beyond relatively narrow questions about how a single European currency is managed lurks the potential for vast institutional changes in the way the EU does business and makes policy. It is an open question whether EU member states will need to develop common policies to regulate labour markets, co-ordinate fiscal policies, and create a sort of 'economic government' to make the euro work. EMU could well accelerate the pace of European integration. The problem for the UK is that its influence in discussions about how and how far such a push might go is limited by its refusal to sign on as a founder member of the euro. Eventually, it is not unimaginable that some of the benefits of the single market might be denied to states that refuse to help shoulder the burden of maintaining and managing a single currency. Euro membership clearly will bring privileges, as well as risks, and non-members simply will never participate in the European project as equals.

Globalization and Britain PLC

Rising interdependence and new threats to traditional ideas of sovereignty are perhaps most perceptible in Europe, but they are also visible on a global scale. The idea of 'globalization' is notoriously fuzzy. Much of the literature that is devoted to it does little to clarify its meaning or effects. Simply defined, globalization is 'a set of processes that result in the increased interdependence of previously separate national economies' (Peterson and Sharp, 1998: 5). It results primarily from liberalized capital markets and increased cross-border investment; the modernization of infrastructures in telecommunications and transport; the emergence of 'information-based' economies; increased alliances between firms; and new regional and global projects to free trade, such as the WTO. All conspire to make the global economy an increasingly seamless, organic whole. The obvious political effect of globalization is to challenge the existing Westphalian model of an international system based on sovereign states.

   In many respects, Britain has been at the forefront of globalization in doctrinal, historical and policy terms. The two economic thinkers primarily responsible for developing the idea of 'comparative advantage' were both British: Adam Smith and David Ricardo. Their influence on nineteenth-century British economic diplomacy was clear: government policy was distinctly *laissez-faire* with the state essentially standing aside to let private enterprise and cross-border trade flourish. While Britain's GNP increased by more than 1000 per cent, British policy fostered the emergence of an essentially 'global' nineteenth-century world economy. In Carr's (1945: 13) judgement, the era's 'progressive [economic] expansion was the product not of the principle of universal free trade (which was never applied, and whose application would have been found to be intolerable) but of the open British market'.

In the post-war period, Britain's *laissez-faire* tradition fell victim to frequent attempts, many of them desperate and blatantly protectionist, to arrest Britain's rapid post-war economic decline (Gamble, 1990). The Thatcher years marked a return to the instinctual association of free trade with prosperity. Britain pioneered liberalization, privatization and deregulation as modern policy ideas. The EU's '1992 project' to create a truly single European market drew substantial inspiration from Thatcherite principles (Cockfield, 1994).

However, the 1992 project was indicative of a more general, structural, global shift in power from governments to markets. This shift was dramatically illustrated after the election of François Mitterrand in 1981, who campaigned to be President of France with a promise to initiate a 'rupture with capitalism'. Using the traditional Keynesian tools of demand management, the French Socialists sought to tax and spend France's way out of the recession of the early 1980s, while subsidising and protecting French industry. The results were disastrous. France was punished ruthlessly by global markets, which abandoned the French franc and quickly channelled investment elsewhere. After an astounding policy U-turn, Mitterrand and the French Socialists embraced the 1992 project. Even in France, the major European country with the weakest tradition of *laissez-faire* economic policy, it became accepted that 'socialism in one country' was no longer possible in the face of global markets.

The 1990s brought accelerating increases in trade and cross-border investment. The end of the cold war reduced the number of non-capitalist states to only a handful, and made political boundaries less of a barrier to transnational capitalism than at any time since before 1914. The idea of 'security' itself was fundamentally redefined, with national economic dynamism beginning to supplant, or even supersede, military strength as a primary source of international power.

In many ways, the UK was well placed to thrive under these conditions. It continued to attract far more direct investment from Asia and America than any other European country. Its highly trade-oriented industrial sector was more entrepreneurial and internationally oriented than were those of most other EU states. Perhaps above all, Britain probably offered leadership on trade policy at the EU level more often than in any other area of policy, thus stamping its own imprint on how the world's largest trade power conducted itself in international economic diplomacy.

Still, globalization prompted deep insecurities, in Britain as elsewhere. Despite enjoying the lowest unemployment rate (by far) in Europe, Britain was the only European country in which the number of hours worked by the average worker was rising: to nearly 44 hours per week by 1998. Over half of all British workers were expected regularly to work overtime, but only one-third of all overtime worked was compensated. Consistently, nearly two-thirds of British workers expressed fears of losing their jobs, a higher share than in most of the rest of Europe (Eatwell, 1997: 64).

In Britain, as elsewhere, it was possible to link the pessimism of ordinary citizens about the consequences of globalization with their rising alienation from governments and public institutions. The advent of globalized markets made it increasingly difficult for governments to deliver what Western citizens most wanted: economic security. In particular, young people in Britain expressed profound cynicism about political life. Incredibly, in the months before Labour's landslide victory in 1997, only 2 per cent of a large sample of Britons aged 12–25 reported feeling an affinity with any British political party (Stevens, 1997).

Meanwhile, the 'European project' became remote from the concerns of ordinary people, particularly in the headstrong rush to the euro. The EU, along with most western states, struggled to develop new ideas on the issues that mattered most to citizens: jobs, training and education. In political as well as policy terms, the primary task of the EU in the twenty-first century seemed likely to be reforming European institutions to adapt to globalization, while protecting European citizens from its vagaries. In key respects, Britain seemed better suited to lead in this quest than other major EU states, where 'globalization ha[d] become a cliché which embattled politicians utter[ed] to explain away Europe's many ills and their own inadequacies' (Ludlow, 1997: 13). Witness, for example, the warning of Philippe Séguin, the leader of France's neo-Gaullist party, that 'savage globalization . . . would transform the planet into a gigantic casino' (quoted in *Financial Times*, 3 February 1998).

It was debatable whether the EU sustained globalization, by freeing trade among its members and extending it to others, or shielded Europe from globalization through a combination of protectionism, interventionism and corporatism. On the political right, Eurosceptics argued that Britain could rediscover its role as a promoter of globalized free trade and cross-border exchange only if it disentangled itself from the EU. Even the Blair government openly expressed doubts about 'how well Europe worked' in preparing the EU for a twenty-first century economy, which demanded highly skilled, flexible workforces and deregulated, liberalized national economies.

An EU bogged down with major internal disputes over agricultural reform, the euro and enlargement is far from unlikely in the early twenty-first century. Meanwhile, Britain's strong cultural affinities with America and the Commonwealth will continue to foster the conviction that there exist genuine alternatives to the European project. In military terms, Britain is unlikely to surrender its status as America's staunchest ally, even when it means isolation from the rest of Europe (and even most of the Commonwealth). This point was amply illustrated in policy towards Iraq in 1998, a time when the personal affinity of Blair and Bill Clinton led to a revival of old homilies about the 'special relationship' between Britain and America.

Yet, the UK's international standing in the twenty-first century is likely to depend above all on its ability to maximize its influence within the EU. Even the Clinton administration made no secret of its view that London's influence in Washington was directly proportionate to its influence in Brussels, Paris and Bonn. As such, the stakes involved in the decision not to be a founder member of the euro were high. Though there were uncertainties about whether the euro would succeed, it was clear that the EU would remain, for the foreseeable future, the world's largest single capitalist market and a leading international trading power. It was less clear whether the UK could retain its status as Europe's leading recipient of foreign direct investment or its forcible position in international economic diplomacy if it remained long outside a successful euro. Despite its flaws, the EU was the most logical – and perhaps only – springboard for the projection of a British vision of a liberal, modern, peaceful international order which combined open markets with adequate social, environmental and consumer safeguards.

More generally, ensuring order in a globalized world may require something like Bull's (1995: 245) vision of a 'new medievalism', or a 'system of overlapping authority and multiple loyalty'. Already, modern governance occurs at multiple levels: the United Nations for global environmental questions, NATO handles peacekeeping, the EU has authority on most economic matters, national capitals deal with social questions, and local or regional capitals are responsible for most cultural issues. As such, especially in Europe, the modern world resembles the pre-Westphalian world in which no ruler, state or church was fully 'sovereign'.

At the level of the citizen, the loyalties of a modern Glaswegian might well be split between Glasgow, Edinburgh, London, Brussels, and perhaps even New York and Hong Kong. Similarly, the pre-modern subject of the Middle Ages often owed a 'slice' of loyalty to feudal princes, Catholic vassals, the Pope and the Holy Roman Emperor. At the end of the twentieth century, Bull's (1995: 245) essential prerequisite for 'new medievalism' – the willingness of states to share their ability to command loyalties – was still in short supply and the concept of sovereignty had not 'ceased to be applicable'. Still, globalization clearly posed major, perhaps lethal, threats to traditional notions of sovereignty.

Conclusion

British exceptionalism has sometimes invited superciliousness. The tendency to assume and even insist that other states should replicate British ways and institutions has often worked to Britain's disadvantage in international relations. The problem has not only been one of backlash against hectoring from a nation viewed as hidebound by tradition, addicted to overcentralized power and generally in decline. Superciliousness becomes increasingly costly in a world where states must 'earn' their influence by being seen, in the eyes of the world, to foster both economic success and political legitimacy.

The point has become especially salient as 'policy transfer' has become a more significant practice in modern governance. Policy transfer is what happens when governments learn from each other: it is 'a process in which knowledge about policies, administrative arrangements, institutions etc. in one-time and/or place is used . . . in another time and/or place' (Dolowitz and Marsh, 1996: 344). Policy transfer occurs frequently and almost naturally as globalization reduces the role of the 'positive', interventionist state, while accentuating its regulatory role. As rule-making replaces taxing and spending, international competition takes place not only between economic producers but also between regulatory regimes (Majone, 1997). Investment is attracted to areas where businesses find an amenable regulatory climate. High-skilled workers are attracted to areas where the environment is clean, consumers are protected, and crime is low. Politically sophisticated Western citizens demand political regimes that strike the right balance between public and private interests.

As such, one of the most compelling and convincing arguments for international cooperation is that it encourages governments to compare notes, share experiences and draw lessons from each other. The scourge of late twentieth century western Europe – stubbornly high unemployment – became a matter not so much of EU competence as policy transfer. After 1997, European governments agreed to table national (not common or 'EU') 'action plans' annually on what they were doing to fight unemployment domestically, and what measures worked. The methodology combined peer pressure, policy experimentation and information-sharing in a way that was, by this time, routine at the EU level.

The Blair government appeared to learn that this methodology was incompatible with the traditional (perhaps instinctual) British practice of trying to export a 'British model'. During the 1998 British EU Presidency, Gordon Brown, the Chancellor of the Exchequer, echoed Blair's call for a 'third way' between draconian, US-style capitalism and over-regulated, European-style corporatism. Crucially, however, Brown also conceded that Britain had problems of its own and that EU states had 'a great deal to learn from each other' (quoted in *Financial Times*, 22 January 1998).

Just as policy transfer promotes innovative governance, so do strong local governments or states' rights in federal systems. Smaller units of government become 'laboratories' for policy experiments, with successful policies studied, adapted and widely adopted. Postwar Britain missed out on most of the 'good governance' effects of this process: in contrast with virtually all other west European states, the UK became more and not less centralized in the late twentieth century. Meanwhile, British political institutions became increasingly incongruous with a progressively less homogenous British nation. The inexorable, if erratic, rise of Scottish and Welsh nationalism and the emergence of a truly 'multicultural society' in many urban areas raised new questions about Britain's national identity, and its compatibility with a state that was enormously centralized by international standards.

As such, the Blair government's embrace of constitutional reform, beginning with the creation of a Scottish Parliament and Welsh Assembly, was not only overdue but more of a boon to Britain's international standing than was often realised. Despite hesitations about conceding large amounts of power to new sub-national authorities, Labour's programme for constitutional reform started with the concession that Britain's institutions were not faultless and, in some cases, needed modernization. Constitutional reform complemented the Blair government's more constructive, if not uncritical, approach to European integration. For perhaps the first time in its history, a British government seemed prepared to acknowledge that nation states – the products of bloody conquests, historical accidents or the fusion of much smaller political units – did not represent some 'ultimate form of government' (Ludlow, 1997: 7). British sovereignty was no longer confused with British independence. Potentially, at least, Britain seemed poised to make an important contribution to solving the global conundrums of governance in the twenty-first century: reconciling small government with strong government, and embracing globalization while preserving national (even European) values.

13

Ideas, Ideologies and the British Political Tradition

MICHAEL KENNY

This chapter is concerned with the relationship between political ideas and political practice, one of the most interesting but complex themes in the study of British politics. Much analysis in this context is conducted on the assumption that ideas are of secondary value in explaining political developments, and that the interests of political actors or the impact of structural phenomena should weigh more heavily in the calculations of analysts. Yet rival traditions of scholarly interpretation have for a long time explored the significance of ideas and ideologies, both in shaping actors' perceptions of their 'interests' and in generating frameworks through which the political world that they inhabit is made comprehensible and alternative possibilities imagined. This chapter looks at some of the different interpretations of British politics which have argued that doctrine, of different kinds, has been central to the history and character of this polity. It explores whether the leading political ideas should be understood in terms of a 'political tradition' rooted within the peculiarities of British history and culture as some (mainly conservative) intellectuals and politicians have claimed. It then turns to consider if liberalism can be said to have played a fundamental role within the modern period, and, in particular, if 'the British political tradition' is more liberal or conservative in orientation. The chapter concludes by discussing the advantages and limitations of attempts to characterize a particular tradition of ideas at the core of the modern British polity, and by offering some general reflections on how ideas and ideologies might be considered fundamental to the comprehension of political action in this setting.

Tradition or Ideology?

Before embarking on a brief survey of the principal interpretations of
the so-called 'British tradition', it is worth observing an important
interpretative divide among those who assert the significance of
political ideas. This is between those intellectual historians who
subscribe to the belief that there is a core tradition within political
life which can be understood in terms of the recurrence of a particular
set of ideas and values and those who present ideology as the key
interpretative tool for understanding modern political discourse. 'The
British tradition' has frequently been characterized as a non-ideological entity and sometimes as trans-ideological. Lurking beneath such
commitments is an unspoken philosophical distinction between
authentic political cultures, which are deemed to have emerged as
organic expressions of the national psyche, on the one hand, and
ideological paradigms, on the other, which have been viewed as alien
imports into domestic political life. As we shall see, this kind of
argument has generated some potent and longstanding interpretations of a putative 'British tradition', though important differences
persist about how this ought to be understood.

   The implications of thinking about political ideas and culture in
terms of 'traditions' have figured prominently in the study of Western
thought, with leading philosophers like Alasdair MacIntyre elaborat-
ing the importance of conceiving individual actions and thoughts in
relation to rich traditions of 'practice' (MacIntyre, 1985: 204–25).
Different commentators have, for instance, asserted that in thinking
about the political ideas associated with the Labour Party, it is
important to supplement discussion of formal doctrine (the publicly
stated beliefs of leading figures in the party and party programmes)
with consideration of the underlying 'ethos' that binds the membership and underpins a powerful sense of collective identity and fellowship (Drucker, 1979). In a similar vein, some commentators propose
that it is the shared understandings, or ethos, which persists under the
surface of political life and emerges periodically into the open that
constitute the interpretative key to modern British politics.

   Other critics have opted to embrace 'ideology', not just in the
obvious normative sense of promoting the claims of a particular
school of political thinking, like socialism or conservatism, but as an
analytical framework which points to underlying patterns and continuities within the many strands of political argument and discourse
in a particular community (Freeden, 1997; Appleby, 1992). The

notion of ideology, it is suggested, helps us understand the recurrence through time of clusters of shared understandings of the meaning of concepts like democracy, rights and liberty. This clustering of a set of interrelated concepts appears to be an essential feature of political discourse in modern politics, allowing us to consider the emergence of ideological 'families' like liberalism, conservatism and socialism in different national contexts. Though understandings of ideological paradigms vary markedly, it has been possible in recent years to discern a move among commentators to reject the interpretation of ideology as a number of core beliefs to which true believers should be expected to adhere. Instead ideology has been presented as sets of 'idea-practices' which undergo a process of continual and subtle refinement and modification in the hands of intellectuals and ideologues. This constitutes an important alternative way of conceiving the relationship between political ideas and action in the British context. It challenges the view that a 'non-ideological' tradition can be recuperated from history and reinvigorated in the present.

Defining 'the British Tradition'

Oakeshott

Perhaps the most influential interpretative school which points to the importance of a prevailing tradition of political life in Britain takes a lead from the philosopher Michael Oakeshott (1901–90) and has its origins in earlier thinkers like Edmund Burke (1729–97). The impact of Oakeshott's reflections upon political culture and practice stemmed from his attempt to characterize the British tradition in terms of some of the most pervasive myths and self-perceptions of the English. Every political community, Oakeshott argued, can be said to have developed a 'tradition' of political life; as Andrew Vincent puts it:

> a mixture of preferences and aversions, approvals and disapprovals, anxieties, fears and beliefs ... This 'multi-voiced' entity does not constitute a creed or rationally self-consistent doctrine. A tradition does not appear as a set of maxims, rules or propositions (Vincent, 1994: 214)

A tradition does not therefore correlate with one of the blocks of modern ideology to which analysts and activist adhere, being both broader and more diverse than a single ideological paradigm. Yet ideologies do play an important and, in certain ways, unavoidable role as 'abridgements' of such traditions – simplifications of richer and more nuanced sets of practices, values and ideas designed to facilitate political argument and understanding (Oakeshott, 1962). Ideologies are likely to be especially appealing in situations where political experience and wisdom are either lacking or distrusted, hence the appeal of reformist socialism in British politics in the 1940s, following the discrediting of the political elite and associated political orthodoxies in the preceding decade.

Developing a deep understanding of 'the British tradition' and deriving the correct kinds of intimations from it are, thus, important tasks facing the academy and polity alike. Policies based upon 'alien', overly schematic ideological systems are likely to do more damage than good to the interwoven fabric of custom and culture that constitutes civil society. For Oakeshott, the British tradition involves a preference for the pragmatic handling of social problems, an aversion to the intrusions of rationalist dogma and a commitment to the rule of law which enables the flourishing of what he termed a 'vital civil association'. These values are embodied in the 'practices' of political life – the core institutions and associated cultures which ensure they are passed from generation to generation.

Such thinking also provided a high-minded version of a frequently uttered piece of 'common-sense' wisdom – that ideology is in fact alien to British culture and experience and has had largely harmful consequences when imported. This concern has a long historical pedigree, stretching back at least to Burke's hostile response to indigenous radicals enamoured by the model of the French Revolution. Kenneth Minogue has forcefully argued that ideologies are 'alien powers' – modes of thought abstracted from political traditions and realities which seek to impose totalising systems in the place of organic traditions (Minogue, 1985). This kind of argument was deployed against proponents of communist and fascist ideology when these emerged as serious and potentially influential belief-systems in the first half of the twentieth century – they were frequently portrayed as unworkable and alien in the distinctive British context. Some commentators still maintain that British political thought either has contributed little to the broad range of continental European ideological systems or has remained broadly unaffected by them.

The characterization of a powerful indigenous tradition in terms of a cluster of non-ideological values, prejudices and ideas has, in addition, come from intellectuals of very different political persuasions. There have been recurrent laments about the empiricism, anti-intellectualism and pragmatism of the British intelligentsia, body politic or working class, and the shared belief that the systems of modern political thought are, by and large, foreign elements in the British context which is shaped by indigenous traditions of thought and argument. This kind of claim should alert us to the ideological malleability of the concept of tradition. It can and has been deployed as effectively by political radicals seeking to revive hidden, suppressed or marginalized traditions of thinking as it has by conservatives.

Greenleaf

A fascinating and fertile deployment of the Oakeshottian model can be found in W. H. Greenleaf's major study of *The British Political Tradition* (Greenleaf, 1983a; 1983b; 1987). Greenleaf differed from those who characterized the British tradition as non-ideological in nature, by positing a trans-ideological pattern or dialectic at the heart of domestic political life. Like Oakeshott he regarded a tradition of political activity as implying 'a unity in diversity: a complex amalgam of different forces and opposing choices, and therefore of internal tensions, which is at the same time in a continual state of flux and development but which nevertheless constitutes a recognizable and acknowledged whole' (Greenleaf, 1983a: 13). Struck by the English constiutionalist A. V. Dicey's (1835–1922) observation that political life in the early twentieth century was being reshaped by tides of collectivism (see Chapter 7), Greenleaf presented the British tradition as a 'basic tension between libertarianism and collectivism'. Indeed, '[t]he dialectic between the growing processes of collectivism and the opposing libertarian tendency is the one supreme fact of our domestic political life ... over the past century and a half' (Greenleaf, 1983b: 3).

The normative purpose of Greenleaf's study is barely concealed:

> Why, in Britain, has a libertarian, individualist society sustaining a limited conception of government been in so many ways and to such a degree replaced by the positive state pursuing explicit policies of widespread intervention in the name of social justice and the public good? (Greenleaf, 1983a: 42)

Libertarianism was defined as an assemblage of values, central to which was the 'notion of a natural harmony in society achieved without recourse to state intervention'. Four central characteristics were identified: 'stress on the basic importance of individuality, that is, on the rights of the individual and his freedom from both social supervision and arbitrary political control', a commitment to limiting the legitimate arena for government intervention, a corresponding suspicion of concentrations of power 'likely to be dangerous to this sacrosanct zone of individual choice and activity', and the security offered by the rule of law. Collectivism, on the other hand, signalled the 'idea of an artificial identification of human interests resulting from legislative or other political regulation', and was often articulated through a primary concern with the 'public good' and the achievement of common security (Greenleaf, 1983a: 15–17). The story Greenleaf told was of a shift in the balance from libertarian to collectivist ideas as the modern state expanded in function and capacity. In the second volume of his enterprise, Greenleaf surveyed the principal ideological streams flowing through modern British politics – conservatism, liberalism and socialism – and showed how 'our three main political doctrines have both stimulated and reacted to the growth of government intervention and the proliferation of public agency; and how they have dealt with the problems of individual liberty involved' (Greenleaf, 1983b: xi). Each of these ideologies contained exponents of both libertarian and collectivist perspectives and were to be understood as inevitably marked by the clash of these competing perspectives.

Greenleaf's analysis has generated some innovative interpretations of these paradigms and associated thinkers, and inspired some influential analysis of modern British politics (Beer, 1982). Yet a number of analytical and interpretative queries have been raised about Greenleaf's arguments and these are pertinent for similar characterizations of the British tradition. Interpretation of political discourse in the nineteenth and twentieth centuries through the push-and-pull of libertarian and collectivist expressions gives rise to inadequate intellectual history as these categories are too starkly drawn to account for the unfolding of patterns of thought which straddle and undermine this divide. Many so-called collectivists can, on closer inspection, be found to adhere to forms of ethical individualism. The example of the 'New Liberal' theorists of the late nineteenth and early twentieth century is discussed below. The general problem is that Greenleaf's analytical framework tends to obscure the ways in which different theorists connect accounts of the nature and moral attributes of the individual with visions of the political community. The simple prioritization of one over the other is rare in political thought.

Dispositional Conservatism

Invocations of certain kinds of tradition as the trans- or non-ideological heart of British politics are most likely to emerge from within the conservative ideological family. The invocation of 'tradition' plays a significant role in all the strains of conservative thinking. Many British conservatives have suggested that their views do not amount to a system of belief like other ideologies, but are better understood (following one of Oakeshott's famous essays, 'On Being Conservative') as the expressions of a disposition or set of intuitions; hence the well-known assertion of the former Conservative minister Sir Ian Gilmour that 'British Conservatism ... is not an "ism". It is not a system of ideas. It cannot be formulated in a series of propositions, which can be aggregated into a creed. It is not an ideology or doctrine' (Gilmour, 1978: 121). This is one of the foundations of many paternalist or one-nation strands of conservative thinking which construct the putative British tradition around one or more of the following: the belief in the wise governance of the established political and social elites; the values embodied in leading institutions; and the good, pragmatic sense of 'the British people'. Variations of this conservative 'tradition' have played an important role in shaping the self-understanding of sections of the political elite.

Problems with 'the British Tradition'

These different arguments share a number of interpretative weaknesses. The contents of the putative tradition always seem to be assembled in a 'normative' way, marginalizing some recurrent elements, like socialism or radicalism, yet offering no convincing account of the criteria governing inclusion and exclusion. On what interpretative basis – apart from partisan preference – are some elements of political discourse expelled from the tradition that such intellectuals construct?

It is tempting to explain such theorizing from a historicist perspective, so that the relatively unbroken historical development and absence of protracted political and socio-economic ruptures which characterize the British historical record in comparison with other states can be seen to have encouraged this kind of reinvention of a continuous unfolding tradition. Yet, more recently, such arguments have come under increasing examination and seem to be working against the grain of contemporary intellectual reasoning. The most obvious reason for this is the reappearance of different kinds of conflict in British social and political life in the late 1970s and early 1980s and the resurgence of ideologically founded political differences. Equally important has been renewed contestation about the character and identity of the British tradition in the wake of Thatcherite attempts to 'colonize' this for highly political and ideological ends, a project which generated a polarized and critical reaction. A further explanation may well lie in the increasingly evident problem of the difficulty of assigning certain practices and ideas 'core' status as British civil society has been shown to have always been a radically pluralized and conflictual arena. Where many conservative commentators saw shared cultural understandings, historians point to persistent value conflicts and differences. Certainly some conservative critics are now less confident that the nexus of customs, sensibilities and ideas that shaped tradition in the British context still survives (Gray, 1993).

A range of social and cultural developments have arguably brought about the demise of a 'common culture', or more accurately the dream of such an entity. British civil society (the domain of associations and organizations that lie between and connect the individual and the state, including the church, trade unions and political parties) has never been the benign and consensual realm that some claim. Yet it has arguably never been as divided between competing value systems as it is now. Moral debate is shaped by the clamour of many competing voices and in this environment self-standing cultural enclaves, such as gay villages, internet user communities and self-help groups, have prospered. These are just a small number of the proliferating identities that can be sustained and reproduced in ways that allow individuals to lead their lives outside or beyond any obviously defined cultural norm. Andrew Vincent is right to question whether conservative appeals to a pre-modern tradition can survive meaningfully in a secular context where different values coexist often uncomfortably and claim different, competing lineages (Vincent, 1994). An interesting, associated problem for students of modern British political ideas to consider is whether both rulers and ruled have now lost faith in the stories about British exceptionalism and innovation that were bound up with received accounts of 'tradition'. Such narratives have arguably played an important rule in helping legitimate the somewhat archaic character of the British state in the modern period.

The foundations underlying arguments about 'the British tradition' have begun to crumble for another important reason – the historiographical revolution that has occurred in the last twenty years about the nature and history of 'Britain' (see Chapter 6). How meaningful is it to talk in historical terms of British political discourse when many longstanding assumptions have been overturned by the recovery of independent histories of Ireland, Scotland and Wales (Kearney, 1989). Britain has come to be seen as itself a cultural construct, frequently imagined through prevailing English values. Once the historical narratives that have been stitched together to create our sense of Britain are 'deconstructed' in this way, there are some important implications for the historical consideration of political thought in the British Isles. For a start, there are separate stories to be told of Scottish and Irish political discourse, though these should still be understood as mediated by and informing prevailing English ideas and values (Boyce *et al.*, 1993). Moreover, the notion of a tradition of discourse underpinned by a single political culture seems far less likely. Although theorists of both left and right have begun to observe that the pluralization of cultural life and national diversification within the United Kingdom are central facts of contemporary British life, this has in fact been a *longstanding* characteristic of the multinational British state, built as it was 'from a number of disparate components, as an ancient heartland had been reinforced by the addition of marches, principalities or provinces' (Clark, 1990: 38–9). 'British' political discourse, in other words, ought to be understood as having been forged against the background of multiple identities, interests and national perspectives.

Individualism

A related but somewhat different understanding of 'the British tradition' reveals the continuing influence of conservative elements but also the rich legacy of liberalism. The notion of a political culture shaped around the values of 'individualism' has figured prominently in scholarly interpretation of social, cultural and intellectual history from the seventeenth century onwards, and has been at the heart of some important historiographical controversies. The classic formulation of the individualist thesis is to be found in C. B. Macpherson's account of the underlying unity of the disparate strands of English political thought from the seventeenth to the nineteenth centuries, a unity he characterized as 'possessive individualism' (Macpherson, 1962). This represented a series of interlinked theoretical positions which were developed, he claimed, through the work of major figures like Thomas Hobbes (1588–1679) and John Locke (1632–1704), and even in the more politically radical writings of the Levellers and James Harrington (1611–77).

In Macpherson's account, the central assumptions of the individualist tradition comprise a conception of liberty defined in terms of the absence of restraint upon the will and actions of an individual, combined with an understanding of the subject as the proprietor of his or her own person and capacities. All of these thinkers shared the assumption that human society was constituted as a series of market relations. These commitments, he suggested, corresponded broadly with the realities of seventeenth-century market society and provided the cornerstone of modern liberal doctrines. The vital backdrop to the emergence of the hegemony of individualism were the political crises of the second half of the seventeenth century, in the course of a protracted struggle in Parliament, a civil war, a series of republican experiments, a restoration of the Monarchy and a final constitutional revolution. But whereas in this period individualist ideas succeeded as a legitimating doctrine for existent power relations, particularly through disseminating the conviction that all individuals are equally subject to the operations of a market economy, this function was eroded from the late nineteenth century onwards as liberalism underwent a more collectivist orientation in response to the pressing and structurally embedded socio-economic difficulties of that era.

In the wake of this interpretation, numerous commentators have discerned a tradition of economic individualism as a distinguishing feature of British political culture, and have explored the intersection of such ideas and the development of the socio-economic arrangements that emerged as agrarian or 'gentlemanly' capitalism (Marquand, 1988; Cain and Hopkins, 1993). The strength of arguments which posit the emergence of possessive or economic individualism in the socio-economic context of the early modern period stems from the focus upon the values and political culture which underwrote the British economic order prior to industrialization.

A different kind of 'individualist' tradition has been posited by some conservative critics, notably the historian Jonathan Clark. He ventures the notion of 'authoritarian individualism' as a description of the nexus of values underlying British political culture in an argument which seeks to undermine the conventional historiographical picture of the seventeenth and eighteenth centuries in which British parliamentary sovereignty is contrasted with the absolutist systems of other European states. Individualism, he asserts, needs to be detached from its association with the marxist understanding of the transformation from feudalism to capitalism: 'in respect of ownership, economic enterprise and the family [individualism] was there all along, fully consistent with strong structures and ideologies of political authority in a variety of forms over several centuries' (Clark, 1990: 34). This individualism was 'authoritarian' in kind, guaranteed by robust forms of political authority and, crucially, legitimated by loyalty to the Anglican church. One of the many implications of the arguments synthesized by Clark and echoed by others, is that an '*ancien régime*' survived in cultural and political terms into the nineteenth century, and was not simply displaced, as much historiography proposes, by a modern, capitalistic order in which individualist doctrine was central. The individualism that Clark describes is of a relatively complex kind, subject to changing patterns of regulation and shifts in status, order and deference. 'Authoritarian individualism', he claims, has been 'sustained by a variety of political systems from medieval mixed monarchy through Tudor and Stuart absolutism and the ancien régime of 1660–1832' (Clark, 1990: 39).

Commentators like Clark assume that individualism is a potent tradition that offers a unique and distinguishing pattern to British historical development. Perhaps the major methodological problem with such a characterization of the 'essence' of British culture is that political cultures are notoriously difficult to delineate and their characterization raises some tricky interpretative issues. Definition depends greatly upon the level of generality and abstraction adopted by the analyst. Viewed panoramically, British history may be interrogated to reveal a series of elements that apparently distil a reasonably coherent 'culture'. Yet observed from the bottom upwards, from the perspective of the marginal or parochial, or if a cultural cross-section is taken at a given historical moment, no such singularity is observable. Even within a community where some important historical continuities can be observed, it should be clear that the many regions and localities which make-up Britain have always contained clusters of opposing and contrary cultures and values. Indeed some would argue that it is through these differences that cultures are constituted, providing the soil within which ideologies flourish.

Though Oakeshott and other interpreters of the British tradition
accept the inevitability of diversity within a cultural system, such
differences are seen as ultimately contained within the overarching
totality of a national tradition.

There are other problems with the individualism thesis. Counter-
readings have been offered of each of the thinkers cited by Macpherson. These stress the inadequacy of 'individualism' as an analytical
category through which to approach their ideas. This is no more true
than in the case of Locke. For Macpherson he was the originator of
an influential 'political theory of appropriation' based upon his
ahistorical notion of a social contract, yet according to Dunn and
others, this is to overstate the impact of what was a marginal and not
particularly radical project (Dunn, 1969).

A fundamental objection to the individualist thesis comes from
critics who echo the objections to the Oakeshottian and conservative
'traditions' considered above. The reconstruction of the possessive or
authoritarian individualist lineage seems to depend upon some
equally longstanding traditions of a rather different kind – of
assocational, socialist and collectivist thinking – being consigned to
the margins of our analytical attention. But why should this be so?
For every influential doyen of 'individualism' since the seventeenth
century, one can find an equivalent public intellectual bemoaning the
social and ethical effects of economic individualism, and indeed one
can see both strains in the same thinkers, for instance writers in the
influential Scottish political economy tradition of the eighteenth
century, like Adam Smith (1723–90) and Adam Ferguson
(1723–1816). Moreover, generations of intellectuals have forged what
the critic Raymond Williams construed as a vibrant counter-tradition
of intellectual discourse concerned with the themes 'Culture' and
'Society' (Williams, 1958). Uniting the ideologically disparate exponents of these themes – Williams connects Burke (commonly understood as a progenitor of conservatism) with, among others, William
Godwin (a utopian anarchist) – is an adamant rejection of forms of
individualist doctrine, such as utilitarianism, which legitimate the
exchange relations at the heart of the market economy.

Individualism or Republicanism?

A range of studies have drawn our attention to the potency of
different traditions of political thought in the periods when individu-

alism has been said to reign supreme. In recent years, a very different lineage has been 'recovered' within early modern political discourse. The consequence of the recovery of a rich tradition of republican discourse is that the story of individualism told by numerous social and political historians is now undergoing serious revision.

The leading account of this heritage has been supplied in J. G. A. Pocock's reconstruction of the 'Atlantic Republican' lineage (Pocock, 1975b). Pocock argues that a vision of a republic imagined as a 'structure of virtue' recurred within the political thought of the early modern period and had origins in Ancient Greek and Roman sources. Virtue was defined in these quarters as a sense of civic excellence generated by an active citizenry. A related motif was an emphasis on liberty, understood as the absence of domination in the life of an individual (Pettit, 1997), in particular that which an absolute monarch exercised over a citizen. This theme even found its way into the writings of seventeenth-century Tories like Lord Bolingbroke, as well as political radicals and the many independent gentry who lamented the corruption and patronage that were disfiguring the contemporary state. Quentin Skinner has recently elaborated upon the significance of the 'neo-roman understanding' of liberty and citizenship in the early modern period, arguing that it:

> rose to prominence in the course of the English revolution of the mid-seventeenth century. Later it was used to attack the ruling oligarchy of eighteenth-century Britain, and still later to defend the revolution mounted by the American colonists against the British crown. (Skinner, 1998: ix)

This nexus of ideas reached Britain through the writings of figures such as Harrington (who, as we saw above, is claimed by Macpherson for the possessive individualist tradition), who imported them through an engagement with the political writings of the Italian writer, Niccolò Machiavelli (1469–1527). As monarchical government in England collapsed, Harrington pointed to the lessons of 'ancient prudence' embodied in the Roman Republic. Historians have thus set about recovering traces of such thinking in locations where it has been assumed that individualism predominated, and have focused especially on the political ideas of the Whig political faction and other critics of both the Hanoverian and Stuart monarchies. Some have even suggested that the impact of republican sentiment can be detected into the eighteenth and even nineteenth centuries.

These interpretations have done much to reshape historical understanding of the political discourse of the early modern period and
have persuaded many historians of the significance of the battle over
political language and ideas that characterized the politics of these
years. There are different implications for the individualist thesis.
Most obviously, Macpherson's 'tradition' has been robbed of several
of its members, Harrington and the Levellers most notably. More
subtle considerations arise from the question of the relationship
between these apparently antithetical lineages. Did 'individualist'
doctrines, with their related ideas about liberty defined as non-
interference – a conception crucially different from non-domination,
carrying very different philosophical and political implications –
displace the republican tradition in the eighteenth century as Skinner
and others suggest? Or did republicanism survive as an alternative
source of ethical and political thinking into the nineteenth century,
for instance in the writings and propaganda of radical democratic
groupings, like the Chartists? Historians continue to debate these and
related matters, yet it does seem that the notion of a hegemonic
'individualist' political culture emerging with agrarian capitalism is in
need of substantial revision. While the recovery of republican sentiment has been in fashion in the 1990s, one can detect a counter-
reaction to this thesis too within historical circles. Pincus has point-
edly observed that civic republicanism is itself a highly ideological
construct, which appeals to those 'hostile to the description of
political personality central to the liberal, social-democratic, and
Marxist traditions', and the impact of which may have been over-
stated (Pincus, 1998: 708).

Liberalism

Many students of political ideas regard liberal ideology as the
quintessential character of the values of individualism, though, as
we have seen, there is a strong conservative claim to this heritage. One
of the biggest problems with the alignment of individualism and
liberalism is that this captures only one variant within the liberal
family, neglecting collectivist and communitarian strands. Yet the
thesis that liberalism has been the fundamental ideological paradigm
in British politics is convincing only when the eclecticism of this set of
doctrines is stressed.

The origins of British liberal thought are multiple and can be traced back well before the nineteenth century when the word 'liberal' was first used (to describe a political party in Spain in 1810). Important sources include the theories of the origins of political authority and nature of political obligation developed in the work of Hobbes and Locke, the philosophical treatment of the rational capacities of individuals in European culture since the sixteenth century, the rejection of religious hierarchy pursued by radical Protestant sects and the ideas of the Whig political faction in Parliament. A distinctive feature of 'early' liberalism was the articulation of a belief in the universal natural rights of individual 'men'. This theme can be traced back to the Civil War period in England, a further indication of the richness of the mid-seventeenth century for subsequent lineages of political thinking. It was given its most extensive articulation by the late eighteenth-century writer and agitator Tom Paine (1737–1809) in his reply to Burke's defence of an organic British tradition in the wake of the French Revolution. However, it was in the early nineteenth century that liberalism emerged as an independent and recognisable body of doctrines, a great synthesis of different lineages and arguments. Agitation for the disestablishment of the Church of England throughout the nineteenth century informed liberal perspectives, while, within the political elite, Whiggish politics offered a subtly different, though not entirely unrelated, account of the British tradition to Burke's. The British parliamentary system, Whig historians asserted, had proved uniquely adaptable and supple in its responses to a range of external social and economic pressures which were headed off with subtle evolutionary political change (Butterfield, 1931). Out of such beliefs grew the conviction that the British political model, enshrined at Westminster, embodied social and political progress – the impressive epitaph of a talented political elite, the rule of which would obviate the need for mass democracy.

Nineteenth-century political thought has been extensively assessed in terms of the prevalence of liberal ideas, and their impact upon public policy has figured in many learned accounts (Williams and Pearson, 1984). The diverging and conflicting strains of nineteenth-century liberalism need to be addressed in considerations of the effects and nature of this tradition. Commentators often talk of the emergence of 'classical liberalism', usually understood in terms of a commitment to '*laissez-faire*' political economy, involving a circumscribed role for the state in economic and social matters and with the concept of individual liberty prioritised and understood in a predominantly 'negative' sense as the absence of (usually physical) constraint. Though such a normative combination was undeniably influential in the mid- to late nineteenth century and recurs repeatedly in political writing and public discourse, this cluster of ideas was open to different interpretations and conceptual connections. Among the 'philosophic radicals' of the early nineteenth century, the utilitarianism of Jeremy Bentham (1748–1832) was blended with the classical political economy of David Ricardo (1772–1823), Adam Smith and Thomas Malthus (1766–1834), and the jurisprudential ideas of Bentham and John Austin (1790–1859). This combination of ideas was translated by some into support for universal suffrage in order to counteract the undue influence of elite groups within the community (Thomas, 1979). Yet some liberals within and beyond this grouping, most notably John Stuart Mill (1806–73), remained far less convinced that mass democracy was compatible with the priority of individual liberty.

Mill was perhaps the leading theorist of this period and figures prominently in accounts of political philosophy as well as public policy in the nineteenth century. He can be seen as a 'hinge-figure' within the history of liberalism, signalling the onset of new emphases in liberal thought that emerged in the late decades of the nineteenth and early twentieth centuries, yet always harking back to the philosophic radical inheritance which his father, James Mill (1773–1826), incorporated in his education. Moving beyond the premises of utilitarian philosophy, though never breaking from it entirely, the younger Mill introduced the quality of self-development into his conception of the liberty of the individual, supplementing the notion of self-determination (Rees, 1985). This view led him away from the democratic arguments of other philosophic radicals as he came to equate the coercive power of public opinion in modern contexts with the tyranny of arbitrary government over the citizen. While utilitarian philosophy famously calculated interests in terms of pleasure and pain, Mill introduced a distinction between higher and lower pleasures in relation to the development of the individual. Freedom was thus conceived in terms of the pursuit of valuable purposes (higher pleasures) so that each citizen came to pursue the 'good' in a unique way. Viewed thus, liberty might be impeded by a range of obstacles – lack of education for instance – while its exercise provided an essential precondition for the creative and self-enhancing activities most likely to benefit individual and community. Individuals who became secure in their independence and progressed in the struggle for self-development were likely to contribute valuably to the public welfare.

'New Liberalism'

Such thinking provided a platform for several generations of theorists, at the turn of the nineteenth and twentieth centuries, who became known as 'New', or sometimes 'social', or 'progressive', liberals (Freeden 1978). This new synthesis constituted a shift, though not a rupture, in ethical and political emphasis within the history of British liberalism. In the wake of the social and economic problems that characterized urban life, as well as the rise of labour as an independent social interest, this grouping tended to reject the understanding of individuals as self-sufficient and competitive wealth-maximisers. Individuals were mutually dependent, as well as competitive. Above and beyond individual interest, and particularly the self-interest of dominant social groupings, was a public 'good' which could be secured and maintained only by the community. This shift was frequently translated into a stress upon public provision and associated welfare rights. Moving away from the political economy of some earlier economic liberals, the New Liberals advocated political intervention in the economy to tackle the failings of the market.

But there were important differences of emphasis within and between the generations of 'New' liberalism, as well as continuities with earlier liberal arguments. According to the philosopher Thomas Hill Green (1836–82), liberty needed to be understood through the notion of self-realization; the individual sought to emancipate herself from tradition by closing the gap between the actual conditions in which she lived and her potential in terms of rational and moral conduct (Vincent and Plant, 1984). This transformation could only occur once the narrow horizons of the pursuit of individual interest were transcended by participation in a shared way of life. In political terms Green believed that the impediments to citizenship could be removed with the defeat of the aristocratic social interest.

The generation of liberals who followed Green shifted further from classical political economy in targeting the unregulated market as the site and source of the absence of liberty in the contemporary world. Leonard Hobhouse (1864–1929) blended liberal concerns with the fashionable evolutionary theories of the Social Darwinists to generate a complex argument about the physical and moral 'unfitness' of the working classes which was reinforced by state passivity (Meadowcroft, 1994). He therefore envisaged welfare policies financed by taxation. Like other New Liberals he perceived the rule of law as the precondition for, not constraint upon, individual liberty, and he tied this value to a commitment to responsible government and universal suffrage. These examples of some strands of 'New' liberalism reveal both the shifts and continuities represented by this current. The commitment to individual liberty remained part of the core vision they elaborated, yet this was now defined as dependent on, not the antithesis of, the political expression of the community.

The emergence of 'New Liberalism' sowed the seeds of increasing discord within this particular ideological family. According to some historians, it is subsequent arguments between different kinds of liberals that have shaped the course of some important developments in the character of public policy in the twentieth century. New Liberalism has thus been identified with some of the most important innovations in social policy in the twentieth century, particularly the pre-1914 social reforms of the Liberal Party and even the construction of the National Health Service by the post-1945 Labour administration via liberal ideological intermediaries like William Beveridge (1879–1963). Beveridge wrote several influential reports on social and economic issues in the 1940s, and these played an important role in shaping the thinking of the political elite about welfare. His recommendation of measures such as comprehensive social insurance, free health care, and a minimum wage place him squarely in the lineage of New Liberalism.

Even more influential an intermediary, perhaps, was John Maynard Keynes (1883–1948). Keynes revolutionized the discipline of economics, particularly with his *General Theory of Employment, Interest and Money* (Keynes, 1936) which justified a range of fiscal and monetary measures by government (though not deficit spending as his critics and supporters have claimed) to stimulate activity in the economy. Although he rejected the socialist alternative to capitalism, Keynes provided a sharp critique of the 'economic anarchy' of a *laissez-faire* economy. He called for an enlargement of government functions, particularly through the overall management of investment and consumption. His ideas played a crucial role in helping legitimate the emergence and acceptance of collectivist philosophies in public life, from the 1930s onwards, but particularly in the decades after the Second World War. This period, labelled by some as the era of the 'Keynesian welfare state', was marked by an unusual degree of consensus between the main parties over the framework within which

economic management and welfare expenditure ought to be conducted, though the degree of consensus and the actual impact of
Keynes's own theories on policy-makers in the 1950s and 1960s are
still fiercely debated.

Liberalism in the 1980s and 1990s

Arguments about the influence of liberal philosophy have resurfaced
in discussion of contemporary politics, long after Keynesian orthodoxies have waned in academic and policy circles. Some commentators have considered the emergence of apparently 'new' political
formations, notably the 'New Right' of the 1980s and, latterly, the
Labour Party in its 'New Labour' guise, as involving the recirculation
of elements of liberal discourse from the rich stock of ideological
resources developed in the early years of the twentieth century
(Barker, 1997).

The impact of the New Right on British politics, first through the
rather disparate ideas of a number of intellectual figures and think-
tanks, and as a key source of influence upon the Thatcher administrations of 1979–90, has been the subject of vigorous debate. Indeed
there has been little agreement as to the essential features of this New
Right, or even its relationship with the conservative and liberal
lineages (Green, 1987). For some, the New Right was a form of
'neo-liberalism', though it is probably better understood as a somewhat unstable mixture of economically liberal and socially conservative ideas. For all its internal differentiation, this current was united
around its rejection of the collectivist orthodoxy which it thought had
entrapped the British economy. Some of its leading advocates, therefore, perceived the New Right in terms of the recovery of the
suppressed traditions of individualism and libertarianism discussed
above.

On the left of the political spectrum, liberalism has been an
important backdrop to ideological development. Commentary on
British socialism, a rich and diverse body of traditions, has frequently
pointed to the absorption of liberal concerns within indigenous
socialist writing: 'from the 1890s onwards liberal and socialist positions have interwoven far more than representatives of party politics
have been willing to concede ... strong liberal undertones may be
found in much British socialist thinking ...' (Freeden, 1990: 12). We
can also fruitfully compare some of the strands of social-liberalism

represented in the work of Hobhouse and Bernard Bosanquet (1848–1923) for example, with the ideas of social democrats like Anthony Crosland (1928–77) whose 'revisionist' socialism was highly influential in Labour circles in the late 1950s and more recent figures like the former deputy leader of the Labour Party, Roy Hattersley.

This theoretical intermingling is in stark contrast with developments at the level of party politics where the Labour Party emerged from under the wing of the Liberal Party as an independent political body in the years following the First World War, and in the 1920s and 1930s slowly replaced it as the main opposition to the Tories. One of the consequences of this competition between the parties was to render 'liberalism' an antithetical political ideology to socialism in political parlance. The label 'liberal' became a powerful insult to throw at opponents within socialist ranks for much of the century. Yet recent developments in British politics have seen the completion of a 'circle' in the history of relations between the Liberal and Labour parties. Tony Blair and some of his advisers have reintroduced into Labour politics the notion of the Liberal Party as natural allies and, if united, the Lib-Lab coalition as the potential hegemon in British political life. In intellectual terms too, one of the most consistent themes in Blair's own writings and speeches is the inspiration the 'centre-left' should still draw from the New Liberal tradition. This stance has encouraged some commentators to regard New Labour as the political reincarnation of the ideas of thinkers like Hobhouse, Bosanquet and Green – the delayed progeny of an illustrious intellectual tradition (Vincent, 1998). Pursuing this line of interpretation, we may well be tempted to regard contemporary ideological arguments between New Labour and the Conservatives as a repeat of earlier conflicts among groups of liberals; with 'New' liberalism once more being marshalled against the rigid orthodoxies of classical liberalism. If liberalism has been the fundamental ideological tradition within British politics, it is because of this lineage's permeable boundaries, substantial internal differences and malleability, especially its openness to combination with elements across the ideological spectrum.

Yet there are several reasons to hesitate before we crown liberalism as the ruling tradition of British political life. The most pressing stems from the resilience and significance of non-liberal ideas within the British political universe. Socialism and conservatism have rich and broadly independent histories in this century despite the impact of liberalism. Scholars have documented the rich vein of democratic socialist and social-democratic thinking which developed in Britain from the late nineteenth century, and the various offshoots of these lineages, like guild socialism in the inter-war years or the ethical socialist tradition stretching back to the 1880s (Wright, 1985). Equally, conservative thinking passed through a series of subtle mutations and recombinations, in which different strains, for instance, one-nation, paternalist and free-market expressions, vied for hegemony within the political and intellectual parameters of conservative ideology, and exercised a crucial influence upon the Conservative Party.

Some of the most creative and radical ideas and movements to have emerged in twentieth-century politics have come from these lineages and have arisen in opposition to the hegemony of collectivist liberalism/social democracy in the years after the Second World War. On the left, there developed from the mid-1950s onwards several generations of a New Left movement, which was characterized by its lively sense of intellectual adventure and opposition to the orthodoxies of consensus politics (Kenny, 1995). The New Left underwent a number of mutations and instigated some important political projects up to the 1980s, both in relation to the Labour Party and beyond. Its adherents fused a sense of frustration with political and cultural radicalism, drawing on older socialist traditions, and mingling them with newer themes and ideas, such as psychoanalysis, cultural studies and feminism. Uniting this disparate current was the rejection of collectivism and the political culture of the post-welfare state settlement in British politics. In terms of the traditions we have examined here, it was individualism – but of a left kind – which the New Left wished to rehabilitate.

It is not insignificant that the New Right's attitude towards liberal collectivism resembled that adopted by the New Left. While liberalism did provide one source of ideas within the latter, for instance through the influence of the émigré economist Friedrich von Hayek, who is himself regarded as a conservative in some quarters, the British New Right was far more influenced by neo-conservative and socially authoritarian ideas than its American counterpart. The restoration of 'traditional' forms of moral conduct and understanding, the call for the restitution of the 'law and order' society, the stress upon 'Victorian values' and the demonization of a feckless and work-shy 'underclass', all reconnected conservatives in the 1970s and 1980s with earlier parts of the conservative heritage. According to some commentators, these were the prevailing parts of the New Right agenda, and were developed in direct opposition to the moral decline and economic decay blamed upon welfare collectivism. The New Left and New Right are but two examples of the antipathy to liberalism that intellectuals and political actors were able to express in the years after 1945 and their significance lies in the energy and appeal that they embodied.

The appearance since the late nineteenth century of bodies of political ideas associated with the public emergence of new social constituencies and identities – notably feminism, anti-racism, lesbian and gay politics, and environmentalist/animal welfare perspectives – has also been significant in this regard. These have developed at different rates throughout the century, and while their coherence and intellectual independence remain debatable, all draw sustenance from their critique of some of the leading strands of liberal political discourse. Feminist theorists and activists in Britain have undermined the bifurcation between the public domain and private issues under-pinning conventional liberal discourse (Lovenduski and Randall, 1993). Questions about domestic violence, the sexual abuse of chil-dren and the safety of women in public places have emerged as central concerns on the contemporary political agenda. Feminism has con-structed a diverse and neglected 'tradition' which cuts across the ideological and intellectual alignments of the modern period – including Mary Wollstonecraft's (1759–97) call to liberate women from the slavery of sensualist accounts of femininity by reclaiming a natural, genderless reason, as well as Harriet and John Stuart Mill's mixture of liberal and proto-feminist arguments. Feminist political theorists continue to explore the intellectual and ideological potential of mixing feminist and liberal discourse as well as the limitations of the latter.

A different reason for caution about the liberal hegemony thesis is that in some forms it presents the relationship between ideology and policy in a misleadingly simplified way (Freeden, 1990). One example is the causal link suggested by some historians between the creation of the welfare state and liberal collectivist doctrines. In her analysis of the different intellectual sources which played a role in the Attlee government's construction of a National Health Service, the historian Jose Harris shows that the principal debates and arguments that provided the backdrop to actual policy initiatives did not shape up according to neatly drawn ideological alignments (Harris, 1986). Policy was a result of the subtle interaction of these and the interests and calculations of various actors, not the straightforward translation of ideology into policy. This example illustrates some of the difficulties facing those who have sought to demonstrate that liberal ideology has substantively shaped British public policy. Such a commitment depends upon prior philosophical claims about the relationship between ideas and behaviour about which many social scientists and historians, with their entrenched suspicions of 'idealist' explanations, remain sceptical.

The Left–Right Ideological Spectrum

Perhaps the biggest challenge to the liberal hegemony thesis comes from those who maintain that ideology is always positioned on a spectrum, and that no single ideology can command unchallenged ascendancy given the conflicting and plural nature of political discourse. Much of the political history of the twentieth century has been written with the assumption that liberalism waned as both an ideological and political force with the demise of the Liberal Party after the First World War, and that political life subsequently reflected a battle between the ideas of the left and right poles of the spectrum, with occasional 'truces', such as in the 'consensus' years of the 1950s and 1960s.

This approach differs from the others examined here in that its origins lie in a model of ideological division which originated in France in the late eighteenth century; the spatial idea of a plane from 'left' to 'right' originated in the seating plan of the post-1789 revolutionary assembly. This representation of ideological development (with communism and fascism neatly added on to the extreme ends of the spectrum) has proved popular with social scientists and has been exported to all sorts of political contexts beyond France, though it is rare to find considered defences of this spatial conception of political ideas and identity (Eatwell, 1989). Indeed this framework has been wielded in numerous analyses of modern British politics. The oscillation between Conservative and Labour administrations that has characterized the twentieth century has been understood as shadowed by ideological conflict between right and left with the balance of power shifting at key moments between the two. Unlike the other interpretations of ideology presented here, such a perspective recognises conflict and contestation as lying at the heart of political life. The contributions of key intellectual figures, political actors and party manifestos are frequently placed at points along an

imaginary one-dimensional spectrum and their meanings consequently sought in these terms.

Considering politics in terms of an ongoing argument between the
ideologies of left and right has become far less fashionable in recent
years, particularly when party leaders are rushing to declare such an
ideological divide irrelevant. In interpretative terms, the utility of the
left–right spectrum has long been questioned. When particular events
or themes in the history of British politics are examined closely, the
picture nearly always seems more complex than the left–right model
pretends. When our ideological categories are deployed to interpret
sets of political ideas and their changing character throughout the
nineteenth and twentieth centuries, it is increasingly clear that a story
which posits shifts from right to left and back again, as from
collectivism to libertarianism, is unlikely to yield sufficiently pene-
trating analyses of the changing contours and dynamics of political
debate. A particular problem facing those who adhere to this model is
that it appears meaningful, if at all, only for a particular segment of
the modern period, specifically what Eric Hobsbawm terms the
'short' twentieth century – 1914–91 (Hobsbawm, 1995). But from a
longer historical perspective, the centrality of the left-right divide
looks relatively short-lived and was preceded by lineages and traditions which, though subterranean in this century, appear to have been
reactivated more recently.

Do these problems mean then that we should abandon the notion of
an ideological spectrum when studying British political thought?
There are many analysts who would say that we should. Yet a case
can be made for the usage of such a metaphor in the analysis of
political ideas, if deployed in a way that brings out the complexities,
ambiguities and overlaps within and between different patterns of
discourse. If ideologies are regarded as clusters of interlinked concepts
and ideas, all interpreted in subtly differing ways within and between
each tradition, it remains useful to imagine *one* of the axes along which
these are developed in left-right spatial terms. Difficulties follow,
however, if we imagine that in any historical period this is the only
dimension upon which ideological and conceptual development occur.

Conclusion

It would seem that no single interpretation that we have reviewed can
be adopted '*in toto*', and some seem seriously flawed. There are strong

reasons to doubt the assumption that traditions of thought exercise translate directly into policy and political action. The belief that traditions directly shape action comes perilously close to a determinist argument and neglects the dimensions of agency which political actors can exercise in relation to the traditions they inherit, selecting elements within them and combining ideas from different traditions. Yet this does not mean that traditions and ideologies cannot be incorporated into the historical and analytical accounts of British politics, merely that nuanced and more humble interpretations ought to be adopted (Bevir, forthcoming). The distinguished American observer of the British political scene, Samuel Beer, suggested that a crucial dimension of political agency stems from a dimension of the human personality that political science, in its more technical forms, rarely captures – the imagination (Beer, 1982). This is the site and source of the values that have played a critical role in transforming the modern world. Today's political scientists would thus do well to remember Beer's account of political culture, in which ideas, values and ideologies collide, as one of the main variables of British political system.

Recent scholarly work throws up further interpretative possibilities. For some commentators, the agency of political actors and parties lies, in part, in the ways in which they abridge, reinvent and modify existent traditions of thought and practice to aid them in the face of changing circumstances. One interesting possibility here, which students of political ideas need to address more fully, is that traditions are absorbed and reworked in unconscious and unwitting as well as self-conscious ways. Analysts need to consider carefully the claim at the heart of several of the theses examined here that a prevailing ethos or philosophy of governance has been reproduced through the institutional and cultural 'codes' at the heart of the British state. Other interpreters point to the creative and significant work which political actors and thinkers put into closing down and 'controlling' the core concepts of political debate, like 'liberty' or 'community', and the impact of this ongoing struggle in terms of the legitimation and delegitimation of political projects.

Beyond these methodological suggestions, some more substantive conclusions about political ideas in the British polity can be offered. The first is that the dream of recovering or reconstructing a singular British tradition ought to be regarded as a mistaken way of understanding the contours and content of political discourse. This approach necessarily neglects the pluralized and contested character of traditions in a political system. The search for *the* single hegemonic tradition as the key to modern political development is only likely to generate a continuous array of alternative candidates, the merits and limitations of which are quickly revealed by critics. The desire to recover 'the British tradition' should be regarded as an example of 'reification' – 'a process of thought whereby human relationships are falsely regarded as relationships between things, and thereby endowed with spurious objectivity and immutability' (Miller, 1991). The tradition of 'individualism', or 'the British way' represented by thinkers like Oakeshott, are quintessential reifications: they are endowed with an objectivity and immutability which careful consideration of the historical record belies. And they are granted these attributes because such representations of tradition serve to buttress ideological readings of the British past. It is the task of students of political ideas to understand and move beyond such constructions, while noting and absorbing some of the insights they undoubtedly possess.

Acknowledgements

I would like to thank the editors, an anonymous reviewer, Steven Kennedy, James Meadowcroft, Michael Braddick and Claire Annesley for their comments and suggestions. I am also grateful to the fellows of Wolfson College, Oxford, who, in appointing me to a Charter Fellowship from 1997 to 1998, provided a congenial and conducive environment in which to reflect on these issues.

Guide to Further Reading

Chapter 2   State, Economy and Society

Perry Anderson's famous essay 'The Origins of the Present Crisis' which influenced so many of the later debates on the character of the British state is reprinted in Anderson (1992). It should be read alongside the rejoinder by Thompson (1965), the later analysis of Britain as an *ancien régime* in Nairn (1977) as well as the different perspectives in Ingham (1994) and Clark (1990). Anderson's later reflection on the debate, 'The Figures of Descent', is also reprinted in Anderson (1992). Other seminal reflections on the relationship of state and economy in Britain can be found in Beer (1965), Olson (1982), Hall (1986), Kennedy (1988), and Esping-Andersen (1990). For theories of the state see Dunleavy and O'Leary (1987), and at a more advanced level Jessop (1990). Oakeshott's distinction between the state as a civil association and an enterprise association is set out in Oakeshott (1975). The debate on decline is revisited in English and Kenny (1999) and Coates (1994). Important recent contributions on the nature of the British state and whether it requires reform include Marquand (1988), Mount (1992) and Hutton (1995).

Chapter 3   The Constitution

There are two ways of approaching the study of the British Constitution. One is essentially historical in focus, the other more explicitly concerned with contemporary debates about the Constitution and proposals for its reform. It is wise to pay some attention to both approaches, if only for the sake of putting current preoccupations into a broader context. The 'landmark' historical texts are Bagehot's 1867 study of the English Constitution (Bagehot, 1963) and Dicey's famous work of 1885 (Dicey, 1959). The former offers a supremely political and realist view of the Constitution, claiming to uncover its 'efficient secrets'. The latter presents a jurist's account of the legal foundations of the Constitution, but with important political elements also recognised. Dicey is, however, not easy reading and those who find him hard going might prefer to turn to Jennings (1959) for a shorter treatment of law and the Constitution. A still persuasive account of the principles of the British Constitution is provided by Birch (1964), whilst the importance of conventions is dealt with fully in Marshall (1986). A sharp critique of the political foundations of the British Constitution is to be found in Johnson (1977). Jowell and Oliver (1994) offer a sound introduction to most aspects of the contemporary Constitution, and thus to the reformist writing of the past decade or so. Mount (1992) and Bogdanor (1997) provide contrasting approaches to the debate about reforming the British Constitution, whilst Cornford (1993) offers a carefully elaborated statement of what a radical reform might look like if enacted. Brazier (1991) provides another discussion of reform possibilities, whilst Turpin (1985) remains a useful source of original materials (cases, extracts from official reports and so on). Wade and Bradley (1985) are useful for those wishing to pursue the specifically legal dimensions of the modern British Constitution.

Chapter 4   The Growth of the State

Greenleaf (1983a, 1983b, 1987) is the best general introduction to changing attitudes towards the state from the nineteenth century onwards. Pugh (1994) provides a useful historical overview from the late-Victorian period. Stevenson (1984) is an accessible social history of the twentieth century. Vincent (1991) provides a succinct account of the state's increasing involvement with the problem of poverty. Harris (1977) sheds light on the role of William Beveridge and his ideas in the evolution of the British state. Helm (1989) is an interesting collection of essays focusing on the state's economic role.

Chapter 5   The Institutions of Central Government

For a classic account of the British system of government Jennings (1966) provides a useful example. For a sophisticated reappraisal of the 'Westminster model' it is worth revisiting Mackintosh (1977a). Crucial for understanding the British system of government and demonstrating the way parliamentarianism underpins the core executive is Judge (1993). The role of the constitution is tackled by Dearlove (1989) and the impact of constitutional principles is further dissected by Beattie (1995). An examination of the ethical dimension is provided by O'Toole (1990) and Richards and Smith (1998). The Cabinet Office and coordination is discussed in detail by Lee *et al.* (1998) and the role of the Treasury is provided with detailed analysis by Thain and Wright (1995). New approaches to the core executive are outlined in Rhodes and Dunleavy (1995), Burch and Holliday (1996) and Smith (1999).

Chapter 6   Territorial Politics

For the place of Ireland in and out of the union, see Beckett (1966), Buckland (1981) or Quinn (1993). For Scotland and the union, see Brown (1992) or Mackie (1978). For a recent analysis of Wales and the union, see Griffiths (1996). On politics in England see Rose (1989). For the UK in the EU, see Geddes (1999), Nicoll and Salmon (1994) or Nugent (1999). For stimulating interpretations of UK territorial politics, see Bulpitt (1983), Colley (1992), Hechter (1975), Kearney (1989), Kendle (1997) and Nairn (1977).

Chapter 7   Law and Politics

On the dominant tradition and the impact of the growth of government see Loughlin (1992). The classic study of the politics of the judiciary is Griffith (1997). The traditional legal exposition of the English Constitution is given by Dicey (1959) and criticised by Robson (1951) and Jennings (1959). A specifically legal account of administrative law and judicial review is offered by Cane (1996) and a broader account is given by Harlow and Rawlings (1997). On the recent controversy over judicial review between politicians and judges see Rozenberg (1997). On EC law and policy see Weatherill (1995). On the European Convention of Human Rights see Jacobs and White (1996). On the attitudes of the British judiciary to the European Convention see Hunt (1997). On these issues generally see contributions to the journal *Public Law*.

Chapter 8   Order and Discipline

A comprehensive and stimulating discussion of the 'problem of order' in social and political theory can be found in Wrong (1994). An excellent critical discussion of the law on 'public order', informed by sociological and political research, is Lacey and Wells (1998). Townshend (1993) is a useful overview of British state strategies for maintaining order. Discussions of the problems of measuring crime and disorder can be found in Reiner (1996) and Maguire (1997). The history of crime, disorder, and control in modern Britain are authoritatively reviewed in Sharpe (1984), Emsley (1996) and Emsley (1997). Theories of social control are critically analysed in Hudson (1997). General studies of policing include Reiner (1992), Reiner (1997), Morgan and Newburn (1997) and Waddington (1999). The definitive account of police history is Emsley (1996a). Garland (1990) is the leading analysis of social theories of punishment. The contemporary politics of law and order are discussed in Downes and Morgan (1997b). Research on the media and crime is surveyed in Reiner (1997b). Stimulating interpretations of current trends in order and discipline are Garland (1996), Cohen (1997), and Sparks (1997).

Chapter 9   Estates, Classes and Interests

The potential further reading for this chapter is especially wide ranging because the chapter tries to connect the conduct of government to deep social and cultural forces, and argues that there is a complex connection between these forces and the creativity of political leaders. If this argument has credence then the starting point for further reading – superficially a surprising one – should be Cowling (1971). In a more orthodox vein, Perkin (1969) is a good start on the social historical background. McKenzie (1963) is authoritative on the historical evolution of the political parties. Anybody interested in contemporary social patterns should spend a long time browsing in the annual publication *Social Trends* (for example, Office for National Statistics, 1997). Beer (1969) is seminal on the evolution of class politics, as is Birch (1964) on the history of representation. Grant (1993) is a very useful introduction to issues about business representation. Ingham (1984) is a fine study of the City–Industry issue. Grant and Marsh (1977) are still standard on the CBI. Moran (1986, 1991) describes change in the City of London, while Brazier *et al.* (1993) sketch the stresses in state–profession relations. Marsh (1992) is excellent on trade unions.

Chapter 10   Electoral Representation and Accountability: The Legacy of Empire

The outstanding historical treatment of 125 years of critique of the plurality-rule system is Hart (1992), which shows in detail how close reform came in

1917 and 1931. For an example of the position criticized here, see Harrison (1996), a beautifully written statement of the 'two-party club' orthodoxy as applied to contemporary British history. Despite its contentious argumentation and patchy coverage of the really key political changes, Harrison's book brings a large amount of material together in one volume. On the concept of representation, see Manin (1997). On electoral systems, see Dummett (1997). On parties and party systems, see Sartori (1976). On constitutional reform, see Bogdanor (1997).

Chapter 11   Citizenship and Identity

The best guide to the history of citizenship and its contextual nature is Heater (1990). Oliver and Heater (1994) is a straightforward and comprehensive guide to the main, general issues of citizenship and how they play out in ideas and jurisprudence in Britain. There are separate assessments of civil liberties in different parts of the UK, but Gardner (1997), while focusing on England and Wales, refers to Northern Ireland and Scotland from time to time. Klug *et al.* (1996) identify some of the adverse impacts of the weaknesses of British rights on different groups and nationalities. But, as these books point out, law and practice fall into abeyance, may be resurrected or change fairly regularly; so no account is ever likely to be wholly accurate. Commentaries covering most aspects of current political debates about citizenship practice in the UK can be found in Andrews (1991). The general contours of past and present debates about the meaning of citizenship in the UK are captured well in Finlayson (1994), Clarke (1996) and, from an explicitly centre-left intellectual point of view, Marquand (1997). Questions of pluralism and identities in the context of centre-right and centre-left conceptions of citizenship are dealt with by Miller (1995). Parekh (1991) and Hall (1992) deal with ethnic minorities, the latter with particular reference to identities. Lister (1997) is perhaps the most useful book of all, since although her purpose is to discuss women and citizenship, she critically reviews virtually all the literature on the subject of citizenship and identities. Thus, not only does she bring together numerous and important contributions on women, identities and citizenship, but she also explains the general implications both of post-modernism and identity politics.

Chapter 12   Sovereignty and Interdependence

Wallace (1986) and Bull (1995) remain two of the most thoughtful and stimulating works on sovereignty and interdependence, and Hoffmann's (1995b) foreword to the latter work is essential. Hoffmann's (1995a) own omnibus collection of essays also pays dividends, for historical as well as conceptual reasons. On imperial Britain and its decline, see Rhodes James (1977), Morgan (1984), Kennedy (1988) and Davies (1996). Carr (1945) is a classic which predates the European unity movement yet offers a powerful rationale for it. Howe (1990) and Nugent (1998) both offer interesting treatments of British sovereignty in the context of European integration. Glimpses of Europe's future are available from Dogan (1994), Caporaso (1996) and Ludlow (1997), while the broader issue of state sovereignty in international relations is well treated by Thomson (1995), Cooper (1996) and Doyle (1997). The practitioner's view is always worth seeking, in this case from Howe (1990), Churchill (1994), Cockfield (1994), Renwick (1996) and Shackleton (1997).

Chapter 13   Ideas, Ideologies and the British Political Tradition

Greenleaf's multi-volume study of the British political tradition is a fascinating starting point for consideration of these issues (1983a, 1983b, 1987). See also his perceptive discussion of Oakeshott's thought in Greenleaf (1966). For further consideration of the ideologies discussed here, see especially Barker (1997) and Freeden (1997), as well as Leach (1991). Excerpts from some of the thinkers discussed here can be found in Eccleshall (1986), as well as in Wright (1985). For discussion of some of the recurrent traditions within British political thought, see Collini *et al.* (1983) and, for consideration of recent political ideas, Garnett (1997).

Bibliography

Abercrombie, N., Hill, S. and Turner, B. (1980) *The Dominant Ideology Thesis,* London, Unwin.

Ackerman, B. (1991) *We the People,* Cambridge, MA, Belknap Press.

Addison, P. (1994) *The Road to 1945: British Politics and World War Two,* rev. edn, London, Pimlico.

Addison, P. (1996) *British Historians and the Debate over the 'Post War Consensus',* Austin, Texas, Humanities Research Center.

Allen, J., Livingstone, S. and Reiner, R. (1998) 'True Lies: Changing Images of Crime in Postwar British Cinema', *European Journal of Communication,* 13:1, 53–75.

Almond, G. and Verba, S. (1963) *The Civic Culture,* Princeton University Press.

Amery, L. (1947) *Thoughts on the Constitution,* London, Oxford University Press.

Anderson, B. (1991), *Imagined Communities: Reflections on the Origin and Spread of Nationalism,* rev. edn, London, Verso.

Anderson, D. and Killingray, D. (eds) (1991) *Policing the Empire: Government, Authority and Control, 1830–1940,* Manchester University Press.

Anderson, P. (1992) *English Questions,* London, Verso.

Andrews, G. (ed.) (1991) *Citizenship,* London, Lawrence & Wishart.

Appleby, J. (1992) 'Ideology and the History of Political Thought', in J. Appleby, *Liberalism and Republicanism in the Historical Imagination,* Cambridge, MA, and London, Harvard University Press.

Armstrong, R. (1997) 'Minutes of Evidence, 12 November 1996', *House of Lords Select Committee on the Public Service Session 1996–97,* London, HMSO.

Ascherson, N. (1988) *Games with Shadows,* London, Radius.

Ashford, D. (1982) *British Dogmatism and French Pragmatism: Central–Local Policymaking in the Welfare State,* London, Allen & Unwin.

Ashford, D. E. (1986) T*he Emergence of the Welfare State,* Oxford, Blackwell.

Ashford, D. (1989) 'British Dogmatism and French Pragmatism Revisited', in C. Crouch and D. Marquand (eds), *The New Centralism: Britain out of Step in Europe,* Oxford, Blackwell, 77–93.

Bacchi, C. (1990) *Same Difference. Feminism and Sexual Difference,* Sydney, Allen & Unwin.

Bagehot, W. (1963) *The English Constitution,* London, Collins.

Baker, K. (ed.) (1993) *The Faber Book of Conservatism,* London, Faber.

Baldwin, D. A. (1993) 'Neoliberalism, Neorealism and World Politics', in D. A. Baldwin (ed.), *Neorealism and Neoliberalism: The Contemporary Debate,* New York, Columbia University Press.

Ball, G. (1968) *The Discipline of Power,* New York, Council on Foreign Relations.

Barker, R. (1997) *Political Ideas in Modern Britain*, 2nd edn, London, Routledge.

Barnett, A. (1997) *The Defining Moment: Prospects for a New Britain under Labour*, London, Charter 88.

Bauman, Z. (1988) *Legislators and Interpreters*, Cambridge, Polity Press.

Bauman, Z. (1997) *Postmodernity and Its Discontents*, Cambridge, Polity Press.

Bayley, D. (1994) *Police for the Future*, New York, Oxford University Press.

Beattie, A. (1995) 'Ministerial Responsibility and the Theory of the British State', in R. A. W. Rhodes and P. Dunleavy (eds), *Prime Minister, Cabinet and Core Executive*, London, Macmillan.

Beattie, A. and Dunleavy, P. (1995) 'Imperial government and the formation of the British ministerial state', in J. Lovenduski and J. Stanyer (eds), *Contemporary Political Studies 1995*, Belfast, UK Political Studies Association, pp. 120–31.

Beck, U. (1992) *Risk Society*, London, Sage.

Beckett, J. C. (1966) *A Short History of Ireland*, 3rd edn, London, Hutchinson.

Beer, S. (1965) *Modern British Politics*, London, Faber.

Beer, S. (1969) *Modern British Politics*, 2nd edn, London, Faber.

Beer, S. (1982) *Britain Against Itself: The Political Contradictions of Collectivism*, London, Faber.

Berlin, I. (1969) *Four Essays on Liberty*, Oxford University Press.

Beveridge, W. (1953) *Power and Influence: An Autobiography*, London, Hodder & Stoughton.

Bevir, M. (forthcoming) 'On Tradition', in K. Brzechczyn and J. Topoloki (eds), *Idealization in History: Poznan Studies in the Philosophy of the Sciences and the Humanities 63*, Amsterdam, Rodopi.

Bew, P. and Meehan, E. (1994) 'Regions and Borders: Controversies in Northern Ireland about the European Union', *Journal of European Public Policy*, 1, 95–113.

Birch, A. H. (1964) *Representative and Responsible Government: An Essay on the British Constitution*, London, Allen & Unwin.

Blackburn, R. (1995) *The Electoral System in Britain*, London, Macmillan.

Blair, T. (1998) *The Third Way: New Politics for the New Century*, London, Fabian Society.

Blake, R. (1985) *The Conservative Party from Peel to Thatcher*, London, Methuen.

Bogdanor, V. (1995) *The Monarchy and the Constitution*, Oxford University Press.

Bogdanor, V. (1997) *Power and the People: A Guide to Constitutional Reform*, London, Gollancz.

Boyce, D. G., Eccleshall, R. and Geoghegan, V. (eds) (1993) *Political Thought in Ireland since the Seventeenth Century*, London, Routledge.

Bradley, I. (1979) *The Optimists: Themes and Personalities in Victorian Liberalism*, London, Faber.

Brazier, M., Lovecy, J., Moran, M. and Potton, M. (1993) 'Falling from a Tightrope: Doctors and Lawyers Between the Market and the State', *Political Studies*, 41, 197–213.

Brazier, R. (1991) *Constitutional Reform*, Oxford University Press.

Brazier, R. (1998) *Constitutional Reform: Reshaping the British Political System*, 2nd edn, Oxford University Press.

Brewer, J. and Styles, J. (eds) (1980) *An Ungovernable People*, London, Hutchinson.

Briggs, A. (1961) *The History of Broadcasting in the United Kingdom: Volume 1: The Birth of Broadcasting*, London, Oxford University Press.

Brittan, S. (1977) *The Economic Consequences of Democracy*, London, Temple Smith.

Brown, A. (1996) 'Women and Politics in Scotland', in J. Lovenduski and P. Norris (eds), *Women and Politics*, Oxford University Press, 28–42.

Brown, A., McCrone, D., and Paterson, L. (1996) *Politics and Society in Scotland*, Basingstoke, Macmillan.

Brown, K. M (1992) *Kingdom or Province? Scotland and the Regal Union, 1603–1715*, Basingstoke, Macmillan.

Bruce-Gardyne, J. and Lawson, N. (1976) *The Power Game*, London, Macmillan.

Buckland, P. (1981) *A History of Northern Ireland*, Dublin, Gill and Macmillan.

Budge, I. and Urwin, D. (1966) *Scottish Political Behaviour: A Case Study in British Homogeneity*, London, Longmans Green.

Bull, H. (1995) *The Anarchical Society: A Study of Order in World Politics*, 2nd edn, London, Macmillan.

Buller, J. and Smith, M. J. (1998) 'Civil Service Attitudes Towards the European Union', in D. Baker and D. Seawright (eds), *Britain For and Against Europe*, Oxford University Press.

Bulpitt, J. (1983) *Territory and Power in the United Kingdom: An Interpretation*, Manchester University Press.

Bulpitt, J. (1986) 'The Discipline of the New Democracy: Mrs Thatcher's Domestic Statecraft', *Political Studies*, 34, 19–39.

Burch, M. (1988) 'British Cabinet: A Residual Executive', *Parliamentary Affairs*, 41, 34–47.

Burch, M. and Holliday, I. (1996) *The British Cabinet System*, Hemel Hempstead, Prentice-Hall.

Butler, D. and Kavanagh, D. (1984) *The British General Election of 1983*, London, Macmillan.

Butler, D., Adonis, A. and Travers, T. (1994) *Failure in British Government: The Politics of the Poll Tax*, Oxford University Press.

Butterfield, H. (1931) *The Whig Interpretation of History*, London, Bell.

Byrne, P. (1996) 'The Politics of the Women's Movement', in J. Lovenduski and P. Norris (eds), *Women and Politics*, Oxford University Press, 57–72.

Cabinet Office (1997) *Ministerial Committees of the Cabinet: Membership and Terms of Reference*, London, Cabinet Office.

Cabinet Office (1998) *The Civil Service Year Book 1998*, London, HMSO.

Cain, P. J. and Hopkins, A G. (1993) *British Imperialism: Volume I: Innovation and Expansion 1688–1914*, London, Longman.

Campbell, C. and Wilson, G. (1995) *The End of Whitehall: Death of a Paradigm*, Oxford, Blackwell.

Cane, P. (1996) *An Introduction to Administrative Law*, 3rd edn, Oxford, Clarendon Press.

Cannadine, D. (1995) 'British History as a "New Subject"': Politics, Perspectives and Prospects', in A. Grant and K. Stringer (eds), *Uniting the Kingdom? The Making of British History*, London, Routledge, 12–28.

Caporaso, J. (1996) 'The European Union and Forms of State', *Journal of Common Market Studies* 34, pp. 29–52.

Carr, C. T. (1941) *Concerning English Administrative Law*, New York, Columbia University Press.

Carr, E. H. (1945) *Nationalism and After*, London, Macmillan.

Chester, D. N. (1953) *Morant and Sadler: Further Evidence*, London, Institute of Public Administration.

Chester, D. N. (1981) *The English Administrative System 1780–1870*, Oxford, Clarendon Press.

Chibnall, S. (1977) *Law and Order News*, London, Tavistock.

Churchill, W. S. (1994) 'The Tragedy of Europe', in B. F. Nelsen and A. C.-G. Stubb (eds), *The European Union: Readings on the Theory and Practice of European Integration*, Boulder, CO, Lynne Rienner, speech delivered at Zurich University on 19 September 1946.

Clark, J. C. D. (1990) 'The History of Britain: A Composite State in a *Europe des Patries*?', in J. C .D. Clark (ed.), *Ideas and Politics in Modern Britain*, Basingstoke, Macmillan, 32–49.

Clarke, M. (1981) *Fallen Idols: Elites and the Search for the Acceptable Face of Capitalism*, London, Junction Books.

Clarke, P. (1978) *Liberals and Social Democrats*, Cambridge University Press.

Clarke, P. B. (1996) *Deep Citizenship*, London, Pluto Press.

Clifford, C., McMillan, A. and McLean, I. (1997) *The Organization of Central Government Departments: A History 1964–1992*, ESRC.

Cm 3579 (1996/7) *Next Steps Agencies in Government: Review 1996*, London, HMSO.

Coates, D. (1994) *The Question of UK Decline*, London, Harvester Wheatsheaf.

Cockett, R. (1995) *Thinking the Unthinkable: Think-Tanks and the Economic Counter-Revolution 1931–1983*, London, Harper Collins.

Cockfield, Lord (1994) *The European Union: Creating the Single Market*, London, Wiley.

Cohen, S. (1972) *Folk Devils and Moral Panics*, London, Paladin.

Cohen, S. (1985) *Visions of Social Control*, Cambridge, Polity Press.

Cohen, S. (1997) 'Crime and Politics: Spot the Difference' in R. Rawlings (ed.), *Law, Society and Economy*, Oxford University Press.

Cohen, S. and Scull, A. (eds) (1983) *Social Control and the State*, Oxford, Martin Robertson.

Cohen, S. and Young, J. (eds) (1973) *The Manufacture of News*, London, Constable.

Cohn, B. (1983) 'Representing authority in Victorian India', in E. Hobsbawm and T. Ranger (eds), *The Invention of Tradition*, Cambridge University Press.

Colley, L. (1992) *Britons: Forging the Nation 1701–1837*, London, Yale University Press.

Cooper, R. (1996) *The Post-Modern State and the World Order*, London, Demos, paper no. 19.

Cornford, J. A. (1993) *A Written Constitution for the United Kingdom*, London, Institute for Public Policy Research.

Cowling, M. (1971) *The Impact of Labour 1920–1924: The Beginning of Modern British Politics*, Cambridge University Press.

Cox, M. (1997) 'Bringing in the "International"'; the IRA Ceasefire and the End of the Cold War', *International Affairs*, 73, 671–93.

Cradock, P. (1997) *In Pursuit of British Interests*, London, Murray.

Cranston, R. (1985) *Legal Foundations of the Welfare State*, London, Weidenfeld and Nicolson.

Crick, B. (1996) 'The Politics of British History', *Political Quarterly*, 67, 261–5.

Critcher, C. and Waddington, D. (eds) (1996) *Policing Public Order*, Aldershot, Avebury.

Critchley, T. A. (1970) *The Conquest of Violence*, London, Constable.

Cronin, J. E. (1991) *The Politics of State Expansion*, London, Routledge.

Crossman, R. (1963) 'Introduction' in Bagehot (1963), 1–57.

Daalder, H. (1963a) *Cabinet Reform in Britain 1914–63*, Stanford University Press.

Daalder, H. (1963b) 'The Haldane Committee and the Cabinet', *Public Administration*, 41, 117–35.

Dahl, R.A. (1985) *Controlling Nuclear Weapons: Democracy versus Guardianship*, Syracuse, Syracuse University Press.

Dahrendorf, R. (1985) *Law and Order*, London, Sweet & Maxwell.

Davies, N. (1996) *Europe: A History*, Oxford University Press.

Dearlove, J. (1989) 'Bringing the Constitution Back In: Political Science and the State', *Political Studies*, 37, 521–39.

Denman, R. (1996) *Missed Chances: Britain and Europe in the 20th Century*, London, Cassell.

Denver, D. (1994) *Elections and Voting Behaviour in Britain*, London, Harvester Wheatsheaf.

Devine, T. M. (1994) *Clanship to Crofters' War: The Social Transformation of the Scottish Highlands*, Manchester University Press.

Dicey, A. V. (1915) 'Introduction' in *An Introduction to the Study of the Law of the Constitution*, 8th edn, London, Macmillan.

Dicey, A. V. (1959) *An Introduction to the Study of the Law of the Constitution*, 10th edn, Basingstoke, Macmillan.

Dietz, M. (1992) 'Context is All: Feminism and Theories of Citizenship', in C. Mouffe (ed.), *Dimensions of Radical Democracy*, London, Verso.

Dogan, M. (1994) 'The Decline of Nationalisms in Europe', *Comparative Politics*, 26, pp. 281–305.

Dolowitz, D. and Marsh, D. (1996) 'Who Learns What From Whom: A Review of the Policy Transfer Literature', *Political Studies*, 44, 343–57.

Donzelot, J. (1980) *The Policing of Families*, London, Hutchinson.

Downes, D. and Morgan, R. (1997) 'Dumping the "Hostages to Fortune"? The Politics of Law and Order in Post-War Britain', in M. Maguire, R. Morgan and R. Reiner (eds), *The Oxford Handbook of Criminology*, Oxford University Press.

Doyle, M. (1997) *Ways of War and Peace*, London and New York, Norton.

Drucker, H. (1979) *Doctrine and Ethos in the Labour Party*, London, Allen & Unwin.

Dummett, M. (1997) *Principles of Electoral Reform*, Oxford University Press.

Dunleavy, P. (1981) *The Politics of Mass Housing in Britain, 1945–75: Corporate Power and Professional Influence in the Welfare State*, Oxford, Clarendon Press.

Dunleavy, P. (1981) *Democracy, Bureaucracy and Public Choice: Economic Explanations in Political Science*, Hemel Hempstead, Harvester-Wheatsheaf.

Dunleavy, P. (1995) 'Policy Disasters: Explaining the UK's Record', *Public Policy and Administration*, vol. 10, no. 2. pp. 52–71.

Dunleavy, P. and Husbands, C. T. (1985) *British Democracy at the Crossroads: Voting and Party Competition in the 1980s*, London, Allen & Unwin.

Dunleavy, P. and Margetts, H. (1995) 'Understanding the dynamics of electoral reform', *International Political Science Review*, vol. 16, no. 1, pp. 9–29.

Dunleavy, P. and O'Leary, B. (1987) *Theories of the State*, London, Macmillan.

Dunleavy, P. and Rhodes, R. A. W. (1990) 'Core Executive Studies in Britain', *Public Administration*, 68, 3–28.

Dunleavy, P., Jones, G. W. and O'Leary, B. (1990) 'Prime Ministers and the Commons: Patterns of Behaviour, 1868 to 1987', *Public Administration*, 68, 123–40.

Dunleavy, P., Margetts, H. and Weir, S. (1992) *Replaying the General Election of 1992: How Britain would have Voted under Alternative Electoral Systems*, London, LSE Public Policy Group.

Dunleavy, P., Margetts, H. and Weir, S. (1997) *Making Votes Count: How Britain would have Voted under Alternative Electoral Systems in the 1990s*, Colchester, Democratic Audit of the UK.

Dunn, J. (1969) *The Political Thought of John Locke: An Historical Account of the Argument*, Cambridge University Press.

Eatwell, R. (1989) 'The Rise of "Left-Right" Terminology: The Confusions of Social Science', in R. Eatwell and N. O'Sullivan (eds), *The Nature of the Right: European and American Politics and Political Thought since 1789*, London, Pinter, 32–46.

Eatwell, R. (1997) 'Britain', in R. Eatwell (ed.), *European Political Cultures: Conflict or Convergence?*, London, Routledge, pp. 50–68.

Eccleshall, R. (ed.) (1986) *British Liberalism: Liberal Thought from the 1640s to the 1980s*, London, Longman.

Edgerton, D. (1991) *England and the Aeroplane*, London, Macmillan.

Elbaum, B. and Lazonick, W. (eds) (1986) *The Decline of the British Economy*, Oxford University Press.

Elton, Lord (1945) *Imperial Commonwealth*, London, Collins.

Emsley, C. (1996a) *The English Police: A Political and Social History*, London, Longman.

Emsley, C. (1996b) *Crime and Society in England 1750–1900*, London, Longman.

Emsley, C. (1997) 'The History of Crime and Crime Control Institutions', in M. Maguire, R. Morgan and R. Reiner (eds), *The Oxford Handbook of Criminology*, Oxford University Press.

English, R. and Kenny, M. (1999) *Rethinking Decline*, London, Macmillan.

Esping-Anderson, G. (1990) *Three Worlds of Welfare Capitalism*, Cambridge, Polity Press.

Farran, S. (1996) *The UK Before the European Court of Human Rights: Case Law & Commentary*, London, Blackstone.

Finer, S. E. (1952) *The Life and Times of Sir Edwin Chadwick*, London, Methuen.

Finlayson, G. (1994) *Citizen, State, and Social Welfare in Britain 1830–1990*, Oxford, Clarendon Press.

Foster, C. D. (1997) *A Stronger Centre of Government*, London, Constitutional Unit.

Foster, C. and Plowden, F. (1997) *The State Under Stress*, Milton Keynes, Open University Press.

Fraser, D. (1979) *Power and Authority in the Victorian City*, Oxford, Blackwell.

Freeden, M. (1978) *Reappraising New Liberalism: An Ideology of Social Reform*, Oxford, Clarendon Press.

Freeden, M. (1986) *The New Liberalism: An Ideology of Social Reform*, Oxford, Clarendon Press.

Freeden, M. (1990) 'The Stranger at the Feast: Ideology and Public Policy in Twentieth Century Britain', *Twentieth Century British History*, 1:1, 9–34.

Freeden, M. (1997) *Ideology and Political Theory: A Conceptual Approach*, Oxford, Clarendon Press.

Friedberg, A. (1988) *The Weary Titan; Britain and the Experience of Relative Decline, 1895–1905*, Princeton University Press.

Gallagher, A. M. (1995) 'Equality, Contact and Pluralism: Attitudes to Community Relations', in R. Breen, P. Devine, and G. Robinson (eds), *Social Attitudes in Northern Ireland: The Fourth Report 1994–95*, Belfast, Appletree Press, 13–32.

Gamble, A. (1990) *Britain in Decline*, London, Macmillan.

Gardner, J. P. (ed.) (1994) *Hallmarks of Citizenship: A Green Paper*, London, Institute for Citizenship Studies/British Institute of International and Comparative Law.

Gardner, J. P. (ed.) (1997) *Citizenship: The White Paper*, London, Institute for Citizenship Studies/British Institute of International and Comparative Law.

Garland, D. (1990) *Punishment and Modern Society*, Oxford University Press.

Garland, D. (1996) 'The Limits of the Sovereign State', *British Journal of Criminology* 36:4, 445–71.

Garnett, M. (1996) *Principles and Politics in Contemporary Britain*, London, Longman.

Garrard, J. (1983) *Leadership and Power in Victorian Industrial Towns 1830–80*, Manchester University Press.

Gatrell, V. (1980) 'The Decline of Theft and Violence in Victorian and Edwardian England', in V.Gatrell, B.Lenmen and G.Parker (eds), *Crime and the Law*, London, Europa.

Gatrell, V. (1990) 'Crime, Authority, and the Policeman-State', in F. M. L. Thompson (ed.), *The Cambridge Social History of Britain 1750–1950 Volume 3*, Cambridge University Press.

Geary, R. (1985) *Policing Industrial Disputes*, Cambridge University Press.

Geddes, A. (1999) *Britain in the European Union*, 2nd edn, Tisbury, Baseline.
Gerbner, G. (1995) 'Television Violence: The Power and the Peril', in G. Dines and J. Humez (eds), *Gender, Race and Class in the Media*, Thousand Oaks, CA, Sage.
Giddens, A. (1990) *The Consequences of Modernity*, Cambridge, Polity Press.
Giddens, A. (1994) *Beyond Left and Right*, Cambridge, Polity Press.
Giddens, A. (1998) *The Third Way: The Renewal of Social Democracy*, Cambridge, Polity.
Gilmour, I. (1977) *Inside Right: A Study of Conservatism*, London, Hutchinson.
Gilmour, I. (1978) *Inside Right: A Study of Conservatism*, London, Quartet Books.
Goldsworthy, D. (1971) *Colonial Issues in British Politics, 1945–61*, Oxford University Press.
Gough, I. (1979) *The Political Economy of the Welfare State*, London, Macmillan.
Grant, W. (1993) *Business and Politics in Britain*, 2nd edn, Basingstoke, Macmillan.
Grant, W. (1997) *The Common Agricultural Policy*, Basingstoke, Macmillan.
Grant, W. and Marsh, D. (1977) *The CBI*, London, Hodder & Stoughton.
Gray, J. (1993) *Beyond the New Right: Markets, Government and the Common Environment*, London, Routledge.
Green, D. (1987) *The New Right: The Counter-Revolution in Politics, Economics and Social Thought*, London, Harvester Wheatsheaf.
Green, T. H. (1879) *Lectures on the Principles of Political Obligation*, London, Longman.
Green, T. H. (1883) *Prologemena to Ethics*, New York, Cromwell.
Greenleaf, W. H. (1983a) *The British Political Tradition, Volume One: The Rise of Collectivism*, London–New York, Methuen.
Greenleaf, W. H. (1983b) *The British Political Tradition, Volume Two: The Ideological Heritage*, London–New York, Methuen.
Greenleaf, W. H. (1987) *The British Political Tradition, Volume Three: A Much Governed Society*, London–New York, Methuen.
Greenleaf, W. H. (1966) *Oakeshott's Philosophical Politics*, London, Longman.
Griffith, J. A. G. (1993) *Judicial Politics since 1920: A Chronicle*, Oxford, Blackwell.
Griffith, J. A. G. (1997) *The Politics of the Judiciary*, 5th edn, London, Fontana.
Griffith, J. A. G. and Ryle, M. (1989) *Parliament: Functions, Practices and Procedures*, London, Sweet & Maxwell.
Griffiths, D. (1996) *Thatcherism and Territorial Politics: A Welsh Case Study*, Aldershot, Avebury.
Gurr, T. R. (1981) 'Historical Trends in Violent Crime: A Critical Review of the Evidence', in M. Tonry and N. Morris (eds), *Crime and Justice Volume 3*, Chicago University Press.
Hailsham, Lord (1978) *The Dilemma of Democracy: Diagnosis and Prescription*, London, Collins.
Hall, P. (1986) *Governing the Economy*, Cambridge, Polity.

Hall, S. (1992) 'The Question of Cultural Identity', in S. Hall (ed.), *Modernity and Its Futures*, Cambridge, Polity Press, 51–70.

Hall, S., Critcher, C., Jefferson, T., Clarke, J. and Roberts, B. (1978) *Policing the Crisis*, London, Macmillan.

Hanham, H. J. (1978) *Elections and Party Management: Politics in the Time of Disraeli and Gladstone*, 2nd edn, Hassocks, Harvester.

Harlow, C. and Rawlings, R. (1997) *Law and Administration*, 2nd edn, London, Butterworths.

Harris, D. J., O'Boyle, M. and Warbrick, C. (1995) *Law of the European Convention on Human Rights*, London.

Harris, J. (1977) *William Beveridge*, Oxford University Press.

Harris, J. (1986) '"Contract" and "Citizenship"', in D. Marquand and A. Seldon (eds), *The Ideas that Shaped Post-War Britain*, London, Fontana, 122–38.

Harrison, B. (1996) *The Transformation of British Politics, 1860-1995*, Oxford University Press.

Hart, J. (1972) 'The Genesis of the Northcote-Trevelyan Report', in G. Sutherland (ed.), *Studies in the Growth of Nineteenth-Century Government*, London, Routledge & Kegan Paul, 63–81.

Hart, J. (1992) *Proportional Representation: Critics of the British Electoral System*, Oxford University Press.

Harvie, C. (1984) 'Revolution and the Rule of Law', in K. O. Morgan (ed.), *The Oxford Illustrated History of Britain*, Oxford University Press.

Hayek, F. A. (1960) *The Constitution of Liberty*, London, Routledge.

Heater, D. (1990) *Citizenship: The Civic Ideal in World History, Politics and Education*. London, Longman.

Heath, A. and Topf, R. (1988) 'Political Culture', in R. Jowell, Witherspoon and L. Brook (eds), *British Social Attitudes, the 1987 Report*, Aldershot, Gower, 51–69.

Hechter, M. (1975) *Internal Colonialism: The Celtic Fringe in British National Development, 1536–1966*, London, Routledge & Kegan Paul.

Helm, D. (ed.) (1989) *The Economic Borders of the State*, Oxford University Press.

Hennessy, P. (1986) *Cabinet*, Oxford, Blackwell.

Hennessy, P. (1990) *Whitehall*, London, Fontana.

Hewart, G. (1929) *The New Despotism*, London, Benn.

Hill, R. L. (1929) *Toryism and the People 1832–1846*, London, Constable.

Hindess, B. (1971) *The Decline of Working Class Politics*, London, MacGibbon & Kee.

Hirst, P. and Thompson, G. (1995) 'Globalization, Foreign Direct Investment and Economic Governance', *Organization*, 1, 277–303.

Hobbes, T. (1996) *Leviathan*, Oxford University Press.

Hobsbawm, E. (1969) *Industry and Empire*, Harmondsworth, Penguin.

Hobsbawm, E. (1994) 'Barbarism: A User's Guide', *New Left Review*, 206, 44–54.

Hobsbawm, E. (1995) *Age of Extremes: The Short Twentieth Century 1914–1991*, London, Abacus.

Hoffmann, S. (1995a) *The European Sisyphus: Essays on Europe 1964–1994*, Boulder CO, Westview Press.

Hoffmann, S. (1995b) 'Revisiting the Anarchic Society', foreword to H. Bull, *The Anarchic Society*, 2nd edn, Basingstoke, Macmillan.

Hogwood, B. W. (1995) 'Regional Administration in Britain since 1979: Trends and Explanations', *Regional and Federal Studies*, 5, 267–91.

Holland, R.F. (1985) *European Decolonization, 1918–1981: An Introductory Survey*, London, Macmillan.

Home Office (1995) *Digest 3: Information on the Criminal Justice System in England and Wales*, London, Home Office Research and Statistics Department.

Home Office (1997) *Rights Brought Home: The Human Rights Bill*, Cm. 3782, London, HMSO.

Honigsbaum, F. (1970) 'The Struggle for the Ministry of Health 1914–1919', *Occasional Papers in Public Administration* 37, London, Bellhalth.

Hoogenboom, B. (1991) 'Grey Policing: A Theoretical Framework', *Policing and Society*, 2:1, 17–30.

Hoskyns, C. (1996) *Integrating Gender: Women, Law and Politics in the European Union*, London, Verso.

Howe, G. (1990) 'Sovereignty and Interdependence: Britain's Place in the World', *International Affairs*, 66, 675–95.

Howell, D. (1986) *A Lost Left: Three Studies in Socialism and Nationalism*, Manchester University Press.

Hudson, B. (1997) 'Social Control', in M. Maguire, R. Morgan and R. Reiner (eds), *The Oxford Handbook of Criminology*, Oxford University Press.

Hunt, M. (1997) *Using Human Rights Law in English Courts*, Oxford, Hart.

Hunter, B. (ed.) (1995) *The Statesman's Year-book: Statistical and Historical Annual of the States of the World for the Year 1995–1996*, London, Macmillan.

Hutchison, I. G. C. (1996) 'Government', in T. M. Devine and R. J. Finlay (eds), *Scotland in the Twentieth Century*, Edinburgh, Edinburgh University Press, 46–63.

Hutton, W. (1995) *The State We're In*, London, Cape.

Ignatieff, M. (1991) 'Citizenship and Moral Narcissism', in G. Andrews (ed.), *Citizenship*, London, Lawrence & Wishart, 26–36.

Illich, I. (1973) *Deschooling Society*, London, Penguin.

Ingham, G. (1984) *Capitalism Divided: The City and Industry in British Social Development*, Basingstoke, Macmillan.

Ingham, G. (1994) *Capitalism Divided*, London, Macmillan.

Jacobs, F. G. and White, R. (1996) *The European Convention of Human Rights*, 2nd edn, Oxford, Clarendon Press.

Jefferson, T. (1990) *The Case Against Paramilitary Policing*, Milton Keynes, Open University Press.

Jenks, E. (1923) *The Government of the British Empire*, London, John Murray.

Jennings, I. (1966) *The British Constitution*, Cambridge University Press.

Jennings, Sir Ivor (1959) *The Law and the Constitution*, 5th edn, London, University of London Press.

Jessop, B. (1990) *State Theory*, Pennsylvania University Press.

Johnson, N. (1977) *In Search of the Constitution: Reflections on State and Society in Britain*, London, Pergamon.

Johnson, N. (1992) *The Political Consequences of PR: The British Idea of Responsible Government*, CPS Policy Study no. 30, London, Centre for Policy Studies.

Johnson, N. (1997) 'Opposition in the British Political System', *Government and Opposition*, 32: 4, 487–510.

Johnson, N. (1998) 'The Judicial Dimension in British Politics', in H. Berrington (ed.), *Britain in the Nineties: The Politics of Paradox*, London, Cass, pp. 148–66.

Johnston, L. (1992) *The Rebirth of Private Policing*, London, Routledge.

Jones, G. (1975) 'Development of the Cabinet', in W. Thornhill (ed.), *The Modernisation of British Government*, London, Pitman.

Jones, H. and Kandiah, M. (eds) (1996) *The Myth of Consensus: New Views on British History 1945–64*, Basingstoke, Macmillan/ICBH.

Jordan, B. (1989) *The Common Good: Citizenship, Morality and Self-Interest*, Oxford, Blackwell.

Jowell, J. and Oliver, D. (eds) (1994) *The Changing Constitution*, 3rd edn, Oxford University Press.

Judge, D. (1993) *The Parliamentary State*, Sage, London.

Kavanagh, D. (1986) *Mrs Thatcher: A Study in Prime Ministerial Style*, Glasgow, University of Strathclyde.

Kearney, H. (1989) *The British Isles: A History of Four Nations*, Cambridge University Press.

Keith-Lucas, B. (1952) *The English Local Government Franchise: A Short History*, Oxford, Blackwell.

Kemp, P. (1993) *Beyond Next Steps: a Civil Service for the 21st Century*, London, Social Market Foundation.

Kendle, J. (1997) *Federal Britain: A History*, London, Routledge.

Kennedy, P. (1988) *The Rise and Fall of the Great Powers*, London, Unwin Hyman.

Kenny, M. (1995) *The First New Left: British Intellectuals after Stalin*, London, Lawrence & Wishart.

Keynes, J. M. (1936) *The General Theory of Employment, Interest and Money*, London, Macmillan.

King, A. (1976) *Why is Britain becoming Harder to Govern?*, London, BBC Publications.

King, A. (1981) 'The Rise of the Career-Politician in Britain and Its Consequences', *British Journal of Political Science*, 11: 3, 249–85.

King, A. (1985) 'Margaret Thatcher: the Style of a Prime Minister', in A. King (ed.), *The British Prime Minister*, Basingstoke, Macmillan.

King, D. (1995) *Actively Seeking Work: The Politics of Unemployment and Welfare Policy in the United States and Great Britain*, Chicago and London, University of Chicago Press.

Klug, F., Starmer, K. and Weir, S. (1996) *The Three Pillars of Liberty, Political Rights and Freedoms in the United Kingdom*, London, Routledge.

Lacey, N. and Wells, C. (1998) *Reconstructing Criminal Law*, London, Butterworths.

Laundy, P. (1979) 'The Speaker and his Office in the Twentieth Century', in S. A. Walkland and M. Ryle (eds), *The House of Commons in the Twentieth Century*, Oxford University Press.

Laws, J. (1993) 'Is the High Court the Guardian of Fundamental Constitutional Rights?', *Public Law*, 59–79.

Lawson, N. (1992) *The View from No. 11*, London, Bantam Press.

Lawson, N. (1994) 'Cabinet Government in the Thatcher Years' *Contemporary Record*, 8, 440–7.

Le May, G. H. (1979) *The Victorian Constitution: Conventions, Usages and Contingencies*, London, Duckworth.

Le Sueur, A. (1996) 'The Judicial Review Debate: From Partnership to Friction', *Government and Opposition*, 31, 8–26.

Leach, R. (1991) *British Political Ideologies*, London, Philip Allen.

Lee, J. M. (1963) *Social Leaders and Public Persons: A Study of County Government in Cheshire since 1888*, Oxford, Clarendon Press.

Lee, J. M, Jones, G. W. and Burnham, S. (1998) *At the Centre of Whitehall: Advising the Prime Minister and Cabinet*, London, Macmillan.

Lee, S. (1995) 'Imagining England', paper presented to a workshop on Englishness and Questions of National Identity, at Annual Conference of Political Studies Association of the UK, York University.

Lenman, B. P. (1992) *The Eclipse of Parliament*, London, Arnold.

Leonard, M. (1998) *Rediscovering Europe*, London, Demos in association with Interbrand and Sorrell.

Ling, T. (1998) *The British State Since 1945*, Cambridge, Polity Press.

Lister, R. (1990) *The Exclusive Society: Citizenship and the Poor*, London, Child Poverty Action Group.

Lister, R. (1997) *Citizenship: Feminist Perspectives*, Basingstoke, Macmillan.

Livingstone, S. (1996) 'On the Continuing Problem of Media Effects', in J. Curran and M.Gurevitch (eds), *Mass Media and Society*, London, Arnold.

Lloyd, J. (1998) 'Time to Say Goodbye', *New Statesman*, 12 June, 10–11.

Loughlin, M. (1992) *Public Law and Political Theory*, Oxford, Clarendon Press.

Loughlin, M. and Scott, C. (1997) 'The Regulatory State', in P. Dunleavy, A. Gamble, I. Holliday and G. Peele (eds), *Developments in British Politics 5*, London, Macmillan, 205–19.

Lovenduski, J. and Norris, P. (eds), (1993) *Gender and Party Politics*, London, Sage.

Lovenduski, J. and Norris, P. (eds), (1996) *Women in Politics*, Oxford University Press.

Lovenduski, J. and Randall, V. (eds) (1993) *Contemporary Feminist Politics: Women and Power in Britain*, Oxford University Press.

Lowell, A.L. (1908) *The Government of England, Volumes I and II*, New York, Macmillan.

Ludlow, P. (1997) *Preparing Europe for the 21st Century*, Brussels, Centre for European Policy Studies, CEPS 3rd IAC Annual Report.

Lustgarten, L. (1986) *The Governance of the Police*, London, Sweet & Maxwell.

Lyon, D. (1994) *Postmodernity*, Buckingham, Open University Press.

MacDonagh, O. (1977) *Early Victorian Government 1830–1870*, London, Weidenfeld and Nicolson.

MacIntyre, A. (1985) *After Virtue: A Study in Moral Theory*, London, Duckworth.

Mackay, F. (1996) 'The Zero Tolerance Campaign: Setting the Agenda' in J. Lovenduski and P. Norris (eds), *Women and Politics*, Oxford University Press, pp. 208–22.

Mackie, J. D. (1978) *A History of Scotland*, 2nd edn, Harmondsworth, Penguin.

Mackintosh, J. P. (1962) *The British Cabinet*, London, Stevens.

Mackintosh, J. P. (1977a) *The Politics and Government of Britain*, Hutchinson, London.

Mackintosh, J. P. (1977b) *The British Cabinet*, 3rd edn, London, Stevens.

Macpherson, C. B. (1962) *The Political Theory of Possessive Individualism: Hobbes to Locke*, London, Oxford University Press.

Maguire, M. (1997) 'Crime Statistics, Patterns, and Trends: Changing Perceptions and their Implications', in M. Maguire, R. Morgan and R. Reiner (eds), *The Oxford Handbook of Criminology*, Oxford University Press.

Maidment, R. and Thompson G. (eds) (1993) *Managing the United Kingdom*, London, Sage.

Maitland, F. W. (1908) *The Constitutional History of England*, Cambridge University Press.

Majone, G. (1997) 'From the Postitive to the Regulatory State: Causes and Consequences of Changes in the Mode of Governance', *Journal of Public Policy*, 17, 139–67.

Manin, B. (1997) *The Principles of Representative Government*, Cambridge University Press.

Mann, M. (1986) *The Sources of Social Power Volume I: A History of Power From the Beginning to A.D. 1760*, Cambridge University Press.

Mann, M. (1993) *The Sources of Social Power Volume II: The Rise of Classes and Nation-States, 1760–1914*, Cambridge University Press.

Marenin, O. (1983) 'Parking Tickets and Class Repression: The Concept of Policing in Critical Theories of Criminal Justice', *Contemporary Crises* 6(2), pp. 241–66.

Mark, R. (1977) *Policing A Perplexed Society*, London, Unwin.

Marquand, D. (1988) *The Unprincipled Society: New Demands and Old Politics*, London, Fontana.

Marquand, D. (1997) *The New Reckoning: Capitalism, States and Citizens*, Oxford, Polity Press.

Marsh, D. (1992), *The New Politics of British Trade Unionism*, Basingstoke, Macmillan.

Marshall, G. (1986) *Constitutional Conventions: The Rules and Forms of Political Accountability*, Oxford University Press.

Marshall, T. H. (1950) *Citizenship and Social Class*, Cambridge University Press.

Marx, K. (1976) *Capital Volume I*, Harmondsworth, Penguin.

Massey, A. (1993), *Managing the Public Sector: A Comparative Analysis of the United Kingdom and the United States*, Cambridge University Press.

Mathiesen, T. (1997) 'The Viewer Society: Michel Foucault's "Panopticon" Revisited', *Theoretical Criminology*, 1:2, 215–34.

Matthew, H. C. G. (1984) 'The Liberal Age', in K. O. Morgan (ed.), *The Oxford Illustrated History of Britain*, Oxford University Press.

McKenzie, R. T. (1963), *British Political Parties*, London, Mercury.

Meadowcroft, J. (ed.) (1994) *L. T. Hobhouse, 1864–1929: Liberalism and Other Writings*, Cambridge University Press.

Meehan, E. (1995) 'Civil Society', in M. Clarke (ed.), *The State of Britain*, Birmingham, School of Public Policy for Economic and Social Research Council and the Royal Society of Arts, 59–70.

Meehan, E. (forthcoming) 'British–Irish Relations in the Context of European Union', *Review of International Relations*.

Messerlin, P. (1996) 'France and Trade Policy', *International Affairs*, 72, 293–309.

Miliband, R. (1984) *Capitalist Democracy in Britain*, Oxford University Press.

Miller, D. (1991) 'Reification', in D. Miller (ed.), *The Blackwell Encyclopaedia of Political Thought*, Oxford, Blackwell, 428.

Miller, D. (1993) 'In Defence of Nationality', *Journal of Applied Philosophy*, 10, 3–16.

Miller, D. (1995) 'Citizenship and Pluralism', *Political Studies* 43, 432–50.

Miller, W.L. (1989) *Media and Votes: The Audience, Content and Influence of Press and TV at the 1987 General Election*, Oxford, Clarendon Press.

Minogue, K. (1985) *Alien Powers: The Pure Theory of Ideology*, New York, St. Martin's Press.

Moore, B. (1966) *The Social Origins of Dictatorship and Democracy*, Harmondsworth, Penguin.

Moran, M. (1979) 'The Conservative Party and the Trade Unions since 1974', *Political Studies*, 27, 38–53.

Moran, M. (1986) *The Politics of Banking*, London, Macmillan.

Moran, M. (1991) *The Politics of the Financial Services Revolution*, London, Macmillan.

Morgan, J. (1987) *Conflict and Order*, Oxford University Press.

Morgan, K. O. (1980) *Portrait of a Progressive: The Political Career of Christopher, Viscount Addison*, Oxford, Clarendon Press.

Morgan, K. O. (ed.) (1984) *The Oxford Illustrated History of Britain*, Oxford University Press.

Morgan, R. and Newburn, T. (1997) *The Future of Policing*, Oxford University Press.

MORI (1998) Poll conducted for The European Movement on 'Attitudes Towards the European Union', 23–26 January, accessible at < http://www.mori.com >

Morris, R. J. (1976) *Cholera: The Social Response to an Epidemic*, London, Croom Helm.

Mouffe, C. (ed.) (1992) *Dimensions of Radical Democracy*, London, Verso.

Mount, F. (1992) *The British Constitution Now: Recovery or Decline?*, London, Heinemann.

Nairn, T. (1977) *The Break-Up of Britain: Crisis and Neo-Nationalism*, London, New Left Books.

Newburn, T. (1997) 'Youth, Crime and Justice', in M. Maguire, R. Morgan and R. Reiner (eds), *The Oxford Handbook of Criminology*, Oxford University Press.

Newburn, T. and Jones, T. (1998) *Private Security and Public Policing*, Oxford University Press.

Nicoll, W. and Salmon, T. C. (1994) *Understanding the New European Community*, Hemel Hempstead, Harvester Wheatsheaf.

Nicolson, I. F. (1986) *The Mystery of Crichel Down*, Oxford, Clarendon Press.

Nordlinger, E. (1981) *The Autonomy of the Democratic State*, Cambridge, Mass, Harvard University Press.

Norman, E. (1976) *Church and Society in England 1770–1976*, Oxford, Clarendon Press.

Norris, P. (1990) *British By-Elections: The Volatile Electorate*, Oxford, Clarendon Press.

Northcote, S. and Trevelyan, C. (1954) 'The Northcote-Trevelyan Report', reprinted in *Public Administration*, 32, 1–16.

Nozick, R. (1974) *Anarchy, State and Utopia*, Oxford University Press.

Nugent, N. (1996) 'Sovereignty and Britain's Membership of the European Union', *Public Policy and Administration*, 11: 2, 3–18.

Nugent, N. (1999) *The Government and Politics of the European Union*, 4th edn, London, Macmillan.

O'Toole, B. (1990), 'T. H. Green and the Ethics of Senior Officials in British Central Government', *Public Administration*, vol. 68/3, London, Blackwell, 337–52.

Oakeshott, M. (1962) *Rationalism in Politics and Other Essays*, Indianapolis, IN, Liberty Press.

Oakeshott, M. (1975) *On Human Conduct*, Oxford University Press.

Office for National Statistics (1997) *Social Trends 27*, London, HMSO.

Oliver, D. and Heater, D. (1994) *The Foundations of Citizenship*, Hemel Hempstead, Harvester Wheatsheaf for the Citizenship Foundation.

Olson, M. (1982) *The Rise and Decline of Nations*, London, Yale University Press.

Parekh, B. (1991) 'British Citizenship and Cultural Difference', in G. Andrews (ed.), *Citizenship*, London, Lawrence & Wishart, 183–204.

Parekh, B. (1994) 'Discourses on National Identity', *Political Studies*, 42, 492–504.

Parry, G., Moyser, G. and Day, N. (1992) *Political Participation and Democracy in Britain*, Cambridge University Press.

Pateman, C. (1988) *The Sexual Contract*, Oxford, Blackwell/Polity Press.

Pateman, C. (1989) *The Disorder of Women*, Oxford, Blackwell/Polity Press.

Paterson, W. (1994) 'Britain and the European Union Revisited, Some Unanswered Questions', *Scottish Affairs*, 9, Autumn, pp. 1–12.

Perkin, H. (1969) *The Origins of Modern English Society*, London, Routledge.

Peterson, J. (1997a) 'Britain, Europe and the World', in P. Dunleavy, A. Gamble, I. Holliday and G. Peele (eds), *Developments in British Politics 5*, Macmillan, Basingstoke.

Peterson, J. (1997b) 'States, Societies and the European Union', *West European Politics*, 20: 4, 1–23.

Peterson, J. and Sharp, M. (1998) *Technology Policy in the European Union*, Basingstoke, Macmillan.

Peterson, J. and Sjursen, H. (eds) (1998) *A Common Foreign Policy for Europe? Competing Visions of the CFSP*, London, Routledge.

Pettit, P. (1997) *Republicanism: A Theory of Freeom and Government*, Oxford, Clarendon Press.

Phillips, A. (1993) *Democracy and Difference*, Cambridge, Polity Press.

Pierson, P. (1994) *Dismantling the Welfare State? Reagan, Thatcher, and the Politics of Retrenchment*, Cambridge University Press.

Pincus, S. (1998) 'Neither Machiavellian Moment nor Possessive Individualism: Commercial Society and the Defenders of the English Commonwealth', *American Historical Review*, 103, 705–36.

Pinto-Duschinsky, M. (1981) *British Political Finance, 1830–1980*, London, American Enterprise Institute.

Pocock, J. G. A. (1975a) 'British History: A Plea for a New Subject', *Journal of Modern History*, 47, 601–21.

Pocock, J. G. A. (1975b) *The Machiavellian Moment: Florentine Political Thought and the Atlantic Republican Tradition*, Princeton, NJ, Princeton University Press.

Prest, J. (1990) *Liberty and Locality: Parliament, Permissive Legislation, and Ratepayers' Democracies in the Nineteenth Century*, Oxford, Clarendon Press.

Pryce, S. (1997) *Presidentializing the Premiership*, London, Macmillan.

Pulzer, P. G. J. (1967) *Political Representation and Elections in Britain*, London, George Allen & Unwin.

Quinn, D. (1993) *Understanding Northern Ireland*, Manchester, Baseline.

Rawls, J. (1972) *A Theory of Justice*, Oxford University Press.

Rees, J. C. (1985) *John Stuart Mill's On Liberty*, Oxford, Clarendon Press.

Reiman, J. (1979) *The Rich Get Richer and the Poor Get Prison*, New York, Wiley.

Reiner, R. (1991) *Chief Constables*, Oxford University Press.

Reiner, R. (1992) *The Politics of the Police*, Hemel Hempstead, Wheatsheaf.

Reiner, R. (1994) 'The Dialectics of Dixon: The Changing Image of the TV Cop', in S. Becker and M. Stephens (eds), *Police Force, Police Service*, London, Macmillan.

Reiner, R. (1996) 'The Case of the Missing Crimes', in R. Levitas and W. Guy (eds), *Interpreting Official Statistics*, London, Routledge.

Reiner, R. (1997a) 'Policing and the Police', in M. Maguire, R. Morgan and R. Reiner (eds), *The Oxford Handbook of Criminology*, Oxford University Press.

Reiner, R. (1997b) 'Media Made Criminality', in M. Maguire, R. Morgan and R. Reiner (eds), *The Oxford Handbook of Criminology*, Oxford University Press.

Reiner, R. and Cross, M. (eds), (1991) *Beyond Law and Order*, London, Macmillan.

Renwick, R. (1996) *Fighting With Allies: America and Britain in Peace and War*, London, Macmillan.

Rhodes James, R. (1977) *The British Revolution: 1880–1939*, New York, Alfred A. Knopf.

Rhodes, R. A. W. and Dunleavy P. (eds) (1995) *Prime Minister, Cabinet and Core Executive*, London, Macmillan.

Rhodes, R. A. W. (1988) *Beyond Westminster and Whitehall*, London, Unwin Hyman.

Rhodes, R. A. W. (1994) 'The Hollowing Out of the State', *Political Quarterly*, 65, 138–51.

322   *Bibliography*

Rhodes, R. A. W. (1995) 'The New Governance: Governing without Government', in M. Clarke, (ed.), *The State of Britain*, Birmingham, School of Public Policy for Economic and Social Research Council and the Royal Society of Arts, 29–45.

Richards, D. and Smith, M. J. (1998) 'The Gatekeepers of the Common Good, Power and the Public Service Ethos', *EGPA Yearbook* 1998, EGPA, Brussels.

Richards, D. (1997) *The Civil Service Under the Conservatives*, Sussex, Sussex Academic Press.

Riddell, P. (1998) 'Does Anybody Listen to MPs?', *The Times*, 23 March.

Riley, P. W. J. (1978) *The Union of England and Scotland: A Study in Anglo-Scottish Politics of the Eighteenth Century*, Manchester University Press.

Robinson, A. (1978) *Parliament and Public Spending*, London, Heinemann.

Robinson, C., Scaglion, R. and Olivero, M. (1994) *Police in Contradiction*, Westport, CT, Greenwood.

Robson, W. A. (1948) *Public Administration Today*, London, Stevens.

Robson, W. A. (1951) *Justice and Administrative Law: A Study of the British Constitution*, 3rd edn, London, Stevens.

Rock, P. (1997) 'Sociological Theories of Crime', in M. Maguire, R. Morgan and R. Reiner (eds), *The Oxford Handbook of Criminology*, Oxford University Press.

Rokkan, S. and Urwin, D. W. (1982) 'Introduction: Centres and Peripheries in Western Europe', in S. Rokkan and D. W. Urwin (eds), *The Politics of Territorial Identity: Studies in European Regionalism*, London, Sage, 1–17.

Rose, N. (1996) 'The Death of the Social? Re-figuring the Territory of Government' *Economy and Society*, 25:3, 327–56.

Rose, R. (1982) *Understanding the United Kingdom: The Territorial Dimension in Government*, London, Longman.

Rose, R. (1989) *Politics in England: Change and Persistence*, 5th edn, London, Macmillan.

Rose, R. and Peters, B. G. (1979) *Can Governments Go Bankrupt?* Basingstoke, Macmillan.

Rosevere, H. (1969) *The Treasury: The Evolution of a British Institution*, London, Allen Lane.

Rozenberg, J. (1997) *Trial of Strength: The Battle Between Ministers and Judges over Who Makes the Law*, London, Cohen.

Sartori, G. (1976) *Parties and Party Systems: A Framework for Analysis*, Cambridge University Press.

Savage, G. (1996) *The Social Construction of Expertise*, Pittsburgh University Press.

Scarman, Lord (1981) *The Brixton Disorders*, London, Penguin.

Schaffer, B. B. (1957) 'The Idea of the Ministerial Department: Bentham, Mill and Bagehot', *Australian Journal of Politics and History*, 3, 59–78.

Schlesinger, P. and Tumber, H. (1994) *Reporting Crime*, Oxford University Press.

Schumpeter, J. A. (1992) *Capitalism, Socialism and Democracy*, London, Routledge.

Scottish Office (1997) *Scotland's Parliament*, Cm. 3658, London, HMSO.

Sedley, S. (1994) 'Governments, Constitutions, and Judges', in G. Richardson and H. Genn (eds), *Administrative Law & Government Action: The Courts and Alternative Mechanisms of Review*, Oxford, Clarendon Press, 35–43.

Sedley, S. (1997) 'The Common Law and the Constitution', *London Review of Books*, 8 May 1997, 8–11.

Seeley, J. (1909) *The Expansion of England*, London, Macmillan.

Semmel, B. (1960) *Imperialism and Social Reform*, London, Allen & Unwin.

Shackleton, M. (1997) 'The Internal Legitimacy Crisis of the European Union', in A.W. Cafruny and C. Lankowski (eds), *Europe's Ambiguous Unity*, Boulder, CO, and London, Lynne Rienner.

Sharpe, J. (1984) *Crime in Early Modern England 1550–1750*, London, Longman.

Shearing, C. and Stenning, P. (1983) 'Private Security: Implications for Social Control' *Social Problems*, 30:5, 493–506.

Signorielli, N. (1990) 'Television's Mean and Dangerous World: A Continuation of the Cultural Indicators Perspective', in N. Signorielli and M. Morgan (eds), *Cultivation Analysis*, Newbury Park, Sage.

Skidelsky, R. (1989) 'Keynes and the State', in D. Helm (ed.), *The Economic Borders of the State*, Oxford University Press.

Skinner, Q. (1978) *The Foundations of Modern Political Thought*, vols 1, 2, Cambridge University Press.

Skinner, Q. (1998) *Liberty before Liberalism*, Cambridge University Press.

Smith, M. and Corrigan, J. (1995) 'Relations with Europe' in R. Breen, P. Devine, and G. Robinson (eds), *Social Attitudes in Northern Ireland: The Fourth Report 1994–95*, Belfast, Appletree Press, pp. 84–105.

Smith, M.J. (1994) 'The Core Executive and the Resignation of Mrs Thatcher', *Public Administration*, 72, 341–63.

Smith, M.J. (1998) 'Reconceptualizing the British State: Theoretical and Empirical Challenges to Central Government', *Public Administration*, 76, 45–72.

Smith, M.J. (1999) *The Core Executive in Britain*, London, Macmillan.

Sparks, R. (1997) 'Recent Social Theory and the Study of Crime and Punishment', in M. Maguire, R. Morgan and R. Reiner (eds), *The Oxford Handbook of Criminology*, Oxford University Press.

Stanworth, P. and Giddens, A. (1974) *Elites and Power in British Society*, Cambridge University Press.

Stevens, J. (1997) *Speaking Up, Speaking Out!*, London, the Industrial Society with MORI.

Stevenson, J. (1990) *British Society 1914–1945*, Harmondsworth, Penguin.

Stevenson, J. and Cook, C. (1977) *The Slump*, London, Cape.

Stewart, J., Kendall, E. and Coote, A. (1994) *Citizens' Juries*, London, Institute for Public Policy Research.

Steyn, Lord (1997) 'The Weakest and Least Dangerous Department of Government', *Public Law*, 84–95.

Stokes, E. (1959) *The English Utilitarians and India*, London, Oxford University Press.

Stone, B. (1995) 'Administrative Accountability in Western Democracies: Towards a New Conceptual Framework', *Governance*, 8, 505–25.

Storch, R. (1975) 'The Plague of Blue Locusts: Police Reform and Popular Resistance in Northern England 1840—1857', *International Review of Social History* 20:1, 61–90.

Strange, S. (1971) *Sterling and British Policy*, Oxford University Press.

Subrahmanyam, G. (1995) 'Effortless rule and military realities: The British imperial state in 1891', in J. Lovenduski and J. Stanyer (eds) *Contemporary Political Studies 1995*, Belfast, UK Political Studies Association, pp. 132–44.

Sumner, C. (1997) 'Social Control', in R. Bergalli and C. Sumner (eds), *Social Control and Political Order*, London, Sage.

Taylor, A. J. P. (1965) *English History, 1914–1945*, London, Oxford University Press.

Taylor, A. J. P. (1970) *English History 1914–1945*, Harmondsworth, Penguin.

Thain, C. and Wright, M. (1995) *The Treasury and Whitehall*, Oxford, Clarendon.

Thane, P. (1990) 'Government and Society in England and Wales, 1750–1914', in F. M. L. Thompson (ed.), *The Cambridge Social History of Modern Britain, 1750–1950, Volume 3 Social Agencies and Institutions*, Cambridge University Press.

The Economist (1998) 'Britain and Europe', 3 January, pp. 27–30.

Thomas, W. (1979) *The Philosophic Radicals: Nine Studies in Theory and Practice, 1817–1841*, Oxford, Clarendon Press.

Thompson, E. P. (1965) 'The Peculiarities of the English', *Socialist Register*.

Thompson, E. P. (1980) *Writing by Candlelight*, London, Merlin.

Thompson, E. P (1975) *Whigs and Hunters*, London, Penguin.

Thomson, J. E. (1995) 'State Sovereignty in International Relations: Bridging the Gap Between Theory and Empirical Research', *International Studies Quarterly*, 39(2), 213–33.

Thornton, A. P. (1957) *The Imperial Idea and Its Enemies*, London, Macmillan.

Townshend, C. (1993) *Making the Peace: Public Order and Public Security in Modern Britain*, Oxford University Press.

Tuchman, B. (1966) *The Proud Tower*, Englewood Cliffs, NJ, Prentice Hall.

Turner, B. S. (1990) 'Outline of a Theory of Citizenship', *Sociology*, 24, 189–217.

Turpin, C. (1985) *British Government and the Constitution: Texts, Cases and Materials*, London, Weidenfeld and Nicolson.

Twine, F. (1994) *Citizenship and Social Rights: The Interdependence of Self and Society*, London, Sage.

Vasey, C. M. W. (1986) 'The European Free Trade Association (EFTA)', in R. Mayne (ed.), *Western Europe*, New York and London, Facts on File Publications.

Vincent, A. (1994) 'British Conservatism and the Problem of Ideology', *Political Studies*, 42, pp. 204–27.

Vincent, A. (1998) 'New Ideologies for Old?', *Political Quarterly*, 69, 1.

Vincent, A. and Plant R. (1984) *Philosophy, Politics and Citizenship: The Life and Thought of the British Idealists*, Oxford, Blackwell.

Vincent, D. (1991) *Poor Citizens*, London, Longman.

Waddington, D. (1993) *Contemporary Issues in Public Disorder*, London, Routledge.

Waddington, P. A. J. (1990) *The Strong Arm of the Law*, Oxford University Press.

Waddington, P. A. J. (1994) *Liberty and Order*, London, UCL Press.

Waddington, P. A. J. (1999) *Policing Citizens*, London, UCL Press.

Wade, E. C. S. and Bradley, A. W. (1985) *Constitutional and Administrative Law*, 10th ed, London, Longman.

Wallace, W. (1996) 'What Price Interdependence? Sovereignty and Independence in British Politics', *International Affairs* 62(3), pp. 367–89.

Waltz, K. (1979) *Theory of International Politics*, Reading, MA: Addison-Wesley.

Walzer, M. (1992) 'The Civil Society Argument', in C. Mouffe (ed.), *Dimensions of Radical Democracy*, London, Verso.

Wartella, E. (1995) 'Media and Problem Behaviours in Young People', in M. Rutter and D. Smith (eds), *Psychological Disorders in Young People*, London, Wiley.

Weatherill, S. (1995) *Law and Integration in the European Union*, Oxford, Clarendon Press.

Webb, S. (1890) *Socialism in England*, London, Swan Sonnenschein.

Webb, S. and Webb, B. (1963) *English Local Government*, vol.1 'The Parish and the County', London, Cass.

Weber, M. (1964) *The Theory of Economic and Social Organisation*, Glencoe, IL, Free Press.

Weinberger, B. (1991) *Keeping the Peace?*, Oxford, Berg.

Weinberger, B. (1996) *The Best Police Force in the World?*, London, Scolar.

Welsh Office (1997) *A Voice for Wales: The Government's Proposals for a Welsh Assembly*, Cm. 3718, London, HMSO.

Wilford, R. (1996) 'Women and Politics in Northern Ireland', in J. Lovenduski and P. Norris (eds), *Women and Politics*, Oxford University Press, 43–56.

Williams, G. and Pearson, R. (1984) *Politial Thought and Public Policy in the Nineteenth Century: An Interpretation*, London, Longman.

Williams, R. (1958) *Culture and Society, 1780–1950*, London, Chatto & Windus.

Williams, R. (1961) *The Long Revolution*, London, Chatto & Windus.

Willson, F. M. G. (1955) 'Ministries and Boards: Some Aspects of Administrative Development Since 1832', *Public Administration*, 33, 43–57.

Wright, A. (1985) *British Socialism: Socialist Thought from the 1880s to 1960*, London, Longman.

Wright, M. (1972) 'Treasury Control 1854–1914', in G. Sutherland (ed.), *Studies in the Growth of Government*, London, Routledge & Kegan Paul.

Wright, P. (1987) *Spycatcher*, New York: Viking.

Wrong, D. (1994) *The Problem of Order*, Cambridge, MA, Harvard University Press.

Young, O. (1969) 'Interdependencies in World Politics', *International Journal*, 24, 726–50.

Index